THE MAN LISZT

THE MAN LISZT

A STUDY OF THE TRAGI-COMEDY OF
A SOUL DIVIDED AGAINST ITSELF

by

ERNEST NEWMAN

. . . . *"Nil fuit unquam*
Sic impar sibi."   HORACE

TAPLINGER PUBLISHING COMPANY
NEW YORK

Published in the United States in 1970 by
Taplinger Publishing Co., Inc.
New York, New York

© *Copyright 1935 by Charles Scribner's Sons*

ISBN 0 8008 5095 5

Library of Congress Catalog Card Number 74-119622

Printed in Great Britain

TO VERA

CONTENTS

		Page
FOREWORD		xi
MAIN SOURCES AND REFERENCES		xviii
CHAPTER I	THE UNRELIABILITY OF THE OLDER LISZT BIOGRAPHIES	1
II	THE BEGINNINGS OF THE D'AGOULT AFFAIR	16
III	THE DEVELOPMENT OF THE D'AGOULT AFFAIR	54
IV	THE END OF THE D'AGOULT AFFAIR ..	85
V	*BÉATRIX* AND *NÉLIDA*	112
VI	LISZT AND THE PRINCESS WITTGENSTEIN ..	157
VII	THE SEPARATION FROM THE PRINCESS: THE DUALITY OF LISZT'S SOUL	190
VIII	PULL FRANCISCAN, PULL ZIGÉUNER ..	220
IX	THE QUESTIONABLE EVIDENTIAL VALUE OF LISZT'S LETTERS: THE OLGA JANINA EPISODE	248
X	THE ACTOR	280
POSTLUDE	LISZT'S PERSONALITY AND HIS ART ..	297
INDEX	.. ..	307

LIST OF ILLUSTRATIONS

To face page

FRANZ LISZT AS A YOUNG MAN 74

COUNTESS D'AGOULT 75

LISZT IN 1842 90

PRINCESS WITTGENSTEIN WITH HER DAUGHTER
PRINCESS MARIE 91

FRANZ LISZT IN THE WEIMAR PERIOD .. 186

LISZT IN 1863 187

PRINCESS CAROLYNE SAYN-WITTGENSTEIN, IN
LATER LIFE 202

LISZT IN 1885 203

FOREWORD

The impulse to embark on the present study came to me without any conscious volition on my part in the course of my work upon the second volume of my *Life of Wagner*. Research into that subject necessarily brought me on a hundred occasions into contact with the figure of Liszt. In that figure I have long been deeply interested for its own sake; and the publication, within recent years, of a good deal of autobiographical and epistolary material that was unknown to the older Liszt biographers had often made me wish that some student with a thorough knowledge of it all would try his hand at a new life-size portrait of this extraordinary man, who is perhaps the most elusive psychological problem in all music. As his career touched that of Wagner at so many points, I felt myself under the necessity, in the course of my second Wagner volume, of defining Liszt himself more accurately than I could persuade myself had yet been done. I soon found, however, that to attempt this with even the smallest prospect of success meant devoting a disproportionate amount of space to Liszt in what is, after all, a Life not of Liszt but of Wagner. Then, finding myself with so much Liszt material on my hands, and becoming more and more fascinated with the contradictions of his complex nature, and more and more conscious that none of the existing biographies, not even the admirable recent one of Peter Raabe, takes stock of all we now know about Liszt, I was suddenly assailed by the temptation to make him the subject of a full-length psychological study. The temptation was all the more irresistible because of my growing interest, during the last few years, in the general problem of musical biography. The Liszt subject attracted me, indeed, not only by its intrinsic interest but by its peculiar difficulty.

This book can be confidently counted upon to displease three classes of readers—those who object on principle to all musical biography, those who object to frank biography, and those who object to the destruction of a biographical legend in which they have been brought up to believe. To the first class—the people who assure us that nothing in connection with an artist matters but his art—I can only reply that many of us have a profound interest not only in art but in human nature and human adventure; these good people must therefore go their own way and allow the rest of us to go ours. What right, asked Tennyson, has the public to know of the follies of Byron? The poet, he said, has given us some fine poems, and we ought to be satisfied with those. Precisely why we "ought" to be satisfied, Tennyson does not tell us; we may reasonably suggest that if our interest in human nature justifies our reading about a fictitious Maud or Galahad or Merlin, it equally justifies our wanting to read about a Byron, whose real life was much more fascinating than the fictive life of any of the Tennysonian worthies. As for the objection that is sometimes raised to the frankness of modern biography, the sufficient answer to that is that if we are to have biographies at all they may as well be veracious ones. By frankness I do not mean the mere malicious or impertinent dwelling upon features in the subject's character or career that lend themselves easily to the sorry business of showing that the greatest or the best of men have their weaknesses or their vices. By frankness I mean the refusal to ignore the plain evidence as to these weaknesses or vices for no better reason than because they cannot be made to fit in with a preconceived scheme for exhibiting the subject as all hero or all saint.

As M. André Maurois has pointed out in his thoughtful book, *Aspects de la biographie*, the modern literary world is in revolt against the complacent type of biography associated with the nineteenth century, in which the subject was conceived centrally as the representative of this or that virtue, and everything in his life that seemed to clash with that conception was either dwelt lightly upon or suppressed. "The modern biographer," says M. Maurois, "if he is honest, refuses to say, 'Here is a great king, a great minister, a great writer. About his name a legend has been constructed; and it is this legend, and this alone, that I intend to set forth.' No: what he says is this: 'Here is a man. I possess a certain number of documents and testimonies concerning him. I am going to try to paint a true portrait of him.

What will this portrait be? I do not know: I do not wish to know until it is finished. I am ready to paint my model just as a long contemplation of him has made me see him, and to retouch the portrait in accordance with any new facts about him that I may discover.' . . . We do not desire that the biographer shall allow his judgments to be dictated by preconceived ideas; we desire that the observed facts shall of themselves lead to general ideas, and that these general ideas shall be verified afterwards by fresh impartial researches, conducted carefully and without passion. We desire that every document shall be made use of that can throw a new light on the subject, and that neither timidity, admiration nor hostility shall impel the biographer to neglect or pass over in silence a single one of them.''

M. Maurois proceeds to debate the question whether biography is, or should be, an art or a science. Into his searching examination of that question I do not propose to follow him, for my own purpose in the present study of Liszt has not been consciously to produce either wholly a work of science or wholly a work of art. For the latter, the deliberate adoption of a certain point of view on the part of the biographer is necessary. If his intention is to make a pure work of art of his portrait of his sitter he must "compose" his picture, deciding, more or less arbitrarily, what is the central significance of the mass of material he has accumulated with regard to him, and shaping and lighting the mass in such a way as to give it a unity and a salience imposed upon it from without as much as from within. A scientific biography, on the other hand, would simply set forth all the known facts with the coldness of a treatise on the structure and habits of an insect or a plant. If the present volume partakes to some extent of the character of each of these types, it has not been because, in writing it, I have consciously striven after a compromise of this kind. I have had before me, in the first place, the purely scientific ideal of accumulating all the relevant facts and setting them before the reader without prepossession and without prejudice. If a scientific word must be found for my method of procedure, perhaps I may be allowed to say that it has been inductive rather than deductive: I have not started, in the nineteenth century manner, from a definite point of view in my reading of Liszt's character and then used the arbitrarily selected material to drive this point home to the reader; I have marshalled the material and then tried to allow it to impose upon me the conclusions that seemed to me immanent in it.

I say "tried" because, to quote M. Maurois once more, the biographer who plumes himself on his complete scientific "impartiality" is as likely as not to be the victim of self-delusion on that point: do what he will, he cannot hope to escape entirely from the unconscious urge to "compose" his sitter, to draw from the assembled facts a conclusion that is the product of subconscious forces within himself, a conclusion, therefore, that may not appeal with the same force to others. But a biographer will not trouble himself greatly about a danger of this kind if he recognises that in scientific biography, as in every other science, no such thing as finality is possible. He has performed his task to the best of his ability if he has set before his readers the results of his enquiry in such a form that it becomes easier for them than it was before to go over the ground afresh on their own account. That has been my sole purpose in the present volume—to correct past errors in Liszt biography; to bring into the one focus a great number of facts, old and new; to suggest, on the basis of these, a possible explanation of an exceedingly complex personality; and then to leave the construction, as I have attempted it, to be confirmed, rectified, or expanded by later students.

To the third class of objectors to which I have referred— those who resent, on sentimental grounds, the shattering of a biographical legend that has acquired almost the authority of Holy Writ—I can only say that at some time or other every legend must submit to critical examination, and if it is found to be inconsistent with the facts it is the legend, not the facts, that will have to go by the board. As for the inception and propagation of the current Liszt legend, one can only hold up one's hands in pious amazement at the credulity alike of the old-style musical biographer and of his readers. It does not seem to have occurred to anyone to ask what was the authority for the Liszt legend that has held the field for so long. As will be shown in the following pages, the prime source of it was information, largely false, and, where it was not actually false, cunningly and tendentiously coloured, supplied to Liszt's first biographer, Lina Ramann, by the Princess Wittgenstein and, to a smaller extent, by Liszt himself. That fact of itself ought to have put both the later biographers and the general reader on their guard, more especially as regards Liszt's earlier years. The mere fact that in connection with some ten of the most vitally formative years of his life—the period of his association with the Countess d'Agoult—not a single first-hand document was open to investigation ought at least to have made both readers and biographers walk warily through that dark forest. A completely new aspect of that matter came to light when the *Mémoires* of the Countess d'Agoult and the Liszt–d'Agoult correspondence were recently published for the first time. A reading of these was sufficient not only to make us revise all our previous notions of the life and the character of Liszt, but to generate a profound distrust of most musical biography; for who can persuade himself, after this revelation of the complete change that can be effected in our point of view by the publication of a single set of first-hand documents, that we know anything like the truth as to the life of any musician in connection with whom first-hand documents are scarce or nonexistent? And one becomes positively dazed when one reflects that by the merest turn in fortune's wheel these new and vital Liszt documents might have vanished from mortal ken for ever; they have been preserved only because they passed, by inheritance, into the custody of one over whom neither Liszt nor the Princess Wittgenstein had any legal control—the grandson of the composer and the Countess d'Agoult, M. Daniel Ollivier. Had Liszt or the Princess destroyed them, as they would probably have been tempted to do had they acquired possession of them, we should have been the victims in perpetuity of the legend that has falsified Lisztian history for the last half-century.

It is not only in connection with the d'Agoult affair, however, that the older biographies of Liszt can be shown to be in great part unreliable. Speaking generally, the biographers have either not been aware of the mass of significant material scattered about in Liszt's own correspondence and in the reminiscences of contemporaries, or else they have chosen to pass it over in silence because it could not be made to square with the fallacious simplification and idealisation of Liszt's character that constituted the Liszt legend. In collecting the relevant evidence as to the whole Liszt my intention has not been anything in the nature of that "debunking"—an odious word for an odious thing—that is so much to the taste of certain modern biographers who, unable to see or to understand the complexity of human nature, take merely a malicious delight in exposing a great man's weaknesses or absurdities. It is because Liszt is so complex that his character becomes so fascinating a study to the modern biographer.

We can readily comprehend the unwillingness of a great man's friends to dwell publicly upon anything but the ideal aspects of his character: they are reluctant to contemplate him except from the angle of their love for him. But in the process of the years the man passes into history, and then it becomes the business of biography to try to see him as he really was and as a whole. In this connection a passage at the end of Fanny Lewald's reminiscences of Liszt (published in book form in her *Zwölf Bilder nach dem Leben*) may be taken as a parable. In the last years of Liszt's life an American sculptor made a life-size bust of him that distressed Frau Lewald-Stahr by its realism. In that period of his life Liszt was no longer the Apollo whom artists and sculptors had so long loved to paint and to model. He had grown very stout; his head had sunk flaccidly into his shoulders; his face had become puffy as the result of his long indulgence in wine and spirits. The American sculptor had not only modelled him just as he was in these respects but had done full justice to the warts that stood out so prominently on his face. Fanny Lewald was revolted by the bust: in her opinion the sculptor ought to have shown to posterity the ideal Liszt as his friends still saw him—the head carried high as in the days of his beauty and pride and confident power, the eye flashing command, and, above all, no warts. Liszt was philosophical enough to take the sculptor's part. A man who, in his old age, still feels within himself something of the glow of youth, he said, too easily deceives himself as to his appearance; his mirror does not tell him the truth. This truth is equally hidden from his friends, who habitually see before them not the real man of the moment but the man they have long known and loved. So it is perhaps good for them all, said Liszt, when a stranger comes who looks objectively at him with eyes free from illusion, and says to him, "See, my friend! This is how you look to us! This is what you are!"

It is the biographer's task, when his subject has long passed into history and can no longer suffer in himself from frankness, to try to model him not as he imagined himself to be, not as his friends, by a process of loving selection among his contradictory traits, would fain persuade themselves they saw him, but as he actually was. The biographer is justified in attempting this complete reconstruction of him so long as he bases that reconstruction on nothing but facts for which there is first-hand documentary evidence. If the reader of the present volume, unwilling to surrender his belief in the old Liszt legend, feels angered at the portrait presented in the following pages, it is no use his merely abusing the photographer. He must either give good reason for disputing the facts adduced, or must show that the writer's interpretation of them is wrong.

This volume was virtually ready for the printers at the commencement of the present year, but was held over because it came to my knowledge that M. Ollivier was contemplating the publication of a second volume of the Liszt–d'Agoult correspondence, dealing with the relations of the pair between 1840 and their final parting in 1844. This second volume having been issued in July of the present year, it was merely a matter of a few days' work to build the new information into the tissue of Chapter IV of the present study. I have to express my grateful thanks to M. Ollivier for his kind permission to quote to the extent I have done from the three notable contributions he has made to Liszt literature—the two volumes of the Liszt–d'Agoult letters to which I have just referred (1933 and 1934), and the *Mémoires* of the Countess d'Agoult (1927).

E.N.

July, 1934.

B

MAIN SOURCES AND REFERENCES

A

ABB = A. W. AMBROS: *Bunte Blätter*. 2 vols. Leipzig, 1872, 1874.

AM = COUNTESS D'AGOULT ("DANIEL STERN"): *Mémoires, 1833-1854; avec une introduction de Daniel Ollivier.* Paris, 1927.

AN = COUNTESS D'AGOULT ("DANIEL STERN"): *Nélida.* 2 vols. Brussels, 1846.

AS = COUNTESS D'AGOULT ("DANIEL STERN"): *Souvenirs, 1806-1833.* 2nd ed. Paris, 1877.

B

BAL = THEODOR VON BERNHARDI: *Aus dem Leben Theodor von Bernhardis.* 9 vols. Leipzig, 1893-1896.

BAS = HANS VON BÜLOW: *Ausgewählte Schriften, 1850-1892, herausgegeben von Marie von Bülow.* Leipzig, 1911.

BAYB = *Bayreuther Blätter*, 1907.

BB = HANS VON BÜLOW: *Briefe.* 7 vols. Leipzig, 1899-1908.

BBE = H. DE BALZAC: *Béatrix.* Paris, n.d.

BBL = MARIE VON BÜLOW: *Hans von Bülows Leben, dargestellt aus seinen Briefen.* 2nd ed. Leipzig, 1921.

BC = *Correspondance de Honoré de Balzac.* 2 vols. Paris, 1877.

BHZL = *Briefe hervorragender Zeitgenossen an Franz Liszt, herausgegeben von La Mara.* 3 vols. Leipzig, 1895-1904.

BLW = MARIE VON BÜLOW: *Hans von Bülow in Leben und Wort.* Stuttgart, 1925.

BNB = HANS VON BÜLOW: *Neue Briefe, herausgegeben und eingeleitet von Richard Graf du Moulin Eckart.* Munich, 1927.

BRR = ROBERT BORY: *Une retraite romantique en Suisse; Liszt et la Comtesse d'Agoult.* Paris, 1930.

BSF = GERTRUD BÄUMER: *Studien über Frauen.* Berlin, 1920.

C

CAB = PETER CORNELIUS: *Ausgewählte Briefe, nebst Tagebuchblättern und Gelegenheitsgedichten, herausgegeben von seinem Sohne, Carl Maria Cornelius.* 2 vols. Leipzig, 1904, 1905.

CFL = FREDERICK CORDER: *Ferencz (François) Liszt.* London, 1925.

CMC = CARL MARIA CORNELIUS: *Peter Cornelius.* 2 vols. Regensburg, 1925.

CSB = *Les Cahiers de Sainte-Beuve.* Paris, 1876.

D

DMCW = RICHARD GRAF DU MOULIN ECKART: *Cosima Wagner, ein Lebens- und Charakterbild.* Munich, 1929.

E

EDFM = JULIUS ECKARDT: *Ferdinand David und die Familie Mendelssohn-Bartholdy.* Leipzig, 1888.

F

FMSG = AMY FAY: *Music-Study in Germany.* London, 1904.

FSC = "ROBERT FRANZ" (COUNTESS OLGA JANINA): *Souvenirs d'une Cosaque.* 5th ed. Paris, 1874.

G

GFL = AUGUST GÖLLERICH: *Franz Liszt.* Berlin, 1908.

GRT = FERDINAND GREGOROVIUS: *Römische Tagebücher, herausgegeben von Friedrich Althaus.* Stuttgart, 1892.

H

HFL = JAMES HUNEKER: *Franz Liszt.* London, 1911.

HLR = NADINE HELBIG: *Franz Liszt in Rom.* (In *Deutsche Revue*, Feb.-March, 1907.)

HPD = MARCEL HERWEGH: *Au Printemps des Dieux.* 2nd ed. Paris, 1929.

HZVM = KARL HILLEBRAND: *Zeiten, Völker und Menschen.* 7 vols. Berlin, 1874-1885.

K

KBG = LUDWIG KARPATH: *Begegnung mit dem Genius.* Vienna, 1934.

KE   = BERTHOLD KELLERMANN: *Erinnerungen, ein Künstlerleben, herausgegeben von Sebastian Haussmann und Hellmut Kellermann.* Zürich, 1932.

KFL = JULIUS KAPP: *Franz Liszt.* Berlin, 1909. (Revised edition 1924.)

L

LAR = RUDOLF LEHMANN: *An Artist's Reminiscences.* London, 1894.

LCD = J. C. LOBE: *Consonanzen und Dissonanzen; Gesammelte Schriften aus älterer und neuerer Zeit.* Leipzig, 1869.

LCS = BERTHOLD LITZMANN: *Clara Schumann . . . translated by Grace E. Hadow.* 2 vols. London, 1913.

LGW = *Aus der Glanzzeit der Weimarer Altenburg: Bilder und Briefe aus dem Leben der Fürstin Carolyne Sayn-Wittgenstein, herausgegeben von La Mara.* Leipzig, 1906.

LMMM = LA MARA: *Marie von Mouchanoff-Kalergis (geb. Gräfin Nesselrode), in Briefen an ihre Tochter.* Leipzig, 1907.

LZAC = *Correspondance de Liszt et de la Comtesse d'Agoult, 1833-1864, publiée par Daniel Ollivier.* 2 vols. Paris, 1933, 1934.

LZB = *Franz Liszts Briefe, herausgegeben von La Mara.* 8 vols. Leipzig, 1893-1905.

LZBL = FANNY LEWALD: *Zwölf Bilder nach dem Leben.* Berlin, 1888.

LZBM = *Franz Liszts Briefe an seine Mutter, aus dem Französischen übertragen und herausgegeben von La Mara.* Leipzig, 1918.

LZPR = FRANZ LISZT: *Pages romantiques, publiées avec une introduction et des notes par Jean Chantavoine.* Paris, 1912.

M

MJJ = ANDREAS MOSER: *Joseph Joachim, ein Lebensbild. Neue, umgearbeitete und erweiterte Ausgabe.* 2 vols. Berlin, 1908, 1910.

N

NLW = ERNEST NEWMAN: *The Life of Richard Wagner.* Vol. I. London and New York, 1933.

P

PCC   = ADOLPHE PICTET: *Une Course à Chamounix: Introduction de Robert Bory*. Geneva, 1930.

R

RFL   = LINA RAMANN: *Franz Liszt als Künstler und Mensch.* 3 vols. Leipzig, 1880-1894.

RJR   = HELENE RAFF: *Joachim Raff, ein Lebensbild.* Regensburg, 1925.

RLAM = LINA RAMANN: *Franz Liszt, Artist and Man, 1811-1840,* translated by E. Cowdery. 2 vols. London, 1882.

RLL   = PETER RAABE: *Liszts Leben.* Stuttgart, 1931.

RLS   = PETER RAABE: *Liszts Schaffen.* Stuttgart, 1931.

RML   = Special Liszt Numbers of *La Revue Musicale.* Paris, May and June, 1928.

S

SFL   = BRUNO SCHRADER: *Franz Liszt.* 2nd ed. Berlin, 1921.

SJI   = GEORGE SAND: *Journal intime (Posthume); publié par Aurore Sand.* Paris, 1926.

SLE   = KARL SCHORN: *Lebenserinnerungen.* 2 vols. Bonn, 1898.

SLPK = ARNOLD SCHERING: *Ueber Liszts Persönlichkeit und Kunst* (in *Jahrbuch der Musikbibliothek Peters,* 1926).

SLRB = KURD VON SCHLÖZER: *Letzte Römische Briefe, 1882-1904.* Stuttgart, 1924.

SNW   = ADELHEID VON SCHORN: *Das Nachklassische Weimar.* 2 vols. Weimar, 1911, 1912.

SRB   = KURD VON SCHLÖZER: *Römische Briefe, 1864-1869, herausgegeben von Karl von Schlözer.* Berlin, 1924.

SRS   = EUGENIE SCHUMANN: *Robert Schumann: ein Lebensbild meines Vaters.* Leipzig, 1931.

SSPS = CAMILLE SAINT-SAËNS: *Portraits et Souvenirs.* Paris, n.d.

SWJ   = ADOLF STAHR: *Weimar und Jena.* 3rd ed. Oldenburg, n.d. [1892?]

SZM   = ADELHEID VON SCHORN: *Zwei Menschenalter, Erinnerungen und Briefe.* Berlin, 1901.

T

TPT   = MODESTE TCHAIKOVSKY: *Life and Letters of Peter Ilich Tchaikovsky, edited from the Russian by Rosa Newmarch.* London, 1906.

W

WBB = *Richard Wagners Briefe an Hans von Bülow.* Jena, 1916.

WEWL = WENDOLIN WEISSHEIMER: *Erlebnisse mit Wagner, Liszt, und vielen anderen Zeitgenossen.* Stuttgart, 1898.

WFL = COSIMA WAGNER: *Franz Liszt, ein Gedenkblatt von seiner Tochter.* 2nd ed. Munich, 1911.

WFLR = JANKA WOHL: *François Liszt, Recollections of a Compatriot, translated from the French by B. Peyton Ward.* London, 1887.

WML = RICHARD WAGNER: *Mein Leben, kritisch durchgesehen, eingeleitet und erläutert von Wilhelm Altmann.* 2 vols. Leipzig, n.d.

WMM = *Memoirs of Alexander Wolkoff-Mouromtzoff (A. M. Roussoff).* London, 1928.

THE UNRELIABILITY OF THE OLDER LISZT BIOGRAPHIES

I

Musical biography has always tended to the diffusion of a romantic legend rather than to an impartial record of the sober truth. For the musical world is divided into clans, and each clan swears such unquestioning loyalty to its adopted chieftain that it is almost as much as the outsider's life is worth to hint that the Big Chief may have had a human as well as a heroic or a sacred side to him. This touching tribal loyalty, uncritical as it may be, is after all quite understandable: the biographer, and those of the musical public who have passed through much the same experiences as his with regard to a given composer's work, owe so much of what is best in their own spiritual life to a Beethoven or a Wagner that they are only too ready to imagine the actual man to have existed always on the same high plane as his artistic ideal, and to resent any attempt to see him as he really was in himself. So it comes about that musical biography in general is, to use the historic phrase of Nietzsche *à propos* of Wagner, "merely *fable convenue*, or worse." The enquiring student comes to believe, in time, that there is more in Mr. Henry Ford's dictum—"history is bunk"—than even that accomplished scholar and refined stylist ever realised.

The Wagner legend we all know: it takes no account of his very human failings—his frequent ingratitude towards bene-factors, his insensitiveness in the matter of money obligations, his egoism where other people's rights to their own lives were concerned, his occasional untruthfulness in the matter of his autobiography. The Beethoven legend we all know: it takes no account of his lack of ideal probity now and then in his dealings with publishers, his pathetic obtuseness in many matters not connected with his creative work, his arrogant ill-breeding, his loudly expressed contempt for the weakness of a love of decorations in others while all the time childishly delighting in anything of the kind that came his own way, his democratic insistence that one man was as good as another, a dustman the equal of a duke, while aristocratically raging at any sign of other people being lacking in respect to himself, his blind egoism where his nephew was concerned, his readiness to defame the moral character of anyone who, like his sister-in-law, refused to bend unquestioningly to his imperious will. And now it becomes evident that all these years there has been in circulation a Liszt legend that corresponds no more with the reality than the legends that had crystallised round Beethoven and Wagner correspond to the men as they actually were. Our consolation is that in each case the real man turns out to be psychologically much more fascinating than the old saintly figure posturing in the stained glass window.

About Liszt the composer critical opinion has always been, and probably always will be, sharply divided. From his own day onwards there have been some who, like Schumann and Joachim, were repelled by his attitude-striking and the too plentiful suggestions of flashiness and bombast in his music; they instinctively felt that there was something spiritually unwholesome in it, for all the sincerity of his ideal of progress in art. There are others who are either constitutionally insensitive to these defects in Liszt's music or deliberately turn a blind eye on them, preferring to contemplate only his significance as an original harmonist, his innovations in the sphere of musical form, and the splendid part he played in the onward movement of music in the mid-nineteenth century. (There is a third group that tries to give due weight to all these considerations, and is neither Lisztian nor anti-Lisztian, but sees him objectively as a historical phenomenon, a force which one neither "likes" nor "dislikes" but simply studies, as one studies today the diplomacy of Metternich, let us say, or the socialism of Karl Marx. Needless to say, the members of this detached group come in for the cross-fire of both the others!). About Liszt the man, however, there has hitherto been virtually only one opinion: the legend has been imposed upon the popular imagination of one who, whatever of tawdriness there may have been in his music at times, was in his private and in his public life a Bayard not only without fear but without reproach, about the nearest thing to St. Francis of Paula (whom, indeed, he adopted as his patron saint) that the imperfect modern world has seen. It will be the purpose of the present book to enquire what foundation there is for that legend.

2

The Liszt that is best known to the ordinary music lover of the present day is the Liszt of the vital Weimar years (1848-61), whose record indeed is glorious: this is the Liszt who befriended not only Wagner but almost every other European composer who was worth encouraging, the Liszt of not only the open mind but the open purse, the Liszt whom no contumely on the part of the critics could cause to swerve an inch from his course, the Liszt whom no ingratitude on the part of some of those he had helped—Clara Schumann, for example—could either sour or provoke to reprisals. The Liszt of the last quarter-century of his life is to most people less well known; for popular biography he became, during that period, a figure with more and more of St. Francis about him, drawing ever nearer and nearer to the monastic ideal of poverty, obedience, and renunciation. Least known of all, until quite lately, was the Liszt of the first thirty-five years of his life. Everyone knew, of course, that his eleven-years' liaison with the Countess d'Agoult had ended unhappily; but the complacent assumption was made, by all the biographers, that the faults were all on one side, and that not Liszt's. The current view of the affair and of the personages involved in it was expressed in its extremest form by the late Mr. Frederick Corder:

"After this religious (or anti-religious) phase which young men go through, came the inevitable amorous period. . . . That so brilliant and attractive a creature as Franz Liszt would be beset by those many libidinous females of French society who kept what they were pleased to call *salons*, but which were better called by a coarser term, might be taken for granted; that his romantic attitude of fidelity to his early love [Caroline de St. Cricq] and religious renunciation of marriage was an impossible one every human [*sic*] man knows; it is sufficient to state in the fewest words that the woman who captured him permanently was Marie-Catherine-Sophie, Countess d'Agoult, a literary person of many experiences, who, recklessly abandoning her husband, children and worldly position, forced herself upon Liszt, in one of those erotic crazes common to her sex, and became his 'wife in the sight of heaven,' as they say on the stage, for ten years. . . . The actual results were, firstly, a distinguished family was humiliated, secondly, the position of a great artist was severely compromised for ten years, and thirdly, the world was encumbered with three superfluous children, who had to be 'legitimised.' . . . Madame d'Agoult is said to have possessed great beauty and literary talent, though there is no evidence extant of either quality.(1) She was 'highly temperamental'—in other words, she had a violent temper—there is ample evidence of *that*, and she can hardly be said to have justified her existence in any way. Liszt seems to have behaved towards her as a gentleman should do in the circumstances, and to have accepted the results of his unfortunate escapade without complaint."(2)

Thus are musical history and biography written, in England, by "professors of composition". Neither Mr. Corder nor any of the other biographers who take the traditional line with regard to the Liszt-d'Agoult affair could be expected to know the whole truth about it, for the two vital collections of documents bearing on the case—the *Mémoires* of the Countess and

---

(1) Her beauty, grace and high breeding are praised by many of her contemporaries, even the women among them: George Sand used to become quite lyrical over her. As for her literary gifts, it is evident that Mr. Corder had not taken the trouble to read a single one of her books. Lina Ramann, whose information on this point was of course derived, directly or indirectly, from Liszt himself, describes her as "beautiful, indeed very beautiful—a Loreley. Slender, of distinguished bearing, bewitchingly graceful and yet stately in her movements, with a proudly carried head covered with a profusion of blond hair that fell over her shoulders like a shower of gold, a profile of classical symmetry . . ." (RFL, I, 322, 323)

(2) CFL, p. 53, 54.

the two volumes of the *Correspondance de Liszt et de la Comtesse d'Agoult, 1833-34*—were not published until 1927, 1933 and 1934 respectively. But in the absence of any first-hand documents bearing on this episode in Liszt's life the biographers might at least have proceeded warily. Ordinary caution should have suggested a suspension of judgment. Instead of that, the judges gave their verdict in favour of the prosecutor without even asking whether any evidence could be called for the defendant. They had virtually nothing to go upon but the account of the matter given in the official *Life of Liszt* by Lina Ramann, the first volume of which was published, during the composer's lifetime, in 1880, the second in 1887 (a year after his death), the third in 1894. The material for the first volume, in which, of course, the d'Agoult episode falls, was perhaps supplied partly by Liszt himself but mainly and more directly by the devoted partner in his second extra-matrimonial adventure, the Princess Carolyne von Sayn-Wittgenstein;(3) and common prudence would have prompted the reflection, on the part both of the biographer and the reader, that possibly only half the story may therefore have been told. All later biographies of Liszt were, in the main, founded on that of Lina Ramann, especially as regards the first third of his career.

---

(3) Liszt's daughter, Cosima Wagner, hints that the Princess actually wrote some portions of the *Life* (See WFL, p. 18). Du Moulin Eckart says that there is no longer any doubt that this was the case. "A veil," he says, "has been drawn over this lovely and noble figure [the Countess d'Agoult] in the biography [of Liszt] by the Princess Wittgenstein's henchwoman [Lina Ramann] . . . The remarkable correspondence between the Princess and her faithful Ramann is now in the Weimar archives: it is not to be opened till fifty years after the Princess's death. It will furnish a complete explanation of the relation between the Princess and this strangest of all biographies. . . . The book cannot be absolved from the charge of calumny . . ." (DMCW, pp. 9, 10). But in that calumny Liszt is inextricably involved. Even if he himself did not supply Lina Ramann with deliberately false information, even if he did not see the first volume of the book in proof, we know he saw it afterwards, for his own copy, with his annotations, still exists in Weimar. Yet he not only acquiesced in what he must have known to be a tissue of falsehoods about Madame d'Agoult, but in almost every recorded reference to her in his conversations in later life he repeated these falsehoods.

3

The verdict of the court was given to Liszt in virtue of his "character", though it was precisely this "character" of his that was at stake! That character being what it was supposed to be, any calling of evidence for the other side was regarded as a pure superfluity. It has always been a matter for wonder how Liszt, whose plentiful nobility of soul no one will dispute, could in later years have behaved so callously, so unforgivingly, where the Countess was concerned. He, who was generally so abounding in toleration to those who had behaved badly to him, was in this case pitiless. An attempt had been made by Louis de Ronchaud, in his preface to a new edition of the Countess's *Esquisses Morales* (1880),(4) to show that in the Liszt affair she had been at least as much sinned against as sinning. But the biographers would have none of this. The fact that Ronchaud was the favourite friend of the Countess in her later years was held by the all-too-partisan Liszt biographers to convict *him a priori* of partisanship: and his generous estimate of her literary significance was regarded as of itself sufficient to discredit his judgment by the very people who admit that Liszt himself grossly over-estimated the intellectual capacity of his adored Carolyne.

There could therefore be no discussion of the question whether Liszt had been "good" in the d'Agoult affair—because his unvarying and incorruptible "goodness" was the first principle of the Lisztian faith! So we find Julius Kapp, for example, loftily ruling that these suggestions that there may possibly have been another side to the story "reveal little knowledge and understanding of the nobility of Liszt. A man of such gentleness and chivalry as Liszt was does not judge a woman, thirty or forty years later, with such personal irritability as he did, for example, at the news of her death."(5) The bare possibility that in this one matter Liszt, for some reason or other that might be

---

(4) She wrote under the pseudonym of "Daniel Stern".

(5) KFL, p. 64. Kapp, in the preface to the revised edition (the 19th, 1924) of his book (first published in 1909), claims that his object throughout has been to tell "the absolute truth." "I forbore," he says, "to write Liszt's life as it *might* have been, or as many people today would

worth investigating, had failed to be either noble, gentle or chivalrous apparently does not seem to have occurred to the biographers. It was humanly natural that he and the Princess Wittgenstein should try to present the case to posterity in the colours most favourable to him, for no man tells his biographer the whole truth about himself, even when he knows it; but whether this procedure was ideally "chivalrous" in the present instance may be held to be open to question. It has been said, again, that Liszt showed his chivalry by never saying anything *in public* to the detriment of the Countess. It might fairly be argued, however, that to set a false legend going in private, thus giving the victim of it, or her friends, no chance to comment publicly upon the accusations, was even less chivalrous than an entry into the public lists would have been.

Liszt tells the Princess, in a letter of 13th April, 1866,(6) that he has just seen Madame d'Agoult in Paris, and that she had informed him that she was preparing her memoirs for publication. According to his own account he told her rather brutally that they would be nothing but *poses et mensonges*. This phrase about "postures and lies" has become a *locus classicus* in Liszt biography. While the first-hand documents bearing on the case were still unknown, the phrase was regarded as deciding in advance the incurable unveracity of the Countess. Now that these documents are published, however, not only do they put a very different complexion upon the whole affair but they raise the suspicion that Liszt, fearing the telling of the uncompromising truth about himself, wanted to prejudice posterity in advance

---

like to picture it as having been; I made no scruple about demolishing many a halo that had been created by friendly hands or illegitimately maintained by an adroit use of tradition; I tried to construct, instead of an ideal figure bathed in incense, a figure of flesh and blood just as it walked the earth, illuminated by the nobility of its own being, but also burdened with human weaknesses." The newest documents bearing on the case, however, show that Kapp, in spite of all his care and all his zeal for the truth, took, as previous biographers had done, too much for granted as to the "ideal" side of Liszt's character. It is yet another illustration of the sad and sobering fact that no finality in biography is attainable.

(6) LZB, VI, 111.

against his former love by hinting that whatever she might have to say about him was bound to be falsehood. And, as we have seen, the device succeeded to perfection—for a time. A breach was made in it by the publication of the Countess's *Mémoires*, and it was finally routed by the appearance of the first volume of the Liszt-d'Agoult *Correspondance* six years later. Not only does the whole episode now call for drastic re-writing, but, as we shall in due course see, the basic truth of the Countess's view of Liszt in his younger days is confirmed by what we know of him, from the most authentic sources, in the later stages of his life, as well as by his own letters to her during the period from 1833 to 1840.

4

There always co-existed in the one organism, in fact, not one Liszt but two Liszts—perhaps more than two; and it is hardly surprising that his biographers have not been able to harmonise them, seeing that he himself never succeeded in so doing. That was his real tragedy, both as man and as artist. Everyone who has thought seriously and sympathetically about him has been struck by the dualism of his nature. One always speaks of his cardinal qualities in contradictory pairs or threes. He himself used to say he was "half Zigeuner, half Franciscan." Henry Thode describes him as "one-third minstrel, one-third chevalier, one-third Franciscan." Other descriptions of him have been "half saint, half charlatan," "half priest, half circus-rider." Always, after studying him, there remains the impression of a soul hopelessly divided against itself.(7) The romantic falsification wrought by the biographies has come about through the

---

(7) In 1863, *à propos* of a remark in one of Brendel's articles in the *Neue Zeitschrift für Musik*, to the effect that "the artistic nature, when it is genuine, supplies its own self-correction as a result of its own shifting antitheses," Liszt writes to Brendel, "I agree with this. . . . This much is certain, that few men have had to labour at the wearisome task of self-correction as I have, for the process of my intellectual development has been, if not impeded, at all events made considerably more difficult by reason of a multiplicity of occurrences. Some twenty years ago a gifted man said to me, not inaptly, 'You really have to deal with three men in you, who run counter to each other—the convivial man of

selection only of the traits and the anecdotes that reveal the priest rather than the circus-rider, and the bland ignoring of everything that hints at the other aspect of him. The legend has been sedulously diffused that after a period in which, admittedly, he was more of a virtuoso than a thoughtful artist, he purged himself of all impurities and became an inflexibly virtuous high priest of art. Always, however, some incident or other crops up that suggests that his conversion was never quite so complete as would appear on the surface, that, cloister and scourge himself as he would, the old Adam in him was never wholly subdued. The biographers would have us believe that even when he sinned against art in his flaming youth he was simultaneously conscious of his sin and repentant of it. We all know, for example, the story of how, after his playing of a Beethoven work in Paris, the audience unanimously demanded his Fantasia on *Robert the Devil*, and how he was compelled to give way, muttering angrily "I am the servant of the public, that goes without saying!"(8) There is ample evidence, however, that in general he delighted in his showy Fantasias for their own sake as well as for the spell they exercised over his more superficial hearers, and that rather than lose the applause that, for all his idealism, was the very breath of his nostrils, he was perfectly willing to exhibit himself as the circus-rider pure and simple. This, indeed, was one of the elements in him that

---

the salons, the virtuoso, and the thoughtful creative artist. If you ever manage to come to terms with one of them, you will be able to congratulate yourself on your luck.' Well, we shall see!" (Letter of 7th September, 1863, in LZB, II, 50, 51.)

We shall find, in the course of the present study, good reason for doubting whether Liszt ever succeeded in even approximately harmonising these three elements of his being.

(8) His irritation on this occasion is understandable: the incident took place at one of the concerts given to raise funds for the Beethoven monument in Bonn. He had no scruple, however, about adding to *Adelaïde* what he describes as "an enormous cadenza of three pages in small notes, and a whole coda that is almost as long": all this, he tells Breitkopf & Härtel in a letter of 7th May, 1841, in which he offers them his handiwork for publication, he has played, "without being hissed, at the concert at the Paris Conservatoire in aid of the Beethoven monument, and I mean to play it again in Germany and Russia". (LZB, I, 41.)

made the soberer musicians of the period a trifle suspicious of him; moreover, there is good reason to suspect that even his playing of the great classics was often marred by the defects of his uncontrollable Zigeuner temperament, to say nothing of his unwarrantable alterations of, and interpolations in, the text.

Mendelssohn, for instance, writes thus to Ferdinand David on 5th February, 1842, after a recital of Liszt's in Berlin:

"Liszt has not pleased me half so well here as he has done in other places: he has forfeited a considerable portion of my esteem through the tomfool pranks he played not only with the public —which doesn't matter—but with the music itself. He performed works by Beethoven, Bach, Handel and Weber in such a pitiably imperfect style, so uncleanly, so ignorantly, that I could have listened to many a middling pianist with more pleasure. Here six bars were added, there seven were omitted; here wrong harmonies were played and then, later, cancelled out by others equally false, there a horrible fortissimo was employed in the softest passages; and there were all sorts of other lamentable misdemeanours."(9) "As likely as not," says Moser, "if the applause after, say, a Beethoven sonata was not as vociferous as usual, he would plunge straight into a quite empty piece in which he could display his diabolical art as a pianist; the applause followed, and the honour of the virtuoso was saved."(10) The same oscillation between extremes was visible in his daily life: Schumann, as late as 1846, records a conversation with Mendelssohn in which the latter spoke of

---

(9) EDFM, p. 164. In fairness to Liszt, however, it has to be recognised that "misdemeanours" of this kind were common at that time. See NLW, Chapter VIII, for evidence as to the pranks even the leading instrumentalists in orchestras were in the habit of playing with their music in order to draw attention to themselves. Ferdinand David himself had a good deal on his conscience. Jahn, in an article in the *Grenzboten* (1855), charged him with "introducing all sorts of cheap affectations to give piquancy to the works of Haydn and Mozart". In a letter of 1st February, 1844, to Mendelssohn, David himself boasts that the success of a performance of Beethoven's triple concerto (by himself, Hiller, and Rietz) was due to the fact that they had played the last movement with "all possible coquetry and *chicane*".

(10) MJJ, I, 113.

"Liszt's way in everything—a perpetual fluctuation between scandal and apotheosis; with him, every man is either god or devil."(11)

5

The popular impression is that after settling down at Weimar and becoming, along with Wagner, the leader of the "New German School," Liszt turned his back for good upon the follies and vulgarities of his youth. The truth is, however, that even the strength of his new ideals and the influence, in some ways beneficent, of the Princess Wittgenstein upon him were insufficient to keep him from reverting frequently to his old musical loves of the more sinful kind: the virtuoso was too strong within him for that. In 1850, the year that saw the composition of his *Prometheus* and the second version of *Ce qu'on entend sur la montagne*, the *Heroïde funèbre*, the *Pater Noster*, and other works in his most ideal vein, he wrote also his enormous *Fantasia and Fugue on Ad nos* (the chorale sung by the Anabaptists in Meyerbeer's *Le Prophète*). No doubt many of his friends wondered secretly at this excursion into a field upon which he was supposed to have turned his back; but it was reserved for his pupil and secretary, the eleven-years-younger Raff, in a letter of December of that year, to indulge in the plainest of plain-speaking to him with regard to it:

"I have gone through the *Prophète* Fugue with the greatest interest. Do you know, it is a mystery to me how you could bring yourself to expend so much painful labour on a theme of this kind? With the same expenditure of invention you could easily have produced an original composition of the first importance, and then people would not be saying that you have to fasten upon Meyerbeer because of a lack of original invention. I know you will reply, 'This is my will.' To that there is no objection to be raised except the one you yourself will make at other times, that hours and days no more come to us as gifts than ideas do, and that you ought no longer to clamp yourself to other big names now that everyone looks to you to begin the *Movens* of a new epoch. . . . Has one ever heard of a man

---

(11) LCS, II, 120.

riveting a new frigate to an old brig to make it sail faster? What I am saying now is not merely a personal presumption on my part—I would not be guilty of that with regard to you—but the view of *the artist*, a view you will incidentally get also from Joachim, David, or anyone else. It comes solely from a sense of your artistic position. . . . I ask pardon for remarks such as these, that are wrung from me simply because I am impatient to see you in the position that is yours by rights."(12)

While his enemies rejoiced over these and similar evidences of a certain weakness in him, for it confirmed their opinion that at heart he was only a brilliant showman, his best friends grieved at them. Joachim, who was sincerely devoted to him in the Weimar days, was saddened by the cynicism with which, when the fit was on him, he would play the mountebank with the classics. "Joachim has repeatedly told me," says Moser, "what a wonderful experience it was to play sonatas or other chamber works with Liszt *for the first time*. At the second or third performance, however, Liszt could not refrain from playing quite simple passages in octaves or thirds, converting ordinary trills into sixths, and indulging in fiddle-faddle of this kind even in such a work as the *Kreutzer Sonata* of Beethoven."(13)

Even Peter Raabe, the sympathetic author of what is in many respects the most reliable biography of Liszt, finds it a little hard to understand how the composer, in his best period, could bring himself to revive some of the works of his worst, or to hark back to a style he had presumably outgrown. In 1853, for example, the year in which he finished the great B minor piano sonata and was working hard at the *Faust Symphony*, he brought out a new and revised edition of the worthless *Gaudeamus igitur* Paraphrase.(14) Raabe surmises, as did Weissheimer long

---

(12) BHZL, I, 154. The *Ad nos* is now recognised as one of Liszt's greater works. Raff's outburst was probably occasioned less by the quality of the work itself than by the feeling that at this stage of Liszt's evolution he ought not to have been reverting to his old practice of taking work —and often inferior work—of other composers as his starting point.

(13) MJJ, II, 339.

(14) RLS, p. 10.

ago,(15) that Liszt, on occasions of this kind, succumbed to the temptation of his publishers and the desire to make a little money. That explanation satisfies, as far as it goes; but it still leaves us wondering why the mature man should have so complacently shown his contemporaries, most of whom were sharply critical of him, the worst side of his talent simultaneously with the best; we can readily understand how, by doing so, he made his own position in the musical world more difficult. Composers before and since Liszt have not disdained to make a slight concession now and then, for money's sake, to the tastes of the less intellectual portion of their admirers; but few of them can have so cynically done violence to their own artistic conscience as he frequently did. Liszt's lapses were all the more dangerous for him because of the loftiness of the ideals to which he would have had his contemporaries believe he had now devoted his life; it made it too easy for those who disliked him and his music to say that, preach as he might about the ideal, he remained the old showman at heart.

6

In the light of what we now know about him, however, it is a not unreasonable assumption that, for him, these works in his older style had actually a virtue that a more refined taste cannot associate with them. Strive as he would, the influence of the first period of his life as an artist, the years in which he was everywhere fêted as the most brilliant concert virtuoso the world had ever seen, was ineradicable. Admiration and applause were at all times a necessity to him. Kurd von Schlözer(16)

---

(15) See WEWL, p. 43. "At first," says Weissheimer, "I could not quite comprehend why Liszt should write such things [as the Fantasias on Italian operas which he used to play at the Princess Wittgenstein's soirées]. Only later did it become clear to me—at a very lavish dinner at which Liszt broke out with 'Ah, if I had written only *Faust* and *Dante* Symphonies I shouldn't be able to give my friends trout with iced champagne!'"

(16) Schlözer was the young Secretary to the Prussian Legation in Rome during the years 1864-69, during which he saw a good deal of Liszt, both privately and in high society. His notes on Liszt are particularly

noted with indulgent irony—for he sincerely admired and loved Liszt—how, when he was playing to an elegant company, the old warrior would revert to a well-known habit of his youth, turning round to his auditors and transfixing them with "a demoniac look," as in the days when, at his recitals, he used to slay pretty princesses and countesses by the score.(17) The tonsure and the cassock—for Liszt by this time had become an abbé—had evidently not by any means subdued the mountebank in him. It is probable, then, that in the matter of his weaker compositions also there still lingered in him a positive liking for what was showy. As the scrupulous Raabe points out, as late as 1868 he could not refrain, in his Rêverie *Les Adieux* (based on Gounod's *Romeo and Juliet*), from adding to the simple piece, that was within the power of any pianist, *ossia* lines "that present not an easier alternative but merely another procedure that had occurred to him. The only conclusion we can come to is that he himself filed away at worthless things of this kind with a certain satisfaction."(18) And, as Raabe says, he had evidently lost the faculty of discriminating between what was worth publishing and what was not. In 1884, two years before his death, the old man of seventy-three brought out a *Bülowmarsch* of which Bülow himself and his Meiningen orchestra made mock when they came to try over the work that had been written in their honour: asked by the publisher of the work why he did not perform it in Berlin, Bülow answered, "Because I only play good music."(19) Two years before that, Bülow had laughed at the folly of a publisher who had paid Liszt 1,500 marks for a *Romance oubliée* which Bülow calls "an unexampled scar on the face".(20)

The Zigeuner in Liszt, in fact, was at war with the Franciscan,

---

valuable because they are not reminiscences compiled years later, and therefore subject to the colouring that all experiences are apt to acquire in the course of time, but appear in letters written to his family day by day.

(17) See SRB, p. 218.

(18) RLS, p 13.

(19) GFL, p. 51.

(20) In a letter to Eugen Spitzweg, in BBL, p. 365.

the natural vulgarian with the natural nobleman, to the end of his days. His weaknesses were ineradicable and incurable. When he was left to himself they always tended to get the upper hand of him. The best that was latent in him was brought out by the Princess Wittgenstein in the twelve or thirteen years in Weimar during which her stronger nature exercised daily sway over his; the fundamental dualism of soul was still in him, but she managed, in the main, to repress some of the paltrier elements of his nature and to encourage some of the nobler. When, in the later years in Rome and elsewhere, her influence was mostly withdrawn, his better self had a hard fight of it with his worse, a fight from which it did not always emerge triumphant. It would not have been very difficult to reconstruct, approximately, the Liszt of the earlier years—the years of the liaison with Madame d'Agoult, about which so little was at one time known—from the copious testimony we have as to the nature of the Liszt of the Weimar and the Liszt of the Rome period. And our conjectural reconstruction of him finds the fullest confirmation in the d'Agoult documents recently published, to the detailed consideration of which we may now address ourselves. We shall see that, from the first, Liszt was a soul divided against itself; that Madame d'Agoult had the best of reasons for realising what was weak and contemptible as well as what was noble in him; and that it was, in large part, the galling conviction that she knew him through and through, was not duped by the actor in him, and would in all probability one day communicate to the world her pitiless observations of him, that filled him with such unappeasable enmity towards her and made him try to forestall the world's judgment by declaring in advance that whatever she might say about himself would be merely *poses et mensonges.*

CHAPTER II

THE BEGINNINGS OF THE
D'AGOULT AFFAIR

I

The reader of any of the Liszt biographies will be familiar already with the story of Liszt and the Countess d'Agoult as told by Lina Ramann, for it was from her that all the later biographers have copied, with, of course, as we have seen in the case of Mr. Corder, fanciful embellishments of their own. Unfortunately it has to be said quite frankly today that Ramann's account of the matter is itself, to a large extent, merely *poses et mensonges*. According to her, the Countess, a mixture of vanity, hypocrisy, and romantic self-delusion, set her cap from the first at the model of adolescent purity that was Franz Liszt, gradually wore down his moral resistance, and finally persuaded him, against his will, to the flight to Switzerland with her. While Liszt himself must have supplied Lina Ramann with certain details as to persons, times and places, the main inspirer of the chapter concerned was undoubtedly the Princess Wittgenstein. It would be no surprise indeed to find it proved that, as Cosima Wagner and others have hinted, much of the actual writing in this chapter was hers, for it bears all the marks of her high-flown literary style, and it is a perfect specimen of the tight-lipped primness that is possible only to a religious woman who knows herself to be a model to the rest of her sex. Her familiar prejudices are visible at every turn—prejudice against all that the French romantic movement of the eighteen-thirties stood for in the matter of life and art, prejudice against the political and cultural views of the Countess (who was inclined to free-thinking, whereas the Princess was a devout Catholic), prejudice against the beautiful and intelligent woman who had played so large a part in Liszt's life before she herself came into it to guide it into what she held to be the true path. One of her grievances against the Countess is that she had wished to play the part of Liszt's "Muse"—a *rôle*, of course, reserved by Providence, in the Princess's estimation, for the Princess.

Her facts and dates relating to this period are frequently wrong. The Countess had not three children by her marriage, but two. It was not to Berne but to Basel that the pair fled first in 1835. These and other details suggest that in general Lina Ramann had been primed by the Princess rather than by Liszt, who would not be likely to blunder over points like these. The climax of misstatement is reached in the remark that while the Countess "had taken the name of the bourgeois artist, her pride would not permit of her giving up a single one of her usual habits of life. She had no income. He had to bear, out of the receipts from his concerts, the expense even of obligations of hers that antedated their intimate relationship."(1) In her preface to the English edition of the first volume of her book (1882), however, Ramann gives us to understand that several new facts had come to her knowledge since the publication of the German original in 1880; and the passage in question was now amended to the following: "Her income consisted only of the interest of her dowry, which the Count d'Agoult *had* paid her very regularly; but what was twenty thousand francs a year to meet the requirements of her luxury, which, according to Liszt's secretary, Belloni, amounted in the course of years to three hundred thousand francs? Liszt covered all these expenses with the proceeds of his concerts. He also took responsibilities of a tenderer nature, which fell into the period of their intimate connection."(2)

2

Thus can musical biography be written without the slightest enquiry into the credibility of the alleged facts! Liszt and the

---

(1) RFL, I, 332.

(2) RLAM, II, 111, 112. It is this later statement of Ramann's that appears in most of the modern biographies. See, for instance, KFL, p. 69. And Miss Cowdery, the English translator, makes the "300,000 francs" apply to "the course of years," whereas the original reads "sometimes 300,000 francs *a year.*"

Countess fled to Switzerland in the spring of 1835: Belloni did
not become Liszt's secretary until the autumn of 1840, so that
he could have had no first-hand knowledge whatever of the
pianist's finances before that date. In 1835 Liszt had practically
no money. After a brief career as an infant prodigy he played
very little in public for a long time; between 1830 and 1834 he
hardly appeared in the concert room at all, but earned a modest
income by teaching. His small savings he had mostly invested
for the maintenance of his mother. Twice in the course of his
correspondence with the Countess in 1834 he mentions his
poverty.(3) He earned hardly any money worth speaking of
between the spring of 1835 and 1839, when he launched upon
his dazzling career as a mature virtuoso. As late as November,
1837, we find him writing to his mother, "We are expecting a
remittance from Madame d'Agoult's attorney. Even if one did
not want it, this kind of thing is always acceptable. It is
luxurious to have 100,000 francs in one's writing desk that one
doesn't know what to do with."(4) In August, 1836, he tells
Mademoiselle Lyde that he has only 200 francs in his purse,
and that he is awaiting a remittance from her father, "to whom
my mother has entrusted my modest quarterly revenue of
1,000 francs."(5) It is tolerably evident that during the first
few years of his association with the Countess it was not his
money but hers that was the main support of the pair.

As for the years between 1839 and the spring of 1844, when
he and Marie finally parted company, the most recent documents
suggest that Liszt's wealth has been over-estimated by the
biographers. Apparently it was not until the winter of 1842-43
that he began to make money in large quantities. The tours
which he and others undertook in England in 1840 and 1841
were failures; we find him writing to the Countess of his
"penury," practising economy, and even selling rings that had
been given him by royalties. He was frequently glad of an

---

(3) He is "as poor as Job," he says (LZAC, I, 113). "I must give up my
    plan to go to Mont Saint-Michel, for I have no permission to do so,
    and too little money." Ibid., I, 124.

(4) LZBM, p. 39.

(5) LZB, I, 15.

engagement of any kind. In June, 1841, he paid off some debts he had contracted in London, and congratulated himself that there now remained only one of 120 louis in Brussels. All through that year he was evidently pressed for money. Meanwhile the Countess's mother had arranged for the immediate transfer to her of some of the money that would ultimately come to her, and on the death of her mother she came into a fortune. There is no supporting evidence whatever for the charge made against the Countess by Lina Ramann. Insignificant as the matter may be in itself, it is an interesting illustration of the general unreliability of the Ramann biography, and of the malice towards the Countess that inspired some sections of it.(6)

---

(6) All the evidence we possess shows that Marie kept urging Liszt to practise economy. We find her trying to dissuade him from even the small expenditure of 1,500 francs or so for a carriage on the ground that they could not afford such an unnecessary luxury. In December, 1839, she urged him to give fewer concerts: was it worth while, she added, for him to endanger his health for a few thousand francs? (LZAC, I, 329). In the following January she tells him once more that her ideal is a simple life of retirement with him: "Oh! Franz, why need we be rich? Why need we live among men?" (LZAC, I, 366). A few months later she gently reproves him—not on her account but on that of his mother—for squandering his money as he notoriously did: "Your mother spoke to me yesterday about her finances. She is not so well off as I imagined; actually her capital is less than 60,000 francs. Remember this when you are tempted to strew your liberalities right and left. I know you are generous beyond words; but though this disposition brings satisfactions of the highest order, it ought to yield to the humble duty of assuring as comfortable an existence as possible to one's mother and one's children" (LZAC, I, 437).

There seems to be no evidence whatever for Belloni's charge of Marie's wasting Liszt's fortune. Was the good Belloni, one wonders, trying to cover up some financial misdeeds of his own? He became Liszt's man of affairs, as we have seen, in 1840. The Brussels banker Dubois, who saw him at close quarters, declared categorically that he was in the habit of "swindling" Liszt over his concert receipts: "I have no hesitation in saying this," he adds, "for I can prove it" (See KFL, p. 165).

The Countess seems to have kept Belloni at a proper distance, and to have warned Liszt against permitting undue familiarity on his servant's part (See LZAC, II, 117). Perhaps this attitude of hers towards him did not help to endear her to Belloni.

But apart from easily demonstrable errors of this kind on
trifling matters of fact, it is clear that the chapter on the
Countess in the Ramann-Wittgenstein *Life* is a deliberate and,
in its way, a clever device to forestall the judgment of posterity
on Liszt. Not only did he himself know that the Countess
intended to write her memoirs(7) but he was well aware that
she had kept a journal in at any rate the early years of their
union, for we find him, in 1840, adding a comment in his own
handwriting to the section dealing with their Italian sojourn.
In 1838 he had himself committed to paper some reflections
upon their life in common, which remained in her possession
as part of her own journal. When, therefore, she told him in
1866 that she intended to write her memoirs he knew too well
how critically she had often judged him during the years of
their association, and how many letters of his, belonging to this
period, remained in her hands, to feel at all comfortable with
regard to the prospect. She had already angered him in 1846,
after their definite rupture, by painting him in a very unfavourable light in her novel *Nélida*, of which more will fall to be said
later. He had almost forgotten and to some extent forgiven this
malicious blow in the course of the years; but he was exasperated
beyond measure when, in 1866, she brought out a new edition
of the book. He took it as a sign of implacable enmity on her
part.

He knew then that, the Countess being what she was, if ever
her memoirs were published they would contain a much less
flattering portrait of him than it was agreeable to him to
anticipate. The obvious tactics, therefore, were to forestall her.
He does not figure *in propria persona* in the *Souvenirs*, which,

---

(7) The reader must distinguish between "Daniel Stern's" *Souvenirs* and
her *Mémoires*. Her complete autobiography was planned by her to
occupy three volumes, dealing with (1) the years from her birth (in
December, 1805) to 1833, (2) the years 1833 to 1848, which cover the
period of her association with Liszt, (3) the remaining years of her life.
The first volume was published, under the title of *Mes Souvenirs*, by
her executors in 1877 (she had died on the 5th March, 1876). The other
volumes were never formally completed, but her journals and reminiscences covering the years 1833 to 1854 were issued in 1927 under
the title of *Mémoires*.

as we have seen, extend only to 1833; and he probably knew that at her death the remainder of the autobiography had not been formally completed. But it was tolerably certain that what had been left would be given to the world some time or other; and in view of this the wells of truth had to be poisoned in advance. The Princess gladly saw to that; her anxiety to be first in the field, indeed, may have been one of the reasons for bringing out the first volume of Lina Ramann's *Life* so early as 1880, six years before Liszt's death, and only four after that of the Countess. And the tactics succeeded, for Ramann's account of Madame d'Agoult and of her relations with Liszt has been received without question by the musical world for close on half a century. The method of procedure was as cunning as it was unscrupulous. The plan was to blacken the Countess's character for veracity before she could be put into the witness-box. She was to be declared, in advance, to be simply incapable by nature of telling the truth or seeing things as they were. With tears in her beautiful Polish eyes the Princess weeps over her predecessor and rival as only a woman supremely conscious of her own virtue—in spite of her having been guilty of the same lapse—can weep over an erring sister. The Countess, it seems, even lacked—in the eyes of the scribbling blue-stocking who is directly answerable for so much that is laughable and detestable in the literary works of Liszt, and who was herself to produce a probably unreadable masterpiece, in twenty-four volumes, on *The Interior Causes of the Exterior Weakness of the Church*—any literary gift whatever.(8) Worst of all, in the

---

(8) The list of the Princess's own literary achievements will give the reader an idea of the cast of her mind. It is as follows:

Buddhisme et Christianisme, 1 vol.

De la prière, par une femme du monde, 1 vol.

Entretiens pratiques à l'usage des femmes du monde:

   Religion et monde, 1 vol.

   L'amitié des anges, 1 vol.

   La chapelle sixtine, 1 vol.

La matière dans la dogmatique chrétienne, 3 vols.

L'église attaquée par la médisance, 1 vol.

Petits entretiens pratiques à l'usage des femmes du grand monde pour la durée d'une retraite spirituelle, 8 vols.

religious Princess's eyes, Madame d'Agoult was inclined towards rationalism; she actually read not only George Sand but
Voltaire. The daughter of a French father and a German
mother, the associate of most of the leading French writers and
thinkers of her day, she was intellectually a compound of a
number of influences, instead of having, like the Princess, the
notable advantage of a purely one-track mind. She was keen to
taste of everything that life could offer, but unfortunately "had
not much feeling for deeper knowledge, and had a feeble eye for
the higher truth," while her imagination caused her to live in a
world remote from reality. She was vain and fantastic and
prone to hypocrisy, we are told, though, as the Princess handsomely enough admits, "it might be maintained that she was
not herself conscious of her hypocrisy, but, on the contrary,
laboured under the delusion that she was anything but a
hypocrite."(9)

---

*Simplicité des colombes, Prudence des serpens:Quelques reflexions suggerées
par les femmes et les temps actuels*, 1 vol.
Souffrance et Prudence, 1 vol.
Sur la perfection chrétienne et la vie intérieure, 1 vol.
Causes intérieures de la faiblesse extérieure de l'église, 24 vols.
This last was not to be published until twenty-five years after her death,
when, she thought, the world might be intellectually and spiritually
ripe for it.

(9) The Princess did more than inspire Lina Ramann's mendacities: she
pumped her prejudice into her literary friends. In 1878, two years after
Madame d'Agoult's death, Karl Hillebrand wrote a study of her that
was republished later in his collected works. Ostensibly this article
deals with Madame d'Agoult as an author; but the practised student of
Liszt literature can see clearly enough that Hillebrand's analysis of her
character, or what he imagined to be her character, has the minimum of
connection with her works, but corresponds so closely with what was
to be said about her, in 1880, in the first volume of the Ramann *Life*,
that there can be little question that it is the result of talks with the
Princess Wittgenstein. We meet with not only the same opinions as
in Ramann's book but occasionally with an almost identical phraseology.
(See HZVM, IV, 76 ff.)
The first really thoughtful and sympathetic modern study of Marie
d'Agoult seems to be that of Gertrud Bäumer (in BSF). Frau Bäumer,
in 1920, had the wit to perceive that on the face of it Lina Ramann's
account is highly suspicious: "It is impossible," she says, "to obtain

The reader will see how cunningly the court was prejudiced in advance; by insisting, more in sorrow, it seemed, than in anger, that the Countess was hypocritical, constitutionally untruthful, and always liable to mistake her romantic fancies for facts, the world was prepared in advance to take it for granted that whatever she might some day have to say on the subject of Liszt was bound to be unworthy of credence. Unfortunately for Liszt and the Princess, however, we have at last the Countess's own memoirs and Liszt's letters to her, and these put quite another complexion on the matter. As I have already said, from all we know of the Liszt of the middle and later years we might have ventured to reconstruct conjecturally the Liszt of the first period, who until lately was so little known to us; and when, after the publication of these first-hand documents, we find that they confirm that conjectural reconstruction to the full, we are driven to the conclusion that the Countess is on the whole what the judges call a witness of truth, and that the untruth, the hypocrisy, the inability to distinguish between fact and fancy, are all on the side of Liszt and the Princess.(10)

---

from this a clear idea of Marie's relations with Liszt"—a conjecture that is now seen to have been correct. "What is said about her in the Liszt biographies," says Frau Bäumer, "is not only banal and coarse-fibred in the matter of perception but untrustworthy in its treatment of matters of fact." And alone among the writers on the subject she guessed that a good deal in the Countess's novel *Nélida* must necessarily be a picture of actual episodes in her life and Liszt's—a point to which special attention will be given later in the present volume.

10) Lina Ramann (1833-1912) was a music teacher in Nuremberg who did a good deal of writing upon music. About 1874 she produced a brochure on Liszt's *Christus* which was sent to the Princess by their common Weimar friend Adelheid von Schorn. On the strength of this she was approved as the biographer of the composer. She went to Rome in the summer of 1876 and spent some weeks with the Princess upon the preparations for the biography. In a letter to Adelheid of 4th August of that year the Princess says that Ramann is a woman of intelligence and erudition, but "her philosophical style would qualify her rather for the analysis of Liszt's works than for his biography. . . . She is still not quite clear as to her task. I hope she will perform it well, but if she does not, I can supply what is lacking myself" (SZM, p. 330). It will thus be seen that the precious pair began work on the biography within a few months of the death of Madame d'Agoult. As Ramann could have

3

Marie Catherine Sophie de Flavigny, the daughter of a French emigré, the Vicomte de Flavigny, and Marie Elisabeth, the daughter—already widowed at eighteen—of the German banker Johann Philipp Bethmann, was born at Frankfort-on-the-Main in the night of 30th-31st December, 1805. In 1809 her father returned to France and settled in Touraine. Marie, after the sudden death of the Vicomte, was sent to the convent of the Sacré-Cœur, in Paris, to be educated. When the girl rejoined her mother, her beauty, her command of languages, her distinction of manner and her quick intelligence at once gave her a position in the aristocratic society of the capital. She fell in love with a peer of France, the Count Auguste de Lagarde, but the pair were separated by some misunderstanding or other. In her grief, hardly conscious of what she was doing, she mechanically accepted, against the advice of everyone, the hand of Count Charles d'Agoult, one of Napoleon's cavalry colonels, a member of one of the oldest families in Provence. Him she married on 16th May, 1827; he was fifteen years older than she.(11) The union proved itself a failure, not because of the difference between their ages but because the young wife had intellectually nothing in common with the kind of company preferred by her husband. She describes herself as one of the victims of the notorious *mal du siècle* that ravaged the France of the eighteen-thirties.

"People were tormented by the desire for the ideal life, and sought in everything for a sign from heaven. Hardly free yet from the formidable struggle [the Revolution and the Napoleonic wars] in which all the assizes of the world had been shaken to their foundations, men still shuddered under the expectation of the unknown, the extraordinary, the impossible. . . . All these warring impulses, these abrupt changes in the experiences of men and of nations delivered up the young to all the winds of doubt. An ardour, a sceptical torment of the senses and of the

known absolutely nothing at first hand about the events of the years 1833-44, the sole sources of her information about the Liszt-d'Agoult episode must have been Liszt and the Princess. The latter never knew Madame d'Agoult personally, or even set eyes on her.

(11) Not twenty years, as the biographies have it.

intellect caused a ferment in them powerful but bitter, compact of sadness and irony." Men fastened greedily on the romantic figures—Cain, Ahasuerus, Werther, Manfred, René, Faust, Hamlet, Obermann, Adolphe—that seemed to speak to them, from the literature of the past and the present, of their own deep trouble of mind and soul.

"It was in these intellectual and moral circumstances," she says, "in this atmosphere charged with electricity, that Franz and Marie met. The love that swiftly flamed within them bore all the marks of the milieu in which it was born. These two, more than others, were bound to come under its influence, for they were both endowed with the sensibilities of the poet and the artist. Strong affinities of race and temperament brought them together, but the extreme differences in their education and their station in life of necessity raised up innumerable difficulties around them. A thousand obstacles arose between them and endowed the passion that drove them towards each other with a dolorous intensity which, in more balanced days than those, love will never again know."(12)

To modern ears, Marie's reference to the difference between Liszt's education and station and her own may sound a little patronising. As regards the former, we have to remember that Liszt's life as an infant prodigy had left gaps in his general education of which he himself was acutely conscious not only at that time but all his life, and which we find him doing his best to repair in later years by wide if somewhat unsystematic reading. As regards the social point, it has to be borne in mind that at that epoch the musician, while welcome enough in the houses of the aristocracy as a paid performer, was never admitted there as a social equal.(13) In her *Souvenirs*, Marie

---

(12) AM, pp. 2-5.

(13) The dividing line between the upper and the lower classes was drawn with particular sharpness in the smaller German capitals in the early part of the nineteenth century. In the Weimar theatre, until 1848, when democratic ideas had begun to make a little headway in Germany, the Court and its satellites and high officials sat on the right side, the ordinary people on the left. When the mother of Adelheid von Schorn, who was herself of the Weimar nobility, wished to marry the art-authority Ludwig Schorn, in 1831, the Grand Duke tore at his hair with both hands in desperation at her folly in thus committing social

describes how concerts in aristocratic salons were arranged in those days:

"Composers and singers still had their place apart: in spite of the eagerness to have them, they appeared in the salons only on the footing of inferiors. If someone wanted to give a fine concert he went to Rossini, who, for a recognised fee—it was small enough, only 1,500 francs if I remember rightly—undertook to arrange the programme and to see to the carrying out of it, thus relieving the master of the house of all embarrassments in the way of choice of artists, of rehearsals, and so on. The great maestro himself sat at the piano the whole evening, accompanying the singers. Generally he added an instrumental virtuoso—Herz or Moscheles, Lafont or Bériot, Nadermann (the leading Paris harpist), Tulou (the King's first flute), or the wonder of the musical world, the little Liszt. At the appointed hour they arrived in a body and entered by a side door; in a body they sat near the piano; and in a body they departed, after having received the compliments of the master of the house and of a few professed dilettanti. The next day the master sent Rossini his fee, and believed he had discharged his obligations towards them and him."

It was only in the less rich houses that there was "rather more affability" between the artists and the *gens du monde*. If an artist, relying on his success with the public, gave himself, in society, anything that looked like airs, he was promptly snubbed: Henriette Sontag, for instance, who, spoiled by the adulation of Germany, arrived late at a great house at which she had been engaged to sing, disdained to make excuses, sang capriciously, and tried to play the *grande dame*, was promptly put in her place.(14) A mere singer could not be permitted to behave like that!

Liszt's pride revolted against this social ignominy from the first; it was answerable for a good deal both of the rather aggressive irony that everyone noted in him at this period and for his meticulous assumption of the grand manner in his dealings with

---

suicide, while the Grand Duchess implored her to reflect that if she persisted in her purpose she would be condemned to sit on the left side of the theatre (See SZM, pp. 11, 12).

(14) See AS, pp. 303, 304.

aristocrats in his later years.(15) Paradoxically enough, it was precisely this social disadvantage that played a decisive part in bringing Franz and Marie together. There was a good deal of her mother in her. The young Frankfort widow's passion for the Vicomte de Flavigny had been so little to the liking of her family that they finally took the step of having him arrested on pseudo-political grounds. The girl's reply to this move was to obtain admission to the prison, spend some hours alone with the Vicomte, and then tell her family that for her reputation's sake they had better give their consent to the marriage at once. This trait of quick decision and resolute action descended, in due time, to Marie's own daughter, Cosima Wagner.

4

Franz and Marie first met at a party in the house of a certain Madame la Marquise L.V. [Vayer], during which Liszt had played to the guests. The next day this lady called on Marie, accompanied by a relative who, noticing the enthusiasm of the ladies for the handsome young pianist, thought it advisable to put in a prudent word about the "eccentricity of artists and the difficulty of admitting them into one's house on terms of equality." This decided the spirited Marie; she asked her friend for Liszt's address and straightway sent him an invitation to her next reception.(16) She found it anything but easy to draft the letter.

---

(15) On the general point of the galling social subservience of the musician in those days see NLW, chapter IX, and particularly the passionate outcry of Liszt against it in one of his articles in the *Gazette musicale de Paris*, 1835. These, however, though signed by him, were probably, in part, the work of the Countess.

(16) This account of the matter in her *Mémoires* is confirmed by a passage in a letter from Marie (in Croissy) to Liszt (in Paris), of 26th May, 1833. "I saw the Duchess for ten minutes only. She told me, laughingly, that she thought you were wandering about in the neighbourhood of Croissy, that society regarded you as being shared with us. Then I told her that they found very ridiculous the footing on which you had established yourself in our salons, this familiarity, etc., etc. . . . Upon which she raised her ducal head haughtily to give me to understand that she would never yield an inch to the silly croaking of these frogs, and that, with her, *les gens aimables avaient toujours raison*." (LZAC, I, 58).

"I had observed in the artist, during our conversation of the evening before, an indefinable sense of umbrage, a kind of haste to remind himself of the difference in ranks, as if he were afraid that *he* would be reminded of it. The remarks of the Marquise's relation had made me conscious of something upon which I had never had occasion to reflect before—that distinction of name, of blood, and of fortune which we owed to the accident of birth and which placed us in a position of superiority to the rest of mankind. At that moment I felt embarrassed by this seeming superiority in my relations with a man whose immense talent and what I thought I already knew of his character placed him, in my esteem, so much above myself. I was afraid, when writing my letter, that the habit of the formulae of my world towards an artist who was not of that world might make me appear to be haughty when I wished merely to say the right thing; but at the same time I was afraid that by ignoring these formulae I might be showing more interest than was decorous in so novel a relation to a man so young and so much of a stranger to all my own people."(17)

Liszt accepted the invitation without sending a written reply to it.

Lina Ramann—or the Princess Wittgenstein—would have us believe that "the alliance between the pair was not the result of one of those flames of love that suddenly kindle in the heart, no one knows how or why. Nor was it the outcome of a mutual inclination germinating in silence and gradually assuming the force of passion, nor the fruit of an understanding in the depths of the heart: it was an accident, a play, a caprice, a misfortune." The intention of the sadly suspect narrative is clear throughout— to persuade the reader that the giddy Countess set her cap at the young prodigy out of vanity, that the virtuous Joseph resisted the designing Madame Potiphar for a long while, even

---

Even well-meant consolation of this kind must have been galling to Liszt, as reminding him of his social inferiority; and at first sight it seems tactless and cruel on the Countess's part to tell him of such things. We have to remember, however, that the question was a serious one in the French society of that epoch. Her object was the kindly one of assuring Liszt that his real friends would not submit to be separated from him by these unjust social conventions.

(17) AM, pp. 22-24.

going so far as to avoid her, but that in the end he succumbed to her wiles. Her one desire, it seems, was to flaunt him as an ornament of her salon, to be his "Muse" before all the world; she "did not realise that the Muse of a genuine artist must be made of other stuff than sensual delights and fantastic vanity"— of the superior stuff, in fact, of which the Princess was modestly convinced that *she* was made.(18) The *Mémoires* of the Countess, however, and Liszt's contemporary letters to her, present the affair in a very different light.

The meeting of the pair took place in 1833, at a critical period in Liszt's life. For one reason and another he had never really liked the profession of public pianist into which he had been thrust virtually from the age of six. He was by nature inclined at least as much to religion as to music, and on more than one occasion in his boyhood he had implored his parents to allow him to enter the Church; his favourite reading as a child was the Bible, St. Thomas à Kempis's *Imitation of Christ*, and the lives of the saints, especially that of his patron saint, Francis of Paula. On many an occasion in later life, a tired, disillusioned and self-reproaching man, he looked back wistfully on the religious aspirations of his boyhood.

"You know, dearest mother," he writes in 1862, "how, during many of the years of my youth, I dreamed myself incessantly into the world of the saints. Nothing seemed to me so self-evident as heaven, nothing so true and so rich in blessedness as the goodness and compassion of God. Notwithstanding all the aberrations and errors of my life, nothing and nobody have ever been able to shake my faith in immortality and eternal salvation, a faith I had won by my prayers in the churches at Raiding [his birthplace] and Frauendorf, the Mariahilf Church in Vienna, Notre Dame de Lorette and St. Vincent de Paule in Paris. . . . When I now read the lives of the saints I feel I am meeting again, after a long journey, old and reverend friends from whom I shall never part."(19)

And once when he re-visited as a man the little church at Raiding he told his companion mournfully that there he would

---

(18) See RFL, I, 327-330.

(19) LZBM, pp. 145, 146.

have passed his life in prayer had it not been for the Magnates of Hungary, whose donations had allowed his father to send him to Vienna to study under Czerny. In his will, made in 1860, he says that in his seventeenth year he begged, with tears in his eyes, to be allowed to enter the Paris Seminary: "I hoped it might be granted to me to live the life of the saints and perhaps die the death of the martyrs."(20) He had continued to play the piano only because, from his earliest years, his parents had been dependent upon his earnings. His father had died in 1827, when Franz was only sixteen. Thirty-seven years later the middle-aged man, in a letter to the Princess, told of the singular prevision shown by his father on his death-bed. "He said I had a good heart and did not lack intelligence, but he feared that women would trouble my life and bring me under their sway. This prevision was strange, for at that time, at the age of sixteen, I had no idea what a woman was, and in my simplicity I asked my confessor to explain the sixth and ninth commandments to me, for I was afraid I might have broken them without knowing I had done so."(21)

5

The father had died at Boulogne. Franz, on his return to Paris with his mother, settled down as a teacher. He fell in love with one of his pupils, Caroline de St. Cricq, the seventeen-years-old daughter of the Comte de St. Cricq, the French Minister for the Interior. Such presumption on the part of a plebeian little piano teacher was not to be tolerated: Liszt was paid his fee and politely shown the door by the father. Caroline was a beautiful, gentle soul whom Liszt held in the highest esteem throughout his life. The shock turned his thoughts once more in the direction of religion; and once more he forbore to enter the Church only out of consideration for his mother. For two years the boy suffered seriously in his health. He rarely went out; in the winter of 1827-28 the report was actually current in Paris that he was dead. He sought consolation in

(20) LZB, I, 365; V, 52.
(21) Ibid., VII, 82.

the company of Christian Urhan, a strange being who combined the loftiest mysticism with the profession of violinist in the orchestra of the Opéra.(22) He was known as "the seraphic counterpart of the diabolical Berlioz"; so strict were his moral principles that he always kept his eyes averted from the stage when a woman dancer appeared. To the influence of Urhan was added that of the Abbé Lamennais, to whom Liszt was greatly drawn during the next three or four years, and with whom he stayed at the Abbé's Brittany retreat of La Chênaie. He managed, however, to fill his mind with not only religious works but the romantic literature of the epoch. He was at last shaken out of his apathy by the stirring events of July, 1830, in Paris; as his mother said, the Revolution cured him.

At this time, then, as so often happened to him in later life, he was divided in his allegiance between the world and religion. "Liszt told me," George Sand notes in her *Journal intime* under the date of November, 1834, "that no one but God was deserving of love." He had never been greatly drawn, he said, to anyone but Lamennais, "and never would an earthly love take possession of him." "Il est bien heureux, ce petit chrétien-là!" she comments drily. He appears, however, to have been sufficiently interested in George Sand about this time, or a little earlier, to arouse the jealousy of Alfred de Musset; and one gathers that there had been some Paris gossip about the trio. The fact that Liszt was really interested, as she says, in no one but God and the Virgin Mary would not quite commend him to the robust George, who, like the Wife of Bath, was an exacting realist in matters of male affection; and she appears to have given the too highly spiritualised young man the sound advice not to think too much about her.(23)

Even at the age of more than seventy Liszt exercised a strange fascination over young women: it is easy to imagine, therefore, the devastation he wrought among them in his flower-like youth,

---

(22) His favourite instruments, however, were the viola and the viola d'amore. It was for him that Meyerbeer wrote the famous viola d'amore solo in *Les Huguenots*. Urhan acted also as organist at the church of St. Vincent de Paule.

(23) See SJI, pp. 21, 22. The *Journal intime* was not published until 1926.

with his slender figure, his finely moulded face, his eloquent
eyes, his broad brow, and the romantic pallor that was so much
in vogue at the time. To Marie d'Agoult, at their first meeting,
he seemed, with his *air distrait et inquiet*, like "a phantom for
whom the hour when it must return to the darkness is about to
sound." She found his conversation, in spite of his somewhat
strange manners, which were not quite that of the world in
which Marie had been accustomed to move, interesting by
reason both of the novelty of his ideas and the vivacity with
which they were expressed. "He spoke impetuously, abruptly;
he gave vehement utterance to ideas and judgments that
sounded bizarre to ears accustomed, as mine were, to the
banality of received opinions. His flashing eyes, his gestures,
his smile, now profound and of an infinite sweetness, now
caustic, seemed to be intended to provoke me either to contradiction or to intimate assent."(24)

He came frequently to her house, for, as she says, after six
years of marriage she enjoyed complete independence:

> "From the commencement our conversations were very
> serious, and, by common accord, quite free from anything banal.
> Without hesitation, without effort, by the natural inclination of
> our souls, we embarked at once upon elevated subjects, which
> alone had any interest for us. We talked of the destiny of man-
> kind, of its sadness and incertitude, of the soul and of God. We
> exchanged grave thoughts on the present time, on the future
> life, and on the promises of religion with regard to this. We
> said nothing that came too near the personal or the intimate;
> but the very tone of our talks showed that we were both ex-
> ceedingly unhappy, and that, young as we were, we had been
> through more than one bitter experience. In these *sous-
> entendus*, these veiled confidences, these outpourings that were
> at the same time very frank and very discreet, Franz spoke with
> a vivacity, an abundance, and an originality of impressions that
> awoke a whole world that had been slumbering in me; and when
> he left me I was sunk in reveries without end. Although his
> education had been very incomplete, he having been compelled
> to apply himself unremittingly to his art from his very infancy,
> he had come to such close quarters with the difficulties of life,

(24) AM, pp. 21, 22.

he had seen the world under so many diverse aspects, from the dazzling celebrity of his public career to the privations of an existence precariously dependent on the mob and its caprices, today dandled, like the little Mozart, on the knees of queens and princesses, tomorrow condemned to isolation and cruel poverty, that he had come to realise more than I had done the inconsequence, the injustice, the folly, the cruel levity and tyranny of public opinion. More adventurous by nature and by the force of circumstances than I was, he had speculatively reached out further than I had done into the sphere of good and evil. Though he was still, in imagination at least, an ardent Catholic, and the rumours of his taking holy orders were not without foundation, the inquietude of his mind impelled him towards heresy. During the last few years he had assiduously listened to the preachings of the sects and schools that announced new revelations. He had frequented the meetings of the disciples of Saint-Simon; under the trees of La Chênaie he had drunk in greedily the teachings of the illustrious *Croyant* [Lamennais] who had been condemned by Rome. In politics, as in religion, he hated mediocrity, and his opinions were audaciously advanced. He despised the bourgeois monarchy [of Louis Philippe] and the government of the *juste milieu;* he cried out with all his being for the reign of justice, that is to say, a republic as he conceived it. With the same effervescence he gave himself up to the new movements in letters and the arts that were then menacing the ancient routines: Childe Harold, Manfred, Werther, Obermann, all the proud or desperate revolutionaries of romantic poetry, were the companions of his sleepless nights. By their aid he rose to a haughty disdain of conventions; like them, he quivered under the detested yoke of aristocracies that were based on neither genius nor virtue; he cried out for no more submission, no more resignation, but for a holy, implacable hate that should avenge all iniquities. . . . The voice of the young enchanter, his vibrant speech, opened out before me a whole infinity, now luminous, now sombre, for ever changing, into which my thoughts plunged and were lost. Nothing of coquetry or of gallantry was blended with our intimacy, as so often happens between fashionable persons of opposite sexes. Between us there was something at once very young and very serious, at once very profound and very naïve."(25)

---

(25) AM, p. 25ff.

6

Soon after their first meeting, Marie went, in the summer of 1833, to her country house at Croissy. There she found herself more than ever conscious that the mind and the personality of Liszt had supplied her with something that had hitherto been lacking in her environment. After six weeks' intellectual solitude she invited him to stay with her. She noted a change in his manner, as if the impression were disagreeable to him, at his introduction to her children, whom he had not seen before. The incident seemed to make each of them curiously self-conscious:

"From that day my relations with Franz took on a new aspect. Henceforth I saw him only rarely, and even then seldom *tête-à-tête;* and there were times when I did not know whether I really desired these meetings or feared them, so disturbing were they to me. Into our briefest conversations, which were often interrupted, something had crept that was no longer entirely us. If at bottom our talks remained the same as before, the tone of them had become something quite different. Franz brought to them a fantastic temper; I was ill at ease. Sometimes there would be long silences between us; at others, Franz would talk with feverish animation, affecting a mocking gaiety that made me uncomfortable. He who had used to be so full of enthusiasm, so eloquent in his talk about the good and the beautiful, so ambitious to give elevation to his life, to consecrate it to great art, so religious in all his thoughts, never spoke of anything now except in tones of irony. He paraded his doubts,(26) he seemed deliberately to merge all the things he

---

(26) About this time, in fact, Liszt coquetted with rationalism, as Joseph d'Ortigue noted in the short biography he wrote of the pianist in the *Gazette musicale de Paris* in 1835.

From internal evidence we may confidently assign to this epoch a note on Liszt in Sainte-Beuve's note-books: "Liszt, who is a young man of talent, though affected, has a way of employing this talent with people that has let me into the secret of his way of playing the piano: his way is to be at the same moment on the most remote keys, by means of a celerity that is almost impossible—now with Lamennais, now the Princess Belgiojoso, now Ballanche, now George Sand, etc. He is less successful, however, in achieving a harmony with these people than with his piano. We detect the *tour de force* and the pretence: and these are

respected and scorned and admired and sympathised with in an all-embracing indifference. He sang the praises of mundane wisdom and the easy-going life; he undertook the defence of free-thinkers. Suddenly, without any apparent reason, he broke out with strange ideas of a kind I had never heard from him before: he lauded what he called my fine life, congratulated me on my brilliant position in the world, admired what he called my royal establishment, the opulence and elegance of everything around me. Was he serious? Was it merely by way of persiflage? His impassive air, his dull accents, made it impossible for me to decide. And strangely enough, his talent seemed to me as completely changed as his mind. When he improvised at the piano it was no longer, as of old, to evoke suave harmonies that opened out the heavens to me; it was to set vibrating discordant, strident tones from those powerful fingers of his."

All this rings absolutely true; it is in complete accordance psychologically with what we know of the Liszt of the later years.

At last his cynicism and roughness brought about an emotional crisis between them in which Marie burst into tears. This melted him: he fell at her feet, embraced her knees, and in dolorous tones implored her pardon. The ice was broken, the veil lifted; they knew now that henceforth each belonged to the other. Franz's manner changed with his new mood. They talked much about themselves: Franz told her of his joyless, undirected childhood, of his temptations, his revulsions and remorse, his desire to flee to the cloister, his scorn for the celebrity he had attained as a pianist, the war that was being waged within him between the flesh and the spirit, between worldly ambitions and an ideal of a life devoted to art in all its purity. He spoke of the passion with which she had inspired him, of his insensate hopes, of the fascination of suicide. They felt that they had been fated for each other; they looked back fondly,

---

the defects also of his playing. But his nature is noble, elevated, and he is generous and enthusiastic" (CSB, pp. 6, 7). Insincerity would perhaps be too crude a word for all this; but certainly there was something in him, then and later, that made many people regard him as insincere.

as lovers will do, upon all that had been doubtful and discouraging in the days before they had realised their mutual predestination. They had long walks in the Croissy park, the quiet of which brought peace to the soul of Liszt, who was for the moment weary of the din and dirt of great cities. As yet, apparently, their relations had no other footing and no other direction than that of a romantic spiritual attachment. But, as Marie says, this was the mysterious calm that precedes and heralds the tempest.

7

Their letters of this period confirm Marie's account of the matter in her memoirs, and give the lie to the Princess's carefully concocted brew of misstatement and insinuation. The earliest letters and fragments of letters that have recently been published are often undated, but the internal evidence is conclusive as to their belonging to the first half of the year 1833. From the beginning, it is clear, Liszt had been powerfully attracted to Marie: "Oh, write to me often," he implores in one of the earliest notes of the series:(27) "you write so divinely, so straight from the heart; your every word burns with an inner flame. . . . There is only one name now that I repeat every hour. I wait for a day to come. . . . Soon, soon, perhaps? The prophets are silent before the coming of the Messiah."(28) He is undergoing one of those crises, that were later to be so frequent with him, in which he longs to retire into himself and forget the hateful world. So he is going into an original kind of "retreat." His friend Erard, who is in London, has placed his apartment in the Rue du Mail at his disposal; there he will read, work and study from morning to night. Only his mother and Berlioz will have access to him; all his other friends will believe he has left Paris. "One passion alone, one faith alone, now has its home in my heart—the faith, the passion, for work." Marie is to write to him care of his mother, who will bring the letters to him. "See, Madame, there are

---

(27) They were both living in Paris at this time.

(28) LZAC, I, 24, 25.

men whom God has branded on the brow, to live and die in vain; eternally deceived and undeceived, even hope becomes for them an ignoble, insupportable torture. Let them fulfil their destiny. Their bed in the grave will be fresh and tranquil for them." It was a fit that was to seize him more than once in his later years, as we shall see.(29)

But in his "retreat" he welcomes every line from her.

"At last," he writes a day or two later, "a letter from you! God be praised! I was beginning to despair. Do not be surprised at the dryness, the cold concision of my letters; you know me, you know all there sometimes is of *derision* in my resignations, of bitterness in this apparent calm of mine (my *second nature*, as you once very truly said)."

His nerves were fretted by the strain of his hectic social life and by his disgust with himself for allowing himself to be drawn into a world against which the better part of him revolted: he goes sometimes to the church of the Petits Pères, which is only a few steps from his retreat; occasionally he takes a walk in the Faubourg Saint-Antoine. He sleeps a great deal, and his health is improving. If his door is closed to his other friends, it is open for Marie: "I will wait for you the whole day here— No. 21 in Erard's street, second floor, the door to the right: I am always alone." (30)

He is divided between a desire to give himself wholly to God and to visit some friends who have offended him and to relieve his feelings by being rude to them. "I do nothing all day but read and work. I feel I am growing! I want six years!" In a later note: "Since midday a great sadness has weighed me down: I feel that there is nothing left for me now but to seek my tomb in silence and shame, sequestering myself more and more from those who are dear to me. This morning a few words of sympathy, of interest in me, aroused me with a start. You

---

(29) His letters to the Princess during the last quarter of his life are full of similar protestations that he loathes the world and desires only to work and pray in solitude: they afford one proof among many that Madame d'Agoult's analysis of his character as a young man is a trustworthy one.

(30) Ibid., pp. 24-29.

know whose was the hand that wrote them: my thanks, Madame."(31)

From August onwards his letters are addressed to Marie at Croissy. He is in the depths of gloom once more. Even his mother seems alien to him: "as regards her and my friends, I retire daily more and more into a sort of cold and sorrowful dignity." Apparently he has seen Marie, for he tells her she was "sublime last Saturday morning," when, apparently, she had read Goethe and Schiller to him—or perhaps sung some musical settings of their verses. "Never have Goethe and Schiller been understood so fully; never has an emotion so vast benumbed my heart and burned my brow. Oh, one ought to die after these hours of enthusiasm, of delirium! . . . You know, Madame, that it is only you to whom I can speak of Art, of Poetry." On 16th September: "Write soon and at length. I am so sad in your soul. You do not know how prodigiously you are loved." In October: "I feel such a need to talk with you, to see you, to hear you say that you pity me. All my friends find me horribly changed: some endow me with a *grande passion*, others say I am going mad. You know that I am neither in love nor a madman. A secret instinct torments me. . . . Away! Away!" On 30th October: "You suffer, you suffer horribly. These last beautiful days have ground you to pieces, eaten you away. It is blood that you weep now . . . and you believe that all is said. . . . No, Madame, no, no! You know that I will always be yours, even to the grave. We two!"

8

On 2nd November he implores her to return to Paris, if she can, for a coming Berlioz concert, so that he may see her. The "sincerity" of her last letter has "profoundly moved him." "I know I have no longer any right to make any demand whatever upon you. . . . But if for once (whether tomorrow, this winter, or later is of no consequence) you would consent out of pity, out of *curiosity* perhaps, to grant me a few minutes' conversation, I would bless you for it, I would give thanks to

(31) LZAC, I, p. 34.

God." "I too see two faces in what you write to me, the one bearing a sorry grimace, shamefully dignified . . . but silence! No more raillery, no more derision. Silence! Let your word be Yes . . . Yes . . . Yes . . . No, no. Anyhow it is perhaps complete madness on my part to love like this!"(32)

A little later he begs for news of her: "I do not know why I am so uneasy; I have not had a moment's tranquillity since our separation. . . . Let me weep a few days longer . . . do not pity me. . . . Remain mine still; who else's hand could lay its benediction on my tomb? . . . I am astonished at my passive courage: the week that has just ended has been frightful for me. How many times has that terrible cry of the poet, 'Horrible, horrible death,' lacerated my breast! . . . Is it not possible for you to write to me every day? If you are afraid of always using the same address, you could write to me sometimes care of Madame Vial, Rue Chantereine 21. I am sure of her, though I have never spoken to her of you."(33)

At this stage we have apparently the first of Marie's letters to him that have been preserved. She addresses him as "Monsieur," and discusses points connected with literature and music. "Adieu, Monsieur," she ends; "I will soon be in Paris to meet my mother: it will be a pleasure to me to present you to her." Then her tone becomes warmer. She thinks of him, she says, wherever she is, whatever she is doing. There have been days when she has thought of suicide. "But God had pity on me. I wanted to say to you that, whatever my sufferings, present or future, you should not weep for them, for they have brought me more of good than they will be able to bring me of evil. You have succeeded in breaking all the bonds that still held me to the world, and you have wakened in my soul a spirit of universal charity, that love for all that had been extinguished in me by the sense of my personal griefs. . . . May this thought be sweet to you to your dying hour."

The dry tone of his letters pains her. She hopes, however,

---

(32) LZAC, I, pp. 37, 40, 43, 47, 48, 49. As will have been seen, the young Liszt is not always quite coherent in his epistolary style.

(33) Ibid., pp. 52, 53.

to see him soon in Paris. "No one could understand the extra-ordinary kind of existence I live here [at Croissy]: the most complete solitude after the whirlwind of the social world, not a soul to whom I can open mine, not even the desire to com-mune with any living being, no correspondence that interests me, not a memory to which I wish to cling, nothing but one thought that takes possession of all my forces and raises me or depresses me, vivifies me, reduces me to despair, or heartens me. Adieu; you wish to know much. Study only eternity. On your knees; pray for me, save me. . . . No, I am not absurd; you are right not to write to me oftener, but sometimes I love you foolishly, and at those times I no longer comprehend that I cannot and should not be for you so absorbing a thought as you are for me."(34)

It will be seen that these documents are in perfect keeping with the story as told in Marie's *Mémoires;* and it is time the quietus was given to the malicious fiction of the Ramann-Wittgenstein chapter on her. The Princess's account of the matter, which can derive ultimately only from Liszt, has no congruity whatever with the facts. It was not, as she makes out, a case of a selfish, erotic, designing woman drawing an innocent young idealist into her toils out of pure vanity. As Marie says in her *Mémoires,* their relations were grave and youthfully naïve: each found in the other a haven of rest from the stupid and vulgar world around them; and of the two it was Liszt who was the more aggressively ardent. For he had far more need of her than she had of him: we come, for the first time, upon the *leit-motiv* that is the key to his whole character and the explanation of his final failure—the dualism in him that made it impossible for him ever to choose decisively between religion and the world, his constant need of a woman stronger in mind and in purpose than himself to take charge of his life for him. We shall see later that the heights to which he rose in his really great period, that of Weimar between 1848 and 1861, were made possible for him only because the stronger hand of the Princess never loosened its grip on his, and that when her hold upon him relaxed, his life went slowly to pieces.

(34) LZAC, I, 52, 53, 55, 56, 57, 58.

9

The letters we have dealt with so far cover the year 1833; and how little the biographers of Liszt have known at first hand of his life at this period is shown by the fact that even Raabe gives 1834 as the year of "the beginning of his relations with the Countess d'Agoult."(35) As we have seen, already in 1833 she had begun to play an important part in his emotional and intellectual life. The year 1834 finds them being drawn still closer together; and Liszt's letters show that, far from recognising, as the Princess would have us believe, that he was in danger of falling into the toils of a calculating woman, and fighting with the whole strength of his better nature against the seductions of the siren, he was not only deeply in love with her but saw in her the one being who—with, of course, a little assistance from Providence—could bring peace to his soul and give his life the balance he knew only too sadly that it lacked. They saw each other comparatively little during this period, for Marie spent a good deal of her time at Croissy, while Liszt was with Lamennais for some weeks at La Chênaie.

At the commencement of 1834 he laments not having been able to see her: "Write me a word. Speak to me of yesterday, of the evening. What was your coiffure? Did you cough? Did you waltz? Tell me all this. Let my illness be a sort of absence, like two days spent apart from you. Let me read you"; for, as he has just told her, "You are the only being in the world who means life for me and whom it grieves me not to see. . . . I love you. I want to see again your golden hair, your blue eyes, to hear you speak, to read your letters. I want to live. I love you; and I will live because I love you." He passes through one of those periods, so painfully frequent with him all his life, when he is angry and dismayed because he cannot

---

(35) RLL, p. 277. On p. 31 he says that the pair met "at the end of 1833." Liszt's earlier letters to Marie are not dated; but as the first to bear a date (8th August, 1833) is the twenty-second of the series, it is evident that they must have known each other since at least the spring of that year. The Countess herself is manifestly in error when she says (AM, p. 18) that they first met "towards the end of the third year that followed the Revolution of 1830."

bend his mind to work. Already we see the central tragedy of his life shaping itself—the distressed consciousness that there was some flaw in the foundations of his soul that hindered him from wholly realising himself either as man or as artist. "You cannot imagine what melancholy and bitterness have been left in my soul by the few foolish illusions of glory and ambition that still persisted in me up to the end of last year. Henceforth I will work only for work's sake": this, he thinks, is "almost Christian." A little later he is again ill, discouraged, suffering. "May God have pity on me! You know that now there is only one glance in the world that means anything to me, only one brow, only one soul. You too have pity on me." "I am as dead, but when I think of you I still have the hope of a few hours of terrible happiness. God have pity on us both!" Then he intones his usual *leit-motiv:* "sweet profound sadness within me, flights of faith, shudders of hope—the world and God united in one life."

In April, apparently, Marie goes to Croissy: there, in the solitude and quiet of the country, a mystical mood takes possession of her—"a kind of desire," she writes to him, "never to see you again. But I love you with all my soul." In her absence he becomes bitter. He is sad and bored, and, as usual with him when the intermittent religious fever dies down in him and he feels the strange impotence that was to assail him so often in later life, he turns once more to the delights of the world. He finds it difficult, he tells her, to think of her. Another facet of *l'enfant du siècle* comes uppermost in him. "Nothing has changed in the depths of my heart, because nothing, neither good nor evil, can change there . . . but . . . see, if you will take the trouble to think again of all this and try to trace the logic of it you will probably arrive at the conclusion that a *fatal* character (as you call it) can never stop at the metaphysical subtleties of love, that he needs *must* embrace life in its entirety, however derisory, however bitter it may be." All his life he was fated to be torn between a desire for solitude and saintliness and an imperious need of the crowd. His present fit of transcendental subjectivity over, it is for the crowd that he now longs. He goes a good deal into society again. He stays for a while with Madame d'Haineville at her house in Carenton, near Bernay, in the Department of the Eure. From there he carries on a correspondence with Marie in which we frequently catch a note of irritation. As we have only his letters, not hers, it is difficult to unravel all the skeins; but we gather that for some reason or other there has been talk, in Paris and elsewhere, about some of his earlier amours, especially that with Countess Adèle de Laprunarède, and he feels it necessary to justify himself.(36) "Speak to me very little about Adèle, and for pity's sake *never* mention other names: it hurts me deeply. If you wish it, I will talk to you again, for the last time,(37) of my life from 1830 to 1833. It is very simple and very sad, not very *donjuanique;* but it is inevitable, in spite of your penetrating mind, that you should judge it falsely."

10

He returns to this theme with increasing exasperation. He admits that his past life has been full of shameful follies, but from Marie he hopes to receive pardon and help. At times he reproaches himself for his conduct towards her: "We will talk again about this some time. But without any poor pleasantries, I hope. These things are solemn and serious, and I fervently desire that we shall understand each other once for all. I know it is largely my fault if we are not in better accord; a hundred times I have brought too much violence, too much impertinence and fury into our discussions; and perhaps you have *feigned* a little bad faith."

---

(36) Some ancient letters of his to women seem to have come into Marie's hands. "I do not know," he writes to her exasperatedly, "by what chance all these letters which you do me the honour to return to me, and which you would have done better to dispose of in some other way, were found in that wretched portfolio. They all date from 1831, an epoch when my mother and Madame D., hoping to calm my excited soul, wanted at any cost to marry me to this dear young lady who—but I must not say anything foolish. It was also the epoch of Hor. . . . and, to a small extent, Madame G. . . ., an epoch of struggle, of anguish, of solitary torments, when I was trying violently to smash, destroy, annihilate the love of Adèle."

(37) This confirms the passage in the *Mémoires* in which Marie says he gave her the story of his past erotic indiscretions (see *supra*, p. 35).

E

But both before the coming of this cloud between them and after the passing of it his letters are full of protestations of his love for Marie and his need for her. "There is no longer spirit, nor life, nor illusion, nor dreams, nor hope for me except in you, wholly you." She has recommended a course of reading to him, and he is spreading his net widely. "In three years I shall have polished myself up a bit." He recognises the tendency of his nature to run to extremes; but at the moment the pendulum has swung again in the direction of faith. "I believe once more in this life, in you, in God. Thanks be to you for this! . . . A thousand joys and benedictions. We have both been rather small; let us grow—grow for the life eternal! . . . Oh come soon if you do not wish me to die!"

So it continues during the summer of 1834. "Let us hope that God in His mercy and His infinite love will reunite us and absorb us wholly. I feel very weak and almost at death's door; we will revive, and our heads will burst the stone of the sepulchre." . . . "Whatever may happen, we will love each other, awaiting with holiness and courage God's day of deliverance." He is "neither gay nor sad nor unquiet nor calm. This negative state of mind is becoming habitual with me. I write to you as I would say my prayers in the morning. It is impossible for me to read or to work as I would like to do. . . . Please God that my activity may open out some day, even if it be in twenty years. I will wait." This feeling of impotence, as we shall see later, was perpetually recurrent with him. He was always greatly dependent on external stimuli to put him in the mood for sustained work: on the present occasion a long talk with the energetic Victor Hugo awakens all kinds of ambitious schemes in him. But he confesses that he is not doing as much as he would like to. "My time is almost wasted. I agitate and torment myself in vain—and certain people find me dry and cold or rhetorical!" He takes refuge from his impotence in "the feeling of bitter and disdainful resignation which, as you know, is usual with me." "Isolation is bad for me"—a discovery he was to make incessantly in after years. "I feel I have no strength left in me," he writes to her in July. "All my memories die out slowly, one by one; I count them bitterly. What are they? Shadows effaced by a shadow. What will they become? What we become ourselves, dust or God. . . . Mutation without end, action without aim, universal impenetrability, that is all we know. And we are told to believe and hope!" His letters, he admits, are dry, and he is touched by the gentleness and depth of feeling in hers. He sees that he is growing drier and harder day by day. "I live in a state of utter discontent. My past years seem to me so shameful, so pitiable! And so many impediments and chains in the present!" Her sage advice to him is to read Plutarch's lives of great men.

II

Then his mood changes once more, presumably at the prospect of seeing her again. His vast love for Mariotte, as he calls her, has restored his confidence in God; there is in him now no longer doubting, cursing, vanity, sarcasm or disenchantment, despair, regret or fears of the future. Life seems once more good to him, and he blesses God. He quotes, as completely applicable to himself during the winter of 1833-34, a passage from one of George Sand's *Lettres d'un voyageur* that has just appeared in the *Revue des Deux Mondes:* "I feel within myself a deplorable fatigue and a strength more deplorable still, no hope, no desire, a profound *ennui*, the faculty of accepting every benefit and every ill, too much discouragement or indolence to seek or to avoid anything at all, a body more inured to fatigue than that of a buffalo, a sombre, proud, exasperated soul, a character that is indolent, silent, calm as the water of this brook that is without a ripple on its surface but which a grain of sand can disturb." The young Liszt, it will be seen, suffered as severely as any of his romantic contemporaries from the *mal du siècle*.

He spends a happy week at Croissy, discussing "literature and high philosophy" with Marie, and comes back to Paris serious and sad, with only one desire—to die: "Oh how ardent, how glowing on my lips is your last kiss! How heavenly, how godlike your sigh in my bosom! To you, dearest beloved, and for you, everything!" He goes to Alençon, on his way to La Chênaie. He is consumed with longing to see her or to hear

from her: "you also have been sad, you also have had to pay
the price for all that happiness, that intoxication, those ineffable,
indescribable ravishments, to expiate them day by day, hour
by hour. *To live and to suffer* was the cry of love of a profoundly
religious soul, to whom the sublime word of St. Teresa ('suffer
or die') seemed cowardly in its resignation. To live and suffer
. . . always suffer . . . always. . . . Oh, may you one day
glorify God for our sufferings!"

Even with the good Abbé at La Chênaie he finds it a torture
to be separated from her: his letters confute the Princess's
story that he had fled to this religious retreat to escape Marie's
malign and oppressive influence. He praises even her calli-
graphy and her "delicious, ravishing, marvellous" epistolary
style. "What prodigies, what miracles of amiability, of wit, of
grace! Truly . . . Mariotte is a woman beyond compare. . . .
Will you believe it, already I can no longer endure the admirable
life I lead here. Thoughtful(38) cannot remain so far from
Mariotte." He prefers a thousand times his Paris existence,
with all its fatigues and boredoms, because in Paris he can see
Marie, whose talk is "a continual feast for the intelligence and
the soul." For all his fondness for Lamennais, for all his
admiration for his character, he is suffering sorely, he says.
Company fatigues him, yet when he is alone he is unhappy.
Only Marie can fill the "hungry abyss" of his heart; one glance
from her eyes would make him young again. "Marie, Marie,
put your arms about my heart, your heart against my breast.
I am bare, I am cold; clothe me wholly with your love. . . .
Kindle infinite ardours in me once more; deliver me for an
instant from all the miseries of the times; revive my soul." In
another two days, he says, he will be back in Paris: "till then, I
suffer and am consumed by a torment almost beyond my power
to bear." From Paris he writes:

"I am here. Thanks, oh God; it seemed to me that henceforth
the poor and mournful realities of life would no longer be
endurable; and yet here I am once more, not too crushed, not
too overburdened. Thanks, oh my God! Thy blessing on her,

---

(38) *Sic*, in English in the original. It was one of the names by which he was
known in the circle that comprised Marie and himself.

Thy blessing on her each day, each hour! I am impatient to receive a word from you. I thirst for it; I am at last alone . . . alone, uneasy, tormented with hopes! I feel in the depths of myself that there is no happiness for me but in you, that apart from you there is nothing true, nothing divine. Thanks to you, remorse for the past is becoming numbed in my soul; the poisoned root of it is drying up, and will die. Oh! Have pity, pity on me! Be mine always."

She is still at Croissy; they seem, indeed, to have met singularly little all this year. In the autumn his dark moods, the old feeling of worthlessness and impotence, take possession of him again. His misery is profound, he writes to her; his inner life becomes more tarnished and sombre every day, while the world without stupefies even while it excites him. Later: "I feel calm and strong this morning. I am almost ashamed of yesterday's sadness and excessive dejection. If it is possible for you to send a few words to your poor friend Thoughtful they would make him* very happy." (Apparently she was in Paris just then). The melancholy motive continues to drag its slow length across the pages. "My days are sad and full of ennui. . . . If it be true that sufficient unto the day is the evil thereof, there are also *good things* for which the day does not suffice. . . . At the risk of not seeing you alone I will call about 2.30. I need to see you. Always without adieu; for we shall never leave each other."(39)

12

Towards the end of October of that year her elder daughter fell ill of an intermittent fever which, on her return to Paris with her mother, developed into a cerebral disorder that proved fatal. Liszt, during the anxious days of waiting, called several times at the house but did not see Marie. After the death of her child the stricken mother—who apparently had had to be restrained at one time from suicide—returned to Croissy. There, she says, she received a letter from Franz announcing rather coldly that he was on his way to the Abbé Lamennais at La Chênaie:(40) this was both characteristic of his tact and the

---

(39) These extracts are taken from pp. 68-132 of LZAC, I.

(40) No such letter, however, is included in the published correspondence.

indication of one of those sudden changes in him to which all his life he was subject; the moral crisis drove him, as crises always did, to thoughts of religion. Meanwhile events were moving rapidly at Croissy. The death of the child (in December) had had the paradoxical effect not of bringing Marie and her husband closer together but of emphasising the disparity between their natures. The other child was placed in a *pensionnat*, her innocent gaiety having jarred on the mother's grief. For Marie there followed six months of angry rebellion against the Fates; then her nerves broke and she sank into a condition of apathy that seemed the prelude to a decline. During all this time she had had no word from Franz, nor had his name been mentioned in her presence. At last there came a brief letter from him in which, she says, he announced his intention of leaving France and Europe, and hoped he might see her once before he left. No such letter is given in the *Correspondance*, and it is not easy to trace his movements in detail at this time. Among the letters to his mother is one vaguely dated, by the editor, "La Chênaie, Autumn, 1834"; and we are told in a footnote to this that "Liszt was for some weeks the guest of the Abbé de Lamennais: during this time he wrote the *Pensée des Morts* (*Harmonies poétiques*), the piano piece *Lyon*,(41) and the unpublished *Fantaisie symphonique for piano and orchestra on themes by Berlioz*." We have a letter of his to Lamennais, dated from Paris 14th January, 1835, in which he says it will soon be four months since he left the Abbé—which would seem to refer to his visit of the preceding September—and says that unless something unforeseen happens he will ask for his hospitality again for a few days in the following July (1835). It is probable that he was concèaling himself from his friends at this time, for a letter of George Sand's to him, dated 19th January, 1835, begins, "I do not know where you are: several people have told me that you are

---

(41) His sympathies had been stirred by the revolt of the Lyons working people in that year against the hard conditions of their life. The *Lyon* appeared, with a dedication to Lamennais, as the first number of the *Impressions et Poésies* in the *1re Année de Pélérinage* (1840). Liszt omitted it from the later redaction of this work, the *Années de Pélérinage, 1re Année, Suisse* (1855).

still in Paris, but wherever you may be I take it that your mother will send my letter on to you."(42) We have, in addition, a letter from Liszt to d'Ortigue, dated conjecturally by the editor of his correspondence "The winter of 1834," and one to Sainte-Beuve, dated Paris, 22nd December, 1834, in which he says that he will be in Paris only another week, and that he particularly wants to see Sainte-Beuve before he leaves.(43)

But though Marie may have erred a little in her chronology when writing her memoirs, there is no reason to question her summary of the psychical facts. At their next meeting, she says, Franz, moved by the spectacle of her misery, declared that instead of his leaving France alone they must fly from the world together. "I also," she makes him say, "am hungry to live! We have had enough of bending under the yoke that bows us down towards the earth; too long have we struggled and suffered in vain. Let us still struggle and suffer, but let it be together and erect. Our souls are not made for the things that can be shared, for those mute resignations in which everything is extinguished in tears. We are young, courageous, sincere, and proud. We need either great faults or great virtues; we must confess, in the face of heaven, the sanctity or the fatality of our love." "A week later," she says, "we had left France."

Once more Liszt's letters confirm the essential truth of her story. The half-dozen brief notes of his that bear on this period are not dated, but they unmistakably fall in the last few days before the flight from Paris. The passion in them is warmer, the tempo faster than ever before.

"My heart," he begins, "overflows with emotions and happiness! I do not know what is this celestial languor, this immense

(42) BHZL, I, 9. The "5" is so indistinct that, as the editor of the volume says, it might be "3"; but the contents of the letter seem to make 1833 an impossible date for it. His letter of "the end of 1834 or beginning of 1835" (LZB, I, 6) may possibly be a reply to this of George Sand's.

(43) Liszt seems to have been very careless in the matter of dating his letters in the earlier part of his life, and the dates have to be more or less guessed at in many instances.

joy, that penetrates and consumes me wholly! I feel as if I had never loved before, never been loved!!! My God, my God, never let us be separated: have pity on us! . . . Oh God, our God, thanks and benediction and adoration to Thee for all Thou has given us and all Thou hast in store for us. . . . This is to be—to be!" In the next letter: "The peace and benediction of God be on you. . . . I live only in you, absorbed and almost deified by you. . . . You have been, you are, noble and grand and sublime. . . . You make me very proud. . . . But silence! . . . listen to the soul of your daughter and console yourself for her flight to heaven!"

Later still:

"Let me then see you again, and, if possible, speak to you once more. What you say is perfectly just and sensible in general, but I cannot accept certain personal assertions. Unless I deceive myself, your whole life is being put to the hazard now. It is therefore worth while reflecting carefully and deciding slowly. Try to come here today or tomorrow at any hour you will."

The result of the interview can be guessed. "Marie! Marie!" he writes,

"Oh, let me repeat that name a hundred times, a thousand times. For three days it has lived within me, oppressed me, burned me. . . . Eternity in your arms. . . . Heaven, hell, all, all in you, and again in you. . . . Oh, let me be mad, insane. . . . Common, prudent, narrow reality no longer suffices for me; we must live with all our life, all our love, all our woes! You believe me capable, do you not, of sacrifice, of virtue, of moderation, of religion? . . . This is to be, to be!!!" "The day when you can say to me with all your soul, all your heart, all your mind, 'Franz, let us blot out, forget, forgive for ever, everything that has been incomplete, distressing and perhaps wretched in the past: let us be all in all to each other, for now I understand you and pardon you as I love you'—that day—and may it be soon—we will fly far from the world; we will live, love and die for each other alone."

As early as March they must have been lovers in material fact as well as in spiritual aspiration, for their first child, Blandine, was born on 18th December of that year.

13

The mendacity of Lina Ramann's story of the early relations between the pair is now apparent. Liszt was not an innocent young Joseph Andrews seduced by a Lady Booby who was his superior in calculation and cunning and heartlessness. From first to last his letters show him to have been the most ardent of lovers, and the final step of flight from Paris was taken on his initiative.

> "The illusory play in which his passion had entangled him now disgusted him," says Ramann; "he felt that the moment for separation had come. He would leave Paris; and as the concert season was drawing to an end—it was the spring of 1835—and he felt the need of rest after the great strain it had put upon him, the present moment seemed to be doubly favourable to the execution of his purpose. He hoped that the Countess d'Agoult would agree with him as to the rightness and the necessity of this step, and co-operate with him in it. But in this he deceived himself. She was so deeply ensnared in the inner web of her own spinning that she could indeed give up husband and children, but not Liszt, could give up her illusion, but not her ideal at that time—to have a 'great passion.' Notwithstanding his representations, and against his wish, she left Paris: his reflection had come too late."(44)

All this we know now to be completely untrue.

In the English edition of the Ramann *Life*, for the changes in which, as her preface shows, the authoress took the responsibility, we are told that "the Countess d'Agoult now undertook a journey with her mother; their first destination was Basel. Madame de Flavigny hoped, by her presence, to prevent a definitely rash step, concluding that, after some time, her daughter would return to her normal position. But in this she was mistaken. One morning the Countess's trunks were, without his previous knowledge, brought to Liszt's rooms; for he had followed the ladies to Basel, but was living in another hotel."(45) This story of Marie's forcing herself upon the

---

(44) RFL, I, 331.

(45) RLAM, II, 110. Even Lina Ramann, as we see, is constrained to admit that Liszt "followed" Marie to Basel. We have a rich embroidery upon

unwilling Franz has been repeated by one biographer after another, without any of them, apparently, asking himself *why* Liszt was in Basel at all unless with the intention of eloping with the Countess. As it happens, however, we now have a letter of his, dated "Basel, May, 1835," in which he tells Marie that from six to eight he will be in the country with Herr Knopp, but makes an appointment with her for "before or afterwards".(46) Then, on 2nd June, Marie sends him a note: "Send me at once the name of your hotel and the number of your room. Do not go out. My mother is here; my brother-in-law has gone. By the time you have read this I shall have spoken to my mother; until now I have not dared to say anything. It' is a last and a hard trial, but my love is my faith and I thirst for martyrdom." Liszt's reply was: "Here I am, since you have called out to me. I shall not go out till I see you. My room is at the Hôtel de la Cigogne number twenty at the first étage—go to the right side. Yours."(47) To complete the record and hammer home the conclusion we have a letter from Liszt (in Basel) to his mother, running thus:

"Surpassing all hope, we have arrived here at ten o'clock this morning. . . . Longinus [one of his names for Marie] is here, also her mother. Nothing has been definitely settled as yet, but presumably we will leave here in about four or five days, taking her *femme de chambre* with us. We are both in fairly good spirits, and have no intention whatever of being unhappy. I am well: the Swiss air strengthens my appetite. . . .

the ancient legend in Schrader: "Liszt, warned by Berlioz, maintained an attitude of reserve towards her [in Paris]; but when he seemed in danger of succumbing his friends advised him to leave Paris and so avoid a scandal. Liszt therefore went in the spring of 1835 to Switzerland. One day when he was sitting at his writing table in Berne [*sic*] the door flew open and the Countess burst in, followed by her servants, who deposited her numerous trunks in the room" (SFL, p. 29). The same fantastic story is found in GFL, pp. 89, 90, and, indeed, in most of the biographies.

(46) These words are in English in the original.

(47) LZAC, I, 136. The whole of the letter, apart from the first sentence, is in English. This may have been intended as a precaution against Madame de Flavigny's reading it.

Adieu: best wishes to Puzzi [his pupil Hermann Cohn] and Madame Sand. I will write to you again soon."(48)

If all this does not indicate that the elopement was decided upon in Paris—no doubt on Marie's discovery that she was pregnant—that Liszt's mother had already been informed of their intention, and that Liszt was in Basel for the express purpose of meeting Marie, words can have no meaning.(49) That Liszt was acquainted with Ramann's untruthful account of the affair is proved by the fact that there exists at Weimar a copy of the first volume of the *Life* in which he has pencilled an occasional correction of a date or place or made a brief comment. He must be held, therefore, to be at least an accessory after the fact in the tissue of lies that Lina Ramann and the Princess had woven on his behalf.

The copious extracts from his letters that have been given above have not been motived by mere curiosity concerning his emotional record. They are vital in two ways—first because they reveal him as already sadly dependent upon a woman for the support and guidance of his inner life, secondly because we find the situation reduplicated later in his relations with the Princess, even to the closest correspondence in the phrasing of some of his letters to her. The basic elements of his character, the sources of all his weakness as man and as artist, are already beginning to come into view.

---

(48) LZMB, pp. 16, 17.

(49) It is worth noting that while Ramann gives the dates of the birth of the two later children, Cosima and Daniel, she gave no hint whatever of that of Blandine. To have done so might have aroused doubts in the reader's mind as to the complete truth of her story of Liszt trying to escape from Marie during the final months in Paris.

According to Liszt's declaration when registering the birth of his child in Geneva, the father was "François Liszt, professor of music, aged 24 years and one month," and the mother "Catherine Adélaïde Méran, *rentière*, aged 24 years, born in Paris"; "both unmarried and domiciled in Geneva." And this in the virtuous city of Calvin! (See BRR, p. 41).

CHAPTER III

THE DEVELOPMENT OF THE D'AGOULT AFFAIR

I

Madame de Flavigny having returned to Paris, the lovers spent three happy months in complete isolation in Switzerland. Far from regarding himself as a captive, Liszt was filled with delight at having at last, as he thought, realised his ideal of escape from a world which, with one half of his perpetually vacillating nature, he hated so sincerely both then and later. "To live alone," says Marie, "we two together, to place a decided distance between us and our past, to change our horizon as we had just changed our life, this was our sole aim. We wanted only solitude, contemplation, work. Franz, wearied and in some ways humiliated by the splendours of a celebrity of which no trace would survive him, tortured by higher ambitions, desired that silence should close in on his name and his life, so that he might give himself up undisturbed to the serious study of the great masters and to the composition of a great work of art." He was particularly engrossed with that ideal of religious music that was to play so large a part in his later life. Their mystical fervour brought them both, at one time, to the point of contemplating a *séparation consentie*, "a final renunciation, a voluntary expiation of our too great happiness. He spoke of the suggestions of the divine spirit that had formerly inclined him to the taking of monastic vows." The separation, "by severing our terrestrial bond, was to prepare us, by the detachment and the purification of the cloistral life, for that celestial union in which those who have loved each other in holy fashion here below shall live, freed now from all trial, for ever inseparable in the bosom of God."(1)

Here, as in a hundred other cases, the Countess unknowingly sketches for us, down to the smallest detail, precisely the Liszt that will emerge later from our analysis of his record in his second and his third periods, the first-hand documents for which are abundant. And the truth of her account of their inner and outer life in the Swiss days is confirmed by the independent evidence we possess relating to it. No letters, says Marie, reached them in their solitude; the outer world was forgotten; and it is a fact that there exist no letters either from or to Liszt belonging to this period. The end of their brief idyll, however, was near at hand. They were reading *Obermann* and *Jocelyn* together at Bex, in the valley of the Rhône, when a touch of autumn cold drove them, about the end of September, to Geneva.(2) There Marie received letters from her mother and her brother urging her to return: her flight was not generally known as yet in Paris, her husband was willing, out of regard for the *convenances*, to return to the *status quo ante*, and the thought of her child was tugging at her heart. But she decided to remain with Liszt, in whom she saw "a being apart, superior to everyone I had ever known. . . . Sometimes, in a kind of mystical delirium, I felt myself called by God, as it were chosen as an offering for the salvation of this divine genius who had nothing in common with the rest of mankind and ought not to be subject to the common law. . . . I could have wished to be a saint for love's sake: I blessed my martyrdom." For a moment,

---

(1) AM, pp. 42-45.

(2) "Geneva," says Marie, "was the nearest town; and it was to there we had given instructions, when we left Paris, for our letters to be forwarded." This is yet another incidental piece of evidence that the elopement had been planned between them in Paris: there was no question whatever of a flight on Liszt's part to escape from her. Yet even to the present day the legend is persisted in that Liszt "wished to fly from the danger" that threatened him, that he "decided to leave Paris, in the hope of putting an end to so perilous a situation, and sought refuge in Switzerland," and that "hardly was he installed there when the Countess, abandoning husband and child, rejoined him". (See, for example, BRR, p. 22).

it would appear from his letters to his mother, Liszt cherished the idea of returning to Paris—perhaps for an interview with Marie's husband or brother: then he tried to persuade his mother to come and live with them in Geneva. That he intended to settle there for some time is shown by his asking her to send him his books and manuscripts; he is, he assures her in November, "happy, very happy, overwhelmingly happy. Only one timid little ambition remains unsatisfied: whence it comes and what its aim is you know."

But while Franz was happy, unhappiness was commencing for Marie, and that, by paradox, for much the same reasons. Wearying, as usual, of a life of retirement after a few months' experience of it, the commoner side of his nature was now longing once more for the world. He soon made acquaintances in Geneva: he was admired and flattered as usual, and the incense that arose to his nostrils was highly agreeable to him. Robert Bory is mistaken when he says(3) that Marie, proud of her conquest of the brilliant virtuoso, and hungry for glory, dragged Liszt into Genevese society. The truth is that she did all she could to avoid this. There was no "conquest" to be proud of on her side, according to the opinion of that epoch. Her flight with a mere piano-player was a shocking misalliance; it was the plebeian Liszt who, proud of *his* conquest, took a delight in displaying the beautiful aristocratic bird he had caught in his net. Marie everywhere suffered greatly from the odium that attached to their union, and particularly from the notoriously narrow bourgeois morality of Geneva. She was glad to leave the town at the first opportunity; she had felt there, she says in a letter of October, 1836, "like a fish out of water."(4)

An interesting light on the Liszt of this period is thrown by the recently published extracts from the journal of one Madame Boissier, who had already met him in Paris, where her daughter had had piano lessons from him. The awkward young plebeian, she noted, had evidently picked up from Marie

---

(3) BRR, pp. 21, 22, 52.

(4) See BRR, p. 110.

something of the *bon ton* of the aristocratic world. "He does not dress with the bad taste that was so noticeable in him in Paris," says the friendly but critical Madame Boissier: "one can see that he has benefited by good feminine advice. He is amiable and good-natured. But he is a poor young man, horribly spoiled by society and by his successes."

His biographers have painted him, at this epoch, as a young man of the loftiest religious aspirations. Marie, on the other hand, has described him (as we have seen) as being dry, ironical, a victim of the advanced ideas of the time. This diagnosis is confirmed by Madame Boissier:

"Liszt's conversation is more fatiguing than agreeable. I would not say that he lacks either ideas or wit; he is even capable of entering into grave and profound ideas, but he loses himself in them. It has been his misfortune to live among literary people of the day who have stuffed him with their dangerous doctrines, their false notions, their incredulity. He rejects the accepted principles and beliefs; but I cannot quite make out what he would put in their place. . . . He shrugs his shoulders at the sacredness of marriage, and other bagatelles of that sort. He abandons himself to his passions with the most complete freedom and unconcern. If need were he would present me to his Countess without blushing. He had, and perhaps still has, a noble soul; but he is crazy." Later she notes that "he has improved in some respects since Paris: he has more ease in his manners and in the ways of society".(5)

One day he received a letter from his fifteen-years-old pupil "Puzzi,"(6) who was finding existence intolerable without the master for whom he felt a fanatical admiration and love, begging that he might come and live in Geneva simply to be near him. Liszt wounded Marie deeply by sending the boy an invitation at once, without consulting her. She foresaw that when Puzzi came there would be an end of the solitude that was now so dear to her: she asked herself in sorrow whether she had torn herself

---

(5) BRR, pp. 31, 32.

(6) This Hermann Cohn was a strange youth who, some years later, after swindling Liszt out of 3,000 francs (see LZAC, II, 183), gave up the idea of being a public pianist and dedicated himself to the Lord.

away from her own child merely in order that a stranger should invade her hearth. Puzzi arrived a week later, and Marie, though she kept her thoughts from Liszt, could only wonder sadly at his lack of delicate perception. Soon their house was invaded by a crowd of new acquaintances, attracted by the handsome young Don Juan whose history was so romantic, not less than by the playing of the famous virtuoso. Not only was the *solitude à deux* to which Marie had looked forward now destroyed, but, the epoch being what it was, she was made to feel far more acutely than he the social consequences of their equivocal union.

2

As is the case with all writers of autobiographies, she no doubt read retrospectively into these early days a good deal of the reflections and experiences of her later life. But though she may have had, in the eighteen-fifties or 'sixties, a clearer sense of the forces that had been slowly making for the destruction of her happiness in the late 'thirties, there is no reason to doubt that even then she felt, however dimly, the chill of the shadow that was already creeping over her life and his. He, for his part, was as yet blind to it, for he was too much absorbed in himself to have discerning eyes for *her* spiritual problems. The Muse who presides so benevolently over biography sent him, with admirable foresight, to Paris, by way of Lyons, in April, 1836. He did not return to Geneva until the end of July, so that the recently published *Correspondance* provides us with a number of letters to Marie that are invaluable for our new understanding of him.

Once more we discover that the Ramann-Wittgenstein account of him in what may be called the d'Agoult days is a tissue of absurdities, a flagitious blend of *suppressio veri* and *suggestio falsi*. Far from his having been decoyed into a prison in May, 1835, and far from his tugging pathetically at his chains the moment he realised that he had been trapped, we find that Marie is still the very centre of his being. His letters are full of laments over his enforced absence from her, of longing to return to her, of cries that show his utter dependence upon her for the steadying and guidance of his inner life. A few typical extracts from the letters will make this clear.

21st April. "Oh, it is an unspeakable joy to me to think that soon we shall be able to travel together! I feel that I am more worthy of this now: little by little my resignation to suffering and the higher life that you have taught me will purify me. I still lack inner clearness: my flesh and my blood need to be regener-ated and vitalised anew. Give me sometimes a little of your compassion, and have pity on my infirmities."

23rd April. "You know I cannot live without hearing from you. Dear Marie, we are so necessary to each other. . . . Fortunately, to console me for all these wearisome distractions, I have your Memorandum. Every evening, when I return to my hotel, I *religiously* read some pages of it. It is my prayer, my poetry, my regeneration. Dear, dear Saas [one of his names for her], you are such a sublime."(7)

End of April. "For the rest, I am tired of humanity and its hubbub. I desire only a little repose. I should like to be able to be quite certain that we shall live at least three or four years in Naples or Rome. A life so full of puerile-agitation as mine is at present would be profoundly antipathetic to me in the future. Whatever you may say, my true vocation is solitude. . . . I am vexed with you for having closed your door [in Geneva] as you are doing. In this you are acting traitorously, for you gave me a formal promise to receive regularly the four or five individuals we know. . . . I am sad without you. . . . I fancy I wrote you a very stupid letter yesterday evening, but you must be used to that by now. You must have known for a long time that I have no sort of intelligence when you are not with me. . . . Write to me often. You are my sole life, my sole hope, and my unique glory. . . . Make something or somebody of me."

30th April. "I am sad and troubled. . . . I could never endure ten days away from you. . . . If I were to listen to myself, you would see me arrive tomorrow evening. I cannot resign myself to this strange solitude. Oh, I will never leave you again! . . . I am going to pray in some church or other."

1st May. "If you knew how furiously and languorously I have need of you! Oh! my God, I can do nothing but dream of you; I cannot talk to anyone, and to you even less than to others!

---

(7) These last words are in English in the original.

F

Oh! if you knew only half the happiness it would be to me to see you here tomorrow, the day after tomorrow, I would not hesitate to say to you, 'Come, come.' . . . Marie, Marie, oh, give me my life again, your love; let your beautiful head bend voluptuously again to mine, let your adorable tears refresh, like dew from heaven, my poor dry and exhausted heart! Do not listen to me if I ever speak to you of anything else but love and happiness; tear out and burn every page in my letters where there happens to be written any name but yours, a thought that is not worthy of you; cast into the dust of the roads and the mud of the gutters every remembrance, every affection, every misery that have crossed and clashed with each other in this life of mine that was so bare, so feeble, so calamitous before you came into it. . . . The day will come when we shall see and comprehend clearly what at present we can only dimly glimpse and hope for in our terrestrial darkness. . . . And then you will recall the burning words that neither you nor I could have held back, for they would have shattered our bones and destroyed our mortal life, those words we uttered one night, in that room in which you came to me.(8) . . . Oh! if you feel any desire to see me again, come: you will find me alone, alone! For without you there is for me no glance, no sun, nor nature, nor God, nor temple, nor life."

— May. "My heart is dry. I long to see you, to gaze on you, to contemplate you, to remain long, long hours at your feet. You will give me back my life again, will you not? But my life regenerated, glorified by you and in you."

23rd July. "I have had a bad day: sadness and weariness are eating away my poor heart. Music exhausts me, humiliates and bores me, and nature without you is merely destruction and reproduction without end. . . . I need to see you again and to commence a new life. I want rest, profound rest. I aspire towards I know not what existence, at once bizarre and simple, common and mystical; an existence entirely ideal, entirely solitary, entirely in you and in God, as I feel Him to be and adore Him. Oh, give me rest, give me *your peace* as Christ gave *His* peace to his Apostles. . . . I am still not yet healed of my past; there are days when my wounds plague me. So lay your kind

---

(8) Referring, presumably, either to their meeting in his room in Paris just before their flight (see p. 50) or to that in the hotel at Basel.

hand on my breast and let me sleep in your bosom, there where I have buried all I have had of sorrow and genius and tenderness."(9)

3

Before we pass on to the next stage in the story we may profitably pause for a moment to glance at another facet of Liszt's character, and one that has mostly escaped observation by the biographers. The world's idea of him has been in large part derived from the imposing figure he presents during his Weimar period. Even this has been insufficiently studied, as we shall see later; for in this period also there were two Liszts—the statuesque creature who played so fine a part in Wagner's life and in musical affairs generally, and the weaker being who is revealed to us in his correspondence with the Princess Wittgenstein and in the comments of some of his contemporaries. The Weimar Liszt, indeed, was half face, half mask, the latter turned towards the world, the former shown only to the Princess and his own glass. The mask was a deliberate cultivation on his part, the product in some degree of his self-defensive reaction to painful circumstances, in some degree due to the actor that was inborn in him taking control and shaping the speech and the outward conduct of the man. The saintly Liszt of the literary legend was not quite the Liszt his friends and associates knew. It was only occasionally, when something broke through the bastions of his acquired self-control, that the mask fell, and the real Liszt, or at all events the other half of the real Liszt, was made visible; and when this happened the spectators were generally astonished at the revelation.(10)

We must do him the credit to recognise that no one was more acutely aware than he was of the defects in his character, and few men have fought so hard as he to purge themselves of their weaknesses and their faults. But of the weaknesses and the

---

(9) LZAC, I, 137-179.

(10) I came to this conclusion as to Liszt's "mask" from my own study of him. Later I discovered that Peter Cornelius, who knew him through and through, had used the same expression in connection with him in the eighteen-sixties. See *infra*, p. 205.

faults most people who came into contact with him, especially in his first and last periods, were sooner or later made aware. We find him more than once apologising to Marie for his temper and for the ugly quality of his speech during his fits of rage. Only rarely did he so far lose control of himself, in his later years, as to give his friends a hint of what he could be when the carefully cultivated St. Francis within him was momentarily edged aside by the natural man. He astonished Wagner, during the few days the latter spent at Weimar on his flight from Dresden in May, 1849, by a sudden volcanic outburst of this kind. After a rehearsal of *Tannhäuser*, Wagner, Stör and the singer Goetze dined with Liszt at a hotel. Apparently the conversation happened to turn upon Weimar society, and especially that section of it that was placing obstacles in the way of Liszt's accomplishment of his ideals; and, for the first time in Wagner's experience of him, the mask fell and a hitherto unsuspected Liszt came into view.

"I had occasion," says Wagner, " to be frightened at a trait in his character that till then had been completely unknown to me. As the result of certain incitements, this man, who was used to making himself appear to be so harmoniously sure of himself, broke out in a way that was truly terrifying, almost gnashing his teeth in his rage at that same world against which I myself was in revolt. Deeply moved by this strange contact with this extraordinary man, but unable to trace the connection of ideas that had led him to so horrible a demonstration, I sat in the utmost astonishment, while Liszt had to recover in the night from a violent attack of nerves."(11)

Occasionally he would amaze his company at Weimar by breaking into a similar frenzy, especially when music critics were mentioned in his presence; and Adelheid von Schorn tells us that she knew, from the Princess, how uncontrollable the fury of this St. Francis *manqué* could be at times, while he himself confessed to Adelheid that once in his youth, in Switzerland, he had smashed a window with his fist in a fit of temper.(12)

---

(11) WML, p. 563.

(12) SZM, p. 365. His cultivated courtliness of manner was always liable to break down under opposition: we find him, in 1843, apologising to

We meet with a further instance or two of the same kind during his be-abbéd Roman years. Adelheid von Schorn was the witness of an unpleasant scene at a soirée in Tivoli in 1880. Liszt began to play the piano, the young son of one of the ladies present turning over for him.

> "Either the young man became bored or he felt he was no longer required: suddenly he moved away with his hands in his trousers pockets and stationed himself at the further end of the piano, where he began to look at some music. I saw Liszt's face cloud: in a moment he abruptly ceased playing, rushed up to the young man and seized him by both his shoulders. I had never seen Liszt like this: his eyes flashed, his hair literally stood on end; he shook the malefactor so violently that the boy could hardly keep his feet, and poured out on him a flood of reproaches for his rudeness and inattention when he, the Master, was playing. Liszt loosed him and stormed out of the room. We were all of us more dead than alive: the ladies trembled, the young man howled. . . . I went after Liszt. I found him on the terrace, where he was striding furiously up and down, his head bare, his white hair streaming in the wind. . . . I ran to him: without saying a word he gave me his arm, and we walked about together for about ten minutes before he calmed down."(13)

St. Francis evidently had a good deal of human nature left in him at the age of seventy, especially when his self-esteem was wounded. Episodes of this kind always led to the bitterest self-reproach afterwards: he was not only grieved at his lapse from his ideal of Franciscan virtue but annoyed with himself

---

the Countess Hanska for having been "so brusque and violent in our discussions (see LZB, VIII, 34). But when he came to years of discretion he was careful to keep every trace of anger or hatred out of his letters. He was aware, as one of the people who knew him best has left on record, that his letters at once became quasi-public property; and he was watchful not to say anything in them that would be likely to clash with the saintly legend he was desirous of building up around himself. It is owing to the tightness of the hand he kept upon himself in his correspondence that this has helped to spread the mistaken notion of him that is now current.

(13) SZM, p. 365.

for having been so lacking in control as to let his mask fall before
others.

We catch glimpses of him labouring, in as yet a tentative
fashion, at the manufacture of his mask during the early
d'Agoult days. It would hardly be too much to say that Liszt
came gradually to make up his character for public appearance
as an actress makes up her face; and in the one case as in the
other the spectator, when the make-up temporarily wears
through, is astonished at the revelation of what the art of the
beauty specialist has concealed. From the time when the
Princess Wittgenstein took him in hand—a time that happened
to coincide with the coming both of more wisdom and of more
self-control on his own part, as the result of a wide experience
of the world and a long struggle to exorcise his own demon—his
letters exhibit practically no trace of temper or malevolence.
In the d'Agoult days he had not attained to such marble
mastery of himself in the presence of others. The object of his
visit to Paris in 1836 was, in small part, to have an interview
with Marie's brother, but in much larger part to square accounts
with a dangerous rival, Thalberg, who had lately been taking
the Parisian musical world by storm. Liszt was still human
enough at that time to feel a little apprehension of a competitor
and a good deal of hatred for him. The story of his dealings
with Thalberg makes rather unpleasant reading, because it is all
so unlike the greater-hearted Liszt of a later day. He had
intended to challenge his popular rival openly; but it was not
until some months later that he publicly entered the lists against
him in Paris and rolled him in the dust. Meanwhile he was
childishly delighted, as his letters show, at any remarks made in
his presence to the other pianist's disparagement, and he complacently repeats to Marie all the flattering things that were said
about his own playing in Lyons and, a few weeks later, in Paris.
He can only bring himself to go to Paris, he writes to Marie
from Lyons in May, because he wants to assert himself against
the upstart Thalberg. "It is a question of *amour-propre*," he
says, "nothing more, nothing less. I certainly do not want to
see Monsieur So-and-so but to put a dash of water in the wine
of Monsieur So-and-so. As it happens, my aim is fully attained

already; it appears that Thalberg had less success at his last concert; the programme was a shameful piece of work. Leave things to Time and all these waves of frenetic enthusiasm will calm down, and Monsieur Sigismond [Thalberg] will take his proper place by the side of MM. Kalkbrenner and Herz." He played a few times himself before invited audiences, and was pleased to find that everyone recognised the immense progress he had made in his art.

He had an interview and an explanation with Maurice de Flavigny, Marie's brother, which fact of itself shows that he regarded his bond with her as permanent. He was decidedly feeling his strength at this time; his letters show that he was prepared to quarrel with anyone who disapproved of him, or anyone who, he thought, had been speaking ill of him. We see him also working hard at the manufacture of one component of his mask—that aristocratic manner the value of which he had learned from his association with Marie and her circle, and which he was to exploit rather too obviously both in society and in some of his letters in after years. He has been making a round of calls in Paris: "I have been remarkably well received," he tells Marie: "if I do not deceive myself, I have constantly maintained a certain worthy and slightly superior simplicity— the kind of thing you like."(14) And in the light of what Ramann tells us about the Countess's extravagant demands on his purse, it is interesting to find him highly pleased when he can make a few hundred francs at a concert in Lyons or else- where. But, as usual, this "man of solitude" cannot refrain from giving a brilliant and presumably expensive dinner to his friends: his guests, he tells Marie, were Ballanche, the Baron d'Eckstein, Montalembert, Meyerbeer, Adolphe Nourrit (the leading tenor of the Opéra), Ferdinand Denis, Leuret (a cele- brated doctor), a "Théophile" whose surname is not given,

---

(14) Twenty years later we find him naïvely asking for the Princess's appro- val of his dignified, mock-modest way of acknowledging the frenzied acclamations of the Pesth public whenever it catches sight of him in the gardens, the casino, etc.: "My bearing is, I think, just what it ought to be—simple and serious" (LZB, IV, 317). Only an actor who was always dramatising himself in public could have written this passage, which links up with several others of the kind in his letters.

Chopin, Delacroix (the painter), Boulanger (another painter),. Barrault (the Saint-Simonian orator) and others whose names are concealed under a comprehensive "etc., etc.". In almost the next breath he resumes his desperate appeal for a life of solitude and contemplation with Marie alone, and an approving Providence in the offing!

4

His letters of this period come to an end in July, 1836, when he returned to Geneva. During the next few months the rivalry of Thalberg became still more menacing: the situation may be gauged from a passage in an Open Letter to Liszt from the notorious Fétis, who seems to have had something of Hanslick's gift for being superbly wrong on almost every occasion when fineness of perception and a sense of future values was in question: "You [Liszt] are a product," said Fétis magisterially, "of a school that has outlived itself and has nothing to look forward to. You are not the creator of a new school. *That* man is Thalberg; this is the whole difference between you two." By December Liszt was once more in Paris, with the lust of combat in him; and before the winter was over he had conclusively proved to the Parisians that however good Thalberg might be within his limits, Franz Liszt was his superior, and that for Franz Liszt no limits existed so far as the piano was concerned. At the end of January, 1837, Marie went to stay with George Sand at her estate at Nohant, where Liszt joined her in May. His letters of this period show him implacably hostile to his rival. "This evening was magnificent for me," he writes triumphantly to Marie after one of his Paris concerts; "you have never seen me so well understood and so much applauded. The public is decidedly veering in our direction. Thalberg was stupefied with amazement. He said out loud, before several people, that he had never heard anything like it. . . . Unless I deceive myself he must be feeling rather unhappy. . . . He shuts himself up in his narrow solemnity. I prefer that it should be so, though he will have to pay for it, and devilishly." This is not quite the Liszt of the legend of a later day! His openly expressed contempt and dislike for Thalberg, however, belong to a period when the mask of the generous, saintly Liszt had not yet been fitted to his face.

Light on his mood, or one of his moods, at this time is thrown by an article from his pen (the first of his *Lettres d'un Bachelier ès Musique*) in the *Gazette Musicale* of 12th February, 1837.(15)

He is sorry, he says, to have left the Alps for Paris, where the enveloping mist seems to say to him, "Give yourself up to your vilest instincts, sully yourself in the uncleanest debauches: the day is gloomy, I come between you and God himself; roll yourself in the mud, for there you will find gold and pleasures of all kinds." "For the third time," he continues, "I find myself caught in this living chaos in which brutal passions, hypocritical

---

(15) The letter is addressed to George Sand. It would appear from certain passages in his correspondence that a good deal, if not all, of some of these Letters was written by Marie. In a letter to her of this period we find him giving her (she was at Nohant at the time) the most detailed instructions as to the lines on which the next article is to run. She is to begin with some remarks about the nucleus of people in Paris who are sincerely devoted to the best art, with "one or two phrases on the impotence of the obstacles and on the necessity for the progress of music in France." Then she is to describe his four concerts in detail—how people listened with "religious attention and passionate interest to pieces that would probably have made the audience at many concerts yawn"; though naturally she is not to talk about *him*, but to praise his collaborators, Urhan, Lafont, Bériot and Batta, not forgetting a nice word for "the beautiful aristocratic salons of Erard" and for Erard's pianos. Although she is "not to say a word about him," she can, if she likes, "speak of the effect I made at the Conservatoire and at the Italiens, where my piano drowned the orchestra; say, which is quite true, that I could not have achieved this effect with any other instrument." And so on. "This matter is important for me: it is a real service I am asking of you." He will publish the article, he adds, under his own name (see LZAC, pp. 193, 194).

It looks, indeed, as if Marie wrote a good deal of what appears under his signature in his articles of this period, just as in the Weimar period the Princess contributed largely to the literary work that was published under his name. In Marie's journal (AM, pp. 103, 104) there is a record of her impressions of a visit of the pair to the Grande-Chartreuse. This passage is reproduced, with slight alterations, in the fourth of Liszt's *Lettres d'un Bachelier ès Musique* (to Louis de Ronchaud), which appeared in the *Gazette Musicale* on 25th March, 1838 (see LZPR, pp. 153ff).

vices, and shameless ambitions clash and struggle pell-mell, mad to destroy each other," though there are voices raised up for better things even in "this city which one would say is vowed to the cult of hell." "It is in a religious mood, a blend of profound sadness and undefined hope, that I come to Paris again. Two phases of my life have already been accomplished there." He describes pathetically—or Marie describes for him— his early years as an infant prodigy.

"A premature melancholy weighed on me at that time: I submitted with an instinctive repulsion to the barely concealed degradation of artistic servitude. Later, when death had deprived me of my father, and when, on my return to Paris, I had begun to have a premonition of what art and the artist might become, I was almost crushed by the impossibilities I saw arising in every quarter into which I projected my thought. Not meeting with a single sympathetic word either from the world of fashion or from artists, who dozed in a convenient indifferentism, and having no knowledge of myself, of the goal towards which I ought to strive and of the forces that were within me, I allowed myself to be swept away by a bitter disgust of art, which, as I saw it, was reduced to a more or less lucrative business, to an amusement for high society; and I would gladly have been anything in the world but a musician in the service of aristocrats, patronised and paid by them, just like a juggler or the learned dog Munito: peace be to his memory!"

He goes on to tell of his two-years' illness at that time, and of his desire to renounce the world for religion.

"But an isolation so complete as this could not last for ever. Poverty, that old go-between between man and evil, tore me away from my contemplative solitude and brought me frequently before a public on which my own existence and that of my mother depended. Young and extreme as I then was, I suffered grievously under the shock of the outer things among which my profession of musician threw me unceasingly, and that wounded so deeply the mystical feeling of love and religion that filled my heart. . . . Tormented by a thousand confused instincts and by a need for vast expansion, too young to distrust myself, too simple to concentrate on myself, I gave myself up completely to my impressions, my admirations, my repugnances. I earned the reputation of being an actor, because I did not know how to play a part but let myself appear just what I was, an enthusiastic child, a sympathetic artist, austerely devout, in a word, all that one is at eighteen when one loves God and men with a soul that is ardent, passionate, not yet deadened by the brutal trituration of social egoisms.''

He tells of his sins against art in those days, the tricks he played with the works of the masters in order to win applause, and of his resolve never to sink into this abyss of vulgarity again;(16) and he proceeds to some sage reflections on the duty of the executive artist towards the creative.

In the second *Lettre*, which appeared in the *Gazette Musicale* on 16th July,(17) he assured his readers that the artist is essentially a solitary: "though circumstances may throw him into the centre of society, he creates for his own soul, amid these discordant noises, an impenetrable solitude to which no voice can penetrate. Vanity, ambition, cupidity, jealousy, love itself, all the passions that sway mankind, remain outside the magic circle he has traced about his thought: there, withdrawn as it were into a sanctuary, he contemplates and adores the ideal type which it will be the object of his whole life to reproduce.'' The artist, it seems, having delivered himself of the work of art that had shaped itself in agony and ecstasy within him, can find no consolation in the approval of the world: "While the entire world is acclaiming the work with enthusiasm, *he* remains only half-satisfied, discontented, and would perhaps destroy it were it not that a new apparition turns his gaze away from what has been accomplished towards those fresh ecstasies, at once celestial and dolorous, that make his life the perpetual *mis-understanding* that seems destined, for a long time yet, to exist between the public and the artist.''

Alas! his life was to be one long series of variations upon this mournful motive; always he was to long to fly from the world

---

(16) As we have seen (p. 10), he was no more able, in the years of his triumphant virtuosity, to keep this promise to his better self than to carry out
   consistently any other of his frequent resolutions for self-reform.

(17) It was written, or purported to be written, on 7th April, the day before
   he left Paris to rejoin Marie at Nohant; he is on the point of setting out,
   he says, "for an unknown land where my desire and my hope have
   long dwelt.''

into the communion of saints, and always something within
him was to make the communion of the saints seem insufficient
without the more fleshly delights of the company of aristocrats
and the eyes and arms of pretty women; always he was to
fluctuate between the ecstasy of virtuous resolve and disgust
with himself for not being able to be content with that ecstasy;
always it was a woman who watched with pain his secret
struggle with himself—first Marie, then the Princess; and each
of them, in her own way, had to give him up, in the end, as
incurable, for the enemy was within his own soul, and it was too
strong for him. The only difference between the two situations
was that the second of these women was growing old when she
at last realised the hopelessness of the task she had set herself,
and experience had taught her charity and the necessity for
resignation where Liszt was concerned; whereas the first of
them was still young and ardent when the veil began to fall from
her eyes, and she was filled with resentment at his having
cheated her of her ideal.

5

The "chivalry" for which the later Liszt is justly famous is
not very evident in his dealings with Thalberg: it is strange to
find him, in his *Lettre* in the *Gazette* of 16th July, actually running his rival down in print. It is true that he begins by making
a parade of the noblest sentiments.

>   "On my arrival in Paris the talk in the musical world was all
> about a pianist the like of whom had never been heard before;
> he was to be the regenerator of the art; both as executant and
> as composer he had opened out a new path along which we ought
> all to follow him. You, who have seen me invariably turn my
> ear towards the smallest hint of progress, and even forestall it
> with the whole of my sympathies, can guess whether my soul
> did not vibrate with the hope of a great impulse being given to
> the whole generation of contemporary pianists. I was suspicious
> only of one thing—the promptitude with which the zealots of
> the new Messiah forgot or rejected those who had preceded
> him. I must confess that I augured less favourably for M. Thal-
> berg's compositions because I heard them praised to the skies
> by people who seemed to believe that, by the mere fact of his

coming, all previous composers, Hummel, Moscheles, Kalk-brenner, Bertini, Chopin, were consigned to oblivion. I was eager to see and study for myself works so new and so profound, that were to introduce me to a man of genius. I shut myself up for a whole morning to study them conscientiously. The result of this study was diametrically opposed to what I had expected. Only one thing surprised me—the enormous effect produced by works so empty, so mediocre. I came to the con-clusion that the execution of the composer must be prodigious; and, my opinion having been formed, I expressed it in the *Gazette Musicale*(18) with no more perverse intention than that of doing what I have done on many another occasion—to give my opinion, good or bad, on such piano works as I had examined. I certainly had no intention, in this case any more than in others, of lecturing or dictating to public opinion. I was far from arrogating to myself a right so impertinent; I merely thought myself entitled to say, not unbecomingly, that if this is the new school, I am not of the new school; that if this is the direction in which M. Thalberg is going, I had no ambition at all to tread the same path; and finally, that there is not a single germ of the future in his ideas which it is the duty of others to cultivate.

"What I said, I said with regret, driven to it, so to speak, by the public, which had made it its business to link our names together, to represent us as fighting in the same arena for the same crown—perhaps also the inner need of men of a certain type of organisation to react against injustice and to protest, even if the occasion be a small one in itself, against error or bad faith, had impelled me to seize my pen and express my frank opinion. After having done so in public, I repeated it to the composer himself when we happened to meet a little later. It was a pleasure to me to do justice to his talent as a player, and he seemed to realise better than others had done the loyalty and frankness of my conduct. The word went round that we were *reconciled;* this was a new theme, that was subjected to as many stupid variations as that of our *enmity* had been. As a matter of fact there was neither enmity nor reconciliation. Because one artist does not rank another as highly as the crowd, in its exaggerating fashion, has done, are they necessarily enemies? Are they reconciled because outside matters of art they appreciate and esteem each other? . . .

(18) Of 8th January, 1837.

"When I wrote those few lines on M. Thalberg's compositions I foresaw at any rate a part of the indignation I was to arouse, the storm that was to break over my head. I confess, however, that I thought that a thousand antecedent events had placed me utterly above the suspicion of envy: I believed—*o sancta simplicitas!* you will say—that the truth ought always to be spoken, and that in no circumstances, even those the most insignificant on the surface, ought an artist to be false to his thought out of prudent calculation of his personal interest. This experience has taught me something, but it will be of no profit to me. Unfortunately I am not one of those *emollient* natures of whom Mirabeau speaks: I love the truth much more than I love myself."(19)

In spite of the purring tone—which leaves us wondering how much of venom there may be concealed under the purring voice and behind the saintly attitude of Liszt towards his rivals or enemies in later years—it is plain that he is very angry. It is in vain that he tries to persuade us that in falling foul of Thalberg in public in this way he was actuated only by the noblest abstract concern for art *qua* art: his letters, as we have seen, show that he regarded Thalberg as a dangerous rival in the career he had marked out for himself, and that he had gone to Paris with his teeth clenched, ready for combat, eager to roll his rival in the dust.(20) No one will think much the worse of him for a feeling so admirably human; what leaves a bad taste in the mouth is the artist's resort to journalism to further his personal ends. Manifestly the Liszt of those days is not the Liszt of the later legend. As time went on he learned, partly by the buffetings of experience, partly by the assiduous cultivation of self-control, to turn towards the world only the face he wished the world to see. As yet the saintly mask was not available: the more profane side of him was too strong to be suppressed.

---

(19) LZPR, pp. 123-126.

(20) "Thalberg is practically dismounted," he writes gleefully to Marie in February, 1837: "he does not know where to give his concert." And a day or two later: "I shall probably arrange to give my concert at the Opéra. I repeat that it would be a huge mistake for me to leave Paris just now. Thalberg is virtually routed. I know that the other day, when he heard I had arrived at Zimmermann's [a pianist and composer of the time], his eyes filled with tears" (LZAC, I, 190, 191).

6

And no one knew better the dualism of his nature, or grieved over it more, than Marie. In Switzerland he had found in her a sympathetic listener when he confided to her his dreams of a life to be devoted not to dazzling the public with his virtuosity as pianist and as transcriber but to the composition of the original works of which he and she believed him to be capable. To her profound regret, however, she saw more and more clearly how incapable he was of struggling for any length of time against the lower element in his nature that drew him irresistibly towards the world and its cheaper prizes. It pained her to see him still writing showy transcriptions, though for this, as she says, there was an excuse to be found—he needed money, and publishers demanded saleable things of the type associated with his name. "Franz derided these mercantile exigencies or was irritated by them, but in the end he had to submit; and not wishing, as he said, to profane purer art by contact with these commoner things, he had abruptly ceased to occupy himself with serious work."(21) The Princess had often to grieve over the same situation in the later years in Rome—yet another proof that Marie's diagnosis of Liszt in the earlier days is a correct one, and she herself a trustworthy witness. "He put out of his sight the compositions of his own that he had sketched. But he could not so easily put them out of his mind; and so, in his exasperation, drawn as he was in opposite directions, he sought, in order to escape from himself, distractions in the outer world, whence I used to see him return more and more dissatisfied, more and more out of equilibrium."(22) Owing to the demands made on his time by the rapidly increasing number of their acquaintances in Geneva, she says, "he could no longer find the leisure, the concentration, necessary for the big works upon which he had wanted to embark."(23)

Her critical eye observed that the disharmony of his soul

---

(21) AM, pp. 66, 67.

(22) Ibid., p. 67.

(23) Ibid., p. 66.

showed itself also in his piano-playing: rage as he might against
the vulgarity and inanity of the public, as soon as he sat down in
front of it the mere virtuoso in him, anxious to dazzle and to be
applauded, came uppermost again. She attended a concert he
gave in Lausanne. The enthusiasm was immense, but it left
her sad at heart. Being sensitive with regard to her equivocal
position in the world, she had taken a seat behind a screen.
As soon as he began to play, some impulse or other prompted
her to move the screen, and her eyes met his. "How can I
describe what I felt?" she says. "It was Franz I saw, and yet it
was not Franz. It was as if someone were personating him on
the stage, with great art and verisimilitude, yet had nothing in
common with him except the facial resemblance. And his
playing disturbed me. His prodigious, brilliant, incomparable
virtuosity was indeed there, but I felt it nevertheless as something alien to me. Where were we? Was I dreaming? Was I
the victim of a delirium? Who had taken me there? For what
purpose? I felt an inexpressible anguish. From that day a
change was wrought in my existence; it brought with it a new
and difficult trial of my courage."(24) The success of the
virtuoso led, of course, to the irruption of a crowd of new
acquaintances into what she hoped would be the solitude for
which Franz was always crying out.

From May to August, 1837, the lovers were with George
Sand at Nohant. We have consequently no letters bearing on
this period. We have, however, a journal kept by Marie during
these months, in which she records not only her love but her
admiration for him. As always when the outer world did not
intrude on them, she was relatively happy. On 7th June we
find her enthusiastically chanting Liszt's praises—his personal
beauty, the angelic sweetness of his attitude towards her, the
nobility of his piano playing when the three of them are alone,
his "purity of intention," his "rectitude of will," his "loving
comprehension of human infirmity." Evidently he was for the
moment in one of his saintly moods, the mood in which he was
filled with love and pity and charity for all mankind: "If it
were necessary for one soul to be damned," he said to her,

(24) AM, p. 64.

F. Bruckmann

FRANZ LISZT AS A YOUNG MAN

From a drawing by Ingres

COUNTESS D'AGOULT

"I would volunteer to be that one." Undoubtedly he was sincere; undoubtedly he would have offered himself up for the sacrifice—providing there was not too long an interval between his offer to the cosmos and the acceptance of it, an interval during which the carnal delights of the world, the applause of the public, the dinner talk of titled friends, the invitation to the alcove which he could read in the eyes of infatuated women, could turn him from his saintly purpose.

Marie, for her part, felt that a life such as that lived by the three of them at Nohant, with an occasional visitor from Paris, would solve all the problems that tormented and perplexed her. Liszt was showing only his most charming side, and she could not imagine life without him. "I like travelling," she writes in her journal—she and Liszt were then at Bourges, on their way to Italy—"because it gives me a feeling of the unity of my life. When I visit in his company places I did not know before, I feel that he is my sole support, my sole guide, that my destiny is in him alone, that I have voluntarily and gladly placed it in his hands, that truly I have neither temple nor country except in his heart."(25) Lina Ramann (or the Princess) sneers at her for "wanting to be his Muse". The ambition was surely a laudable one, for it meant encouraging him to turn his back on the superficial public that saw only the piano virtuoso in him, and to devote himself to original composition. Moreover he himself, at this time, though he forgot the fact later, gratefully recognised her as his Muse. "I cannot go a month without seeing you," he had written to her from Paris in February: "so come here, and come as soon as possible: understand me and love me. But what need is there for me to tell you this? Am I not wholly yours? Is it not you who multiply my ambition a hundredfold? Is it not for you that I struggle and fight? Oh, Marie, Marie, you can still love me. In spite of all my past faults, in spite of men, in spite of everything, I will be worthy of you."(26)

---

(25) AM, pp. 73-98.

(26) LZAC, I, 191.

G

7

From about August, 1837, to the autumn of 1839 the lovers lived in Italy, for the most part in Milan, Venice and Rome. In Bellaggio they found again, for a brief period, the solitude they desired: "What is there in all the world," Marie writes in her journal on 6th September, 1837, "but work, contemplation and love?"(27) For the moment Liszt is quite happy in his abstraction from the world:

"I am astonished," Marie confides to her journal on 5th October, "to find him so constantly gay, so happy in the absolute solitude in which we are living. At an age when everything impels a man towards outer activity, when movement and change are almost a condition of existence, he, whose mind is so communicative, he, whose occupations have always taken him into the world, he, the artist, that is to say the man of sympathies, of emotions, of imagination, concentrates all his faculties within the narrow frame of a life of *tête-à-tête*. A bad piano, a few books, the conversation of a serious woman, suffice for him. He renounces all the joys of *amour-propre*, the excitement of combat, the amusements of social life, even the delight of being useful and doing good: he renounces them all without even appearing to be conscious that he is renouncing."(28)

He writes what she calls his twelve Preludes—"a fine work," she notes, "that makes a worthy beginning of his original compositions." Remote from the world, he can persuade himself that the world is good: he awaits, "in religious confidence, the solution of the great problems of humanity, the extinction of evil, the reign of God." The mood, of course, was far too virtuous to last. In Milan he plunged into society again, to the regret of Marie, who found the Milanese aristocrats empty-headed and uncultured. Franz also had no great respect for them in this regard; but his attitude towards society, then and always, was the same as his attitude towards his pipes and cigars and coffee and alcohol—he knew full well that they were bad for him, but he could not live without them. Differences had evidently arisen between him and Marie on this subject of

---

(27) AM, p. 114.
(28) Ibid., pp. 118, 119.

his passion for society, for we find her noting in her journal, in the spring of 1838, "My heart and my mind are dry; it is a malady I brought with me on my entry into the world. Passion elevated me for a moment, but I feel that the principle of life is lacking in me. I feel that I am a shackle on him; I do not benefit him; I cast sadness and discouragement on his days."(29)

The storm she heard muttering in the distance was not long in bursting. In Venice, in April, 1838, he suddenly announced his intention of going to Vienna to play for the benefit of the sufferers by the Danube floods; he would be away, he said, no longer than a week. The biographers have told us of the sensation created by his playing. He found himself admired and fêted as no performer had ever been before; and the adulation turned his head. Alone in Venice, with her perceptions sharpened by a serious illness, Marie sensed already the beginning of the end of their idyll. His letters were full, she says, of accounts of his triumphs;(30) and as she read them she realised that the outer world, with its material prizes and its paltry vanities had taken complete possession of his divided soul once more. "This world about which it now seemed a necessity that I should hear, these aristocratic names, these princes, these emperors—it was all like a false note in harmony. We had gone into solitude; now he had returned in triumph once more into the world he had so despised and disdained, and from which he had wanted to fly with me."(31)

He prolongs his absence indefinitely, his plea being that he cannot well leave Austria while his services are in such demand. But she has no illusions about him: she knows that the real pull on him there is threefold—the desire to make money, the intoxicating flattery of aristocratic society, and some facile love affairs. "Franz had abandoned me," says Marie in her *Mémoires*, "for such small motives! It was not to do a great work, not out of devotion, not out of patriotism, but for salon successes, for

(29) AM, p. 140.

(30) This statement is confirmed by his letters of this period to her.

(31) AM, p. 144.

newspaper glory, for invitations from princesses." When at last he returns she finds him changed:

"The way in which he spoke about his stay in Vienna brought me down from the clouds. They had found armorial bearings for him—a republican, living with a *grande dame*! He wanted me to be heroic. The women had thrown themselves at his head; he was no longer embarrassed over his lapses, he reasoned about them like a philosopher. He spoke of necessities. . . . He was elegantly dressed; his talk was about nothing but princes; he was secretly pleased with his exploits as Don Juan. One day I said something that hurt him: I called him a *Don Juan parvenu*. I summoned up my pride as a woman, as a *grande dame*, as a republican, to judge him from above. He had made money easily; he had left it(32) for the victims of the floods; but he had realised that in two years he could make a fortune."

Manifestly the life he had been living in Vienna and Hungary appealed to him immensely; dissolved into thin air were all his aspirations for a life of solitude, of mystical contemplation, of the slow gestation of great original works.(33) He hinted that Marie ought to return alone to Paris, and dwelt plausibly upon the satisfaction she would find, or ought to find, in resuming her place there as a leading light in society. He suggested her taking a certain Theodoro as a lover.

Her reply to all this was "Let us try again." As she was weak after her illness, and felt a longing for sea air, they decided to go to Genoa. He went there in advance: when she arrived

---

(32) But not all of it, by any means, as the biographies have led us to believe.

(33) The Empress of Austria thought of inviting him to play at Court, but before doing so she wanted to know something about this young man of whom she had heard strange reports from Paris. The Grand Duke Ludwig accordingly set the Police Minister, Count Sedlnitzky, to work. The latter reported that Liszt had attracted unfavourable attention to himself in Paris by his association with George Sand, Lamennais and other persons of dubious repute, and by his elopement with a certain Countess d'Agoult. In Italy and Vienna, however, he had done nothing to cause him to be suspected of holding revolutionary opinions. "Rather does he appear to me simply a vain and frivolous young man, who affects the fantastic manners of the young Frenchmen of today, but good-natured, and, apart from his merits as an artist, of no significance" (see KFL, pp. 108-110).

she found that this ardent apostle of solitude and contemplation had rented a magnificent villa, bought himself horses, and plunged once more into the whirl of fashionable life. He confessed having been unfaithful to her, but promised never to fall again. One day she discovered that, without consulting her, he had entered into engagements to tour Germany as a pianist; and once more, under the convenient plea that *she* could never endure a life of that kind, he tries to win her round to his plan of her settling in Paris with her family and leaving him free to go where he will. "My family?" she replied. "Have I one now? Would my daughter recognise me? My only talent was my love for you, the desire to please you." "A tear coursed down his cheek. He reproached me with being lacking in precision; he pretended not to understand what it was I wanted, what it was that was making me suffer, the points upon which we felt differently. In six months he had forgotten much and travelled far!"(34)   •

8

So much for Marie's journal. Let us now see how far Liszt's letters of this epoch confirm or refute her account of his conduct and his motives.

The year 1838 was obviously the beginning of the crisis within him that was to extend all through 1839 and 1840, and after that to lead inevitably to a breach between him and Marie. The fundamental dualism of his nature becomes more and more apparent as time goes on. At first we see him writing from Milan to Marie (in Como) to assure her, as usual, that after his brief re-entry into the world he is already weary of it. "How I long," he says, "to return to my shell in Como! I can live only in one way, and you know what that is. For a long time you have been mistaken as to my needs and my tastes. Now you know me better, do you not? You *must* know that I am happy with you and with you alone." In spite of his success at his Milan concert he is sad at heart because he cannot be always and exclusively occupied with her, and only her. Why, he plaintively asks, should he be subject as he is to the crude

_____
(34) AM, pp. 143-149.

necessities of this poor life: why has he not taken her into some solitude inaccessible to the rest of mankind: why has he ever deceived himself as to their true needs? "In spite of all my faults and all my misdeeds, you have given such happiness to our intimate seclusion! Yes, dear good Marie, you are an angel, and I am hardly worthy of you. . . . Make me day by day less unworthy of you." All the same, it is a great satisfaction to him to tell her that he has been presented to the Duchess Litta, to the Marquise D. . . ., to the Trivulzi, etc. Liszt always loved to see his notepaper sprinkled with the names of royalties and aristocrats.

On 7th April he sets out for Vienna, leaving Marie in Venice. His letters show that his unparalleled success there and elsewhere had gone to his head. There is hardly a word in them about the ostensible object of his journey—to raise funds for the sufferers by the Danube floods. His talk is all of the terrific sensation he is making; of the money that is rolling in; of his determination to humble Thalberg once more; of his satisfaction when he is assured that he has made the Viennese forget his rival; of his further successes in Pressburg and Pesth; of the adulation that is poured out on him wherever he goes; of the "brilliant business" he is doing; of how he is decidedly "l'homme à la mode"; how his room is never free of admirers, so that he can hardly get a moment to himself or to write to Marie; how his portrait is selling in immense numbers; how pleased he is that after being at first ignored by the Court (no doubt because of his illicit relations with Marie), he is at last invited to play there; and much more in the same feverish and sometimes rather fatuous strain. But combined with this familiar motive, in double counterpoint, now one of them, now the other, sounding the upper part, is the other motive that by now is equally familiar to us, and that will become more so in the course of the present study—that of his weariness of this kind of life, of his "mortal sadness," of the pain it gives him to know that she is ill and unhappy, of how he never forgets her for a quarter of an hour, of the impossibility of his living without her, of his "thirst for the impossible," of his sense of isolation in the midst of the admiring crowd that surrounds him. He belongs only to her, he tells her. "Why did I not leave here after the first few days? Or rather, why did I ever decide to come here? I assure you, my good, my only Marie, I do not think that I have done wrong. I suffer as you do, less nobly but just as profoundly. I still feel myself worthy of your love, your compassion." But still he cannot tear himself away; his vanity, his love of flattery, of high living and patrician company, are too strong to permit of that. Marie's last letter to him during this period is dated 24th May; the "week" had drawn itself out to nearly two months. And when he did return, Marie, as her journal shows, noticed a decided change for the worse in him.

9

The Princess, and all the modern writers who have been misled by her mendacities, would have us believe that Madame d'Agoult was a hindrance to the development of the better Liszt. When we come to the consideration of the novel in which Marie has drawn herself and him we shall see that one of her grievances against him was that he too often allowed the shoddier elements in his nature to get the upper hand of the better ones, that instead of settling down in retirement to the writing of the big works he was always longing to write he exhausted body and brain and disharmonised his soul by too much social intercourse, too high living, and too much piano-circus-riding in public. And that her diagnosis of him in her novel was accurate in this respect is now proved by certain passages from a contemporary journal of his own that are incorporated in her *Mémoires*. These passages date from the summer and autumn of 1838 and the early part of 1839, that is to say, the period following his return from Vienna.

"She said to me today," he writes in August, 'You ought to make better use of your time—work, learn, take exercise, etc.' Often she has scolded me, in her own way, for my indolence, my indifference; and these words of hers sadden me. Work? Make use of my time? But what can I do with my time? At what can I and ought I to work? Reflect as I will, grope as I will, I do not feel a vocation within me, nor can I discover one outside me. . . . I have all the *amour-propre* and all the pride of a high destiny; what I have not is the calm and sustained conviction of

such a destiny. . . . There is a storm in the air, and my nerves are irritated horribly. I feel I want a prey. I feel an eagle's claws tearing at my breast; my tongue is dried up. Two opposed forces are at war within me: one of them impels me towards the immensities of infinite space, high and ever higher, beyond all the suns and all the heavens; the other draws me towards the lowest, darkest regions of calm, of death, of annihilation. And I stay nailed to my chair, equally wretched about my strength and my weakness, not knowing what will become of me. Why have I squandered my fine gifts for some paltry feminine idols, that must of necessity laugh at me for it? There have been many days in which I have not written a single line: I sometimes suffer bitterly at my inability to handle speech as I can the keys of my piano. It would be so sweet to be able to express nobly, simply, and powerfully what I have thus felt in certain hours of my life. . . . I am like the she-wolf in Dante,
> . . . che di tutte brame
> Sembiava carca nella sua magrezza.(35)

He attributes a good deal of his melancholy and irritability to tea, coffee and tobacco, especially the two latter, without which he cannot live. But sometimes, he says, he wearies of them, "as I do of my best friends," and sometimes they disturb and torment him strangely. His pipe at once soothes and frets him; he sits half paralysed in his chair, thinking mournfully of the past, the present and the future, turning over his memories, gazing at his "shattered hopes". When he is in one of these moods only one thing can bring him consolation and strength— a word from Marie, however insignificant: "her speech is the sweetest light and the whitest of stars." Yet it is of this period that biographers like Schrader can say that Liszt "had become another, a nobler man, while the Countess had remained the vain nullity she had always been"!(36)

A little later he laments his inability to rouse his soul from its torpor: he asks of God nothing but to be allowed to sleep and to be forgotten. Later still, in Milan:

"Why despair? But why hope? Why the 'why'? The forces that dominate us obey laws we have not yet discovered. . . .

---

(35) "That in its leanness seemed to be burdened with every desire."
(36) SFL, p. 38.

In the torment of my hours of anguish, when everything is cracking in my heart, everything is being rent and violently uprooted, a single thought remains with me, a single remorse— I should have made her happy! I could have done so! But can I now?" Upon this there follow some lines in Marie's hand-writing: "Lay your hand on your heart and answer: 'Vermag die Liebe alles zu dulden, so vermag sie noch viel mehr alles zu ersetzen.'(37) A noble and beautiful reply, though at another diapason."

On 14th November there is an entry in his journal that seems to point to a crisis arrived at and passed through. Apparently there had been some serious difference between the pair, and Liszt had ceased to wear a ring that Marie had given him.

> "She asked me to wear her ring again. Do the diverse phases of our life join up together harmoniously? Are there not violent shocks of this kind, despairing cries that seem to rupture all one's unity? Are so many catastrophes, so many tears, necessary for the development of our moral energy? I do not know; but when I put the ring on my finger again it seemed to me that I was suddenly healed of a long malady, and I gave myself up to the vast confidence of my first youth, when we met for the first time."

In February, 1839, he writes: "If I feel the needful life and strength in me, I will attempt a symphonic work based on Dante, then another on Faust, say in three years. Meanwhile I will make three sketches—the Triumph of Death, after Orcagna, the Comedy of Death, after Holbein, and a Dantesque fragment. I am attracted also by the Pensiero."(38)

---

(37) "If love can endure all things, still more can it compensate for all things" (Goethe).

(38) The *Dante Symphony* does not seem to have taken any kind of definite shape in Liszt's mind until about 1847, though the opening theme of it is to be found in an early song of his, *Le vieux vagabond*. It was only in 1855 that he really set to work at it, completing it in July of the following year. The Faust subject occupied his mind intermittently from about 1846 or so; but the Symphony was not written until 1854. *Il Pensieroso* (for piano) dates from 1839. If by "a Dantesque fragment" Liszt means the *Fantasia quasi Sonata, après une lecture du Dante* (gracefully translated on the wireless recently, by the way, "After a lecture by Dante"), this was finished some time in 1839.

This, then, was the Liszt of the early years, the Liszt whom Marie knew, the self-divided Liszt whose greatest enemy tortured him and gibed at him from the centre of his own unhappy soul. Did he forget, when he allowed his own tongue and those of others to slander Marie in the later years, all she had been to him, all she had suffered, by his own confession, through him, all the comfort and guidance her stronger spirit had been to his? Or was it, perhaps, that he remembered only too well, and that, as I have suggested, knowing that there was a possibility of her completing her *Mémoires* and of their being published some day, he wanted to prejudice the world against her in advance by spreading the legend that she was not to be believed in anything? For in his heart of hearts he knew that he was just the weak, divided kind of creature she was certain to show him to be—weak, behind his mask, even in the great Weimar years, and weaker still in the Roman years that followed his escape from the directing hand of the Princess Wittgenstein.(39)

---

(39) In 1911 Daniela Thode (Bülow's daughter by Cosima) brought out a German edition of "Daniel Stern's" book *Dante and Goethe*, with an introduction by herself in which she breaks a lance for her much-maligned grandmother. The Countess's idealism, she says, was disappointed in Liszt: "she sought the artist and found the virtuoso: she desired the completion of him as master and found only an extravagant talent whose innermost genius, not yet revealed to the world, was necessarily misjudged by her by reason of her disillusionment" (quoted in RLL, p. 41).

CHAPTER IV

THE END OF THE D'AGOULT AFFAIR

I

Looking back today upon the correspondence of the pair, we can see now that the decisive moment in their story was Liszt's departure for Vienna in 1838; though their union was to last, in outward form, for another six years, it was already virtually over in inner fact, though neither of them seems to have been fully conscious of this at the time.

Liszt had returned to Venice and Marie at the end of May, 1838. After brief stays together in Lugano and Milan, his concert journeys separated them a good deal until January, 1839, when they met again in Rome. The summer of that year was spent mostly in Lucca and San Rossore: in October Liszt set out for Vienna once more, Marie staying for a while in Florence and then returning to Paris with her two little daughters. Liszt toured in Austria, Hungary and Germany until April, 1840, and then returned to Paris, where he gave two private concerts. In May he set out for London, where the Countess rejoined him in June.

We shall see later that as soon as circumstances brought about a temporary separation between Liszt and the Princess Wittgenstein (in May, 1860, when she went to Rome to try to obtain a divorce from her husband), Liszt found his liberty to indulge his Zigeuner instincts so much to his liking that he was secretly resolved never to wear his chains again. Evidently the same thing happened with regard to Marie after the hectic Vienna days of the spring of 1838. In spite of his protestations, when he was away from her, that she is the sole sun of his life, it is clear enough from their letters that such love as still remained between them was mostly on her side. There are plentiful hints that, under the pretence of a noble regard for her "liberty", he kept urging her to seek consolation in other quarters for his absence. "I could never love anyone again," he writes to her from Genoa on 25th June, 1838; "but why should I deprive *you* of a love that might prove a new source of life for you?" He has, he assures her, "a profound respect for her liberty". When she was settled in Paris, where she managed, in time, to make her salon once more a resort of the *littérateurs* and philosophers and artists of the day, she seems to have fascinated Henry Bulwer Lytton (later Lord Dalling, brother of the novelist Edward Bulwer Lytton), at that time Secretary to the English Embassy in Paris. Liszt did his best to manoeuvre her into Bulwer's arms, assuring her that if she was inclined to take him as her lover he, Franz, for his part, would always be a brother to her. But whatever passing regard she may have had for Bulwer, her letters make it clear that she loved no one but Liszt, and that the central desire of her life was to be with him always. This, of course, was impossible so long as he was engaged in touring Europe as a pianist; the world might smile indulgently at his notorious amours so long as they were of the casual and frankly immoral kind, but it would have held up its virtuous hands in horror had he been accompanied everywhere by a devoted woman who was his wife in everything but name. Liszt was fully conscious of the difficulty, and he welcomed it because it gave him an excuse for following his inclinations. He loved the excitements of his wandering life too much to wish to give them up for the milder delights of domesticity; and it was comforting to be able to make it appear, both to Marie and to himself, that in urging her on no account to leave Paris to rejoin him in Germany or Austria he was behaving in the most chivalrous way imaginable towards her. And so, while she was rebuilding her broken world in Paris, he drained to the dregs the cup he really loved, the cup of high living, wild excitement, gross adulation, and piquant amours. His letters during this period show him to be drunk with vanity and reeking with vulgarity.

2

The quasi-saintly Liszt of the later legend, let it be said once more, has no resemblance whatever to the real Liszt of the end of the 'thirties and the early 'forties. He was in a constantly hectic condition, the result partly of overstrained nerves, partly of excessive indulgence in stimulants and narcotics, partly of the self-disgust that would sometimes take possession of him as he contrasted what he was with what he longed to be. In Milan, in August, 1838, he had been angered at some criticism of his conduct by Pixis, whom he had met at a dinner. "He annoyed me," he writes to Marie: "I said nothing, but later I will get even with him and make him pay for this a hundred-fold." His vanity, so copiously fed by his frenzied admirers, especially the feminine portion of them, made him unable to bear the slightest contradiction. Marie warns him more than once to mend his ways. His arrogance, she says, has made him many enemies in Paris and elsewhere: Potocki, for instance, has told her that he has to avoid him so as not to be provoked into challenging him to a duel, so intolerable does he find Liszt's arrogance: "he says you argue with him in so bitter and so rude a way that he keeps asking himself whether he ought to allow it to pass."(1) She warns him that if he hopes to re-establish himself socially in critical Paris he must change his tone: "I do not doubt you can make a good position for yourself here, but you will need more dexterity than anywhere else. Above all you must put the extinguisher on, for the general complaint against you is in connection with your sharp tone, your passion for domination, and your exaggerations."(2) Ronchaud finds him "ferociously irritable and domineering." "Take care of my love," Marie writes to him in 1840, "if you can; it is yours as completely now as ever in the old days. I fear that trouble will come from the fact that you can no longer endure to hear the truth and that you are unwilling to submit to any curb. Surrounded as you have been by Puzzis of all kinds, the only language you have been willing to listen to is the language of

(1) LZAC, I, 340.

(2) Ibid., p. 375.

utter flattery. I am afraid this will not be for your benefit, for I cannot believe that a man ought to surrender himself blindly to all his instincts."(3) He denies it all, of course, especially the charges that he is vain and cannot exist without flattery; but his own letters supply the fullest proof of the justice of Marie's diagnosis of him and of that of the contemporary world in general.

3

He loses no opportunity of telling her of his colossal success and his "good business," as he calls it. At Bologna there has been nothing like it since Malibran was there; and even Malibran did not create such a furore. In Vienna he has "smashed" Bériot, with whom he has played a duet in public, and that in spite of the fact that the piano part was in itself insignificant.(4) There is never a word about anything so idealistic as art for its own sake: he can talk about nothing but the sensation he makes everywhere, "especially among the aristocrats and the women," who seem, indeed, to be his sole concern and his sole standard of value. How deeply he had been mortified in his youth by reason of his plebeian birth, and at the same time how vulgar his own standards were, is shown by the constant delight he takes in reeling off lists of aristocratic names the owners of which have dined him or been dined by him. "The flower of the Hungarian aristocracy," he tells Marie exultantly, has given a banquet in his honour. After his concert in Pressburg he has dined with Count Casimir Esterhazy, "and about four o'clock we all got into our carriages. We were quite an aristocratic caravan—Casimir Esterhazy, in whose excellent coupé I was sitting, Baron Venckheim, two Counts Zychyi, the Festetics. . . ." Later, in Pressburg again, he is asked out to dinner in some "charming houses," where he meets "the most elegant and most aristocratic society." In Vienna "it would be impossible to ask more in the way of satisfaction of one's vanity: the greatest people . . . have not

---

(3) LZAC, I, pp. 425, 426.

(4) Ibid., p. 310.

only received me with all possible consideration but have been the first to express the wish to meet me."(5) As for the women, "they are everywhere crazy about me."

In Pesth he visited the Hungarian theatre, where they were giving *Fidelio*. "When I entered my box, the whole audience rose and clapped and shouted *Eljen, Eljen!* I acknowledged the applause three times, no more, no less, in the style of a king. All this is something unheard of in Hungary, or, I should say, anywhere else." He gives the most expensive entertainments to his titled admirers—on one occasion a dinner with twenty-two covers, on another a supper with forty-five; and to cut the figure of a dandy that he feels to be necessary he is "ruining himself with the tailors.". In Vienna he gives "a veritably aristocratic supper" at which the mere names and titles of his guests give him such a thrill that he spaces out the list for Marie's benefit:

> Prince PÜCKLER.
> Prince Fritz SCHWARZENBERG.
> Count APPONYI.
> Count HARTIG.
> Baron REISCHACH.
> Count SZÉCHENI.
> Count WALDSTEIN.
> Count Paul ESTERHAZY.
>   Etc., etc. . . .

"It will be a little frigid, perhaps," he says, "but in the best style."(6)

In Prague he notes that the "classical party" is not well disposed towards him; but he can cheerfully dispense with the approval of these mere musical purists, seeing that "the whole of the feminine and of the aristocratic public is everywhere for me, warmly, violently; and with these a man can go far." A little later he repeats with evident satisfaction that "the Bohemian aristocracy, the proudest in the whole monarchy, has been most charming towards me, and here, as elsewhere,

---

(5) LZAC, I, 311, 363, etc.

(6) Ibid., p. 373.

the women are all for me. . . . Yesterday I entertained at supper the Prince de Rohan (with whom I have become most intimate), Prince Lichtenstein, Count Schlick, the Counts Thun, etc. There were about a dozen of us."(7) It is the same story when he goes to London: "I am the lion of the London season."(8)

4

So vain was Liszt, so hungry was the vulgarian in him for worldly "honours," that he lent a willing ear to the suggestion that in Hungary he might be ennobled. Of course, he assures Marie, in his usual mock-humble style, the honour is not of his seeking; but his letters show how passionately his heart was set on this scheme, which, as it happened, came to nothing. Like every other parvenu who dreams ecstatically of a patent of nobility, he discovers that as a matter of fact his ancestry can be traced back to the most aristocratic sources: "the authentic documents exist in the hands of the Fiscal of Ofen. Out of curiosity I will make myself acquainted with them one of these days." He asks Marie to design a coat of arms for him.(9)

---

(7) LZAC, I, pp. 405, 406.

(8) Ibid., p. 427. I have a suspicion that Liszt's venom where Thalberg was concerned came in part from the fact that the latter, as the reputed natural son of Prince Moritz Dietrichstein and the Baroness von Wetzlar, was admitted freely into aristocratic society everywhere. (According to another story, he was the natural son of Metternich). Liszt, in a conversation in his old age with his pupil August Göllerich, denied this paternity: according to him, Thalberg's father was an Englishman. Whether that were so or not, the fact remains that Thalberg was everywhere credited with a princely origin, and that on the strength of this he was everywhere treated socially in a different way from pianists of humbler birth, just as Mendelssohn's musicianship was forgiven him because he was a rich man who had no need to take a fee when he performed in the great houses. Liszt's real grievance against Thalberg comes out unconsciously in his remark to Göllerich that "he [Thalberg] was very much patronised and polished by the aristocracy, while I was regarded as very uncouth and ill-bred" (see GFL, p. 21).

(9) Ibid., I, 331, 347. He recurs to the subject in 1843. Somebody in Berlin—apparently another of those obliging persons who, for a consideration, will undertake to prove that any of us is descended in the direct

LISZT IN 1842

From " Franz Liszt," Dr. Julius Kapp, Hesse-Verlag, Berlin

PRINCESS WITTGENSTEIN, WITH HER DAUGHTER
PRINCESS MARIE

He was in the seventh heaven of delight when a number of Hungarian aristocrats publicly presented him with a magnificent sabre of honour;(10) he sent Berlioz the newspaper accounts of the glorious proceedings, for reproduction in the *Journal des Débats;* and his vanity was offended at the flippant tone in the ironical comment of a writer in the *Gazette musicale*—presumably Berlioz—"a most flattering gift, but a rather strange one for a man of peace." The sword and the hoped-for patent of nobility, indeed, became the joke of Paris society and the French press, for in both quarters Liszt was by this time a figure of absurdity by reason of his notorious vanity and his insatiable passion for titled society: Heine, Alphonse Karr, and many another wit greeted the episode as a heaven-sent one for epigram.(11) All this was not at all to the taste of the well-bred Marie, whom we find warning Liszt once more against giving too free play in public to these notorious weaknesses of his. He must beware of making himself too ridiculous: this kind of thing may be all very well in Germany, she tells him, but Paris is another matter altogether: "there has been a good deal of merriment here over the sabre and the ennoblement; people say you are puffed-up with your successes."

He was making himself universally ridiculous in another way—by his amours, the stories of which were public property. His infidelities were a grief to Marie, who was constantly

---

line from Charlemagne or William the Conqueror—had sent him "the coat of arms of the Liszt family." This he adopted and had engraved forthwith (see his letter to Marie, LZAC, II, 273). Peter Raabe decides curtly that "there is no evidence whatever that, as Lina Ramann says, Liszt's family had at one time belonged to the Hungarian nobility" (RLL, p. 1).

(10) The sabre is now in the Franz Liszt Musical Academy in Budapest. It is described in an exhibition catalogue thus: "Hungarian court sabre. Damascus blade, curved in Turkish fashion, inlaid on each side with gold arabesques. The curved hilt is partly of black bone, partly of gilt silver set with precious stones. The scabbard is gilt, with a design of wrought and engraved leaves" (see RLL, p. 241).

(11) Liszt was so nettled by all this persiflage that he sent a long letter to the *Revue des Deux Mondes*, in which he explained that a sabre had a symbolic significance in Hungary.

H

receiving the irritating condolences of friends and acquaintances. She was not only hurt by his escapades themselves but saddened at the complacent vulgarity that made him boast of his "bonnes fortunes." But in spite of it all she seems to have retained her love for him, though now there creeps into her love the anxious note of a mother grieving for her peccant child. Again and again she implores him to give up the wine, tobacco and coffee in which he admits he is indulging to excess, and that were largely the cause of his irritability. "Your letter has arrived. My God, what a state to be in! On my knees I beg you not to hesitate any longer: give up for a few weeks coffee, tobacco and wine. Do this for my sake; even if it seems to you absurd and useless, Franz, I ask it of you more urgently than I have ever done before." And again a little later: "So you are smoking again! My God, shall I never be able to obtain from you the sacrifice of your cigars? Can it not be said that for once at least you will grant my request? You have renounced prayer, but you will not renounce cigars!"(12)

5

As usual with him, he loathed his flaming life and his weak self in the hours when the more idealistic side of him came uppermost, or even when he was merely physically tired and disgusted. In hours like these he turns in exasperation from the brilliant first subject of his symphony—his delight in titles and adulation—and flings himself into the luxuriant development of his contrasting second subject—the desire to flee from the world with Marie. Only with her and for her, he says, can he endure the burden of existence: in Milan, in September, 1838, he wanders through the crowd "with my heart big with emotion,

---

(12) LZAC, I, pp. 324, 338. His cigars must have been not only bad for him but a trial to everyone within range of them. In his Weimar days we find him ordering them at 20 to 25 thalers a thousand, and stipulating that they shall not be "too thin or too mild." Even allowing for the difference in prices between that day and this, it is doubtful whether, at less than a penny each, Liszt's cigars were really first-class. We are consequently not surprised to learn that when he was living in Weimar there was a law prohibiting smoking in the streets.

my head a blank, asking myself why I came here. Everything
hurts me, jars on me, irritates me." He wonders if he has lost
Marie, who was formerly his refuge, his consolation, "the ever-
welling stream in this arid desert." Is the magic that once lay
in her name dispelled? he asks; is it he who has "broken their
lives"? He cannot, should not, exist with anyone but her:
"without you, everything that is good, elevated, vital in me
perishes."(13) He knows, he says, that his youth has been
wasted in "puerile agitations," that he has "misused the
powers that God gave him," that too often he has been "miserably lacking," and that only she, his "noble angel," can save
him. At Padua he remembers the "divine compassion, the
celestial hope for him," that shone in her eyes.(14) This divided
soul, that is perpetually driven by an overmastering appetite
towards the pleasures of society, is also perpetually moaning
that his irritability comes from the fact that he is "never
alone." He is over-burdened and sad, he writes from Vienna
in December, 1839, because his life is "so empty, so destitute
of real, profound, intimate joys"; and in these moments he
recalls mournfully the divine days he had spent with her at
Como and Florence. His delight in his stupendous "success,"
his "good business," alternates with a loathing of himself and
his profession: "I have conceived a disgust for my piano; I wish
I could play only for you; I do not know why the crowd listens
to me and pays me."(15) He is exhausted by his way of life,
which does not allow him "a quarter of an hour of liberty."
His existence since he left her has been "a perpetual excitement
without object and without satisfaction"; the trade he has
chosen seems to him generally "either ridiculous or odious:
it is impossible for me to get any serious work done."(16) "Dear,
adored Marie, all my being is but silence and prayer before you.
You have given me everything, and I have preserved it all in
the profoundest depths of my heart. I will begin to live only

---

(13) LZAC, I, p. 238.

(14) Ibid., pp. 241, 247.

(15) Ibid., pp. 327, 344.

(16) Ibid., pp. 386, 387.

when I see you again, no matter where or how." Almost in the
same breath in which he tells her that he is the lion of the
London season he cries to her to save him from himself. He is
"profoundly bored" in London, where he remains only from
necessity; he longs to lay his head on her breast and forget his
"bitter ennui," his "fatal remorse," in the "immensity of her
love."

<h1 style="text-align:center">6</h1>

One gathers from their correspondence that after the Vienna
and Milan episodes of 1838 a crisis had arisen between them
which each, in his own way and to his own degree, vaguely
hoped to surmount.(17) On her way from Italy to Paris in
October, 1839, Marie has seen a magnificent sunset followed by
the rise of the pale moon in all its melancholy: she took it, she
tells him, as a symbol of their beautiful past and "of the future
that has begun so sadly but will become calm and pure."(18)
From Paris, in November, she tells him she is startled to learn
that he has been reading her journal, for he will find in it many
things that will astonish and pain him: "in the cruel conflict
that we allowed to develop between us I have often been wrong,
above all through my not being willing, or not knowing how, to
suffer through you: the expression of my sorrow in the journal
has often been harsh and vindictive.(19) Try not to judge all
this with your reason but to excuse it in the name of our
love, for indeed I have perhaps suffered more than I have
offended."(20) But he remains, she assures him from Paris,
her only source of life, though his conduct has been imprudent;
"you have not understood my nature, or you have attempted by
violence to mould it to your own." He has unceasingly tried
to destroy her ideal of duty in love: this ideal, which has been

---

(17) Perhaps the immediate cause of it was the "Zepponi" incident that
    figures in *Nélida*. See *infra*, pp. 134 ff.

(18) LZAC, I, pp. 263, 264.

(19) Correlate with this the passage (*infra*, p. 136) in which Guermann reads
    Nélida's journal.

(20) Ibid., pp. 290, 291.

necessary to her being, he has "treated harshly and roughly."
"You will never realise how much ill you have done me and
are still doing. But forgive me for saying this: you are my sole
resource, and I feel that it is to you that I must complain of
you."(21)

In February, 1840, she looks forward delightedly to seeing
him again: "I feel that I shall say to you what I said five years
ago—let us go into the desert and be all in all to each other."(22)
It is clear from a later letter that she looks forward to marriage
with him if circumstances should make that possible.(23) She
recognises that their natures are "diametrically opposite";
"you need distant horizons, the infinite, the illimitable, the
unforeseen, while I want order, the frame well filled, the sense
of duty accomplished, of one's steps being regulated. Each of
us has made an error of judgment—each has judged the other
by himself: what could have been simple for one has never been
so for the other, and *vice versa*." It depends upon him whether
she is to solve her problem: she has two vital desires, to find
some means by which their children shall be really hers, and
that he shall set her a task of definite work, to which she will
submit at first out of pure obedience, but that will soon become
a pleasure, even a passion.(24) Apparently she was longing to
give a solid centre and an assured direction to her broken life;
as she says, by her own act she had lost her husband, the child
of her marriage, and her family, while hard necessity had now
separated her from Liszt and her children by him. She is
devoured by "the need for passion, the need for solitude, the
need for you, for you alone . . . you, nothing but you, you for
ever." In response to cries of despair and hope like this she
had to read the complacent declarations in his letters that
wherever he went the "aristocracy" was "most charming"
towards him, and the women "all for him."

---

(21) LZAC, I, pp. 365, 366.

(22) Ibid., p. 393.

(23) Ibid., p. 396.

(24) Ibid., p. 399.

7

It is manifest that the pair had arrived at the stage that
is the most mournful of all in the lives of lovers, when they can
maintain a tone of aspiration, of idealism, or merely of mutual
toleration only so long as they are corresponding with each
other but are not together in the flesh. Marie and Liszt met
again in Paris in April, 1840. Reading once more between the
lines, we surmise that the old misunderstandings soon raised
their heads again, particularly over the subject of Liszt's
"bonnes fortunes," for in a letter of 17th May (by which time
Liszt was in London) we find Marie once more protesting
against being the subject of the insulting condolences of her
friends, this time, seemingly, in connection with an actress.
"I can well understand *your* not being scandalised by any
scandal," she tells him, "seeing that you are the object of it; we
never condemn what flatters us."(25) Yet she welcomes with
joy his suggestion that she shall join him in London, where, he
says, he will take a house in the country for her from 7th June
to 7th July, after which they will go to Baden together for the
remainder of the summer. "Why fear our differences of
opinion? Why be always fearing and never hoping?" he writes
to her. "My heart is filled with joy at the thought of seeing you
again." He installed her at Richmond, for of course it would
have been difficult for both of them, in the eyes of English
society, had they occupied the same quarters in London.

One day in June the storm burst. What led up to it we do
not precisely know, though there are indications that, as on
so many occasions in the past, Marie wanted merely to be alone
with Liszt when he was not performing, while he was bent on
indulging his insatiable appetite for rich society. Forced to
respond politely to the suggestion of one of his English friends
that he should call on her, she begs Liszt exasperatedly to
plead at the last moment that she is too unwell to receive, or,
alternatively, to bring a number of other people with him—
"better five or six nuisances than one. Do not take a box for
me on Monday, for I shall not be in London. Just now, and

_____

(25) LZAC, I, p. 435.

perhaps for ever, I am capable of only one thing—being
absolutely alone." That these words rankled in Liszt is shown
by his quoting them in his bitter reply to her letter. "This is
what you have to say to me! This is the end you have reached
after six years of the most absolute devotion!" If he was
implying that the "most absolute devotion" had been on his
part, the inveterate actor must have been deluding himself
strangely: while if he recognised that the devotion had been
on Marie's part, it is not very clear why he should have found
such cause for resentment in her unwillingness to be dragged at
his heels into a company in which she would be sorely conscious
of her equivocal position as Liszt's "mistress." There had
previously been a painful scene between them during a drive
from Ascot to Richmond, probably due to the same cause—
her desire for solitude with Liszt. The rift between them
opened out more widely than it had ever done before. Liszt,
in his letter to her at Richmond, rides off into some high-flown
verbiage about the real nature of love, especially in a being
"whose soul has need of the absolute and the infinite," which
no doubt made Marie ask herself ruefully what connection there
was between a need of the absolute and the infinite and the kind
of life Liszt had been living for the last two years and was now
bent on living, against her wish, in London.

8

The recently published (26) second volume of their correspondence enables us to reconstruct, rather better than was
formerly possible, the events and the moods that led up to the
final rupture between the pair in the summer of 1844. The
correspondence is not ideally complete: a few of Liszt's letters
appear to be missing altogether; comparatively few of Marie's
are given; while in several letters there are words that are now
illegible, and gaps that suggest excisions. Who is answerable
for these last we are not told: some may have been the work
of Marie herself, or of her friend Louis de Ronchaud, into
whose custody the letters seem to have passed after her death.

---

(26) In July, 1934.

Ronchaud, in his capacity of "Conservateur des Musées," lived in the Louvre. André de Hevesy tells us that at the news of Ronchaud's death "one of his female relations hastened to his room, impelled partly by curiosity to know his last dispositions, partly by the desire to destroy anything that might shock her austere virtue. She had already begun to deal drastically with the papers in the room when a young attaché of the Louvre, Georges Lafenestre, happened to enter. He offered his arm to the pious lady, now engaged on her work of destruction, and had seals placed on the doors of the room. Thanks to his intervention, what remained of the Liszt-d'Agoult papers could be handed over to M. Daniel Ollivier."(27) The losses, however, cannot have been very serious; and the story told in what remains is clear enough.

In spite of all the differences between the pair, their love for each other was evidently great: one feels justified in saying, indeed, that Marie was the only woman for whom Liszt ever felt a really profound love. He had liaisons by the score, but these were merely fugitive matters of the flesh. He loved, for a time and in a way, the Princess; but his feeling for her was nourished by her blind devotion to him and her lavish flattery of him, and even she ended by slightly boring him. In the case of Marie, however, he was more or less tied, during the most egoistic years of his youth, to a critical woman who, though she loved him sincerely, made no secret of her dissatisfaction with many elements in his nature and many points in his conduct: yet the wounds she was perpetually dealing his self-esteem seem to have been incapable of destroying the fascination she had for him or undermining the respect he had for her character. His comments on her in his later life are, as we can now see, completely untrustworthy: his contemporary letters reveal the true state of his mind towards her during the often difficult years of their union. Marie knew well what it was that was dividing them—the flaw in Liszt's soul that made him run after the glittering prizes of the world at the same time that he longed for seclusion from it, and the chances presented by his wandering life, and by the adulation brought him by his

(27) RML, May, 1928, pp. 33, 34.

pianism, for the infidelities that were a necessity of his strongly
erotic nature. Again and again she asks him why they cannot
retire into comparative solitude together. He, for his part,
cries out incessantly that she is the one object in life that is
dear to him, that she is "the most delicate, the most charming,
the most adorable thing in the world," that he "will end by
living exclusively for her and for music," that a life for them,
apart from each other, is finally inconceivable.

But the nature of Liszt and the material exigencies of his
career made such a solution of their difficulties impossible.
He has to make money by his playing, not for her sake—for her
own fortune seems to have been sufficient for her needs—but
for his own future and in order to provide for his children. To
make money he has to be away from her for the major part of
each year. His nerves are perpetually on the strain: if, as frequently happened at first in 1840 and 1841, the audiences
are small, he is furious with the public; if he turns a town
upside down with enthusiasm for him, the inevitable corollaries
are late hours, fast living, lavish expenditure, amorous complica-
tions, the perpetual robbery of his strength and his time by the
world—then the resort to wine, coffee, and tobacco, that
alternately exalt and depress him, and leave him finally in a
state of irritable self-dissatisfaction that makes Marie's just
reproaches doubly hard to bear. When he knows that he cannot
answer them soberly he resorts to a dry irony that distresses her
still more. In October, 1840, he tells her that he is "exhausted
with rage and suppressed ambition": "I want to throw myself
into your arms and find repose on your noble breast." Has he
been unjust and violent, as she complains? he asks in one of his
letters. "Have I shown myself lacking in feeling? Perhaps I
have. When I think it over I arrive at a sort of parity between
our two natures. Do not be offended: it is wholly to your
advantage." Time after time he apologises for the "acidity"
or the violence of his letters: his excuse is that he is "profoundly
miserable and must hit out at something." She exasperates him
by her accounts of the men of intellect who are paying court
to her in Paris—Emile Girardin, Sainte-Beuve, Victor Hugo:
this seems to have been her subtle way of riposting to the

stories that reach her ears of his amorous escapades. He is furiously jealous, while unable, for sheer justice's sake, to object to her forming her Paris salon as she likes: "I have always been susceptible," he confesses, "to physical temptations, you to those of the heart and the intellect." When she upbraids him for his riotous way of living, he tells her that she "does not understand and will not excuse the sad exigencies of his life." She has an incomparable art of putting him in the wrong, for her mind is subtler than his, she is a better stylist, and her well-bred self-command enables her to sting without bruising, whereas he resorts to violence or to cumbrous irony. He has no conception of delicacy, she tells him: "you are as sublime and as hard as Alpine granite." He admits his roughness, and surmises that she is inclined to over-value men like Girardin because they have the delicacy which, he acknowledges, he lacks.

Misunderstandings were inevitable in this case of two people who really loved each other but were now separated from each other for practically all but a few weeks in the summer of each year. The correspondence makes it clear that the final breach between them was not, as the Princess tells us through Lina Ramann, because the egoistic Marie was unfitted to be the soul-mate of a genius whose one desire was to reach out to the ideal, but simply and solely because her disgust at his complacent amours was rising steadily during all these years, till at last the flood of it swept her away. From one town after another, letters reached her telling of his association with this woman or that—the Princess Belgiojoso, the actress Charlotte Hagn, the singer Caroline Unger, Madame Samoyloff, the pianist Camille Pleyel, the flaming Lola Montez,(28) and others. Even while living in Paris (though not under the same roof as Marie) in the spring of 1844, that was to mark the end of their association, he

---

(28) Lola pursued him to Bonn in 1845, on the occasion of the unveiling of the Beethoven monument. Recognised by the Berlin singer Mantius, she alleged that she was there at the invitation of Liszt, who, however, did his best to avoid his old flame, at any rate in public. She was refused admission to the leading hotel. She forced herself somehow or other into the banquet—the only woman there—and at one stage of the

4454

was fascinated by the demi-mondaine Marie Duplessis (the famous *dame aux camélias*), who begged him to take her away with him. Marie told him bitterly, in 1843, that she "had no objection to being his mistress, but would not be one of his mistresses." He does not deny his peccadilloes; he cannot do that, indeed, for both Marie and the world are too well informed with regard to them. All he can say in reply to her is, "The distinction is charming, and very just. But allow me to inform you that the alternative has never existed for you. My faults, my wrongdoings and my follies are my own, whatever superficial resemblance they may bear to those of others; and you also are mine, and very much mine. Why talk about the other things?"(29) All of which was hardly calculated to make Marie think any more highly of him.

In his better moments he acknowledged frankly that the real cause of their growing estrangement was his adventures with women in one European town after another; his sole excuse was virtually that fate had decreed that he was to traverse Europe as a piano *saltimbanque*, that women flinging themselves at his head were an inevitable consequence of his success, and that, being the fleshly creature he was, he could not resist them if he would, and would not if he could. He recognised ruefully, in 1843, that the real mischief had been done when they separated in Florence in 1839. "That was my crime and is my profound sorrow; but do not let us re-open that wound!" He regrets that "the acclamations of the crowd, the intoxications and excesses of my life, and the banal and lying embraces of my mistresses," which, "in Vienna, in Hungary, in Trieste, everywhere, indeed, have re-sounded the pitiless funeral bell of that fatal hour" [*i.e.* Florence], have given her abundant cause for

---

proceedings jumped on the table (see SLE, p. 200ff.). (Schorn was in Bonn during the festivities.)

The biographers have waxed indignant over the slight hostility to Liszt that was manifest in some quarters during the Bonn celebrations—to Liszt, who had been partly answerable for the erection of the monument. One wonders today, however, whether his association with Lola Montez may have been at any rate part of the reason for this hostility.

(29) LZAC, II, 271.

dissatisfaction with him; his only plea is that he is not the master of his own destiny.(30) She read him through and through, and never spared him her remorseless analysis of his character. She saw in him, she tells him, a striking resemblance to Bettina von Arnim—"this persistent moral drunkenness, that produces only a *Katzenjammer* of the soul, that is to say, a disgust for all natural affection."(31) She wishes him success with his Weimar schemes: "I have always had the most absolute confidence in your musical genius, even when you doubted yourself. For the rest, I confine myself to one last prayer—try to spare me public vulgarities."(32) This, indeed, seems to have been the true source of all the differences between them—her mounting resentment, year after year, at the public linking of her name with that of a notorious erotic vulgarian.

At last, a couple of months after the writing of the letter last quoted, her patience came to an end. She dismissed him finally in a dignified letter dated "April, 1844."(33) His reply is

---

(30) LZAC, II, 269.

(31) Ibid., 327. Olga Janina, in the later years, had something pungent to say on the *Katzenjammer* of Liszt's soul (see *infra*, p. 260).

(32) Ibid., 328.

(33) An extra ray or two of light has recently been thrown on these last days by the publication of some letters from Marie to Georg and Emma Herwegh.

Liszt, who was in Germany, was evidently in no hurry to keep his promise to join Marie in Paris. She confidently expected him, at last, to dinner on 24th March. She invited the Herweghs, but asked them not to bring a lady friend of theirs with them—a Mme. Miethe-O'Connell—"as Liszt can be insupportable when he does not like a woman." He did not arrive, however, until the end of March or beginning of April: it was probably on 10th April that Marie broke with him. On 17th May Georg Herwegh addressed to Marie the letter quoted *infra*, p. 292.

In reply, Marie writes, "What you say about Liszt does not surprise me: it confirms me in the feeling of the necessity of a separation that shall be absolute and eternal. It would really be too absurd to cherish the shadow of a hope; what have I to do with a 'charming good-for-nothing,' a Don Juan parvenu, half mountebank, half juggler, who makes ideas and sentiments disappear up his sleeve, and looks complacently at the bewildered public that applauds him? Ten years of illusion! Is not that

significant, in the light of the slanders which he and the Princess were later to pour upon her memory. From first to last there is not a complaint on his side against her, not the slightest suggestion of that "insincerity," that passion for "falsehood," which he and the Princess would have posterity believe was the basis of her being and the root-cause of their differences. All this was the malicious invention of after-years. In 1844 he takes his beating like a dog, unable to deny that the punishment is just, even though he may feel that the chastising hand is a little hard. He tells his friends frankly that she has parted from him because she "disapproves of, and condemns, his orgiastic life." A year later he attempts a *plaidoyer*. There was no real necessity, he contends, for her to have dismissed him. He cannot "condemn his past." "That past, Madame," he writes, "was filled every day with a serious and passionate devotion to you; the escapades and the faults that may be found in it never lasted and were not in any way serious. The hand you promise to reach out to me some day, when all is forgotten, I shall be very happy to grasp and to hold tightly for ever; but I cannot, and never will be able to, persuade myself that it ought to have been withdrawn from me for a single instant."(34) This is his sole charge against her at this time—the egoistic one that, much as she had endured from him, she ought to have endured still more.

That it was primarily his infidelities, and the ugly noise they made in the world, not any failure of idealism on her part, that caused the final rupture between them, is shown not only by these letters but by one of February, 1846, in which Liszt rather naïvely contends that a man as busy as he had been during all those years simply could not have led "this alleged life of debauches and immorality that makes it necessary for every honest woman to fly from me and repudiate me." He recalls

---

the very sublime of extravagance? And is there anywhere in the world a mind and a heart that can understand and absolve me? You, perhaps! Adieu: my heart is bursting with bitterness; the spirit of revolt takes possession of me. Since I have not been able to live for *some one*, perhaps it will be given me to die for *something*" (see HPD, pp. 61-75).

(34) LZAC, II, 344.

resentfully a passage in one of her former letters—"I am not taken in by any of your lies," she had told him—and in all simplicity asks whether he *has* been guilty of lying, seeing that he has confessed all his infidelities to her and admitted his plentiful weaknesses of character. Marie's reply to that would probably have been that he had invariably confessed after he had been found out, but not before. It is evident that at this time, and for long afterwards, he never really doubted that he deserved the contemptuous blow she had dealt him in the face of the world. "A strange correspondence, this of ours!" he writes to her in January, 1846. "But since henceforth we can have nothing for each other but words, why not say them? They will not close our wounds, it is true; but neither will they re-open them. To what are we condemned? Do we know? We were noble natures, both of us; you have cursed me, and I am banished from your heart because you have misunderstood mine."(35) Once more we may note that there is not a line in the whole correspondence to justify the chapter on Marie written, or inspired, by the Princess for the Lina Ramann biography. That chapter is pure mendacity; and that Liszt should have acquiesced in it, even tacitly, is an indelible stain on his character.

9

History, however, must do him the justice to try to understand him during those terrible years. Imperfect as the records are, we can still see fairly clearly what was at the back of his mind when he argued that, although Marie's case against him was unanswerable as it appeared to her, it was not the whole case as he himself saw it.

When at last they met again, after many years, one of the points he tried to make against her was that, in spite of all his moral divagations, his life had had the inner unity and the continuity of purpose he had planned for it. In the broad sense that was true. The letters contained in the second volume of his correspondence with Marie enable us, for the first time, to

---

(35) LZAC, II, 345.

form a fairly definite image of what he really was in the years between 1840 and 1844. He was primarily and frankly a pushing young careerist and social climber. He had as yet no inkling whatever of the *rôle* he was destined to play in the musical world of the second half of the nineteenth century, or, indeed, of what that world was to be. Nothing of this became in the least clear to him until about 1848, when the genius of Wagner made it manifest that a new epoch had dawned in music, and Liszt was encouraged to develop certain tendencies of his own that had been more or less latent in him. His main desire in life—and a perfectly comprehensible desire—in the years from about 1839 to 1847, was, firstly, to make money enough to allow him to cease careering all over Europe as a piano hussar, and, secondly, to obtain a post at some German Court theatre or other at which he could produce his own *operas*, for it was in opera that he imagined, at this time, his talent would find its full expression. Apparently he never possessed the fabulous riches we have been wont to credit him with, so that a regular salary was a consideration not to be despised. It is true that the position he accepted at Weimar was virtually honorary; but it is evident now that his main motive in accepting that post was to have the opportunity of acquiring, in comparative seclusion, the experience he needed as orchestrator and conductor. In Weimar he was treated by the Grand Ducal family, and especially by the Hereditary Prince Carl Alexander, with a courtesy and a deference that flattered him; it is with manifest delight that he informs Marie of the occasions when he has been invited to dinner at the Court. In 1844 we find him waxing enthusiastic over Carl Alexander's plans for making Weimar once more the centre of German culture that it had been in the days of Goethe and Schiller. *Aedificanda Vimaria*, he tells Marie, is the order of the day. But his sketch of the new programme for Weimar is curious and significant. The plan was—"to renew in lofty style the traditions of Carl August"; "to allow the various talents [*i.e.* musical, dramatic, literary, pictorial, etc.] to function freely, each in its own sphere"; to take as the Alpha and Omega of their endeavour the triple result of "a Court as charming, as brilliant, as attractive as possible; a theatre and a literature that neither rots in the top of the granary nor drowns in the cellar; and finally a University (Jena). Court, Theatre, University—that is the grand trilogy for a state like Weimar, which can never be of any importance as regards its commerce, its industry, its army, or its navy!"(36)

There is not a word, it will be observed, of Weimar becoming a German musical centre, or of any impending new developments in opera. Liszt must have shared the general opinion, at that time, that a town so tiny as Weimar could neither afford the financial expenditure nor supply the audience necessary to make it of any more account in music than twenty other similar pillbox German capitals were: it was only later, when the name of Weimar suddenly went ringing through Germany as the result of Liszt's audacious productions of *Tannhäuser* and *Lohengrin*, that this new ambition took root in him.

That he at first regarded Weimar only as a stepping-stone to higher things—in the most practical sense of the latter term—is shown by his anxiety, in 1846, to obtain the reversion of Donizetti's post at Vienna.(37) This was one of the two or three most desirable appointments in the German-speaking countries. Liszt's letter of May, 1847, to Marie—he had practically decided at that time to abandon the profession of pianist—shows that the object of his concert tours had been to secure him a permanent income of about 25,000 francs a year. It was a competency, and rather more, in those days; but it was not a dazzling fortune. It is therefore easily understandable that, as he tells Marie in his letter of 14th April, 1846, "an appointment of 10,000 francs [Donizetti's salary at Vienna] for six months' service—or non-service—is not to be disdained; and the Vienna position is undeniably one of the best imaginable."(38)

---

(36) LZAC, II, 323.

(37) In 1845 Donizetti, who had been Court Composer and Court Kapell-meister at Vienna since 1842, began to develop melancholia and to show signs of the paralysis that was soon to overtake him. He died in April, 1847.

(38) LZAC, II, 355.

The post, however, will have to be *offered* to him, he says; he will not apply for it.(39)

This was in keeping with all his conduct of his outer life during these years. His character had hardened, for the time being, under the stress of circumstances. He seems to have forgotten his religion: that was to be revived in him by the Princess during the Weimar years, and, later, by his need of a refuge from the disappointments and disillusionments of his life. His success as a pianist had given him a lively sense of his strength; and he was determined to use that success as a means not only to win a high position for himself in a larger musical world than that of the piano, but also to gratify one of the fundamental passions of his being—the desire to be received in aristocratic circles as a social equal. There is not much of the gentle, kindly, resigned Liszt of the later legend in the hard-driving Liszt of these years of virtuosity: what we see is an aggressive *arriviste*, bent on making his way at any cost and by any means. The natural fury of his disposition comes out agreeably now and then. He is prepared to fight a duel with any of the people who are making Marie's position difficult for her in Paris. He is very angry with a certain Koettlitz, who seems to have wormed himself into the confidence of Liszt's mother and to be exercising a bad influence upon her.

> "Koettlitz is an abominable scoundrel," he writes to Marie. "Go to the Hôtel des Princes and find Beker, who was my *valet de place* when I lived in the Hôtel d'Antin. Promise him 100 francs, and tell him to give Koettlitz a good thrashing of the surest, simplest and most positive kind. Tell my mother that if she does not wish to expose herself to insults from me she must send Koettlitz away at once, and that, even if he should be dying of hunger at the gate of the Rue Pigalle, I forbid her to give him a morsel of bread."(40)

10

Sure now of his position as the greatest pianist of the day, he would occasionally treat his audiences with the utmost

---

(39) On this point see further LZAC, II, 373, 376.
(40) Ibid., 378.

insolence and arrogance. Saint-Saëns tells us how Liszt deliberately arrived late for a concert in Paris, and then ostentatiously went the round of the boxes, chatting and laughing with the fashionable ladies of his acquaintance, until the audience began to show its resentment: he knew that he had only to place his hands on the piano for him to have the whole house at his feet.(41) Schumann has given us some amusing accounts of how Liszt passed through Leipzig like a flaming meteor, growing petulant because, in commercial Leipzig, there were not enough countesses in the audience, turning the sober bourgeois town upside down with his expensive parties, exasperating his friends by arriving a couple of hours late because he had had an invitation from an aristocrat, alternately infuriating everyone with his arrogances and fatuities and winning them over by the irresistible charm he could exercise whenever he chose. From 1843 onwards he had the ball at his feet, and he took care that it was kept rolling. He delighted in his manifest superiority to his competitors. More than once we find him refusing to make the first call on some local magnate or other, partly out of the just pride of the artist in the honourable position he had won for himself, partly in pursuance of his carefully laid and consistently followed plan for getting *réclame*—for high-handed conduct of this kind was something unheard-of in the Germany of that epoch, in which musicians and artists generally were used to being condescended to by notabilities, and were duly grateful for it. He posted off to Paris the glowing press notices of his concerts, asking Marie to try to have them reproduced in the Paris papers. He wanted Marie to write his biography, on the basis partly of information supplied by himself, partly of his flattering press criticisms: the book, however, was to be issued as the work of his secretary Belloni.

One suspects also a little calculation, as well as a sincere desire to do good, in some of his benefactions. A trifle too much, perhaps, has been made of these by his biographers. He was not alone in them: it was the custom of the day for a travelling artist to give an extra concert for some local charitable purpose

---

(41) SSPS, p. 16.

or other; and if Liszt's generosity in this respect made the noise
it did in the world, it was because, his popularity with the
public being so great, the sums he earned in this way for
charity were so much larger than those of other performers.
There is no denying, of course, that he was by nature generous,
and that his numerous benefactions were motived, in large
part, by sheer goodness of heart. But it is impossible not to
feel that there was also a certain element of calculation in
some of them. He knew the effect they made, and was well
aware of how that effect contributed to the end he had in view
and of which he never lost sight—the glory of his name and the
acquisition of a fortune sufficient to enable him some day to
give up the pianistic jugglery that he at once loved and hated.
At Halle, in 1842, an action against him was begun by an
obscure local music teacher for a small matter of four louis d'or
for alleged services in preparing the way for his concert in that
town. Liszt fought and won the case—and then ostentatiously
sent eight louis to the man's wife, who was in childbed. The
result might have been foreseen: "that same evening," he tells
Marie in his complacent account of the affair, "more than three
hundred students gave me a serenade, singing my *Rheinweinlied*,(42) after which they went and made a superb charivari
before the house of the plaintiff's lawyer, which amused me
very much."(43) If any musician ever knew the commercial
advantages of advertisement, it was the Liszt of these years.
Asking Marie to send him details of the success of her *Essai sur
la liberté*, he assures her that he does not share her "superb
indifference in the matter of getting publicity."(44) He had
previously advised her, on her entry into authorship, to exploit
her title of Countess to the full for publicity purposes. "This
seems to me the proper game for you to play. Mine is at the
same time simpler and more complicated. Being nobody,
it is necessary for me to be somebody. This somebody will

---

(42) A setting for male voices of a poem by Georg Herwegh, *Wo solch ein
Feuer*.

(43) LZAC, II, 246.

(44) Ibid., 374.

afterwards do something, and will burst if he does little. Tocqueville's attitude is not a European one; by that route one attains only to a provincial celebrity."(45)

He let no opportunity go by of making a gesture that would at once gratify his own pride and impress the public—for he took good care that the gesture should be made where the whole town would see it. In 1842 he gave, in conjunction with the singer Rubini, a concert at The Hague, at which the King and the Court were present. At the end of it the royal Chamberlain handed the two artists a snuffbox each. Liszt made the annoying discovery that his own was of less intrinsic value than Rubini's: "it does not suit me," he wrote to Marie, "not to be put on the same level as he, at any rate in these matters." He accordingly gave his own snuffbox to Belloni: "this," he complacently remarks, "will no doubt be the talk of the town."(46)

In 1848 a new direction was given to his life by the Princess von Sayn-Wittgenstein. Between 1840 and that year, though he had turned out a large quantity of piano arrangements and fantasias, he had done little in the way of original work, apart from a number of songs, a few piano pieces, and two or three essays in religious music (about 1846). In the years immediately following 1848, however, he worked vigorously at composition on the large scale, either for the piano alone, for the orchestra, or for the two in combination. The germs of many of these works must have been planted in him during the years of his wanderings; and it is clear enough that all through those years he was keeping steadily in view his plan for bidding farewell to the piano and writing himself upon musical history in bolder letters than hitherto. We can understand, then, that his life, as he saw it, was really a consistency and a unity in spite of its apparent outward waste. Seeing himself, as no one else, of course, could see him, from the inside, his follies and vulgarities were to him only the froth on a deep and onward-pressing wave. Marie, caught in the froth and soiled by it, could be forgiven for being less aware of what lay beneath it. Matters

---

(45) LZAC, II, 269.

(46) Ibid., 240.

might have been different between them had he made his
fortune a few years earlier and retired from the world with her
to devote himself to the realisation of his plan for composition
on the great scale. The unfortunate thing was that what he
called the exigencies of his sad life separated him from her
for the greater part of each year; and at a distance she could see,
like everyone else, only the worst of him. How bad this worst
was he himself could not deny; his plea in his own justification
was that in the long run it would be outweighed by the best.
This best, however, was visible during those years to no one
but himself. The Princess was more fortunate than Marie:
she obtained possession of him at a time when, having made all
the money he wanted—and being further fortified by hers—
he could at last carry out his plan for severing himself from the
concert world, when he had become a little weary, temporarily,
of promiscuity in matters of the flesh, when he was in the first
flush of his enthusiasm over new ambitions to be realised, and
when, by reaction from his past life, he was once more cultivating the religiosity that happened to be the very breath of her
own being.

CHAPTER V

BÉATRIX AND *NÉLIDA*

I

All the biographies of Liszt make at any rate passing mention of two novels of the period that have been held—in the one case, I think, with only partial reason, in the other case with considerable reason—to contain portraits of him and the Countess d'Agoult. Balzac's *Béatrix* is dated by its author, at the end of the book, "1838-44"; *Nélida*, published by the Countess under her pseudonym, "Daniel Stern", first appeared serially in the Paris *Revue indépendante* in 1846. It was issued in Brussels, in two volumes, in the same year; and it is to the latter edition that reference is made in the following pages. The novel appears to have had a considerable success: it was even translated into Spanish at the end of 1847.(1)

Janka Wohl, the Hungarian pianist who has left us her reminiscences of Liszt during the last few years of his life, seems to be mainly responsible for a story that has got into circulation of the Countess being angered at Balzac's portrait of her in *Béatrix*. According to Janka Wohl, Liszt himself told.her how Marie urged him to call Balzac out, but was laughed at by the pianist for her pains.

"They once tried to make us quarrel," Liszt is alleged to have said to Janka, "but I wasn't going to allow that. You must have read his novel *Beatrice, or Compulsory Love*.(2) I maintain that I do not figure in it in any way; but Madame d'Agoult was not of my opinion. Shortly after the appearance of the said

---

(1) HPD, p. 145.

(2) The sub-title appears in no edition of the novel known to me.

novel, up gets Madame d'Agoult and goes for me in a flood of weeping.

" 'You can flatter yourself that you have nice friends,' she said to me. 'Here's Balzac writing a novel about me. He traduces me, and makes me ridiculous in the eyes of the world. It's a shame, an infamous shame; you must go and demand satisfaction. Your honour is at stake as much as mine.'

"I was stunned at this sudden outburst. She cried with rage, she stamped her foot, and was altogether beside herself. But I—I didn't see the least necessity to go and fight with Balzac about a novel, and make myself responsible for Madame d'Agoult's conduct. What was the use of picking a quarrel with the author for an imaginary thing which in no way concerned me? . . . 'Is your name in it?' I asked the weeping woman. 'Did you find your address in it, or the number of your house?' 'No!' 'Well then, what are you crying about? What right have you to feel yourself attacked? Let him whom the cap fits wear it.' . . ."

The story continues that he introduced Balzac to Marie, and her anger faded at contact with "our delightful guest. She forgave him for taking his subjects where he found them."

"I seldom read novels," Liszt, according to Janka Wohl, continued, "but I made a point of secretly glancing over the pages of the much-abused work. I could not but admire the intuitive genius of Balzac. Madame de Rochefide is a portrait drawn by a master-hand; it is so accurate a photograph that I, who thought that I thoroughly knew this woman, with her way of courting notoriety as much as other women shun it, was´ amazed, and actually understood her better after reading the book."(3)

One is at first tempted to believe that Janka Wohl has been indulging her feminine fancy rather more than is justifiable in a biographer. On further investigation, however, it appears that there is a basis of fact to her story, though Liszt seems to have confused *Béatrix* with another novel. What is quite clear is that he *did* talk to Janka Wohl on the subject, and therefore that he was given, in his old age, to depreciating Marie very much in the way that the Princess has familiarised us with in the

---

(3) WFLR, p. 67 ff.

Ramann biography. There is no evidence, so far as I know, that anything corresponding to his story happened in the case of *Béatrix;* but his own letters to Marie show that something corresponding to it happened in the case of a novel of George Sand's, *Horace,* that was published in book form in 1842. The Madame de Chailly of this was taken by both Liszt and Marie to be intended as a malicious portrait of the latter. "There is no doubt," Liszt writes to her in December, 1841,(4) "that it is your portrait that Madame Sand pretends to have painted in describing the 'artificial mind,' the 'artificial beauty,' the 'artificial nobility' of Madame de Chailly."(5) Not only Marie but her friends had evidently been outraged by this piece of public malice on the part of her one-time friend and admirer, for a few days later we find Liszt writing to her thus: "If you have any regard for what I can say to you in a matter of this kind, I beg you not to take any notice of the insults launched at the Vicomtesse de Chailly. Please do not give Mme Sand the satisfaction of being offended by them. Ronchaud's idea(6) is absurdly amical. M. de Girardin is much more sensible; yet I do not want any vengeance. No, Marie . . . you must not seek revenge for these little perfidies. No, no; you are too noble, too great—sometimes despite yourself."

One gathers that from the George Sand quarter there had come a series of journalistic attacks on Marie, for in April, 1842, Liszt, now thoroughly angry about it all, tells her that if anyone is to fight a duel on her behalf it must be himself. This he is quite ready to do; and later still he once more exhorts her to be calm, assuring her that when he is in Paris in June he will deal with the matter himself and "settle accounts" with George.(7) Evidently, then, there *had* been talk of a duel at some time or another in his past; and as Janka Wohl would hardly be likely

---

(4) Apparently the novel had been appearing in the *Revue Indépendante* of that year.

(5) We need not take the Madame de Chailly of *Horace* too seriously today: it affords merely another illustration of the cattishness of one woman to another after the former friends have quarrelled.

(6) Probably to make a public reply or take public action on Marie's behalf.

(7) LZAC, II, 186, 190, 192, 209, 215.

to know of this, we may take it as certain that Liszt talked to her as she alleges him to have done. Though he confused, after some forty years, *l'affaire Béatrix* with *l'affaire Horace*, and rather misrepresented his own part in the business, it remains clear that in his old age he was delighted to disparage Marie by associating her with the Madame de Rochefide of Balzac's novel.

2

If he had really managed to persuade himself that Balzac's alleged portrait of Marie was "an imaginary thing which in no way concerned him," he must have been singularly blind to the fact that he himself, as all Paris knew at the time, figures unmistakably in the novel, and that Balzac's portrait of him is far from flattering. However true or false to the supposed original the portrait of Madame de Rochefide may be, there can be no question, in the light of all we now know about the Liszt of the early years, that Gennaro Conti is a pitilessly candid study of him as he appeared to detached observers in Paris about the end of the eighteen-thirties.

The Marquise de Rochefide has left her husband for this Conti, whom Balzac describes as both composer and singer, his claims to consideration, however, resting more on his abilities in the latter than in the former capacity, just as Liszt, at that time, commanded considerably more esteem as virtuoso than as composer. Balzac makes Conti out to be "of Neapolitan origin, but born at Marseilles"—just as Liszt was presumably of German origin but born in Hungary.

> "Conti has plenty of intelligence, and he has some talent as a composer, though he may never reach the first rank.(8) Were it not for Meyerbeer and Rossini he might have passed for a man of genius. He has one advantage over these two—in vocal music he is the equivalent of Paganini on the violin, of Liszt on the piano, of Taglioni in the dance. . . . It is not a voice, my friend, but a soul. When his singing answers to certain ideas, certain states of mind which it is difficult to describe,

_____

(8) The following description of him, it should be said, is put into the mouth of Camille Maupin, another character in the novel, who is studied, in part, from George Sand.

but in which a woman sometimes finds herself, she is lost if
she hears Gennaro. The Marquise conceived a violent passion
for him and took him away from me.(9)

---

(9)   There is good reason to believe, as we have seen, that Liszt was fluttering
round George Sand just before Marie came on the scene.
   In 1838 and 1839, the period in which Balzac was engaged on the first
part of *Béatrix*, George Sand and Marie were already estranged (see the
letters of Marie, published in BRR, pp. 156, 163, 165). One might
reasonably have surmised, therefore, that it was the resentful George
who had primed Balzac with the data on which he based his study of
Conti and of the Madame de Rochefide of the earlier chapters of the
story. This surmise now receives confirmation from a letter from
Marie to Liszt, lately published for the first time. Writing from Paris
on 21st January, 1840, she says: "A week ago Potocki [a friend of hers
and Liszt's] met Balzac at the Opéra. 'Well,' said Balzac, 'I have got
the two women at loggerheads.' [*J'ai brouillé les deux femelles*]. (I have
not mentioned to you previously that Balzac has a new novel on the
stocks, written after he had been *tête-à-tête* with George at Nohant).
'Not really,' replied Potocki, 'for I saw Madame Sand yesterday, at
Madame d'Agoult's.' So this is yet another reason why one should not
quarrel—the amusement it gives to certain people" (LZAC, I, 361).
In February and March, 1838, Balzac was the guest of George Sand at
Nohant: there the pair of realists exchanged confidences, each secretly
studying the other. Balzac has left us an account of their talks in a letter
of 2nd March, 1838, to Madame Hanska, in which occurs this passage:
"It was *à propos* of Liszt and Madame d'Agoult that she gave me the
subject of *Les Galériens*, or *Les amours forcés*, which I am going to treat,
for in her position she cannot do so herself. Keep this secret." This of
itself places it beyond doubt that the material for his study of Madame
de Rochefide and of the relations of Madame d'Agoult and Liszt was
supplied to him at this time by George Sand. Balzac had already known
Liszt for some years. Apparently he did not know the Countess personally at this time.
   The first two parts of the novel appeared in *Le Siècle* in April and May,
1839; they were then published in book form at the end of 1839 (though
the title-page bears the date 1840), and again in 1842. The third part
(*Un adultère retrospectif*) appeared in *Le Messager* between 24th December, 1844, and 23rd January, 1845, under the title of *Les petits manéges
d'une femme vertueuse*, to be issued later as *La lune de miel*. It is clear,
then, that the final section of *Béatrix* as we now have it was an after-
thought on Balzac's part, and that in the interval between 1838-39 and
1844 he had completely lost touch with the Madame Rochefide of parts
1 and 2.
   The Claude Vignon of the novel is said to be a portrait of Gustave Planché.

The stroke is excessively provincial, but in accordance with
the rules of war. She won my esteem and friendship by the way
she behaved towards me. She regarded me as a woman likely
to defend my property; she did not know that, for me, the most
ridiculous thing in the world in a situation of this kind is the
object of the combat. She came to see me. This proud woman
was so captivated that she confided her secret to me and made me
the arbiter of her destiny. She was adorable; she remained both
woman and Marquise in my eyes. Women are sometimes bad,
my friend; but they have secret grandeurs that men will never
appreciate."

Camille would have been faithful to Conti in spite of the fact
that she knew him for what he was.

"It is a nature charming on the surface," she continues, "but
detestable at the core. In matters of the heart he is a charlatan.
There are men . . . who are charlatans on the surface and in
quite good faith. They lie to themselves . . . they pursue
their quackeries with a certain innocence; their vanity is in their
blood; they are born actors, braggarts, as extravagant in shape
as a Chinese vase; perhaps they laugh at themselves. Their
personality is generous. . . . But Conti's trickery will never be
known to anyone but his mistress. He has in him a touch of
the Italian jealousy that led Carlone to assassinate Piola, the
jealousy that led to Paisiello being stabbed. This terrible envy
is concealed under a *camaraderie* of the most gracious kind.
Conti lacks the courage of his vice; he smiles at Meyerbeer and
compliments him, while all the time he would like to tear him in
pieces. He knows he is weak, so he tries to look strong; and he is
possessed with a vanity that impels him to affect sentiments
that are at the utmost possible remove from what is in his heart.
He pretends to be an artist who receives his inspiration from
heaven. For him, art is something holy, sacred. He is fanatical,
sublime, in his mockery with society; you would think his
eloquence came from a profound conviction. He is a seer, a
demon, a god, an angel.

"In spite of the warning I am giving you, Calyste, you will be
his dupe. This man of the south, this exuberant artist, is as cold
as a well-rope. Listen to his talk—the artist is a missionary,
according to him, and art is a religion that has its priests and
ought to have its martyrs. Once he gets going, Gennaro attains
a pathos as dishevelled as any that a German professor ever

disgorged upon his audience. You marvel at his convictions, but he himself believes in nothing. While he is raising you to heaven by a piece of singing that is like some mysterious fluid pouring out love, he will turn an ecstatic glance on you; but he is angling for your admiration; he is asking himself, 'Am I really a god in their eyes?' And at the same time he is saying to himself, 'I have eaten too much macaroni.' You think he loves you; but he hates you, though you do not know why. But I can tell you why—last night he saw a woman, he fell in love with her out of caprice, he insulted me with false love, hypocritical caresses, to make me pay dearly for his enforced fidelity. He is insatiable in his hunger for applause; he apes everything and trifles with everything; he feigns joy as excellently as he does sorrow; but he succeeds admirably. He pleases, he is loved; when he wants to, he can make himself admired. I left him hating his voice, to which he owed more success than to his talent as composer; for he would rather be a man of genius like Rossini than an executant of the capacity of Rubini. . . . Like so many artists, he is dainty; he likes his pleasures and his comforts; he is coquettish, refined, well got up; ah well, I flattered all his passions, I loved this being who is so weak and crafty. . . . My friend, I knew all this. I said to the poor Marquise, 'You do not know the abyss into which you are plunging. You are the Perseus of a sorry Andromeda; you will deliver me from my rock. If he loves you, all the better: but I doubt it; he loves only himself.

"Gennaro was in the seventh heaven of pride. *I* was not a Marquise, *I* was not born a Casteran; I was forgotten in a day. I gave myself the savage pleasure of going to the root of this man's nature. Foreseeing the *dénouement* of it all, I just watched him at his tricks. My poor child, in a single week I witnessed veritable horrors of sentiment, the most odious buffooneries. I will say nothing more to you about it: you will meet this man here. . . . His last and consistent insult is to believe that I am capable of communicating my sad knowledge of him to the Marquise. He is perpetually uneasy, reflective; for he believes in no one's good intentions. With me he still acts the part of one who is unhappy at having left me. You will find him full of the most penetrating cordialities; he is careless, chevaleresque. For him, every woman is a madonna. One has to live a long time with him to pierce to the secret of this false *bonhomie* and to detect the invisible stiletto in his mystifications. His air of conviction would deceive God himself. And you will be ensnared by his feline manners, so that you will never get to the profound and rapid arithmetic of his innermost thoughts."(10)

As we shall see again when we come to the character of the Marquise de Rochefide as Balzac draws her, there is here as much independent creation on the novelist's part as direct portraiture of an actual individual. But too many of the features of the portrait of Conti tally exactly with those observable in the Liszt of these years—the ambition of the mere virtuoso to be a great composer, the vanity, the love of adulation, the angling for applause in the course of a performance, the caressing, feline manner where women were concerned, the inner weakness parading itself as strength, the plebeian snobbishness that made him run after aristocratic women, the odd mixture of religion and worldly ambition and eroticism, the charlatan who is half his own dupe, the vaporous theorist of art as a divine mission and the artist as missionary and martyr—for us to have any doubt that for at least half of the character Balzac was drawing from the life. If Liszt could really persuade himself that the novel did not concern him in any way, he must have been singularly obtuse: but if we are to take it for granted that in his old age he spoke about *Béatrix* in anything like the way Janka Wohl makes him do, the only conclusion we can come to is that Balzac's barb had gone as deeply into his sensitive flesh as that launched in *Nélida* did later, and that in the one case as in the other he tried to deceive first his listeners, and then posterity, by an affectation of lofty superiority to what he wished them and us to believe was pure invention on the novelist's part.(11)

---

(10) BBE, p. 114ff.

(11) On 18th June, 1870, we find him writing to the Princess Wittgenstein *à propos* of the allusions to living people in Disraeli's novels, "For my part I always protest, as I did thirty years ago when Balzac's *Béatrix* and *Nélida* were published, against deductions being made from characters in novels to characters in real life who resemble them. The public can divert itself in this way to its heart's content. As for the supposed models, the wisest thing for them to do is to remain perfectly

3

We get more than one echo of the actual Liszt-d'Agoult affair in Camille's account of how Béatrix (the Marquise de Rochefide) confided to her her intention of running away with Conti, of the low-born singer's ridiculous vanity over having captivated a Marquise, of the tone of Béatrix's letters to her during her two years in Italy, of Conti being compelled, for financial reasons, to write an opera for Italy, and so on. Camille reads to Calyste a letter from Béatrix to her that is in singular agreement with the documents with which we have already become acquainted.

"Our friend [Conti] has had great triumphs at the Scala, the Fenice, and lately at San Carlo. Three Italian operas in two years! You cannot say that love has made him indolent. We have had the most marvellous reception everywhere; but I would have preferred silence and solitude. Is not this the only course of life suitable to a woman who has placed herself in direct opposition to the world? I thought it possible. Love is a master more exigent than marriage; but it is so sweet to obey him! After having made love my very life, I did not know I should have to go back into the world again, even at intervals; and the consideration with which I have been surrounded was merely so many wounds. I found myself no longer on a footing of equality with women of rank; the more regard was shown me, the more my inferiority was implied. Gennaro could not understand these delicate points, but he was so happy that it would have been wrong of me not to immolate petty vanity for so great a thing as the life of an artist. . . . I would rather die than leave Gennaro, for my pardon is in the sanctity of my passion. Between social dignity and my own small dignity, which is a secret for my own conscience, I have not hesitated. If occasionally there comes over me a melancholy like the clouds that pass across the sky, the melancholy to which we women love to surrender ourselves, I conceal it, for it would bear the appearance of a regret. . . . In short, I do not see in what way this

---

indifferent, and to grant generously to the author the right to maltreat them according to his fancy" (LZB, VI, 247).
The inference is that at the time he had been hurt quite as much by the portrait of himself in *Béatrix* as by that in *Nélida*.

fine genius can be at fault. I am rather like those devotees who
debate with their God, for is it not to you, my angel, that I owe
my happiness? . . . But alas, we are poor artists, and the need
of money drags the two Bohemians to Paris. Gennaro does not
want me to be conscious that I have given up my luxury, so he
is going to Paris to rehearse a new work of his, a grand opera.
But you will understand that *I* could not set foot in Paris. I
would not wish to face, at the cost of my love, one of those
glances from a man or a woman that would make me think of
assassinating somebody: I would hack in pieces anyone who
would honour me with his pity. . . . You are the only person
with whom I could bear to be alone without Conti."

The correspondence between these sentiments and those we
have already met with in Marie's letters and her journal is so
complete that there seems no escape from the conclusion that
Balzac derived his intimate knowledge of the matter at first-
hand from George Sand: we are tempted to believe that the
letter from which Camille is reading is Balzac's paraphrase of an
actual letter from Marie to George.

That the Marquise de Rochefide of this stage of the story
is drawn, directly or indirectly, from the Countess d'Agoult is
everywhere clear. Emile Faguet has pointed out that Balzac's
genius was for "the painting of middle or lower-class humanity,
the minute description of commonplace things." . . . "This
picture of mankind, this ample comedy of a hundred diverse
acts of which the scene is the whole world, as his admirers have
so often said and as he himself claimed, is brimful of widely
diverse characters, it is true; and yet they have been gathered
together from a comparatively small circle. His knowledge was
confined to the middle classes, and what he knew of the upper
ten was very slight and obviously of the most superficial
kind."(12) His portrait of the patrician Madame de Rochefide
up to the present point is manifestly based either on general
hearsay about Marie or on what he had been told about her
by George Sand; and it is noticeable that, like all Marie's
acquaintances who have left us their record of her, he lays special
stress not only on her blond beauty but on her grace and the

---

(12) Emile Faguet, *Balzac*, translated by Wilfrid Thorley, pp. 68, 162.

aristocratic dignity of her manner, on "the pride of race" that is evident in the carriage of her head, and so on. Though, as we shall see, Balzac gradually turns against the Marquise as his story develops, he never softens in the slightest degree the hardness of his reading of the character of Conti, who remains to the end possessed of "a nature that is false and deceitful," becoming more and more "weary of his poverty and of his love and disgusted with life, regretting having allied himself so publicly with the Marquise."(13)

4

The character of Béatrix, however, changes considerably as the novel goes on, till at last it bears no relation whatever either to Marie's actual life or to her character as we know it. She had merely served Balzac, for the time being, for a study of aristocratic beauty, pride and breeding, and as the basis for a portrait of a woman who has been the dupe of an artist who, for all his profession of religious idealism, is something of a charlatan in matters of art and of a trickster in matters of life. At this point in the story the actual circumstances of the Liszt-d'Agoult affair as it developed after 1839—the period when Balzac would be at work on the earlier chapter of his novel—cease to have any significance for the novelist, even supposing him to have had any acquaintance with them, which is highly improbable. Balzac's genius now gets to work in its own special way; he creates characters and invents circumstances that have no connection whatever with either Liszt or Marie; the latter now becomes a dry-hearted, scheming woman of the middle-class type that Balzac understood so well, a woman who heartlessly takes the innocent Calyste from Camille, not from love but from sheer vanity and the lust for power, and is finally dragged down by an intrigue, on the part of others, of an artificial complexity of the type in which Balzac delighted. To suppose that the Béatrix of the later stages of the novel is still the Countess d'Agoult is as absurd as to suppose that the Camille Maupin of the later stages, who parts with all her property for the benefit

---

(13) BBE, p. 263.

of Calyste, and retires into a nunnery in order to leave him free
to love the Marquise, is still George Sand. Balzac's method of
treatment of the two female characters is in general the same:
up to a certain point Camille *is* George Sand and Béatrix *is* the
Countess d'Agoult, but after that point the novelist converts
them into creatures that obey no law but the peculiar one of
his own genius, and sets them moving in a world that is entirely
his own creation. We can have little difficulty in believing,
howe *r*er, that the Countess, when the book appeared, felt a
momentary resentment against Balzac. All Paris must have
known that the first part of the novel touched upon herself and
her relations with Liszt. Human nature being what it is, it was
natural that her female friends should take a malicious pleasure
in assuming, or pretending to assume, that the second half of
the novel was also founded on fact, and that Béatrix was Marie
to the very last page. It would take some time for this false
impression to be removed; and while it lasted Marie must have
suffered under it.(14)

---

(14) The second half of the novel is a perfect example of Balzac's tendency
to enmesh himself in a web of his own spinning, to work out a complicated intrigue, psychological and circumstantial, for which we have the
profoundest admiration as an exercise of the constructive imagination,
while at the same time we feel that the peculiar genius of the man has
taken him several degrees away from life as we know it. This aspect of
him was expressed to perfection by Sainte-Beuve in the article he wrote
immediately after the novelist's death in 1850:
"Delicate artist in the moral sphere that he is, he has certainly discovered
new veins—laid bare, and injected, portions of the lymphatic vessels that
have hitherto been unperceived. But he also *invents* these veins. There
comes a moment in his analysis when the real plexus ends and the illu-
sory plexus begins; and he does not distinguish between the two. In a
word—continuing my physical and anatomical image—I would say:
When he really takes hold of the *carotid artery* of his subject he injects
it vigorously through and through: but he injects just the same when he
is mistaken—he goes on creating imaginary plexuses of vessels without
being aware that they *are* imaginary." (*Causeries de Lundi*, 2nd ed. 1872,
II, 351-352.)
No better illustration of this habit of Balzac's of creating plexuses of
nerves and veins that are amazingly like those of real life, but still not
quite those of real life, could be cited than the second half of *Béatrix*.
Anyone who can believe that the Marquise de Rochefide of this second

K

5

For whatever grievance she may have had in this quarter, however, she took an ample revenge in *Nélida*. Only today, nearly ninety years after its publication, can that curious book at last be seen for what it really is. It has always been regarded as the venomous invention of a scorned woman ready to go to any length to injure the lover who had left her. Until the day before yesterday, no biographer of Liszt had anything but censure for the book; even Peter Raabe, who does his best not to be unjust towards Marie in the old confident, unthinking pro-Lisztian way, and who has had the advantage, denied to the older biographers, of reading her *Mémoires*,(15) assures us that "while a novel, especially a novel that turns all the facts upside down, is not a historical document, nevertheless we must regard all the evil things that the Countess says about Liszt as representing her actual opinion; for had she thought otherwise of him, and yet, in a book which every reader would associate with him, had calumniated him against her better conscience, the publication of this novel would be not only a piece of tactlessness—which it truly is—but a baseness of which we could not believe her capable." Raabe believes, as all previous writers have done, that "if we want to understand why Liszt remained so implacable towards this woman, we must look at the caricature of him that she gave to the world."(16)

It is the old story over again: Liszt's unvarying nobility and virtue are to be assumed to be beyond question, and any witness from the past who dares to call that nobility and virtue in question is *ipso facto* discredited in the eyes of the court. But those of us who read *Nélida* years ago, and took the traditional view of it then, look at it through very different eyes since the publication of Marie's *Mémoires* and the correspondence between her and Liszt. It now becomes, in large part, precisely

---

half corresponds even remotely to the Countess d'Agoult, or any other actual person, is capable of believing anything.

(15) Though not the *Correspondance*, which was not published until after his admirable work had appeared.

(16) RLL, p. 42.

what Raabe denies it ever to have been—a genuinely historical document; for so far as Liszt is concerned it does little, as we can see today, but give the form of fiction to the facts of the association of the pair as we now know them beyond dispute to have been. In a letter of 13th April, 1866, to the Princess Wittgenstein, Liszt says that "the character of Guermann is a stupid invention."(17) Either his memory of his own past had forsaken him, or he was saying what he knew to be untrue.

Regarded purely and simply as a novel, *Nélida*(18) is a poor enough performance; the Countess was quite out of her element in this literary form, and one finds it hard, at first, to comprehend how the woman who shows herself so exceptionally intelligent in other fields of literature could perpetrate anything so weak as this. When she has to rely on her imagination for the creation of characters and the construction of her story the book becomes at its best commonplace and at its worst pitiable. But it is paradoxically in the poverty of her invention that the value of the book, as a record of actuality, is to be sought. She can describe convincingly only what she knows, what she has seen and heard and lived through; and accordingly in her account of the relations between Nélida and Guermann she keeps doggedly to the facts of the actual relation between herself and Liszt, as a comparison of the novel with her *Mémoires* and his letters abundantly proves. She has been laughed at, not without reason, for the generous idealisation of herself in the character of Nélida, whom she praises liberally for her beauty, her intellectual endowments, and her virtue: Marie was certainly very self-conscious. That point, however, is of no great importance. What we are concerned with is not the character of Nélida but that of Guermann; and it is now evident that so far from that portrait being a "caricature" of Liszt, as Raabe says, it is a portrait painted with the eye on the object, by an artist who knew her sitter through and through. The portrait may not square with the popular notion of the Liszt of history; but that is only because the Liszt of history is the idealised legendary

---

(17) LZB, VI, 111.

(18) "Nélida," of course, is an anagram of "Daniel" [Stern].

Liszt of a later period. Daniel Stern's portrait is emphatically that of the Liszt of the eighteen-thirties and early 'forties.

6

There is no need to give here the story of the novel in detail,(19) for we are concerned with little else in it but Liszt. Nélida is a girl of noble birth and high aspirations who, after a marriage of convenience in her own class, falls in love with, and flies from the world with, Guermann Regnier, whom, as a boy of humble origin, she had known in her childhood, and who has now developed into a painter of some repute. At the outset, then, we have that clash of the two social ranks that we have already seen to have played so vital a part in the relations of Marie and Liszt. The authoress does not spare Guermann; she insists from the beginning—to our modern notions a little cruelly—on his plebeian birth. But in this connection we have to remember two things. In the first place, Marie had not allowed the disparity between her own station in society and that of Liszt to deter her from the dangerous step of linking her lot with his; she had deliberately affronted a Parisian world that would have merely smiled at illicit love but was wrathful at a serious misalliance, because this flew in the face of all its own traditions of caste; and she had borne with courageous resignation all the sufferings her act had of necessity brought upon her—sufferings of which the more tolerant modern world has some difficulty in estimating the extent. In the second place, she herself never, at any time, thought less of Liszt merely for his bourgeois origin. What grieved and angered her, as the *Mémoires* and the letters show, was the vulgar vanity in him that made him anxious to play a parvenu star part in that aristocratic world which *she* had voluntarily quitted for his sake, a vanity that again and again made him ludicrous in many other eyes besides hers. Having given up the reality of caste for his sake, it was a mortification to her to find him so hungry for a shoddy simulacrum of it. Once more we have to remember

---

(19) A letter from Marie to Georg Herwegh makes it clear that she began the book about March, 1844 (see HPD, p. 62).

that the Liszt with whom she associated was the Liszt of the eighteen-thirties and 'forties, not that of the 'sixties or 'seventies. In the intervening thirty years not only he but Europe had changed. He, for his part, had given the world abundant proofs of his right to respect as a thoughtful artist; while the social status of the musician had so greatly improved, as a result partly of a change in European life in general, partly of the way in which the imagination of men had been captured by Wagner, that the old mutual attitude of condescension in the aristocratic patron of music and of servility in the musician had become a thing of the past.

From the beginning to the end the Countess, as all her writings show, was herself in revolt against the social injustice that placed the merely rich or well-born in a position of "superiority" to beings essentially better than themselves, merely because these happened to have been born into a humbler station in life.

"Strange in the eyes of any sensible person," says Nélida, "is the spectacle presented by *le monde*, that is to say, the section of society which, opulent and proud, endowed with noble leisure, is recognised and saluted by all as the supreme arbiter of what is correct, as the guardian of elegant manners and the spirit of honour, and which, in its superb disdain, with no thought for anything but itself, affects to regard itself as *le monde par excellence*, looking upon everything outside itself as unworthy of its attention or its interest!"(20)

Nélida is in complete sympathy with the young painter's revolt against this society, against its contemptuous patronage of him as a mere artist and therefore a member of an inferior class; and she sees herself as the Beatrice who can inspire him in his struggle.(21) She is shocked, when she visits Guermann, at the sight of the squalid domestic conditions under which he is compelled to live:

"She had no idea of the bitterness of the condition of those whose superior talents, lofty instincts and refined manners have not sufficed to shelter them from need, and who, instead of

(20) AN, I, 73, 74.
(21) Ibid., p. 113 ff.

being able to give themselves up to the noble ambitions that haunt them, see themselves forced to bow beneath the yoke of a mean labour that barely secures their existence. These thoughts came to her for the first time when she entered Guermann's apartment—this man who, she knew, adored her, and to whom her heart secretly awarded the palm of genius. She recalled his words: 'I had to become an artist while remaining an artisan:' "(22)

—almost precisely the words, by the way, that Liszt himself had publicly employed to describe his own fate and that of others of his kind.

"We are pariahs," Guermann says to Nélida later; "society, in its superb disdain, treats us as vile artisans who trade in a block of marble or a few yards of painted canvas; it is convinced that our supreme ambition ought to be simply to win the praise of *grands seigneurs blasés* and to amuse their nerve-ridden wives. I am aware that when they have paid for the work of our hands— which of these heartless creatures ever imagines that there is in it the inspiration of the soul?—when they have thrown us our wages, they turn away from us as from beings of a lower order. . . . Art is great, art is holy, art is immortal. The artist is the first, the noblest among men, for to him it has been given to feel more intensely and to express more powerfully than any other the invisible presence of God in creation. He exercises a priesthood that is august although it is outraged."(23)

This is Liszt himself speaking, the indignant Liszt of the *Lettres d'un bachelier ès musique*.

7

Peter Raabe, therefore, goes completely astray in his comment on a later passage in which Nélida expresses her contempt for the acquired snobbishness that made Guermann, as it did Liszt, run after titles when flushed by his success as an artist. Guermann acquires, by virtue of his genius, the *entrée* into high society in Milan:

"In spite," says Nélida, "of his former affectation of being proud of his poverty, the plebeian artist was dazzled more than

(22) AN, I, pp. 120, 121.
(23) Ibid., p. 142 ff.

he would have cared to admit by the brilliant externals of patrician life. Several times, when describing, in his letters [to
Nélida—who had refused to accompany him into this world]
the fêtes to which he had been without her, he grew animated
and boasted to her, with puerile complacency, of the splendour,
the sumptuosity of the Italian palaces, the lavishness of the
suppers, the luxury of the duchesses, till Nélida asked herself
in amazement if this was the same man whom she had heard
judging with such rigid austerity the pleasures of the children
of the century, the same man who had torn himself away with
such proud simplicity from similar magnificences in order to
lead her into poverty and solitude."(24)

To declaim, as Raabe does, "And this is what the Countess
d'Agoult has to say about Liszt, who, as she well enough knew,
had frequented princely courts, baronial castles, and the houses
of the rich and powerful from his childhood, and therefore
knew almost better than anyone else the brilliance and splendour
of distinguished society!" is to miss the whole point, historical
as well as personal, of Nélida's indictment. The young Liszt
had indeed been admitted into the great houses of Paris, but
only as a musical tradesman, on conditions that incessantly
galled his pride. His first ambition, when his unrivalled virtuosity as a pianist made the fashionable world run after him in
the late eighteen-thirties, was to establish himself in that world
as a social equal, whereas Marie would have preferred him to
hold aloof from it as a superior, to show his contempt for it by
despising its shoddy prizes, its facile gush, its vulgar standards of
value, and retiring into himself in order to create great works of
art. But for a renunciation of that kind Liszt was not big
enough, either then or later; and Marie's contempt for him, her
resentment against him for being false to his own idealism and
hers, took the bitter form of derision, by the real aristocrat, of
Liszt's sham aristocracy. Of what avail had it been for her to
give expression to her own loathing and contempt for the vulgar
rich world in which she had been brought up, by the very
practical step of shaking off its dust from the soles of her feet
and enduring comparative poverty and facing social obloquy for

(24) AN, II, 59, 60.

the sake of the better artist she believed there was in him, if the only result of it all was that in the hour of his stupendous success as a pianist he made the paltry standards of that world his own?

The course of the novel corresponds point by point to that of the union between Liszt and the Countess, for Marie, as I have said, has little talent for invention. Revolted by the cynicism of her husband, Nélida, meeting the humble play-fellow of her childhood again after many years, falls a victim to what she calls "la séduction du malheur." She is fascinated by the boldness of the young man's opinions, and captivated by his character in general. "He was generous; he knew how to give with grace."(25) He, for his part, "loved Nélida passionately, with all his imagination and all his pride—the two powers that ruled his life. To win glory and to win Nélida were one and the same desire in him." His belief in his destiny was so great that "in the depths of his heart he congratulated the beautiful patrician on having fallen to the lot of the illustrious plebeian. Confident that he would conduct her to glory, he saw in his union with her the union of all that is most sublime in the world; and nothing would have astonished him more than to have had it suggested to him that there could be anything wrong in his having necessitated, and accepted, sacrifices the extent of which he had no conception." He saw in his flight with her a means for the gratification

"of all the hatreds, all the resentments, that had rooted themselves in his heart since the day when, for the first time, he had become conscious of social inequality. He would beat down prejudice, show a vanquished and dazzled world the supreme power of genius blotting out all the distinctions invented by men, crushing the pride of the patriciate and submitting to his empire the beauty, the virtue and the honour of the first among women. Nothing seemed easier to him than to shake to its foundations this decrepit old society that had denied him the place he felt to be his due. He firmly believed that, while satisfying his egoistic passion, he was at the same time inaugurating a hitherto undreamed-of era of liberty and equality."

(25) AN, I, 242.

His pride had been mortally wounded; "all his evil passions
were fighting a furious battle in his soul"; he declaimed his
social theories at Nélida in just the way that Liszt used to do at
Marie.(26)

Their first weeks in Switzerland are spent, like those of Marie
and Liszt, in complete solitude, not even a letter reaching them
from the outer world. Guermann orates upon the theme of
"the immense future that lay before them; in flaming terms he
painted for her the happiness of a solitude spent in hard work
and given up to the holy ardour of an unalterable affection.
His talk was a perpetual canticle, an enthusiastic hymn to love."
She, for her part, feels the same exaltation, and willingly
persuades herself that "for such a love, any sacrifice, even that
of conscience, was a small price to pay."(27)

8

The lovers go to Geneva, as Liszt and Marie had done: there,
as was the case with Liszt, Guermann's scanty funds are soon
exhausted, so that he is compelled to give lessons. Nélida is
reluctant to be dragged into society—a feeling Guermann is not
sensitive enough to understand—for whenever she finds herself
in an assembly every lorgnette is directed on her, and the women
lean over to each other to discuss her. Guermann's vanity,
however, is reawakened by the adulation showered on him;
once more "he sees the accomplishment of his dreams, the
world enslaved by his genius, society subjugated." Nélida
discovers with surprise, when taking his arm to return to their
house one evening after he had shone in company, that he was
"possessed by an unaccustomed joy. It was the first discord
sounded in the intimacy of their thought. . . . When she
entered the house she was a prey to profound sadness. She
foresaw her solitude being destroyed, before long, by insolent
glances, her love insulted by scornful words, her sanctuary

---

(26) AN, I, pp. 242-258 (see *supra*, p. 33).

(27) Ibid., II, 6-8. Liszt himself, in a letter to Marie of 24th November,
1839, condoles with her on the fact that from the time of their flight
until 1838 she has been, in the eyes of the world, "a sort of mad woman,
a pariah." (LZAC, I, 302).

invaded by the world from which she had fled, but into which she was suddenly thrown by a pitiless fate."(28)

Nélida's husband, like the Count d'Agoult, shows himself to be a man of tact according to the standards of his caste and of the epoch: her mother writes to her, from Paris, that he philosophically assures his friends that Nélida has always been subject to romantic hallucinations that were apt to degenerate into madness. "For the rest," the mother writes to her daughter, "he no longer mentions your name, but he has given orders that your own income is to be placed at your disposal regularly with my notary, who will render you statements. There was nothing else your husband could do—he could not cut the throat of a man of no account whom we have all had among us in the position of something like a servant. I will not advise you to return. All that is now impossible; the world and your family are closed to you for ever. May God have pity on you! That is the sole hope that remains to you."(29)

As time goes on, Nélida discovers that Guermann is becoming more and more the victim of the romantic literature he reads, and more and more attracted by fashionable society and the easy conquests his talent wins him there. At last he receives a warning from Paris that he must exhibit his great picture "John Huss" there, as his personal standing has been injured by his elopement, and his artistic reputation is threatened by a picture, "Savonarola", by his rival D. . . ., who is obviously Thalberg. Guermann decides that he must at once meet the challenge: "the thought of such a check was more than his lofty *amour-propre* could bear."(30) Like Liszt, Guermann goes to Paris "with his heart ulcerated, dreaming of nothing but success, triumph, vengeance. The artist, his glory menaced, was no

---

(28) AN, II, 20-28.

(29) Ibid., II, 37-88. In this, as in several other cases, internal and external evidence makes it probable that the Countess is quoting from an actual letter. If that be so, we can imagine Liszt's rage at the Count's contemptuous description of him.

(30) The reader will remember that Liszt, in a letter to Marie, had declared that the humiliation of Thalberg was a necessity for the satisfaction of his *amour-propre* (see *supra*, p. 64).

longer sensitive to other sorrows; an instant had sufficed to poison, in this proud soul, the stream of love that had flowed so long."

9

Guermann's letters to Nélida from Paris run on precisely the lines of those of Liszt to Marie. He is filled with hatred and contempt for his rival, with a hot determination to roll the upstart in the mud. Away from Nélida, he protests that he cannot live without her: "I am only silence and prayer in your presence."(31) He learns from friends in Geneva that she is secluding herself, and that her health is suffering. He feels that he ought to return to her; but he is unwilling to do this

> "in the moment of his triumph, the moment when the eyes of all Paris were fixed on him—merely to be involved once more in a foolish affair, to see a sick woman, tacitly reproaching him, and to hear the tiresome gossip of the town. For the first time he feels the *shackles* on his life; this woman who had been the brilliant centre of it, the decisive impulse, the luminous point, had become the obstacle, the *duty*. And to Guermann the thought of duty was a horror. The long journey back was frightful; a concentrated irritation gnawed at him. He arrived in Geneva with his heart more full of rage than of love. But when he saw Nélida's hollow cheeks, her listless eyes, her pale lips, saw that she was still of an incomparable majesty in her sorrow, his worse nature was vanquished. He fell at her feet, clasped her to him with more ardour than on the first day, and in the madness of his transports soon made her forget all she had suffered during his cruel absence."(32)

The picture, we may be sure, is painted directly from life.

They decide to go to Milan, Nélida stipulating that they shall live in strict retirement, to which Guermann consents. But soon his love of applause, his desire to shine, his naïve satisfaction at being admitted into great houses, do their malign

---

(31) Liszt had used these precise words in one of his letters to Marie. A careful comparison of *Nélida* with Marie's journal and Liszt's letters leads to the conclusion that she wrote the novel with these personal documents in front of her.

(32) AN, II, pp. 48-55.

work in him again.(33) He tries once more to drag her into
society, on the plea that it will be good for his interest and fame.
She points out to him that in society she will be the target for
every kind of malice, and asks whether it was for this that she
had given up her own brilliant position in Paris. She feels that
he is not keeping to the terms of their idealistic compact, that
he is sacrificing her for his own selfish and rather vulgar ends.
When she tells him that *he* can live the life he likes, but she
prefers to be alone, to devote herself to study, he is annoyed, not
merely at the refusal but at the uncomfortable secret sense that
she is showing herself morally superior to him. Then there
happens what was so frequently to happen in Liszt's later life.
The excitement of society, the late hours, the too lavish living,
the over-indulgence in coffee, wine and tobacco, begin to tell
on Guermann: he returns to Nélida at night tired and fuddled:
the next day he cannot concentrate, so that all his plans for
worthy work go by the board. But the one thing he *must* satisfy
is his vanity. With the fees that come to him—for his portraits
are in great demand in Milan—he keeps a carriage and gives
splendid suppers; and the more he spends, the more he is
compelled to undertake the flashier kind of work that alone
brings in money. Serious study becomes repugnant to him;
with his brilliant gifts and insinuating manner he finds it easy
to shine at the dinner table or the ball, but when he talks to
Nélida he is made unpleasantly conscious that the better part
of his brain is standing still:(34) his facile paradoxes about life
no longer impress her.

10

Guermann gets caught in the net of a siren, the Marquise
Zepponi. His cynicism on this subject leads to an angry scene
between him and Nélida, who is at last goaded into running over
the long catalogue of her grievances and sufferings and telling
him that she, who has made so many sacrifices, has herself a
right to ask for one now. Guermann's only reply is to tell her,

---

(33) It is at this point that Nélida gives the description of him that will be
     found on pp. 128, 129.

(34) AN, II, pp. 60-65.

coldly and brutally, that Malibran could not have acted the scene better. It is just the kind of reply Liszt would have made, and repeated to his friends with a certain fatuous satisfaction in later years;(35) so we can be tolerably certain that some such incident occurred as that here described. Nélida "received one of those wounds that never heal. . . . Henceforth they were on terms not merely of unavowed misunderstanding: there had come between them a hostile principle of which both were clearly conscious: a germ of hatred had been sown in their love."

In the weeks that followed "they tacitly avoided in their conversations whatever might lead to the mention of the Marquise. Guermann spent three or four hours every day at the Palazzo Zepponi." [He was painting the lady's portrait].

"He made it his duty to pass his evenings with Nélida; but this duty, though self-imposed, weighed upon a nature so impatient of restraint as his. As Nélida refused to receive any-one, these *tête-à-tête* evenings were never interrupted by a third party; and so the conversation was difficult to maintain. Guermann felt that it would be tactless of him to talk to her about his mundane life. He suggested their reading together; but he read with an air of boredom, and she listened without pleasure. Day by day he grew more uneasy, she more taciturn. They had reached that mournful stage in the love of beings who have been drawn inexorably to desire solitude, when destiny, that will grant nothing unconditionally to man, begins to turn against them, with bitter irony, the very force that had made

---

(35) Whenever he felt he had said a good thing, he was not immune from the ordinary human weakness of wishing everyone to hear it. The same stories of his own repartees crop up more than once in his letters. Twice at least, and with a considerable interval between the two occasions, he tells a correspondent how, in his own opinion, he had snubbed Princess Metternich in Vienna. The Princess, who did not like him, had asked him, at the conclusion of one of his concert tours, whether he had "done good business." His reply, which has been quoted admiringly a hundred times in the Liszt literature, was that "Only bankers do busi-ness, Madame." This from the man who, as his letters of that period abundantly show, delighted in giving Marie particulars of how profitable his piano-playing business was from day to day! But the actor in him could never resist the temptation to strike an attitude.

them triumph for a while, and that had seemed to make them invulnerable."(36)

No one who has studied the novel in conjunction with the correspondence, and knows how feeble the Countess is when she tries to invent situations between imaginary beings, can doubt that here once more she is merely painting from the life.

The presence of a third party at length becomes necessary if Guermann and Nélida are to continue to live together in the letter if not in the spirit. They feel it would be better if they were to part for a little while: Nélida accordingly goes to Florence, while Guermann returns to Milan to finish a portrait; he is delighted to feel himself free once more, "delivered, at any rate for a few days, from that most irritating of sights—that of the profound unhappiness of another caused by one's own fault, an unhappiness that will neither complain nor be consoled." Guermann meets the Marquise Zepponi at a ball. She casts her spell upon him again, and gives him a rendezvous for the morrow. He returns to his apartment in a state of fever. There he finds some letters from Nélida that have just arrived. "At the sight of her handwriting he felt a sorrowful emotion that was very near remorse, and that drove him instantly to a resolution more prudent and more loyal than might have been expected of him. He determined not to keep the appointment with the Marquise, but to go immediately to Florence." At this critical moment he happens to open her writing-desk, where he finds her journal. He cannot help looking into it; there springs out at him a passage that has evidently been written recently, a long passage in which Nélida calls out to her Sorrow to be great and calm and to conceal itself from *him;* to her Anger, to be proud and magnanimous and to conceal itself, for it knows it is just; to her Pride, to seal her lips and her soul for ever with a triple seal; to her Wisdom, to refrain from trying to console her.

Guermann feels an uncontrollable rage as he reads this passage:

"His pride had received a mortal blow. He saw himself understood, fathomed, judged, by a pride greater than his own, by a spirit whose strength he had not suspected. The woman

(36) AN, II, 66-70.

who had been his slave had won her freedom; if she still con-
sented to wear her chains, it was no longer in blindness, but
with her eyes open; it was no longer in order to be true to
another, but to be true to herself. This thought exasperated
him. He rang, called for a carriage at once, and, throwing
himself into it as if he feared that something might restrain him,
cried to the coachman in a voice of thunder, '*Strada del Corso,
Palazzo Zepponi.*' "(37)

II

Nélida at last becomes convinced that all her sacrifices have
been in vain. "She had gone to Florence with a thought in her
mind very much like that of her lover; she too had wanted to
place an interval, as it were, between the illusion, the doubt,
the enthusiasm, the despair of the past two years and the calm,
strong acceptance of an unhappiness she had now probed to its
centre. At last she had seen clearly into Guermann's soul.
She no longer felt him to be great enough to justify her fault.
Henceforth there was nothing left to her but to await the future."
While she is in this mood there arrives a letter from Guermann
in which he answers, phrase by phrase, the passage that had so
irritated him in her journal:

"There is a *Sorrow* greater than yours, Madame, if less calm;
it is mine at the discovery that your heart no longer cherishes
any of the feelings of which my own has need.

"There is an *Anger* still more legitimate; it is that kindled in
me by the unjust sentence you pass upon my life.

"There is a *Pride* that will speak to you only this once, for
you have wounded it to the death. It is that of a man whom you
cannot appreciate, because your weak soul and your timid spirit
can understand only an existence shaped to the mean propor-
tions of the common rule.

"There is a *Wisdom* that tells me we understand each other
no longer, and that we ought to separate until your eyes open
to a new light which it will not depend upon me to make
visible to you.

"Your obstinate silence, your irritating protest against my

---

(37) AN, II, 85-101. Liszt himself dated their first serious breach from the
Florence days of 1839 (see *supra*, p. 83).

life during the past year, have wrought an ill in me that would perhaps be irreparable did I not fly in all haste from an influence so hurtful. Do not take this last word in the wrong sense. I leave Milan; I rescue myself for the moment from the destructive influence you exercise over my mind, but my devotion to you is unchanged. Wherever you or I may be, you have only to make a sign and I come to you. But before all things it is necessary for me to save the artist in me, that the flame that vivified my genius shall be relit. It would perish in the atmosphere in which you would have me live.

"I am going to W. . . .(38) The Grand Duke, whom I met in Milan, and who has just built a museum, commissions me to paint the frescoes for the ceiling of a large gallery. . . . This glorious work will show both my friends and my enemies of what I am capable. They thought I was finished—I know that is your thought also—that because I do not live like an anchorite, and because for some time I have produced only works of an inferior kind, I have become incapable of great things. In two years my answer to my detractors, my rejoinder to your injustices, will be written in ineffaceable characters on the walls of a magnificent palace."(39)

Raabe, after quoting all this, surmises that "if ever the correspondence between Liszt and the Countess is published, it would not surprise us to discover that this is an actual letter he had written to her."(40) The same thought will have occurred to many a reader, for Guermann's letter bears all the marks of Liszt's style, and it is most improbable that the Countess should have been able to place herself so completely at his point of view as to enable her to state his case, as he saw it, as plausibly and almost convincingly as this. It has to be recorded, however, that in his letter to Marie of 26th March, 1846, discussing *Nélida*, which he has just been reading, he says, "Just one other question: Was it of me you were thinking when you wrote the reply to your lament, 'O my sorrow, O my pride,' etc.? For you know that I do not stop at these surfaces. 'There is a sorrow

---

(38) Obviously Weimar.

(39) AN, II, pp. 106-114.

(40) RLL, I, 47.

greater but less calm than yours,' etc."(41) Like so many
passages in Liszt's correspondence, this is somewhat obscure;
but it certainly seems to suggest that Raabe is wrong in his
conjecture. At the same time, the pseudo-reply to the entry
in her journal is so thoroughly in the style of many of Liszt's
letters to Marie that we may perhaps assume that she is here
paraphrasing some verbal remarks of his. In any case Marie,
for the purposes of the story, has telescoped her dates at this
point. The Florence quarrel was in 1839; it was not until the
end of 1842 that Liszt entered the service of the Grand Duke of
Weimar.

12

The final breach between the pair came in the spring of 1844.
In the interval two things had happened: Marie had become
more and more disgusted at the public linking of her name with
a pianist who was making himself ridiculous all over Europe
by his erotic mountebankeries, more and more sadly conscious
that the Liszt for whom she had planned so idealistically in
years gone by was lost to her for ever; while he, for his part,
was fighting out within himself, in his own way, the unending
battle between his better and his worse nature. His life as a
virtuoso both attracted and repelled him: he loved the adulation
it brought him, but there gnawed at him for ever the consciousness that he was wasting the better part of himself on things
that were beneath him. He was beginning to feel a new power
of creative composition within him; but this, he knew, he could
not develop during a life of incessant travelling, incessant
piano-playing, incessant abandonment to the nocturnal joys
and fatigues of social intercourse. The new Liszt could be born
only in retirement and tranquillity; hence the growing strength
of the desire in him to give up the piano and settle in some quiet
little German town where he could call his soul and his time his
own. Being as yet none too sure of himself as a composer on the
large scale, he was attracted to Weimar because there, in his
capacity as Kapellmeister, he would have plenty of opportunities of trying out his works in private on the orchestra before

---

(41) LZAC, II, 363.

L

committing them to print or to the judgment of the larger
world.(42) In none of the larger German towns could a post of
any authority in the concert room or the opera house have been
found for him, nor, could one have been provided, would he
have ventured upon it: he was as yet too inexperienced in these
matters. Paris was automatically ruled out; he was not liked in
Parisian society, and the French public, as Berlioz had learned
to his cost, had neither the mentality nor the culture for purely
orchestral music of the serious kind. Works of the type that
Liszt was dreaming of writing could be produced only in

---

(42) The idea of abandoning the piano for the orchestra had evidently been
working within him for a long time. The first occasion on which he held
a baton in his hand seems to have been in Pesth in January, 1840. In
February, 1842, while he was concertising in Berlin, he again tried his
prentice hand at conducting, taking the orchestra through the fifth
symphony of Beethoven and the *Olympie* overture of Spontini. A year
later, in Breslau, he conducted the *Magic Flute*, following this up with
the *Coriolan* overture and the *Oberon* overture in Berlin a week or so
later. It was with the fifth symphony of Beethoven that he made his
début as a conductor in Weimar, on 7th January, 1844. The first opera
he conducted there was Flotow's *Martha*, on 16th February, 1848.

He was too sound a musician not to realise that as yet he had had too
little practical acquaintance with the orchestra to be able to write for it
in anything but a dilettante way. Hence the attractiveness of a post at
Weimar in which he could experiment for a while in private before
launching out in public. For a long time after settling in Weimar
he was anything but sure of himself: in November, 1849, he told Raff
that his intention was "to work for two or three years in absolute
quietness and then produce something [no doubt his opera *Sardan-
apalus*] in Paris" (RJR, p. 77). One of Raff's functions at Weimar—a
function in which he had been preceded by Conradi—was to orchestrate,
in whole or in part, the works on which Liszt was engaged. The question
of the extent of Raff's collaboration is authoritatively dealt with at last in
RLS, Chapter III. Liszt seems to have been mistrustful of himself for
a considerable time after settling at Weimar; as late as 1853 the Princess
had to speak rather plainly to him on the subject of his reliance on Raff
in the matter of the scoring of his music (see the letter published for the
first time in RLS, pp. 78, 79). During all these years, however, he was
gradually acquiring the orchestral mastery that is evident in the score
of the *Faust Symphony* (1854). He used the Weimar orchestra liberally
to try out his works in private before venturing to send them to the
engraver.

Germany; and even in Germany the special opportunities he required for quiet work and tentative private rehearsal with the orchestra were not to be found everywhere. To tiny Weimar, then, he felt himself more and more drawn as the months passed on.(43) But for Marie, as he must have known perfectly well, Weimar was a pure impossibility. The illicit nature of their union would have made it highly improbable that she would be received there either at the Court or in society; moreover, used as she had been from her girlhood to the brilliant intellectual life of Paris, to the company of the most distinguished men and women of the time, she would necessarily be appalled at the prospect of living, even under conditions of the utmost respectability, in a stuffy little provincial German town of some 12,000 inhabitants. It may well be, then, that she had protested energetically against his plan for settling there. He, for his part, possessed with the one idea of realising his ambitions as an original composer on the grand scale, would feel that now she had become merely an obstacle in his path.

Raabe does not state the case fairly when he says that "in her doubtless strong love for him she had never considered that so magical a genius as the young Liszt belongs to the whole world, not to one woman." The evidence is overwhelming that she had done all she could to secure his better genius for the world. Out of sympathy for his difficulties, as a social inferior, in Paris, she had cut herself adrift from her own world, at the cost of many a sacrifice and great suffering to herself, in order to help him to the development of the something better than a mere pianist that she had sensed in him at a time when the rest of the musical world had been content with him as he then was. She had seen him, again and again, defeat all her plans for him, seen him immolate his better self on the altar of his vanities, social and artistic, or lower his mental energy and sap his will-power with stimulants and narcotics. She had grieved at her enforced separation from him for so long a period in each

---

(43) Apparently Liszt told Göllerich, towards the end of his life, that the music-loving Grand Duke of Sachsen-Coburg-Gotha also wanted to secure him for his Kapelle, but the Grand Duke of Weimar approached him first (see GFL, p. 127).

year after 1838, and had been publicly shamed by his too frequent vulgarities of all kinds. And when, at last, his years of
triumph as a virtuoso had wearied him, by pure satiety, of that
kind of life, and, feeling himself maturing inwardly both as
man and as artist, he took the noble resolution to give up the
world and devote himself in retirement to the development and
purification of the soul he had so long and so often trailed in the
mud—as no one knew better than he—his dreams could be
converted into reality only under conditions that made it a sheer
impossibility for her to share his lot. It is little wonder that she
should have felt all her sacrifices of the last ten years to have
been in vain, and that in her rage and despair she sought to
avenge her wrongs in *Nélida*.

13

The final stages of the novel need not detain us for long.
We get a passing glimpse of Liszt as Marie must have seen him
in the last days of their union. Guermann "had not foreseen
the possible consequences" of his decision to settle in W. . . .
"For a long time he had acted and talked like a half-intoxicated
man. His long idleness and the factitious excitement of his
worldly life had set up in him a perturbation that allowed him
to hear nothing but the dull roar of his panting, wounded pride.
He was tormented by a single need, that of escaping at any cost
from the consciousness of his wrongdoing—the inevitable chastisement of a superior organisation when it has been employing
its faculties mistakenly." That is not the whole truth about the
Liszt of that epoch, but it is a good deal of the truth as Marie
and others saw it; unfortunately for them they could not pierce
the future, nor did they realise that sometimes a man's future,
especially when he is an exceptional man, does not follow in
strictly logical deduction from the premises of his past. Marie
was necessarily ignorant of three things that were to be vital
for the Liszt of the future—the imperious strength of the long-
suppressed instinct in him to launch out into the larger forms
of orchestral music, the firm hand that was soon to be laid upon
him by a woman who had not yet swum into his ken—the

Princess Wittgenstein—and the new worlds of music that were to be opened out to his vision later by the works of Wagner.

Marie cannot deny herself a final fling at her plebeian lover's pretensions to gentility. Guermann goes to W. . . . flattering himself that his genius will be a passport to the highest Court society. Instead of that, he finds himself treated like any other servant: to his infinite mortification the Grand Duke's Chamberlain allots him a place at meals at the third table, where the company, according to the German small-town standards of the female domestic whom he questions on the matter, is of an enviable distinction—"the first chambermaid, who has lived three years in Paris, the keeper of the privy purse—an excellent man who is not at all proud, but will be delighted to drink with you to the health of the great Napoleon, of whom he is always talking—the second governess," and so on. Marie, it will be seen, had become decidedly acid by this time; but the very pitilessness of her insistence upon the vanity of Liszt's desire to be a *grand seigneur* indicates what a bone of contention it must have been between them all these years. As we know, events proved her to be wrong. She did not know that a new world was soon to be knocking at the ancient doors. After the revolutionary turmoils of 1848 and 1849, the distance between the German princelings and the artists who served them was considerably diminished. Liszt's character and ideals won him considerable respect at Weimar; the relationship between him and the Hereditary Grand Duke (later the reigning Grand Duke Carl Alexander) came as near the affectionate friendship of equals as the etiquette of their respective stations permitted in that epoch. A certain power was given to Liszt's arm by his association with the Princess Wittgenstein, a rich *grande dame* with powerful aristocratic connections. Finally, Weimar was soon to be endowed with an extraordinary prestige in the eyes of Europe by the linking of its name with that of one Richard Wagner, and by the flocking to it of almost all that was best and most eager in the younger life of a new musical Germany. Poor Marie could, of course, foresee none of these things; in the fifteen years or so that had now elapsed since the first linking of her fortunes with those of Liszt not only had he himself

changed considerably but; thanks largely to Wagner, musical
Germany had entered upon a change that was soon to prove
even more vast. For perhaps the only time in his ill-directed life,
Liszt's instinct had been sound. Neither in Paris nor in any
of the larger German towns, such as Berlin, Vienna or Munich,
could he have brought into full being the new life within him
for which he had been so confusedly longing for so many years:
Weimar, and Weimar alone, was ideally fitted for that spiritual
accouchement.

Meanwhile the only Liszt that Marie could see was the past
and present Liszt, the vacillating Liszt of the Swiss, the Italian,
and the Paris years and the years of wandering; and one or
two of the final touches in her portrait of Guermann evidently
came direct from her observation of her sitter. A young German
painter whom Guermann meets in W. . . . is fascinated by
"the rich nature of Guermann, by the charm of his manner,
and by something strange, incomprehensible in him, by the
intellectual disorder and the vague torment in this soul that
was at once so strong and so weak." The Saint-Simonianism of
Guermann's early days comes to the surface in him once more;
he burns to "chastise the pride of the privileged classes" and
"rehabilitate the class of men who are noble but oppressed."
When he sees the enormous extent of the space he has to cover
with frescoes his heart fails him; he doubts whether the talent
he has so far proved himself to possess in works on a smaller
scale can master the greater problems of design that are now
before him. He has days of heartbroken self-examination:
"incapable of taking up his pencil, incapable of ridding himself
of the load that was weighing upon his soul, he would remain for
whole days with his head sunk in his hands, weeping bitter
tears." Once more Marie is drawing from the life; she had been
the pitying witness of many an attack of self-doubt of this kind,
had listened to many a confession that he was tormented by
ideals of a more ambitious kind than he felt he had the power
to realise; and similar doubts were to assail Liszt frequently
in the years to come, and to generate the melancholy that incessantly gnawed at him underneath the mask of stoicism he had
trained himself to wear in public. If Marie could not invent,

she could certainly observe. The many shrewd comments, in her letters, on Sainte-Beuve, George Sand, Lamennais and a score of other notabilities of her circle proves this to the full; and it is only to be expected that her observation should be at its clearest in the case of the complex artist and human being with whom she had spent so many years of intimacy. She knew the Liszt of 1833-44 as no one else did.

The novel, considered as a novel, peters out in sentimental absurdity: Guermann falls ill, sends for Nélida, and dies in the arms of his guardian angel, admitting the wrong he has done her. Marie could not foresee that very soon after the publication of the book in which she had planned this poetical *Tod und Verklärung* for Liszt and herself. he was to find a new Nélida in the person of the Princess, whereupon, as we shall see, the whole tragi-comedy began afresh, with certain minor variations. Nothing is more conclusive as to the central truth of Marie's account of Liszt than the fact that his letters to her are so often reproduced in close detail in his letters to Carolyne. With that aspect of the matter we shall deal shortly. Meanwhile enough evidence has been brought forward to show not only that the account of Marie given by the Princess to Lina Ramann is wickedly false, but that the character of Liszt himself is indelibly stained by the way in which he spoke of Marie in later years. Far from her journal being, as he said, merely *poses et mensonges*, his own letters prove the complete truth of her account of their relations. The old legend of the super-chivalry of Liszt must go by the board. For all the nobility of his character in some respects there was an ineradicable strain of insincerity in him. Even in his most sincere moments he rarely ceased to be something of an actor; and having cast himself—under the influence of the Princess—for the part of the impeccably good *jeune premier* who had been caught by the wiles of a designing siren who was intellectually and morally unworthy of him, he had no scruple whatever about garbling the text of the play in order to secure for himself all the best lines and leave all the worst to Marie.

14

Her offence—a double offence, indeed—was in his eyes unforgivable: she had seen him accurately, at the closest quarters,

for what he was in the years of his greatest weakness and dis-
harmony, and she had wounded him to the quick in the sensitive
self-esteem that was so marked an element of his character.
He never forgave her; he was wanting even in rudimentary
decency on two or three ocasions when most men would have
felt that it was time to relax, if only for a moment, the harshness
of his attitude towards her. He did not address a word to her
when their children Daniel and Blandine died. He was unmoved by the news of her own death. He did, it is true, indulge
in some conventional religious moralising in his letter to his
son-in-law Emile Ollivier (who had married Blandine): "I
thank you for having sent me a copy of Ronchaud's lines on the
death of Madame d'Agoult. Phrase-making is not in my
character [!]; my memory of Mme d'A. is a sorrowful secret;
I confide it to God, imploring Him to grant peace and light to
the soul of the mother of my three dear children." But even
now he cannot refrain from striking a characteristic attitude:
"In her *Esquisses morales* Daniel Stern has written, 'Forgiveness is only a form of contempt.' This is pretentious and false.
The truth has been revealed to us by the Evangelist with the
sublime sweetness of forgiveness. Let us therefore pray to
Our Father who is in heaven to forgive us our offences as we
forgive those who have offended against us."(44) For all his
unctuous profession of charity, he not only never showed, at
any time, the smallest forgiveness for any offence that Marie
may have committed against him, but he acquiesced in the
publication to the world, during his own lifetime, of an account
of her which he must have known in his heart of hearts to be
false. That we are at last able to get to something like the truth
of the matter is entirely due to the fact that Marie had the foresight to make her young grandson Daniel Ollivier(45) the heir

---

(44) Letter of 27th March, 1876, in LZB, VIII, 309.

(45) It is this Daniel Ollivier who has edited the *Mémoires* and the *Correspondance*.

The singer Marianne Brandt perpetrated a monumental *gaffe* on the
occasion of the Countess's death. Taking the conventional view that
Liszt would be prostrated with grief, she wrote to him on 2nd April,
1876, lauding the character and the literary achievements of Daniel

to her literary property; had Liszt and the Princess been able to obtain possession of her journal, her *Mémoires*, and Liszt's letters to her, it is tolerably certain that they would have been destroyed, with the result that the memory of the Countess would have suffered for all time from the comprehensive blackening it had received in Lina Ramann's biography.

It has been urged, in defence of Liszt's implacability, that Marie had committed an unpardonable offence in bringing out a new issue of *Nélida* in 1866: the book had been almost forgotten by that time, Liszt had earned for himself the respect of a considerable section of the musical world by his greater works and by his splendid achievements at Weimar, and the Countess, it is claimed, stooped unnecessarily low in thus holding him up once more to public ridicule. There is a good deal to be said for that point of view, and it is practically certain that the republication of *Nélida* hardened Liszt against her for the rest of his life. Precisely what drove Marie to this unpleasant step we do not know; she had long harboured resentment against Liszt and the Princess, however, for their having taken her children out of her custody, the pious Carolyne holding that Marie's rationalism made her unfit to have the bringing up of them and the moulding of their minds. Marie, for her part, objected to her children passing completely into the charge of one whom she contemptuously, though apparently not accurately, described as "a Polish Jewess." It was not merely that her own feelings were wounded; she felt that the character of the children would suffer, as she explains in a letter of 30th October, 1856, to Emma Herwegh, published for the first time in 1929:

"The details you give me about Liszt interest me greatly. I never speak about him to anyone, for the simple reason that I do not understand the *rôle* he has played between the children and their mother. As for the differences of our younger days, I have forgotten these; nor have I ever thought that he has

---

Stern, and assuring him that she understood how terribly the news of her death must have pained him! (See BHZL, III, 222). The letter should be a warning to all of us when we take up our pens to write conventional letters of condolence.

acted any worse towards me than many others would have done. But I cannot help asking myself by what strange caprice he has imposed on his children a *chance* mother [*i.e.* the Princess] instead of simply allowing their hearts to follow the natural feelings that would have led them in my direction. By his action he has caused himself many a trouble and confusion that he could have spared himself by coming to an understanding with me, as I asked him to do in our common interest. He has brought trouble into their young minds; he has insisted on appearances and *simulations* in place of real sentiments; he has arbitrarily complicated what was the simplest thing in the world; finally he has missed an honourable opportunity to show some respect to the mother of his children and to repair the wrong he has voluntarily or involuntarily wrought. Occasions of this kind present themselves so rarely in a man's life that I cannot comprehend anyone letting one of them escape him. To sum up, *much ado about nothing* is the only result of Liszt's intervention between his children and myself, and I should have imagined that his active life as an artist would have preserved him from such a weakness."(46)

---

(46) HPD, p. 168. It is impossible to reconcile with the theory of Liszt's "chivalry" towards Madame d'Agoult the references he made to her in the latest years of his life. He told Göllerich that she had objected to the children being brought up in the "bourgeois house" of his mother in Paris, whereupon, according to him, he replied, "They are in their right place there, Madame, for my mother's house is a *sanctuary*, in which my innocent children will do well" (GFL, p. 93). There is nothing to this effect in his letters, or any hint that he did not agree with Marie in her anxiety that the children should acquire a better tone than was possible in the company of his mother, who was a none-too-well educated woman of the people. Marie discusses the question soberly and rationally in her letter of 6th December, 1839: "My heart's solitude is complete: I cannot even talk to your mother about the children or you. During the last two years she has entirely lost all that she probably acquired in the way of distinction and intelligence when you were with her. She has sunk into a shabbiness of thought the expression of which I find very painful. I say this to you because I speak to you so frankly about my own people that I believe I have the right to do so where she is concerned. If I pain you, forgive me; in that case I will not talk to you again on this subject until the question of the children's education becomes urgent—when you yourself have realised how impossible it is for you to let them grow up in this atmosphere of commonness" (LZAC, I, 325).

15

The full extent of the Princess's pious malignity where Marie
and her children were concerned has only become evident in
recent years. After the final parting between Marie and Liszt,
the children lived for a while in the house of old Madame Liszt,
but, of course, in the theoretical custody of their mother. It
was not long, however, before the Princess began to give drastic
expression to the hatred she had already conceived for Madame
d'Agoult, a hatred that nourished itself year by year till it came
to its climax in the infamous chapter on Marie in Lina Ramann's
book. The fundamental weakness of Liszt's character has been
shown by the record of his vacillations during the years from
1833 to 1844. With the Princess he was even weaker than with
Marie; where she was concerned he was merely the rabbit
fascinated by the snake. Not long after they had settled down in
Weimar she prevailed on him to have the children placed in the
entire charge of her own former governess, Madame Patersi,
a grim and prim old lady of over seventy, who left Russia for
Paris to take up her new duties in 1850, at which time Blandine
was about fifteen years old, Cosima thirteen, and Daniel eleven.
Madame Patersi made it the object of her life to influence them
against their mother and turn all their thoughts in the direction
of the Princess. Every letter that went to Weimar had to pass
through her hands; she taught the children to speak of the
Princess as their "mother" in their letters to Liszt, and to
address her by that term in their direct letters to her. They saw
Marie sometimes at a concert, however, and were occasionally
invited to her house. The letters of the little Cosima and Blandine to their father (recently published in Du Moulin Eckart's
biography of Cosima) show the deep impression made on the
children by the grace and beauty of their mother, by the extent
of her library, and by the conversation of the distinguished
people they saw at her house. A note in Cosima's diary of 1876,
made after the receipt of the news of her mother's death, reveals
how strong in her still was the memory of the happy but all too

---

Liszt fully recognised that it was necessary, in the children's interest,
that they should be taken out of his mother's hands (see LZAC, II,
75, 88, 109, 277-278).

rare days that she and Blandine were privileged to spend at the Maison Rose: "I cannot describe," she says, "the impressions those Sundays always made on me. I can still see myself devouring with my eyes my mother's wonderful library; and when we returned to our narrow, strict, suppressed life with two seventy-year-old-governesses the impression remained with us of having returned from the realms of the blest."(47)

Marie, as might have been expected, was the perfection of well-bred tact in her relations with the suspicious old dragon of a Madame Patersi, as the girls, young as they are, are quick to note and assure their father. It was because the children were obviously becoming too much fascinated with their mother that, at the bidding of the Princess, Liszt ultimately had them removed to Germany, in spite of the protests of old Madame Liszt. So anxious had the Princess been to rule out the possibility of any pernicious influence on Marie's part upon her children that she had even had their dresses sent to them from Germany, much to the amusement of Marie, who politely tried to convey to Madame Patersi that garments of that kind really were not worn in Paris—a criticism that must have done more than almost anything else to convince the virtuous Carolyne, whose own rather frumpish taste in dress was the subject of bewildered comment even among the male frequenters of her establishment, that the Countess d'Agoult was a thoroughly worldly woman. With the removal of the children to Germany, Marie, of course, lost all real touch with them. But she saw Cosima again in Zürich in 1858, after the latter's marriage to Bülow; and in view of the fact that the young Hans at that time loved Liszt with a dog-like devotion it is interesting to discover that at his first meeting with Marie, who was then a woman of fifty-three, she cast an instantaneous spell upon him. Like everyone else who ever met her, he was fascinated not only by her beauty but by the famous grace of her carriage and her high breeding.

"Daniel Stern," he wrote to Richard Pohl on 24th July, "has made an impression on me that is as great as it was unexpected. Still marvellously beautiful, and noble in form and feature,

---

(47) DMCW, p. 760.

with white hair, she particularly impressed me by her unmistakable resemblance to Liszt in profile and expression, so that
Siegmund and Sieglinde at once came into my mind. In addition, dignity and nobility of bearing without the least effort—a
fine, elegant *laissez-aller* that sets those who are in her company
perfectly at their ease and stimulates them intellectually, leading
them to bring out what is best in themselves. I confess that I
am quite bewitched by it all, and I cannot help thinking what
an unspeakable satisfaction it would be to see this beautiful
and remarkable woman (who in ten years' time will represent
the ideal matron of lively intellect), by the side of the Unique
One [Liszt], giving social completeness to his Olympian being.
I must not think of it, lest I break out into a rage at the parodistic
caricature [the Princess] which at the present moment acts as
the shadow to his light at the Altenburg. And yet how unjust
it would be to rail against that other woman, who has so much
claim to be warmly defended by those who have to some extent
learned to know her. It is just one's sense of natural outward
beauty that protests and must protest against her."(48)

This citation, by the way, affords an incidental illustration of
how little we can rely upon the first publication of any man's
correspondence, in which a prudent editor is always inclined
to suppress whatever he thinks may give pain to some living
friend or relation of this dead person or that. The words "lest
I break out into a rage at the parodistic caricature which at
present acts as the shadow to his light at the Altenburg" are not
to be found in the official edition of Bülow's letters; they have
only lately been restored to the text by Du Moulin Eckart.(49)
They are invaluable as affording us frank contemporary evidence
of how the plentiful absurdities of the Princess Wittgenstein,
and the dubious nature of her influence upon the feeble Liszt,
struck certain habitués of the Altenburg. That Bülow, adoring
his master and benefactor as he did, should thus wish to see
her place taken by the woman for whom neither Liszt nor
the Princess ever had a good word to say, is significant and
illuminating.

---

(48) BB, III, 186.

(49) DMCW, p. 164.

Each fresh document bearing on the subject that has been published in recent years makes it clearer than ever that Liszt's growing animus against Marie was the Princess's work: he was as weak as water in her hands. It is a little difficult to make out his real reaction to his first reading of *Nélida*. In his letters to Marie concerning it, written immediately after the publication of the book, he professes to take a loftily detached view of it, congratulating her on her success, alternately praising and criticising her style and her handling of the characters, and so on. This, of course, is in large part pure pose. There is no doubt he was pained by the book, which did him a great deal of harm in Germany; much of the later opposition to him and mistrust of him was due to the unfavourable impression *Nélida* had given of him as a man of fundamentally weak character, of dubious morality, and something short of ideal sincerity. But he had already schooled himself by this time in a trait that was later to be cultivated by his daughter Cosima—to say the least about the things that hurt him most. His pride forbade him to allow Marie and her friends—to whom, he was well aware, his letters to her on the subject would be shown—the satisfaction of seeing how deep were the wounds she had dealt him: the obvious tactics, therefore, were to simulate an Olympian indifference to them. No one who has studied Liszt in all his complexities and diplomatic finesses can doubt that all his letters of this period that dealt with *Nélida* were written with a view to effect. In a letter of the summer of 1847 to his bosom friend Prince Felix Lichnowsky we see him trying to conceal his chagrin under a mask of lofty sarcasm. "Nélida has written me a letter full of charm and amenity," he says. "I am always enraptured by her rare and lively mind; and whatever may happen I will always be frankly and sincerely devoted to her"—this last a characteristically Lisztian piece of posing.

"Nélida's book has had a business success, and wins the public over to her more than I had hoped for her. This rejoices me sincerely, all the more as I am convinced that, knowing her as I do, her next book will surpass this one in value and talent. My sincere recognition of the style of the book and of certain points in the construction, about which I have written to her, met with her approval; she even did me the honour to say that she found it admirable. If you feel curious about the matter, ask her to send you the original or a copy of my Nélidean letter, addressed to her from Graz(50) she will make no difficulty about doing so, as she has shown it to several friends who, I do not know why, expected me to regard the publication of this novel as an annoying attack on me."(51)

All this was simply a grandiose theatrical gesture of the kind that was so carefully studied by Liszt; even had we not the testimony of one of his closest friends that he was always very watchful of what he said in his letters, knowing as he did that they passed from hand to hand, we should have no difficulty in seeing that his tactics as against the merciless frontal attack of Marie were to pretend that it had left him unmoved. At the same time we must give their due weight to other forces that were operating in him when he wrote these letters. At that date he was too ruefully conscious of the amount of justice in her case against him to be very angry with her, profoundly hurt as he must have been. And we must bear in mind the point that has already been made in Chapter IV—that he found inner support in the reflection that, although everything Marie had said about him was true, it was not the whole truth as he saw the matter, that within himself he had been steadily pressing towards a worthy end all these years, an end in comparison with which the fatuities and vulgarities of his outer life were of minor account. To the passage quoted above from the letter to Felix Lichnowsky he adds, "Frankly, had I not been firmly and reasonably convinced that there was inside me a different fellow from what many people here and there pretended to find, I would long ago have flung the whole wretched business of my wearisome and miserable career out of the window, and occupied myself with eating other more or less appetising sausages in Debreczin or Temesvar."

In his letters of this period to Marie he takes a sly and wholly pardonable pleasure in hitting back at her over *Nélida* whenever

---

(50) This was evidently his letter of 26th May, 1846, now available in the second volume of LZAC, pp. 360 ff.

(51) *Franz Liszts Briefe an den Fürsten Felix Lichnowsky*, in BAYB, pp. 39 ff.

the opportunity presents itself. One of the charges she was used to making against him was that he was excessively vain; and it gave him great delight to be able to quote at some length, in his letter to her of 26th May, 1846, from a review of the book in the *Journal des Débats*, in which the reviewer, Gâchons de Molènes, though anything but kindly disposed towards Liszt, takes Marie to task for the bouquets she has handed out so liberally to herself in the novel. It is clear, however, that for some time after the publication of the book he felt no particular animosity against Marie. He corresponds with her amicably for another three years. The letters run on much the same lines as those of the earlier period: he gives her details about his own life at Weimar and elsewhere, his successes on his concert tours, the operas he is writing, his plans for the future, his meeting with the Princess Wittgenstein, and so on, and takes a flattering interest in Marie's literary work. In July, 1847, he asks her to write for him, on the basis of notes to be supplied by himself, a preface to his *Rhapsodies hongroises*. "I am greatly interested in this work," he says, "and it is absolutely necessary that the profound and intimate sense of this series of compositions shall be eloquently revealed to the public."(52) As late as August, 1848, by which time the Princess was already settled with him in Weimar, he assures Marie that her portrait still hangs where it has been since 1843—in front of his desk. "I love what you write," he tells her a little later, *à propos* of her *Lettres Républicaines*, " for I have loved you, and, as St. Augustine says, to love is to understand."

Then comes a curious change in him, which is obviously the work of the Princess. There is a gap in the correspondence extending from April, 1849, to July, 1855; and when at last he writes to Marie again, this time on the subject of the children, his manner has altered. His tone is businesslike and hard; there is not a sentence in the old affectionate or even friendly key; he is as insulting as one can be under the mask of polite objectivity. He reaches the climax of brutality and indelicacy in the refusal to meet her in Paris in order to discuss the education

(52) LZAC, II, 389.

of the children and the financial provision to be made for them. He has no time for the journey, he says; he suggests that she shall come to Weimar for forty-eight hours, where she will be quite comfortable, while the thirty-hours' journey will be very agreeable in such fine weather. The Princess was plainly bent on not allowing him to see Marie alone, even to discuss the future of her own children with him. It is impossible to believe that these letters are Liszt's own work: their careful composition shows no traces of his own loose epistolary style, and every-where suggest that of the Princess, especially in their occasional resort to pious platitude. It will be difficult to persuade any instructed reader that the letters were not drafted by the Prin-cess and merely copied out and signed by Liszt; and that he should have been willing to assume the responsibility for them is the most convincing proof possible of that often malign personal influence of the Princess upon him that was the regret of almost everyone who knew the pair. The letters must have left in Marie a rankling resentment, in the light of which her subsequent reissue of *Nélida* becomes more comprehensible now than it was at one time. Probably that second blow was aimed less at Liszt himself than at the woman whom Marie had such good reason to detest.

16

Liszt and the Countess met twice in Paris in 1861, and again in 1866. He gives a long account of their conversation on the second of the former occasions in a letter to the Princess of 29th June, 1861. With Carolyne too far away to cast her evil shadow over them, the two poor ghosts seem to have talked for a moment calmly, rationally, resignedly of their shattered past. "Guermann's walls are already painted," he told her, "and still others will be painted, without the least attention being paid to the stupid things that are said or printed." He described him-self as now living alone. It was a singular delusion on his part, for half his soul was no longer his own but the property of Carolyne, while his time and his energies, then and later, were notoriously wasted on all kinds of unworthy people; but his remark at any rate points to his ideal of a life of solitude and

M

renunciation devoted to good works, however imperfectly he might realise that ideal in practice. Then comes a passage that throws a light on the true source, or one of the sources, of their tragic misunderstanding of each other. Marie's complaint had always been that his life lacked inner direction, that he was not strong enough to cast aside the dross in his complex nature and follow up consistently the golden vein of his better genius as composer. To his thinking—we shall see later to what extent he was labouring under a delusion—he had at last achieved this inner unity and self-direction. He claimed that the course of his life had really been strictly "consequent," as he put it.

"When she heard me speak thus of myself," he writes to the Princess, "of my egoism and ambition, of the part of myself that I gave to the public and the part I reserve for the artist in myself, of the perfect identity of my efforts of former days with my ideas of today, of the permanence of this egoism of mine that she found so 'hateful,' she was deeply moved, and her face was bathed in tears. I kissed her forehead, for the first time for long years, and said to her, 'Come, Marie, let me speak to you in the language of the peasants: May God bless you! Wish me no evil!' For a moment she could not reply, but her tears flowed faster than before. Ollivier had told me that when he was travelling in Italy with her he had often seen her weep bitterly in places that particularly recalled our youth to her. I told her that I had been moved by this. She said to me almost stammeringly, 'I shall always remain faithful to Italy—and to Hungary!' Thereupon I left her quietly."(53)

---

(53) LZB, V, 198, 199.

CHAPTER VI

LISZT AND THE PRINCESS WITTGENSTEIN

I

Liszt must have had constantly before his eyes, in the years between 1840 and 1847, the plan of giving up the career of a piano virtuoso and settling down as a serious composer. But two things were necessary before he could realise this ideal—a woman, and money. He needed a woman of a character stronger than his own to be the recipient of his confidences and to help him to overcome his secret weaknesses, especially the blend of indolence and self-doubt that so often made the spectacle of his empty desk-chair a silent reproach to him. We find him, in 1845, seeking the hand of the Countess Valentine Cessiat, the niece of Lamartine. (The amused reader will note once more his passion for an alliance with an aristocrat). The Countess, however, declined his proposal, as she was unwilling to leave her uncle, who, she felt, needed her care. As for the money question, which is generally the vital one in the affairs of men and of kingdoms, while Liszt, in spite of his numerous bene-factions, had laid aside enough to maintain him comfortably for the rest of his life, the fact that his new love was a very rich woman was probably not regarded by him as, of itself, dis-qualifying her for the post of companion. It is true that he tells Marie, on 10th February, 1847, that there is no truth in the rumour that he is about to marry his latest conquest—that he would find her "three millions" an embarrassment, and that, if ever he should "take the plunge," he will do so, he hopes, "with more grace." All the same, the Princess's financial inde-pendence would not be unwelcome to him in the new circum-stances he had in view.

On 2nd February (Russian style), 1847, he played in Kiev. Among his auditors was the young Princess Jeanne Elisabeth Carolyne von Sayn-Wittgenstein; and the overwhelming impression his playing made on her was added to by a hearing of one of his compositions, a Paternoster, in a local church. She at once lost not only her head but her heart to the brilliant and engaging young man. Fate willed that he should make her personal acquaintance: he had to call on her to thank her for her liberal subscription to the funds of a concert he was about to give, as usual, in the cause of charity. She invited him to her property in Woronince: he stayed there only a few days, his concert engagements calling him for the moment elsewhere. They kept up an eager correspondence during his absence, and some time later, in the summer, they met again in Odessa. By now their mutual passion was no longer to be fought against: after his recital at Elizabethgrad Liszt went back with the Princess (in October) to Woronince, where, apart from a few days in November, he remained until near the end of the following January. He had entered into a bond that was to bring him at first a splendid heightening of all his powers and a concentration such as his life had hitherto never known, later a succession of trials and disillusions that he bore with extraordinary patience, and from which death alone was to release him. It was under the first spell of Carolyne's enthusiasm for his music that he began to work on his *Dante Symphony*, the symphonic poem *Ce qu'on entend sur la montagne*, and several of his finest works for the piano.

2

When Liszt first met her, the Princess was a young woman of twenty-eight. Her parents were Poles domiciled in Russia, where they owned a large property that passed to Carolyne on the death of her father; it carried with it some 30,000 serfs. At the age of seventeen she had married Prince Nikolaus von Sayn-Wittgenstein, a German by origin, but a cavalry captain in the Russian army. (There was one child of the marriage—a daughter, Marie, born in February, 1837, who married, in

October, 1859, Prince Konstantin zu Hohenlohe-Schillingsfürst.) Carolyne's marriage soon proved to have been a mistake,
as her mother's had been. Her parents lived apart: as a child
Carolyne divided her time between her father's estate in the
government of Kiev each summer, and tours through Europe
with her society-loving mother each winter. Even Liszt, during
the years when he worshipped her, never sought to persuade
either himself or others that she was physically beautiful. There
was a suggestion of the Oriental in her features. Adelheid von
Schorn, one of her intimates during the Weimar years, describes
her as having clear blue eyes, a pale complexion, and blond hair;
her almost invariable costume comprised a simple black robe
with a loose jacket, and a black lace cap the lilac ribbons of
which were tied under her chin.(1) Malwida von Meysenbug,
who made her acquaintance in Rome in the winter of 1864-65,
tells us that Carolyne's mother had often been distressed at her
child's plainness, but found a certain prospective consolation in
the assurance that she would be beautiful after the Resurrection.
At an early age Carolyne acquired a passion for strong cigars—
she had contracted the habit through so often sitting up into
the small hours of the morning, reading to her father; she
smoked incessantly until almost her last years, giving it up
only when she observed that it made a Roman lady of her
acquaintance, who was also addicted to cigars, physically plain
and in various ways objectionable.

Liszt was perhaps first attracted to her, in part, by her title:
he collected princesses and countesses as other men collect rare
butterflies, or Japanese prints, or first editions.(2) Her great

---

(1) SZM, p. 67. This was in the Weimar epoch. Later, in Rome, she
decked herself out in the brightest colours, telling Malwida von Meysenbug that in doing so she was gratifying God, who had given all kinds of
colours to His flowers.

(2) As indefatigable in love as in composition, he gave the nineteenth
century not only some of its most notable music but several of its best
musicians. His works in the latter genre, however, were issued to the
world under other signatures than his. It would be indiscreet, of course,
to mention the names of those who are generally credited with the
honour of having owned Liszt for a father.

wealth promised to be at his service for the realisation of his
artistic plans. She shared with him his ideal of a union of the
various arts; and, although the scheme ultimately came to
nothing, she was prepared, in the first days of their union, to
spend 20,000 thalers (about £3,000) on a diorama to accompany
a performance of the *Dante Symphony* which he was then
projecting. He was dazed by her culture, which was considerable for a woman of her class. She read widely all her life and
commented exuberantly and confidently on what she read,
unfortunately not always being content with a verbal revelation,
but committing her views to print. Liszt became sincerely
attached to her, and held a high opinion of her intellectual as
well as her more purely feminine qualities. She, for her part,
expended on him a love that was none the less genuine for the
gushing schoolgirl extravagance in which it often found expression. During the periods when they happened to be
separated in space from each other for a few days she kept him
lavishly supplied with bulletins recording her smallest doings:
Liszt, for his part, tried conscientiously to live up to the
exacting standard she set him in this respect, but was often
hard put to it to find matter enough in sleepy Weimar to pad
out the number of pages she was wont to expect of him. She
was not particularly musical; but he found considerable support
and encouragement for his work in her purely intellectual
qualities, though her intense religiosity is probably answerable
for the excessive development of some of the weaker aspects
of him as an artist. But Liszt, like Wagner, needed feminine
society and feminine belief in him if he was to face the burdens
of existence with courage; and there is no evidence that he ever
became critical of a mode of amorous expression in Carolyne's
letters which posterity finds faintly comic. As Raabe puts it,
"she could express the most intimate of her heart's commotions
only in the bombast and fustian of the most high-flown speech;
year after year, in letter after letter, she literally shrieked her
love into his face." Her normal epistolary style, where Liszt
was concerned, was of this order:

"I kiss your hands and kneel before you, prostrating my forehead to your feet, laying, like the Orientals, my finger on my

brow, my lips, and my heart, to assure you that my whole mind, all the breath of my spirit, all my heart exist only to bless you, to glorify you, to love you unto death and beyond—beyond even death, for love is stronger than death."(3)

And again, in 1853:

"I am at your tiny feet, beloved—I kiss them, I roll myself under the soles of them and place them on the nape of my neck—I sweep with my hair the places where you are to walk and prostrate myself under your footprints. . . . You know that all these things are not Oriental hyperbole but *faits accomplis*. . . . You know how I adore you—O how I long to see you again!—O dear masterpiece of God whom I adore, and how could I help adoring the Good Boze [Polish for God] who created you so good, so beautiful, so perfect, so made to be cherished, adored and loved to death and madness!"(4)

Though other people were apt to find the Princess's rhapsodies upon life, art, literature and religion a trifle tiring—Wagner soon wearied of them, while poor Bülow could never spend an evening in her company without getting a headache—they were wholly to the liking of Liszt, who was himself prone to similar floridities in the style of the prose works of his that were intended for publication. Six years after the commencement of their association he wrote to his mother: "I do not know how Princess G. could tell you that Princess Wittgenstein is not beautiful. I, who claim to be a connoisseur in these matters, maintain that she *is* beautiful, indeed very beautiful, for her soul lends her face the transfiguration of the highest beauty."(5)

---

(3) From a letter in the Weimar archives, published for the first time in RLL, p. 149.

(4) From letters published for the first time in RLL, pp. 149, 255. Schumann's daughter Eugenie has recorded her astonishment when one day the Princess knelt down before Liszt to light his cigarette (SRS, p. 357). This kind of thing, of course, was very much to the taste of Liszt.

(5) LZBM, p. 101. Her daughter, Princess Marie Hohenlohe, in her old age told Ludwig Karpath that her mother, "when she was being painted, would keep on saying 'Not like me, but beautiful!' for she wanted to go down to posterity in a beautiful form" (KBG, p. 266).

And in the same year he writes to the Princess herself:

"I have suffered so much only because I want to give you everything — everything — without reserve or restriction — everything as it is set down in the centre of that symbolical ring of pure gold I gave you on 22nd October, 1847, swearing to myself that I would never be false to it, never let this circle be cut or broken; and I think I have kept this promise, and I still wish to be yours alone, yours with every fibre of my being, every facet of my life, and to give you everything without taking anything from others, without repudiating the debts I contracted on my first entry into life."(6)

3

Liszt had played at Weimar for the first time in the latter days of November, 1841, first of all at the Court, then in a public concert, the proceeds of which latter, amounting to 526 thalers, he had given to a charity. He was rewarded by the reigning Grand Duke Carl Friederich of Sachsen-Weimar with the Cross of the Order of the White Falcon, First Class. On the occasion of the Hereditary Grand Duke Carl Alexander's marriage to Princess Sophie, daughter of the King of the Netherlands, in October, 1842, Liszt was invited to the town. He played at the Court and again in the theatre; and the Grand Duke now conferred on him the appointment of Kapellmeister. He was to be "unattached"; the regular Kapellmeister was to remain undisturbed in his functions as head of the Opera, Liszt merely undertaking to spend three months of each year in Weimar and conduct some concerts there. The salary was nominal—a mere 1,000 thalers, which were apparently paid out of the privy purse of the Grand Duchess Maria Pavlovna. To this there were generally added a few hundred thalers per annum for compositions supplied for Court occasions and

---

(6) He means, presumably, his obligations towards Marie d'Agoult and his three children by her. The letter, which is in the archives of the Liszt Museum at Weimar, is published for the first time in RLL, p. 248.

A curious light is thrown on Liszt's grotesque reverence for titles by the fact that, though the Princess always addressed him with the familiar "Du," he could never bring himself, in spite of her repeated requests, to employ anything but the more formal and respectful "Sie".

for music-making with the ladies of the Grand Ducal family.

Weimar was at that time a tiny town of merely some 12,000 inhabitants. As was the case with most similar capitals of the smaller German Duchies, a certain degree of culture in Court and professional circles was counterbalanced by an almost complete lack of anything of the kind among the people as a whole. Liszt was soon driven to the angry conclusion that "the Weimarers are jackasses." With his experience of big capitals like Paris, London, Vienna and Berlin he must have known from the first that this quaint little place could, at the best, provide him with only limited resources for the realisation of his ideals. But, as it turned out, the association with Weimar had its business and its diplomatic as well as its artistic side: sooner or later there was bound to be trouble with the Russian authorities over his illicit association with the Princess. On the plea that she had been a minor when her marriage took place, and an unwilling party to the contract, Carolyne had hoped to obtain a divorce, and, in spite of her being a Catholic, permission to remarry. The bar to this, however, was her huge fortune; her husband and his relatives were not inclined to let so rich a prize slip through their fingers, and they pulled every possible wire, political and religious, to retain it. Before her flight in March, 1848, she had taken the precaution to realise secretly, in western currency, so much of her property as was completely under her control; but the landed estates in Russia that had come to her from her father were another matter, and, as she soon discovered, her husband was not prepared to let her and her lover derive any benefit from these. The Grand Duchess Maria Pavlovna of Sachsen-Weimar being a sister of the Czar, the Princess and Liszt hoped they could count on her influence with her brother—a hope that was destined to be disappointed, for the estates were sequestrated, and the Czar lent himself to the machinations of the clerical party that made a divorce and a re-marriage to Liszt impossible for the Princess. A great part of the fortune she had saved from the wreck went to her daughter on the latter's marriage, so that all in all the Princess was in the end not much more than very handsomely provided for.

4

On their first settling in Weimar, the Princess, who had
arrived there in July, 1848, took up her abode in a roomy house
that was destined to become famous in the annals of music—the
Altenburg, situated on a little hill near the town. (At first she
occupied only the first floor; later the Grand Duchess bought
the house, and the Princess rented the whole of it from her).
Liszt lived for some time at the "Erbprinz" Hotel. The reigning
house tactfully turned a blind eye on the association of the pair.
No scruple was shown, at first, about receiving the Princess at
Court, but even after Liszt had removed to the Altenburg for
good, all official documents during the remaining twelve years
in Weimar were still addressed to him at the hotel. When, later,
the Princess refused to obey the Czar's order to return to
Russia, she was formally banished from that country, after
which, of course, she could no longer be received at the Weimar
Court, and some of the courtiers found it politic not to associate
with her too openly. The virtuous burghers of Weimar, for
their part, looked askance at what they regarded as an immoral
union; and when the Altenburg became, as it did in time, the
centre of a swirl of life of a kind to which the sober little town
had not been accustomed, they crossed themselves piously at
the thought of such godless goings-on as were reported to them.
The strange appearance of the Princess, her equally strange
habits, her habit of turning night into day, her incessant cigar-
smoking, all made her an object of bourgeois suspicion; while
the sleepy little place was disturbed by the sometimes discredit-
able pranks of the crowd of lively young people, pupils of Liszt
and so on, who soon descended upon the Altenburg. Liszt
suffered acutely at times from the mistrust and ill-will he felt to
be in the air about him, and from the spiritual loneliness to
which he was largely condemned.

It is no part of the purpose of the present volume to tell in
detail the story of the magnificent work Liszt did in Weimar.
To his eternal glory, he recognised almost at once the superlative
genius of Wagner, who, from May, 1849, was a political refugee
in Switzerland. On 28th August, 1850, Liszt gave the first
performance of *Lohengrin*, and at a single bound Weimar

became the centre of what was soon to be known as the New German School. For another eight years he threw himself with the utmost zeal and disinterestedness into the production of works in all genres by composers of all schools. But he was hampered by the paucity of the resources at his disposal in the theatre and by the reluctance of a considerable portion of the Weimar public to follow his lead; while the new Intendant appointed in 1857, Dingelstedt, who was more interested in drama than in opera, is said to have employed every means, fair and foul, to turn the theatre in his own direction. The hissing of Cornelius's *Barber of Bagdad* at its first performance on 15th December, 1858, was the final blow; Liszt, angry and disgusted, gave up the struggle and tendered his resignation to the Grand Duke, though he still continued to live in the town for a while.

Our present concern, however, is not with Liszt as a composer and conductor but with Liszt as a man, and more especially with that dualism in his nature that is the special thesis of the present volume.

5

The Princess's hold upon him was very strong. Being constituted as he was, he was immensely impressed by her title. He was almost equally impressed by her erudition. Again and again in his letters we find him regretting, in mature life, the insufficiency and the haphazard nature of his own early education. Intensively trained as he had been from childhood for the *rôle* of a piano virtuoso, he could hardly have had much experience either of the real world or of the world of books until about 1833, when he was twenty-two years old. He no doubt did a fair amount of reading during the earlier years of his association with Madame d'Agoult; but as his compositions and arrangements during this period are quite numerous it is doubtful whether he had much time for the thorough exploration of other intellectual fields. From 1840 to 1847 his restless touring of all Europe could have left him with little superfluous time or energy, except for a few weeks each summer; and such as he had went into the compositions and transcriptions of this epoch, which were numerous. Though he always handled the written word with some difficulty, he probably exaggerated his deficiencies in general intellectual matters, for his letters show him to have been keenly interested in books of various kinds and in politics.(7) The motive of regret for lost opportunities recurs, however, too often in his correspondence and elsewhere for us to be able to ignore it. We may take it that he was sadly conscious that his non-musical culture was not what it might have been; and so he was in a fit state to be impressed by the wide reading of the Princess and her confident expression of opinion upon every subject under the sun.

Her religiosity, again, gave her great power over him, for religion had been from the beginning as strong a motive force of his being as music. (One of the things that had impressed him most deeply at Woronince had been Carolyne's private chapel, in which the mass was celebrated regularly either by a local or a wandering priest, the Princess or her daughter sometimes reading the prayers). In an annexe to the Altenburg stood Liszt's work room—the "blue room"—and bedroom, and a small oratory. For the most part he and the Princess worked side by side in the blue room, resorting to the oratory in moments when the consolations of religion were necessary to enable them to bear the plentiful trials and disappointments of their lives. In moments of depression and discouragement, therefore, Liszt had temple and priestess close at hand; and as his life in Weimar was one long crescendo of vexations, Carolyne came to be identified more and more with the religious moods that were his ultimate support in times of trouble.

To all these influences emanating from the Princess was added another that was equally strong—the sense of what she had sacrificed for him. Her hopes of a divorce and marriage with Liszt were destined not to be realised; her social position gradually became more and more equivocal in the tiny town, while, as we have seen, her Russian estates had been finally

---

(7) Several times, in his letters, he confesses the difficulty he has always had in expressing himself in words, a difficulty which, he said once, increased with the years. On the other hand, he composed with the greatest facility—sometimes, one fears, with too much facility.

sequestrated by the Czar. Liszt must have had abundant reason to reflect that this was the second time a woman had had to suffer grievously on his account. He was older and less violently egoistic now, and, though he must have occasionally been conscious of his chains, less inclined, for many reasons, to break them. His whole life long he remembered with gratitude the sacrifices Carolyne had made for him, all the slights and sufferings she had uncomplainingly borne for him, and, above all, the fact that it was her strong hand that had kept him steadily at the work of composition. His career as a pianist having been ended, there was nothing now to keep him away from Weimar for any length of time; and Carolyne saw to it that while he was under her charge he really worked. One of the many paradoxes of his nature was the combination in him of an immense capacity and desire for work and an equally immense indolence, at times, where original composition was concerned, an indolence that was due in part to his unappeasable appetite for society, in part, one suspects, to a strain of self-doubt in him that ran like a "fault" through a gold-bearing reef. Out of very shame, as well as out of reverence for the Princess and gratitude towards her, he could not be idle in her presence, for her whole life at Weimar was devoted to the one task of not merely helping but making him fulfil the lofty mission to which she felt he had been ordained.

6

His ambition was certainly boundless: it was in the early Weimar days that he told Fétis that his purpose in life was not merely to write articles (he was no doubt referring mainly to his long essays on the *Flying Dutchman*, *Tannhäuser*, and *Lohengrin*), but to win for himself a permanent place in musical history. And Carolyne was as ambitious for him as he was for himself. She had no great liking for opera, and had the less difficulty in turning Liszt's mind away from his early essays in this genre because he soon recognised that while Wagner had dealt a mortal blow to opera of the older type, in the specifically Wagnerian sphere it would be hopeless for him to attempt to compete with his great colleague. His own gifts, he now felt, could find full realisation only in giving a new direction to orchestral music by infusing a poetic purpose into it; and this ideal chimed to perfection with the ideas of Carolyne upon the nature and the inter-relation of the two arts. She was convinced that Liszt was a greater composer than Wagner,(8) and when the superiority of the latter became manifest to the world in general she became decidedly lukewarm towards the man whom she came to regard as Liszt's "rival": it was largely due to her machinations that for some years there was an estrangement between the two. But with all her faults she cannot be denied the credit of having not only encouraged him to do his best work but virtually stood over him while he did it. It is to the Weimar epoch that we owe the symphonic poems, the piano sonata, the two piano concertos, the *Faust Symphony*, the *Dante Symphony* and other important works, as well as the commencement of *St. Elizabeth*. Under no influence but that of Carolyne, with her triple hold upon him through her religion, her sacrifices, and her belief in him, that was greater than his own belief in himself, would he have produced anything like this quantity of work. It saddened her in later years, when they no longer lived in the same house, to find him disintegrating in this respect. In 1882, when begging the faithful Adelheid von Schorn to care for the lonely and failing old man while he was in Weimar, she described her own struggle with him in the first Weimar years:

"I look upon all you are doing for Liszt as being done for myself, and thank you for it. In this matter you have hit the right nail on the head. For twelve years [in Weimar] I had to

---

(8) "She prophesied a greater future for Liszt's music than for Wagner's. Her *ceterum censeo* was that Liszt would dominate the world; and she would sometimes ask people naïvely in her broken German, 'What will people say of Wagner in another fifty years?' (CMC, I, 162). She was convinced that Liszt's orchestration was better than Berlioz's, a point on which Peter Cornelius ventured to differ from her. See his account to his mother of the episode in his letter of 23rd February, 1855 (CAB, I, 196). Fond as he was of the Princess, Cornelius could not help feeling that it was bad for her to discuss questions of this kind only with her own guests, who, for the most part, agreed with her out of politeness, and so increased her belief in her own infallibility on every subject.

look after him in this way; I had to do my own work in the same
room with him, otherwise he would never have composed any
of the works of this period. It is not genius he lacks, but the
capacity to sit still (*Sitzfleisch*)—industry, prolonged application. Unless some one helps him in this respect he is impotent;
and when the consciousness of his impotence takes possession
of him he has to resort to stimulants. This makes his condition
still worse, and so the vicious circle widens."(9)

It was precisely the situation the Countess d'Agoult had so
often had to face—Liszt's fits of indolence and self-doubt and
his passion for worldly distractions making it difficult for him to
settle to work, despair at his impotence driving him to stimulants or anodynes, and the reaction from these sinking him in
a still deeper pit of depression and self-disgust. The more
evidence we accumulate as to the real Liszt during his middle
and later periods the more it becomes evident that Marie is the
most veracious of witnesses with regard to him. It was well for
the Princess, and for him, that he was an older and slightly
wiser man when he came under her influence, and that his profound sense of obligation towards her made him bend his neck
under the yoke, instead of turning angrily on her, as had been
his way with Marie, to revenge on her the outrage on his self-
esteem that was subtly involved in his own recognition of his
weakness. At the same time it is not improbable that many of
the faults in Liszt's musical work are due to his having settled
down at his desk as a matter of loyalty to Carolyne rather than
under the stress of imperious inspiration. And certainly her
influence upon his art was occasionally dubious, if not actually
harmful. He was at one time very much inclined to attempt an
opera on a text—*Die Kinder der Haide*—that was afterwards
set by Rubinstein; but Carolyne persuaded him against the
plan. It was Wagner's advice to him to let the *Dante Symphony*
die away in ethereal strains; but Carolyne insisted on another
and more showy ending. For the same symphony she drafted
a long Foreword the overloaded sentiment of which has not
exactly helped to commend that work to the musical world.
Under her influence he, in later life the most tolerant of men,

---

(9) SZM, p. 432. More will be said on this subject later.

added to the second edition of his book on the Zigeuner an indiscreet chapter on the Jews, which brought him some violent attacks in the German and Austrian press; and she is directly responsible for many of the purple passages that disfigure his discerning articles on Wagner's operas and his book on Chopin.

We have seen how Carolyne forced him to remove his children from the custody of their own mother, placing them first of all under the care of Madame Patersi, then sending them to Bülow's mother in Berlin. Cosima, in her book on her father, draws attention to the difference in tone between two letters written by him to his son in 1852 and 1854 respectively, after the boy had distinguished himself in his examinations. The second letter, as Cosima says, is "expansive, intimate, tender;" the other is "exceedingly severe in tone, even imperious." The explanation is that the second letter was written, unknown to Carolyne, from Vienna, while the first was written in Weimar under her watchful eye: "we see," says Cosima, "how intent the Princess was on not permitting any pernicious weakness on his part towards his son to get the upper hand in him."(10) It is only one instance among many of the extent to which Liszt was dominated by the stronger personality of the Princess.

7

Two totally different impressions of Liszt can be obtained by the choice, on a biographer's part, of this or that section of his correspondence to illustrate a special thesis. Liszt's letters

(10) WFL, p. 18. The two letters in question will be found in the appendix to Cosima's book. In the Weimar letter, Liszt sternly tells Daniel that he must be ambitious for more and more difficult successes: "you would not be my son, and I should have to renounce you as such, if you were not animated by a sincere passion for work," and so on in the same strain. The letter insists so strongly, almost harshly, indeed, on the need for a man "to acquire his liberty, his morality, his value and his grandeur by the progressive ennobling of his faculties and his nature," on idleness being the mother of all the vices, and so forth, that the Princess's hand is unmistakable. All this to a boy of thirteen! The Weimar letter is quite different in tone: Liszt talks affectionately to his child, pointing out how greatly he himself had suffered in days gone by through the defects in his education, and wishing his son better luck than he has had.

to people in general during his Weimar period show him wearing his mask. He appears to be all energy, courage, will: we see a man of not only extraordinary goodness of heart, bestowing his generosities on all and sundry, the undeserving not less than the deserving, free, as no other musician has ever been or is ever likely to be, from the smallest suspicion of self-seeking, personal enmity, or jealousy, inflexibly bent on returning good for evil, incapable of letting the most flagrant ingratitude on the part of some of those whom he had benefited—Clara Schumann, for example—blind him to such merits as they undoubtedly possessed, the priest, if ever there was one, of a religion of art. But we have only to turn to his correspondence with the women in whose sympathetic presence he did not feel it necessary to wear his mask to see him under quite another aspect. This man who seemed to front the world with a courage that no rebuff could daunt, with an idealism that no obloquy could cause to falter, is seen to be, in his secret self, the same tortured, divided soul that Marie knew.

His cries of despair to Marie are all duplicated, sometimes almost word for word, in his letters to the Princess and to Agnes Street.(11) He tells the latter of his difficulty in settling down to work. He is often sad and weary; on 4th May, 1855, he tells her that for the last week it has seemed to him almost impossible to go on living. Life is a long suicide, he says later, a suicide that has to be transformed into sacrifice by faith. "I suffer terribly, and at the same time I shrink from confessing the wounds with which my heart is bleeding." "You know that my maxim is that one ought to stifle and strangle certain emotions, and give no heed to the call of the something in us that is the very foundation of our life." He spends his days "dreaming and praying," trying to fight down his sadness and discouragement:

"I am mortally sad: I can say nothing and listen to nothing. Only prayer can console me, and that only now and then;

---

(11) Agnes Street (*née* Klindworth) came to study with him in Weimar in 1853, bringing with her her two little sons. Liszt fell in love with her. It is to her that the letters in the third volume of his correspondence—given to the world as *Briefe an eine Freundin*—are addressed. They range from 1855, when she quitted Weimar, to the year of his death (1886).

for I can no longer pray with any continuity, however imperiously I may feel the need to do so. May God give me grace to overcome this moral crisis; may the light of His pity lighten my darkness!" For all the love and care the Princess lavishes on him, he suffers in secret. But he cannot speak to anyone of his sufferings; "I have made it a habit to pour out the abundance of my heart only in music, which is a sort of mother tongue to me."

The same motive runs through his letters to the Princess. To her, as to no one else, he can reveal himself in all his weakness, all his self-doubt. He tells her of all he feels to be lacking in himself—"the difficulties I experience in finding a form that will be even moderately satisfactory for this flux and reflux of feelings, of ideas, of prayers, of lamentations, of supreme hopes that fill my heart, that will never have any witness but you, my dear unique one, you who are my glorious portion, on earth and in heaven." "May God grant," he writes again, in almost the very words with which Marie had been so familiar, "that I may become less and less unworthy of you. There are times when I feel so feeble, so broken, so terribly depressed." And just as formerly he professed to be unable to live when separated from Marie, so now he assures Carolyne that the days when she is not with him are pure wretchedness, while on the days when she is with him he realises his own insufficiency in comparison with her.

He was, in fact, essentially unchanged since the d'Agoult days, except that now he was older and therefore more tolerant. We may be fairly sure that had it still been his lot to spend the greater part of the year away from Carolyne, as had formerly been the case with Marie, other attractions would have proved too much for him. As it was, even in Weimar there were episodes with women that led to much unhappiness between him and the Princess, though she learned, in time, to stifle her resentment, for Liszt had an unlimited capacity for abject repentance. But it was rarely that they were separated for long, so that her hold upon him never relaxed during the twelve years they spent together. Looking at the matter from one point of view, we may reasonably regret, for his sake, that he ever left Weimar. Having at last, after the fiasco of *The Barber of Bagdad*, severed the chains that bound him to public life there, he might conceivably have resigned himself to complete solitude with Carolyne and thrown himself into his work of orchestral composition. It might have meant a gradual estrangement from some of his friends; but at any rate so long as he knelt upon the adjacent prie-dieu to that of Carolyne he would have worked. As it was, the Fates drove both of them forth—and separated them. The reality and the force of Carolyne's influence on him in the Weimar days, and the complete truth of Marie's diagnosis of him, are shown by the way his will and his spirit cracked after leaving Weimar. Even Peter Raabe is constrained to admit that the spring within him was henceforth broken, the spring that had helped him "to remould the technique of the piano, to give life to programme music, to clear the way for Wagner. Henceforth a great task was lacking to him, and his life went to pieces." He was only fifty when he quitted Weimar, and he still had twenty-five years to live—a third of his whole life. He produced some fine work during this period, but on the whole the years from 1861 to 1886 are a lamentable record of disappointment, vacillation, failure. With the removal of Carolyne's strong hand, he was completely unable to regulate his life with anything approaching wisdom. We find him torn between the same conflicting influences, wrecked upon the same reefs, as in the d'Agoult days, the only difference being that the flaws in his character that had formerly, when the sap of life had run more strongly in him, kept him fluctuating incessantly between raw folly and passionate rebellion against his vices, now brought him, for the most part, only to a melancholy religious submission to what he knew to be incurable.

8

The line taken by the Liszt biographers and by the musical historians has always been that the Weimar public as a whole behaved with nothing but the basest ingratitude towards Liszt. That proposition, however, perhaps needs a little reconsideration today: the historians, one ventures to suggest, have been just a trifle too ready to see the matter entirely through Liszt's eyes. There are two sides to every case; and the other side of the present case does not seem to have been given its full due. Carl Maria Cornelius, the son and biographer of the composer of the *Barber of Bagdad*, is apparently the only modern writer on the subject to suggest that there may have been another side to the Weimar case. It has become the fashion to regard Liszt and his circle as a noble band of Samsons surrounded by a horde of Philistines. But in no community, not even the smallest village, does it ever happen that all the wise and virtuous people live on one side of the street and all the fools and scoundrels on the other. Commonsense decides, then, that Carl Maria Cornelius is right when he says that "we must not fall into the old error of the Lisztians, who represented the inhabitants of the Altenburg as independent intellectuals and the inhabitants of Weimar as hidebound Philistines."(12) There were many highly cultivated people in the town and neighbourhood—men of letters, artists, scientists, and so on—whose general culture certainly surpassed that of Liszt in breadth and depth; and it will be tolerably safe to assume that a few of the other denizens of Weimar were not wholly lacking in intelligence. Peter Cornelius, whose contemporary testimony in all matters connected with Liszt, Wagner and other leading personalities of the period is particularly valuable, because of the penetration of his judgment on the one hand and his independence of spirit on the other, steadily refused to believe that the fact that some one in Weimar differed from Liszt and the Princess automatically wrote him down as a fool or a knave. A man of wide culture himself, he could find only one half of his spiritual home in the Altenburg; for the other half he was glad to resort—even at the risk of offending the Princess, to whom he was greatly attached—to the conversation of the anti-Lisztian artists and literary men of the town.

The opposition to Liszt, if all of it is not strictly justifiable at the bar of history, is readily explicable in terms of the place and time. Liszt did not carry the whole town with him in his plans; but what town has ever existed in which the whole of the

---

(12) CMC, I, 157.

inhabitants were willing to give their intellectual and artistic conscience into the keeping of one man, however great, however disinterested? A fairly large section of the Weimar public supported him warmly; if the remainder were apathetic, no more was to be expected of ordinary human nature. The importance of the failure of the *Barber of Bagdad* seems to have been exaggerated by the historians, following the lead of Liszt himself: the records make it clear enough that the opposition was organised by the Dingelstedt clique, which managed to make an uproar quite out of proportion to its numbers. (The same thing happened again in Paris in 1861, when the majority of the audience wanted to listen attentively to *Tannhäuser*, but the Jockey Club phalanx made it impossible for them to do so). As regards the Weimar situation as a whole, people of a different way of thinking from Liszt were surely as entitled to wish the Court theatre to go in their direction as he was to try to turn it in his; and there was a good deal to be said for the local point of view that while the meagre finances of the place made it fundamentally impossible for it ever to become a leading operatic centre, the increased expenditure that Liszt demanded for opera acted as a check on the development of the other side of the theatre—the spoken drama—for the cultivation of which the town was better suited. One need not give the verdict in the dispute unconditionally to Liszt's opponents: but at all events they had a case which only sheer partisanship can induce the modern biographers to ignore.

And if it is the duty of the modern historian to try to see these facts of the case as they presented themselves to contemporaries in 1848 and the following years, not as they appear in the romantic falsification that all historical facts undergo when used later for the purposes of sentimental biography, it is still more his duty to try to see Liszt and his associates as Weimar saw them. People who live in the thick of a movement do not see it from the lofty, detached standpoint of history, but in terms of the personalities of the moment; and the personalities of the Liszt circle were not altogether of the kind to make the New German movement in music popular. Liszt's personality—a passionate and occasionally arrogant one in those days—did not endear him to the multitude. He could be diplomatic enough where the Grand Duke was concerned; but when he was crossed he was somewhat less than ideally polite to the Weimar "asses", as he called them. In the intellectual circles of the town, again, that curious something in his nature and his manner, that suspicion of the theatrical that turned Schumann and Joachim and many others against him, made people of a different type instinctively hold aloof from him. He must have struck the ordinary Weimar inhabitants as an alien intruder. His appearance, says Fanny Ewald, who met him in 1848, was not at all German, although it could not be said to be definitely Slav or Sarmatian. He had lived so long either in France or in an international social world that invariably spoke French that he always had some difficulty even with written German; and in the early Weimar years he misused that language sadly—he spoke "a horrible Viennese-German with a pronounced Hungarian intonation."(13) The little failing was hardly calculated to recommend him to provincial Weimar.

Then there was the Princess. The sober burghers of Weimar might at a pinch have been tolerant of what they regarded as her dubious morals, but they could not reconcile themselves to her manners. She had no friends among the townspeople. Her origin and her appearance—a Polish woman of an Oriental cast of features—were against her. They did not like her habit of smoking in public—an enormity in the provincial Germany of that epoch. She showed her lofty contempt for them too openly, even to the extent of an occasional exhibition of ill breeding. Once she placed her feet on the ledge of her box in the theatre; an indignant attendant tapped her unceremoniously on the shoulder, and said, "You mustn't do that, Frau Kapellmeisterin!" At the Altenburg she was indeed the Princess von Sayn-Wittgenstein; but to the Weimar townspeople, as Carl Maria Cornelius says, she was simply "the mistress of the honorary Kapellmeister."(14) Even in high society there were

---

(13) LZBL, pp. 337-339. "As time went on," says Fanny Ewald, "his German became much clearer and more polished, but to the end he spoke French better."

(14) CMC, I, 157, 158.

few people who liked her. She was conspicuously lacking in feminine charm; while her tactlessness alienated many who were otherwise not ill-disposed towards her.(15) Like most blue-stockings, she was too much given to pontifying.

Add to all this the hullabaloo made in the quiet little town by the wild young students from all quarters who gathered round Liszt, and we have reasons enough for the opposition that a good part of Weimar showed to him, to the Princess, and to all they stood for. Personal reasons were perhaps much more strongly operative than the supposed artistic reasons upon which history, from the other end of a long perspective, loves to concentrate. The Liszt biographers dwell with horror on the fact that not only was the Princess not welcomed in Weimar society but she was sometimes insulted in the streets; but to imagine that all this was due simply to Liszt's purely musical ideals not commending themselves to the "Philistines" of Weimar is to part company from common sense.

9

It so happens that we have a good deal of contemporary light on Liszt and the Princess in the memoirs of the famous politician and military historian Theodor von Bernhardi (1803-87), who spent the winter of 1851-52 in Weimar, where he associated with all the leading people of the town, from the Grand Ducal family downwards. It is curious that the material offered by Bernhardi's second volume has not been made use of by the Liszt biographers. Most of them, it is true, may have not been aware of its existence. But one or two, at least, must have been acquainted with it; and we are driven to the conclusion that they have ignored it simply because it was difficult to make it fit in with the sacrosanct Liszt legend. The value of contemporary testimony like that of Bernhardi and Kurd von Schlözer resides in the fact that these diarists or letter writers knew nothing whatever of that later legend. They set down what they had observed, at the moment of observation; and the Liszt they saw was not at all the Liszt of the later biographers.

---

(15) See LZBL, pp. 360, 361.

Bernhardi, who had lived in St. Petersburg, had married a Russian lady, Charlotte von Krusenstern, who had frequently met Carolyne von Sayn-Wittgenstein when the two were children. As soon as the Bernhardis reached Weimar, the Princess invited them to the Altenburg. Bernhardi describes her in his diary, immediately after his first meeting with her, as "a small, dark, ugly, sickly, very clever and adroit Polish woman, with a slightly Jewish *nuance*." She received him with "gushing *empressement*." (The French words, here and in other citations, are in the original German text). She seems to have taken the view of him that she took of many people at this time—that in so far as he might be able, by reason of his distinguished Russian connections, to further her central object of obtaining a divorce in Russia, he was worth cultivating. Part of her tactics seems to have been to profess poverty: they had been reduced, she said, to depending on "Liszt's fingers." "Very clever!" Bernhardi comments; "I happen to know that she brought two million roubles away with her and has put them in a safe place. . . . She makes herself out to be poor and humble, so as to make her sacrifice look as great and unconditional as possible." He did not like her manner: she assailed him with innumerable tactless enquiries about his private affairs and plans,(16) while being somewhat uncommunicative as to her own real opinions in political and religious matters. "Now and then she thought she heard Liszt moving about in the next room. She would run to the door and cry, 'It is you, dear angel?' At last Liszt himself came in—a very ugly man,(17) *manières décousues*, who makes on the whole a disagreeable impression: he is not a man of transcendent intelligence, but his good nature makes him likeable. I came away with a somewhat uncanny impression."

---

(16) We have more than one testimony as to her rather objectionable habit of "pumping" people about their private concerns. (See, for example, Wagner's remarks in WML, II, 682.)

(17) Liszt's appearance at this time, and later, must often have justified this opinion of his looks: see, for instance, the photograph of him in SNW, II, 160. His spiritual sufferings thinned his cheeks and threw out the craggy lines of his forehead, nose, mouth and chin in sharp relief, especially when he was in an ill humour.

Then comes a little revelation that gives us a faint hint of Liszt as Guermann. At a concert at the Court, Liszt, who acted as Kapellmeister, did not mix with the royalties in the intervals, approaching them only when he was summoned to their presence. "In a word, he is the complete Kapellmeister, without the slightest pretension to be taken as a man of fashion." (The last three words are in English in the original). "The ladies sat in the Goethe room; we others were mostly in the adjacent red room. Liszt played a trio with violin and violoncello accompaniment—marvellously beautiful; there is something ethereal in his touch—I can find no other word for it. Although he is really ugly in himself, he looks handsome at the piano, where his face acquires a peculiar animation."

On 11th November Bernhardi is again at the Altenburg. The Princess makes a painful impression on him. "She is very indiscreet. She asks a great many questions, *pour avoir le secret de tout le monde*, hoping by this means to acquire a certain ascendancy, so that people will not venture to injure her in any way." While pumping Bernhardi, she once more conceals her own views on religion and politics.

> "Liszt joins in. He undertakes the apology for strict canonical Catholicism, which forbids any individual opinion or conviction. It looks as if he *had* to take this line; at any rate while he is talking he keeps gazing into Carolyne's eyes to see how far he can go or ought to go. The reasons he gives for his attitude, however, are purely external, even a matter of the police! He was formerly a freethinker, allied with Lamennais and others; but latterly he has seen that this negative point of view must lead to the extremest revolutionary action—that *la guillotine serait introduite partout comme un instrument permanent de l'orchestre politique;* and therefore he has decided to *se rejetter fortement dans le système catholique.*(18) So that it is not a question, for him, of truth for its own sake, of a genuine conviction of its nature! He assured us that many people in France thought as he does. This religiosity, that springs from fear, is therefore nothing but the wish that others (especially the lower classes) may have faith so that *we* may be left undisturbed!"

---

(18) The sentences in French no doubt reproduce Liszt's own words.

A few days later Bernhardi calls on a Court friend of Carolyne's, Frau von Plötz. "We spoke about Liszt, of whom she
has a very poor opinion; she says he is not particularly intelligent
and is childishly vain. Carolyne, on the other hand, she regards
as an exceptional woman," who credits Liszt with a mind and
virtues which he really does not possess. "It is observable,"
Bernhardi comments, "that in conversation Carolyne always
represents herself as being quite insignificant, and Liszt as
a transcendent, indeed, hitherto quite unheard-of, genius."
According to Frau von Plötz,

"Liszt has treated the Princess badly. In Poland she lived
a very original, isolated kind of life, never going into society,
etc. Business connected with her estate had taken her to Kiev.
Liszt was there; the originality, the intellect, the millions and
the title of the Princess attracted him, and *il lui fit la cour tout
bonnement;* but all that was in his mind was a liaison of the usual
kind, with the usual vows of love, but with each party knowing
from the commencement precisely what it all meant. She,
however, took the matter very seriously, though at first he did
not notice this. He had probably forgotten the matter, and was
living here in Weimar in a hotel with another woman—the
ordinary Parisian *femme entretenue;* they said nothing about it
here, in order to retain him in the town. Suddenly, to his
horror, he receives a letter from Carolyne, telling him that she
has made the sacrifice, and that all that remained was for him
to meet her at the frontier. He *had* to fetch her, for he could not
get out of it—conventional honour forbade that; but he *did*
want to get out of it. He did everything in his power to try to
persuade her to terminate the relation, for without her millions
—and at that time it looked as if she would lose them—
Carolyne did not suit him. She never complains, but I have
often seen her in tears. Carolyne was also badly treated by
Weimar society. Had she merely indulged in an immoral
amorous intrigue with Liszt no one would have objected; but
they cast the stone at her because her desire has been to be
honest in her relations with Liszt."

To this, Bernhardi adds a comment of his own:

"It is wonderful, nevertheless, how completely Carolyne has
brought Liszt to her feet. He is not a man of much character:
she has ensnared him by his vanity; she strews incense about

him perpetually, without proportion and without scruple. Frau von Plötz says that Liszt is childishly vain. He would like to be a *grand seigneur*, the favourite of the Hereditary Grand Duke, in whose graces he has already made some progress. So! this explains why Carolyne declares that she has decided upon Weimar as her permanent place of residence, even after her [matrimonial] affairs have been regulated."

10

All this will grieve the propagators of, and the believers in, the Liszt legend. It certainly clashes with it; but in that case, we cannot help feeling, so much the worse for the legend. Whether Frau von Plötz was right on one or two minor matters we cannot be quite sure. But here is a prominent member of Weimar society and an intimate of the Altenburg telling Bernhardi what she knows of the Wittgenstein affair and of Liszt, and what she thinks of the two people concerned. Which is more worthy of our credence—contemporary testimony of this kind, or the carefully concocted legend of the Liszt idolaters of a generation or two later? As usual when we pass over the biographers and go direct to contemporary documents, weighing the evidence that is implicit in them, we come upon the same main threads once more. Frau von Plötz's remark about Liszt being anxious to play the *grand seigneur* is in complete agreement with all we know of him from his letters of the d'Agoult period and from Marie's comments upon him. The theory that Liszt was originally attracted by Carolyne's title is consistent with everything we know of him as an inveterate tuft-hunter. It is *a priori* credible that, as Frau von Plötz said and others have since maintained, in the first instance he had no thought, in Russia, of anything but a fleeting "affair" with the Princess—an affair of a type with which he was already exceedingly well acquainted; once more he was the "Don Juan parvenu" of Marie's biting phrase. We may recall also that Peter Cornelius, as will be shown later, was always on the Princess's side rather than Liszt's; he thought she had made a great sacrifice for him without any real return, and had been badly treated. But the actor in Liszt—an actor who played his part to perfection in his letters (not without consciousness, perhaps, that the letters would some day be published)—has succeeded in creating a legend that it will take some time to dissipate.(19)

We have little difficulty in accepting Frau von Plötz's statement that Liszt at first had not really desired the liaison with the

---

(19) The more thoroughly we study the Liszt question the more we become convinced that the facts have been manipulated wholesale in order to maintain the legend. The impression has been carefully conveyed that the relations between Liszt and the Princess were strictly platonic. Carl Maria Cornelius asserts roundly that this was not so: "there were three children of the union, who were born in other towns than Weimar, and brought up in Brussels" (CMC, I, 158). This was one of the reasons why the Princess was so anxious to legitimate her union with Liszt.

It used to be common talk in the Liszt circle at the end of the nineteenth century that Franz Servais (who died in 1901) was one of Liszt's sons. This now seems more probable than ever. Franz Servais figured as the adopted son of the celebrated Belgian 'cellist Adrien François Servais (1807-66), who, from 1848 onwards, was professor of the 'cello at the Brussels conservatoire. Franz Servais' resemblance to Franz Liszt was always a subject for amused comment in musical circles: twice in Bülow's letters we find remarks (one suspects them to be ironically suggestive) on the "fabulous" resemblance of the young man both to Liszt and to the latter's deceased son Daniel. After his adoptive father's death, Franz was sent by Liszt (about March, 1869) to study the piano with Bülow in Munich: and Liszt always took a great interest in his development. In a letter of 11th August, 1870, to the Princess (LZB, VI, 259), Liszt speaks of Franz as "a very gifted young man, whose features and blond hair remind me of my poor Daniel. Madame Servais, his mother, whom I have not the pleasure of knowing personally, has entrusted him to my care." This may seem, on the surface, to negate the theory of Liszt's paternity; but the question suggests itself whether the letter to the Princess was not just a piece of humorous *blague* for her benefit and for that of posterity. The boy was the living image of Liszt and of Daniel. Like Liszt, he was named Franz. He was admittedly not the son of Adrien Servais. The compilers of musical encyclopaedias can give us no more exact date for his birth than "St. Petersburg, 1847". Liszt first met the Princess in February of that year. We possess a photograph of her that was taken in St. Petersburg in 1847. On the death of the boy's adoptive father, the widow commits him to the care of Liszt. The reader must be left to draw his own conclusion from these facts.

Princess to be permanent. His sense of chivalry would no doubt have made him marry her in the Weimar days had that been possible; but in his heart of hearts he always shrank from contracting a durable bond. He assured Fanny Ewald, in 1848, that "it was a resolution on the Princess's part to follow me here: I had not expected her." Her friend (and Liszt's), Therese von Bacheracht, ventured to warn him against marriage: "you are not constant by nature," she said, "and you do not know what an unhappy marriage is. In any marriage you would be unhappy and create unhappiness." "Very possibly!" he replied. "In essentials I agree with you. An oath is a serious thing. What a man *has* done, he knows; and that he can swear to. But what a man *will* do or not do, what he *will* feel, he cannot know; and to swear in this regard is a much more doubtful business. Who can take an oath that he will always remain the same? I am sure that the best thing to do with me always is to leave me my freedom—that it is dangerous to bind me either to one person or one place." "He spoke," says Fanny, "partly in jest, partly in earnest"; but the "earnestness predominated" when he made the remark quoted above as to his not having expected Carolyne to follow him to Weimar.(20)

II

On 15th November Bernhardi writes in his diary:

"Frau von Plötz is right. Liszt acts with ambitious purposes in view; now that I have begun to observe matters, I see the whole plan on which he hopes to found his greatness. A beginning is to be made in the literary field. Carolyne sets forth a project, with a deprecatory preface—how the great and brilliant ideas of a genius naturally suffer when they are set forth by a weak woman, and so on."

The Grand Duchess and the Hereditary Grand Duke want to maintain as well as they can the former glory of Weimar. To this end Liszt counsels the founding of a journal in order to influence public opinion, as well as to rope in, as contributors, a number of the cultured people of the neighbourhood who

---

(20) LZBL, p. 350.

otherwise might become dangerous. To obviate any opposition or disfavour on the part of other Courts, politics are to be avoided; "the journal is to live, with childish harmlessness, simply in the region of the ideal!" "If Liszt," Bernhardi adds, "is to be the chief person in this matter, it goes without saying that scientific or critical seriousness is not to be expected. . . . They want to win my adherence to this journal: I am to contribute to Liszt's glory!" Naturally money is lacking in little Weimar for an undertaking of this kind; but the Princess makes it appear as if the small-minded Court officials are unable to grasp the colossal conception of the genius! Liszt, of course, in her opinion, is acting from the most disinterested motives.

"In one particular, however," continues Bernhardi, "Frau von Plötz is mistaken. Liszt himself has no such ambition. He seems to be a man of weak character, who just lets things go as they will; riotous living and a liberal supply of incense for his vanity would probably have satisfied him for ever, or at any rate for a long time. But Carolyne is ambitious for him; she wants to make something of him, and no doubt dreams of playing a *rôle* herself in it all, for she surely cannot delude herself into believing that Liszt is a man who would have an opinion of his own in great matters and difficult situations, or a will of his own in a dangerous situation. She promises herself that she will have an opinion and a will for him!"

Then we get a glimpse of the actor in Liszt.

"Franz Liszt came to see us," writes Bernhardi a few days later. "He is not a man of great intelligence, but he has a certain worldly wisdom, and he possesses in a high degree the tact that goes along with this. It is a settled system with him never to express an opinion upon anything, however unimportant it may be, so as not to compromise himself or offend anyone. He, the favourite of the Prince, has spent this evening in the tap-room of a club in which the musicians of the orchestra foregather from time to time to smoke and drink beer. He smelt horribly of bad tobacco. He also acts as a sort of intermediary between the Hereditary Grand Duke on the one side and Fanny Ewald and Adolf Stahr on the other. He is thus clever enough to have a foot in both camps. Liszt and Carolyne are the sort of persons who conduct their lives not in obedience to a conviction but solely for personal interests. . . . Therefore for them there are no such things as noble and ignoble people, men one can respect or despise, but only people who can be useful or harmful. It follows that their eyes look favourably on a scamp whom they can win over, while honest earnestness is monstrous to them. As Liszt takes me for an out-and-out reactionary, he thinks to trick me by enlarging upon how badly the princes behaved in 1848."

Three days later there is a fresh entry in the diary.

"Frau von Plötz spent the evening with us: she is a very amiable woman. We talked about Liszt—how he will not give his opinion upon anything, least of all upon politics. He simply cannot do that, Frau von Plötz thinks, because at heart he is an absolute revolutionary. . . . Liszt is not one of those men whose convictions have any influence on their lives. The Hereditary Grand Duke may rest assured that his friend Liszt will prove unfaithful to him as soon as the wind blows from the other quarter. It is incomprehensible that he cannot see that he himself is more intelligent than Liszt."(21)

We have the feeling that neither the Liszt nor the Wagner biographies have told us the whole truth, and nothing but the truth, about Liszt in Weimar. It may be admitted at once that the whole truth was not quite as seen by people like Bernhardi or the circle in which he moved during his stay in the town. There was a strong strain of quite unselfish idealism running through Liszt's conduct in Weimar. He had been fairly quick to perceive the stupendous significance of Wagner, and it was undoubtedly to Liszt's production of *Lohengrin* in 1850 that Wagner owed his rehabilitation in German operatic circles after his escapades in connection with the Dresden rising of 1849. Liszt himself had visions of new things to be done in orchestral music; and while it may be true, as Cornelius always held, that he was well aware of the benefit to himself of allying himself with the cause of Wagner, who was clearly the man of the future, it is none the less true that he never for a moment sought anything for himself at the expense of his great colleague: indeed, the exact opposite was the case. He was also sincerely anxious to make Weimar a real operatic centre, and in other ways to revive the ancient cultural glory of the little town.

---

(21) BAL, II, 97-108.

12

But while recognising all this to the full, we cannot get rid
of the suspicion that the inner history of the Weimar years now
calls for a little re-writing. As has been pointed out already, it
simply will not do to assume, in these days, that all the intelligence and the purity of purpose in Weimar were concentrated
in the Altenburg, and all the Philistinism in the remaining part
of the town and neighbourhood. Weimar and the adjacent Jena
were rich in men and women of a culture and a general intelligence at least equal to those of Liszt and the Princess. It is
true that there were musical reactionaries there as elsewhere;
but too much importance can be attributed to this factor. In
spite of the usual opposition of vested interests in the theatre,
the plain fact is that Wagner's cause made decided headway in
Weimar. If Liszt's own cause did not make the same progress,
part of the explanation must be sought in contemporary and
local and personal factors that were vital for the time and place,
though they are apt to be lost sight of or ignored by later
historians of a romantic turn of mind.

The simple truth seems to be that Liszt and the Princess
were not liked and not trusted. The Princess was an alien of
strange appearance and stranger habits, who was suspected, not
without justice, of having descended upon the town for two
reasons only—to impose Liszt upon it as the arbiter of Weimar
culture, and to make use of the fact that the Grand Duchess
was the sister of the Czar in order to achieve her personal end
of a divorce in Russia. She was popular neither in society,
where she was too much inclined to lay down the law on literary,
political and religious subjects, nor in the town, where her
habits and her manners were objectionably exotic. She made
both herself and Liszt supremely ridiculous by her fulsome
adulation of him. As for Liszt, it hardly needs to be pointed out
that the inhabitants of Weimar saw him, in general, just as he
was externally in those years, not through the eyes of the
romanticising biographers of half a century later. He was
manifestly very vain. His escapades with women had for years
made him the malicious joke of Europe; and his liaison with the

FRANZ LISZT IN THE WEIMAR PERIOD

LISZT IN 1863

From a painting by Stella, reproduced for the first time in "Franz Liszt,"
Dr. Julius Kapp, Hesse-Verlag, Berlin.

Princess was regarded, for a time, as only the latest joke of the same sorry kind. He was too obviously given to a certain amount of posturing. Society did not like his exaggerated assumption of the *grand seigneur* manner; still less did it like what seemed to be a plan on his part to bring the rather weak-charactered Hereditary Grand Duke under his influence. Contemporaries, in fact, saw him very much as he appears at his worst in his letters to Marie—a Don Juan parvenu, a piano player of humble origin whose desire was to be taken for one of nature's aristocrats, a man who gave the impression, in many matters, of not being quite sincere, whose acting was rather too obvious. And so, for local and temporal and personal reasons, there sprang up an opposition to him that of necessity took the form of a smaller recognition of his real virtues than was their proper due.

Bernhardi left Weimar in 1852, but returned there for a while in the autumn of that year. His diary for that period throws still further light on the position of Liszt and the Princess in Weimar. It is clear that even Liszt's own bodyguard had at that time no great belief in him as a composer. From conversations with some of them Bernhardi gathered that Liszt "is so poor a general-bassist that he is no good at composition. He gets, as musical princesses do, a good idea for a cantilena, but he cannot give it shape and body (*Rundung und Haltung*), and more particularly the necessary harmonic breadth. Raff helps him out in this, just like the music master of a musical princess."

Bernhardi is made the confidant of the woes of the Russian ambassador in Weimar, Maltitz, who has been pestered over the matter of the Wittgenstein divorce. We get a suspicion that the accepted story of the unfailing wickedness of the husband and his relations, as given in the Wittgenstein-Ramann biography of Liszt, may not be altogether trustworthy. The Princess had been trying to have her marriage annulled on the technical plea that she had been forced into it, a plea to which the Russian ecclesiastical and civil authorities naturally paid scant attention. Maltitz had been informed by the Governor General of Kiev, whose adjutant Prince Wittgenstein was, that the latter was coming to Weimar to confer with his wife and Liszt, and he had been instructed to assist him. Maltitz was not at all pleased

o

to be mixed up in the affair. He could not share Carolyne's ·
optimism as to the result of her plea.

"But the Princess," he lamented to Bernhardi, "knows
everything better than anybody else; she is 'stupidly crafty,'
prefers needlessly crooked paths, and, like a true Polish woman,
thinks that money can do anything. She has offered *me* money!"
he complained. Carolyne had arranged a little while before
with an emissary of the Prince that he was to move for a divorce
in return for the conveyance to him of her Balany estate; but
his lawyer had advised him that such an agreement would be
null and void under Russian law. Thereupon Carolyne had
suggested other courses that were equally impracticable. "She
finesses in the most incomprehensible way," said Maltitz,
"and tactlessly refers them to Liszt, who is to speak and decide
for her! It seems probable that she does not lay much store by a
divorce: it is the *status quo* that she wishes to maintain; she will
lift up her voice loudly enough when it is really a question of her
becoming Madame Liszt."

On 13th September poor Maltitz pours out his troubles once
more to Bernhardi. He has sent word to Carolyne that Prince
Nikolaus has arrived in Weimar. She refers them both to
Liszt, who shows himself "very unruly"—"the Prince is not to
be received at the house, he is not to be allowed (on what
grounds?) to see his daughter: Liszt (the brilliant poltroon) is
going to box the Prince's ears; and so on, until Maltitz asks the
furious couple whether they really believe that they will improve
their case by violences."(22)

A few days later, Bernhardi goes to Berlin, where the Prince
calls on him at his hotel.

"He told me all about Weimar. Everything is arranged, and
in the best possible way. [The Prince wished to marry a widow
Kosen]. He has behaved in such a way that Madame sings his
praises everywhere. He made the first approach, visited the
Princess, by arrangement, in her box at the theatre, and gave
her his hand *in conspectu omnium*—has done everything, in fact,
to smooth out difficulties. He expressed the desire, however,
not to meet Liszt, 'in order to avoid an encounter that might
be unfortunate for him rather than for me. I insisted that

(22) BAL, II, 137, 139, 140.

they should marry: I do not want her to go on bearing my name.'
He also objected to his daughter remaining at the Altenburg
with her mother: as she is a *demoiselle d'honneur*, she ought to
live in the castle under the care of the Countess Fritsch . . .
for the society at the Altenburg is not suitable for a young lady:
'it is a drug!' "(23)

With this entry in his diary Bernhardi's contribution to our
subject unfortunately ends. His observations, however, have
given us good reason for believing that even in the matter of the
relations between the Princess, her husband and Liszt, contemporary observers of the affair, could they revisit the earth
today, would find much to question in the account of it that has
been handed down to us in the Liszt biographies.

(23) BAL, II, 141-142.

CHAPTER VII

THE
SEPARATION FROM THE PRINCESS:
THE DUALITY OF LISZT'S SOUL

I

It seems to have been the desire of the Princess, from the first, to legalise her union with Liszt by marriage. The full details of her long struggle for freedom cannot be given here; but in broad outline the facts are these. By 1860 there was every promise that the thousand wires that had been pulled during the preceding twelve years would at last achieve the desired result. Carolyne left for Rome in May, 1860, to bring fresh pressure to bear on the ecclesiastical authorities there; and Liszt joined her in October of the following year. The marriage was actually fixed for his fiftieth birthday (the 22nd of that month); but on the very eve of it the relatives of Prince Sayn-Wittgenstein intervened once more and persuaded the Pope to order the postponement of the marriage in order that the documents might be examined afresh. It was a blow from which Carolyne never recovered; her superstitious mind read into it the expression of Heaven's disapproval. Even when her husband died (in 1864), thus removing the last material obstacle to their union, she shrank from the legal linking of her life with that of Liszt. She became more and more religious; she shut herself up in a small apartment in Rome and developed into an eccentric, puffing away at her long cigars in a room from which both light and air were rigorously excluded—the curtains being drawn all day—and scribbling incessantly at those books of hers which she firmly believed would be the salvation not only of the Roman Church but of European civilisation.

Liszt, after 1861, lived for some time mostly in Rome, generally spending some part of each day with her. Later he allowed himself to be persuaded by the Grand Duke to reside part of each year in Weimar, where he gathered round him a new generation of piano pupils; and later still he accepted a kind of musical advisory and supervisory post in Pesth. Henceforth his life was a perpetual migration between the corners of what he called his triangle, Rome-Pesth-Weimar, with numerous visits to the country houses of his German and Hungarian friends and to various towns in which some work or other of his was to be performed. He had no real home: when left to himself he lived poorly, often lacking ordinary comforts and being badly fed; and in Weimar he was grossly imposed upon by some of his so-called pupils. It was a disorganised kind of life, over which the Princess grieved incessantly; yet nothing would have persuaded him to change it, because, in its way, it suited him better than anchorage in any one place would have done, and, above all, better than a resumption, in the company of Carolyne, of the chains that had weighed upon him in Weimar in days gone by. His respect for her remained unaltered; he could rarely think of her without gratitude; but all the same, the eternal Zigeuner in him was bent on having his freedom at any cost. There has been considerable speculation, on the part of the biographers, as to why he never made any attempt to persuade Carolyne to the marriage after the last legal and moral obstacle in their path had been removed. As against the theory that he had never really wished for the union there can be cited a passage or two from his letters to her that suggest that had she still desired it he would not have refused. A man of his chivalry where Carolyne was concerned would probably have been prepared to weld his life for ever to hers had she insisted on it. But the simple truth seems to be that in his heart of hearts he wanted his freedom, less from any motive of deliberate egoistic calculation than because his profoundest natural instinct drove him imperiously in that direction.

This instinct was given unexpected play after the Princess left for Rome in May, 1860. It was seventeen months before he rejoined her there: he had spent most of the intervening time in

Weimar, but had also made visits to other towns, including Paris, where he resumed his old brilliant social life and basked in the adoration that had always been so dear to him. By the time he arrived in Rome, in October, 1861, he had probably had ample leisure to realise that to be shut up for the remainder of his life with an eccentric and ageing woman, possessed by a few fixed religious ideas which she pursued with fanatical obstinacy, would mean a servitude against which he was bound to revolt sooner or later. He could best preserve his respect and gratitude for Carolyne by not being with her too often or too continuously in the flesh. We must perhaps not take too seriously the expression, in his letters, of desolation at her absence, sincere as they were—in the sense, that is, in which the term "sincere" is generally applicable to Liszt. We have seen him, during his first period, again and again assuring Marie that his days and nights are one long weariness away from her, and that he desires nothing so ardently as to return to her: nevertheless he makes no effort to return, always finding, when the moment for decision comes, that the delights of the social life are too great to be given up. Similarly, in the period that followed the Princess's removal to Rome, though he may have mourned over her absence he managed to find consolations. He still fervently longed to be a saint, but not too much of a saint, and certainly not too uninterruptedly a saint. There were other elements than the religious in his nature that were constantly calling out for satisfaction. Wine and cognac, especially in quantities not permitted by Carolyne at the Altenburg, were comforting to body and soul, and all over Europe there were gay and beautiful and brilliant women of a type he would not be likely to meet in the Piazza di Spagna or the Via del Babuino.(1) And so, if he wept on the side of his face that he turned towards Carolyne in his letters, he certainly did his best to smile with the other.

2

We get a piquant sidelight on one aspect of the matter in one of Carolyne's letters to him, Raabe's comments upon which are an illustration of how difficult a thesis-running biographer

---

(1) The houses occupied successively by the Princess in Rome.

finds it to see a thing as it really is when he is not modelling his subject from the life but constructing an idealised lay figure.

"We cannot help," says Raabe, "admiring the angelic patience of Liszt, who year after year submitted to the reproaches of this woman [Carolyne] that he was indolent and did not behave properly; and we feel a sense of shame as we see him earnestly defending himself against her charges." Raabe quotes from a previously unpublished letter of hers of 1872 (now in the Liszt Museum at Weimar), in which she tells Liszt that she had read in some newspaper or other that "the first toast was that of the old master Liszt, who comported himself in the company in amiable and unconstrained (*zwangloser*) fashion." "This *zwangloser*," she writes to him, "has lacerated my soul as a dissonant note lacerates the ear. I could see you going about as in 1848 in Niemizov, as in 1858 in the Weimar Town Hall, forgetting that twenty-four years, fourteen years, separate you now from then, and that a man who does not change his manners, his *contegno* [demeanour] in twenty-four or fourteen years has something unnatural in him, like a child who should be in his fourteenth or his twenty-fourth year just what he was as a schoolboy of ten." Liszt replies to this (in a passage that was omitted by La Mara, the editor of his correspondence, from his letter of 6th January, 1872) by telling her tranquilly that if she will look up the meaning of *zwanglos* in a dictionary she will find that her "bitter concern" was superfluous.(2)

But Raabe surely misses the point of this specimen of what he calls the Princess's "schoolmistress behaviour." The vital point is not whether she was right or wrong in this particular instance, but that she is anxiously drawing Liszt's attention to a notorious little failing of his—the tendency to over-indulgence in company, and to somewhat undignified behaviour when the wine was in him—and citing a couple of the most notorious instances of it in his past life. That he was always rather too much dependent on alcohol to keep him going, and occasionally,

(2) RLL, p. 217; LZB, VI, 323. The episode must have occurred either in Vienna or in Pesth.

though rarely, drank to actual excess, is beyond question. He himself admits it in a letter of 8th February, 1861, to Carolyne. He happens to be in one of his religious moods, when he finds it a voluptuous pleasure to confess and pray. He has, indeed, just been to confession, and he gives Carolyne the benefit of his self-examination. He thanks God that he has never loved evil, and whenever he has done wrong he has been "profoundly contrite and humble." As he looks back over the long years he finds that he cannot reproach himself with a single sentiment of pride or envy, still less of avarice or hatred. (On the matter of pride and envy and hatred Marie and Thalberg and one or two others might have had something to say).

"My stone of stumbling," he continues, "is this need for intensity of emotion, which easily leads me into paradox in matters of the intelligence and intemperance in the use of spirituous liquors. I have promised you that I will reform in this respect, but I shall not be able to do so without an effort. This rascally music drives me with fearful force towards this excess, to say nothing of the frequent occasions that present themselves when I am tempted to fall."(3)

Even the devoted Adelheid von Schorn, who mothered him in Weimar while the Princess was in Rome, touches, with regret, on this failing of his. She is speaking primarily of his melancholy last years, when he must often have seemed a lost soul to those who loved him.

"So long as Liszt felt really ill," she says, "he followed the instructions of his physician; one of the chief of these was that he should abstain from cognac. I must say something here about the darker side of Liszt's life—his love of strong drink: if I were to ignore this weakness altogether I would justly incur the reproach of unveracity. In describing Liszt's life and character one need not shrink from mentioning his failings, for there is more than enough of good to counterbalance them. Even during his concert tours before 1848 he had grown accustomed to drinking more than was good for him. The reason for this is to be found partly in the merry company that everywhere gathered round the agreeable and liberal artist, partly in the great fatigue he had to undergo. Today, when the railway makes everything

---

(3) LZB, V, 129.

easy, when the telegraph makes everything possible, people have no conception of the expenditure of time and strength that travelling at that epoch involved. Liszt played almost every evening, and travelled day and night. . . . It is readily comprehensible that often the overstrained man resorted to ostensibly strengthening beverages. In the Altenburg years, matters were better in this respect, for the Princess had seen how bad this way of living was for him, and she kept him away from it by her regular ordering of the household. Later in Rome, again, he mostly kept free of it, but to maintain his strength he needed a certain amount of wine and cognac; without these stimulants he felt dull. He never drank any but small quantities, but if anything happened to excite or vex him he would instantly drain a glass. It at once went to his head, for he could not stand much. So it often came about that when I used to call on him in Weimar(4) in the mornings I would find him excited. I would ask his servant what had happened, and always it was not the wine alone but that he had been upset by the visit of some one or other, a letter, and so on.

"It will be seen from the Princess's letters in the last years that his health was declining. He did not eat enough, because his stomach had been ruined by cognac and strong cigars. The weaker he felt, the more claret mixed with cognac he would drink. It was a vicious circle, from which he escaped only when he was really ill and his physician kept him to wine diluted with water. When he was ill he was never irritable, but gentle and communicative; his better self showed itself in all its beauty. He said to me once, 'I know that cognac is my worst enemy, but I cannot do without it.' "(5)

One's mind is carried back to the d'Agoult days, when he confesses a similar inability to face the difficulties, internal and external, of his life without a harmful excess of tobacco, wine, and coffee.

---

(4) This was in the eighteen-seventies and 'eighties.

(5) SZM, pp. 383, 384. The picture is discreetly underpainted. In his last years he is said to have drunk a whole bottle of cognac or of arrack (a kind of gin) each day.

Fanny Ewald was one of a merry party that made holiday with Liszt in Heligoland in August and September, 1849. She describes how Liszt, becoming excited at a farewell supper, made the waiter pour a couple

Nobody possessed any influence over him in these matters but Carolyne, and that only in the Altenburg days, when, for one thing, she was always present to regulate his indulgence for him, and, for another, could encourage him in the religious reactions that followed on an occasional excess. It is beyond dispute that he steadily declined in fibre after the separation from her, going back to all the old habits that meant the widening of the vicious circle—first of all a hunger for society and for flattering attentions, that meant the waste of his time and the exhaustion of his vitality, then remorse at the indolence he felt to be mastering him, then resort to the bottle to raise his spirits, then a repentant reaction, then a renewed longing for company, in which alone he could forget his physical and spiritual misery; and so *ad infinitum*. Raabe thinks the sufficient answer to the Princess's reproaches is to be found in Liszt's replies to her. Raabe publishes, for the first time, an extract from a letter now in the Liszt archives in Weimar.(6) On 20th March, 1872, Liszt writes to the Princess, evidently in reply to her upbraiding:

> "I can prove that for years I have lived without boon companionship of any kind; neither in Rome nor in Pesth can I be justly reproached with squandering my time or my person. I am never to be seen in cafés, hotels, etc., and the people with whom I consort all have some distinction of talent, character, or position. The tone of my relaxations is wholly the reverse of the good-for-nothing kind (*le genre chenapanesque*); there is nothing equivocal or gossiping or improper about it, and certainly none of the people who know me can boast of comradeship with me."(7)

---

of bottles of cognac into the champagne cup, which he declared to be "too insipid" (see LZBL, pp. 358, 360).

In September, 1881, he told the Princess (LZB, VII, 352) that for more than a year he had suffered from violent nausea on rising each morning. "I know what it comes from," he said—"my irregular *régime*, too many strong cigars, and too much cognac, though not as much as people say."

(6) Raabe is the custodian of the Liszt Museum. His admirable work is based on first-hand knowledge of a good many documents that have not been accessible to other writers.

(7) RLL, p. 217.

But once more the essential point is not whether the Princess was justified in her reproaches in every instance—in her anxiety for him she may well have overshot the mark now and then, thus giving him an easy opportunity to put her in the wrong in the particular instance—but that the reproaches should be made, and made so often. A woman who has lived for twelve or thirteen years with a man can be trusted to know something of his character and habits; and Carolyne would not have fretted so much over him when he was at a distance from her, and so constantly exhorted Adelheid von Schorn to watch over him for her and save him from himself, unless she knew his tendency to drift into a way of life that was bad for him both as a man and as the creative artist she wanted him to be.

3

The seventeen months of separation from her after her removal to Rome in May, 1860, were indeed fatal for him: they determined, perhaps, the whole course of his future life. During that period he had tasted bachelor liberty once more, and found it very much to his liking; he was free to go where he liked, consort with whom he would, and in general live as he chose, without being daily exhorted to master his congenital weaknesses and turn the whole of his energies into the one channel of creative work. The exceptionally clear-sighted Peter Cornelius was probably the only person who divined, at the time, that this temporary separation was the beginning of the end for both Liszt and Carolyne. When she left Weimar she had no intention of settling permanently in Rome; the original plan had been that she was to return as soon as her immediate purpose—that of influencing the ecclesiastical authorities in her favour—had been achieved. But she was detained month after month in Rome by the uprising of one fresh difficulty after another; and meanwhile Liszt, for all his apparent desire to see her efforts crowned with success, allowed his own daily life to take a new orientation—or rather a reversal to that of the pre-Weimar days—almost as soon as he was left to his own devices. He promptly launched into the hectic living that Carolyne dreaded for him. Peter Cornelius, who was in Weimar in April and May

of that year, found Liszt "a mystery." "He must have been in a
notably excited condition," says Carl Maria Cornelius, who
may be presumed, on this as on other occasions, to be speaking
on the evidence of documents or traditions preserved in the
family, "a condition that was probably due to the fact that in
the depths of his soul he was reluctant to enter into marriage
with the Princess. His mood was a blend of melancholy and
frivolity; he sought consolation in cognac; he wanted to nar-
cotise himself."(8) Peter Cornelius, though he loved Liszt,
had always felt most sympathy for the Princess, whose sacrifices
he held to have been the greater; while he was too clear-eyed
ever to see Liszt through the romantic haze that has gathered
round his personality in modern times. With a prescience that
now seems almost uncanny, he declared from the first that the
Liszt-Carolyne union was to all intents and purposes already
at an end. "The Altenburg," he writes from Vienna to a friend
on 23rd July, 1860, only two months after the Princess had left
for Rome, "is an enigma to me. But some day it will be solved,
and I look forward with apprehension to that solution, no matter
in what fine words it may be announced. I ponder a good deal
upon it all. I believe the Princess will end her days where she
now is"—a prophecy that was to be fulfilled to the letter. Hence,
he continues, "Liszt's whole behaviour since her departure.
Take note of my words: this is a separation. God grant that I
may be mistaken!"

Evidently Liszt, now that Carolyne was gone, was not precisely giving observers the impression, by his way of living, that
her departure had dealt him a death-blow. "Ah, the Altenburg!" writes Cornelius to another correspondent on 1st August,
"I have had no letters from there. I know nothing, nothing!
But it is a bad business. Take my word for it, the Princess will
remain in Rome. It was a separation; she is a great and unfortunate soul." In October Liszt was in Vienna, whither he
had gone to try to win over the Papal Nuncio to the Princess's
project. Peter Cornelius records in his diary that Liszt came
into his room one morning with tears in his eyes: he had just

---

(8) CMC, I, 317.

been to mass, and was consequently in one of his emotional
religious moods. The pair drove off to the house of Liszt's
step-uncle Eduard. In the carriage Liszt fell on Cornelius's
neck and wept like a child over the behaviour of the Hohenlohe
family, who, he said, were carrying on the evil work of the
Wittgensteins. But he soon forgot his troubles: he gave a dinner
to a number of his friends, the champagne flowed freely, and
the party did not break up until one in the morning. The
observant Cornelius now believed less than ever in the likeli-
hood of the marriage ever taking place. Liszt wanted him to
visit Weimar once more, but Cornelius was resolved not to do
so; without the Princess, he tells a correspondent on 19th June,
1861, the Altenburg is for him not the Altenburg of old. He
feels that something new has crept into the atmosphere of the
place, and that it bodes no good for her. Greatly as he is devoted
to Liszt, he says, if he must take sides in the matter his place
will be with Carolyne. Then comes a passage that gives us a
hint of something that must have been much clearer to contemporaries than the biographers have succeeded in making it
to us—the marked change in Liszt's nature and in his way of
living. He had surrounded himself with admirers and syco-
phants whose influence upon him Cornelius dreaded: we are
reminded of Marie's remark about the "Puzzis."

> "It annoys me to see the people there [at the Altenburg]
> kicking up the dust they do. Liszt should pull himself together
> and enter upon the necessary final period of his creative work;
> if he does, I will follow him everywhere with love, with en-
> thusiasm, for God knows my heart is full of gratitude towards
> him. But to see him as he is now, among all these people,
> Klitzsch and Lohmann and Köhler and Kahnt and Brendel!
> . . ."

At the end of June, 1861, Cornelius writes to his brother Carl:

> "The Princess W. is said to be living a sad and restricted
> life in Rome. I pity this poor woman from the bottom of my
> heart: all the world is against her, and she has to bear her sorrow
> in silence and alone. But God will give her His grace, for she
> loves truly. . . . Weimar will certainly not see me again if *she*
> is not at the Altenburg. . . . Liszt, I am afraid, has had the

impulse to soar destroyed in him, for with the Princess he has lost the very nerve of his life. She was responsible for all the good work he did. If it was impossible for him to ennoble his moral nature permanently during a union of this kind, his power to achieve the best in him will fail, and he will go under. Of this I was conscious from my personal observation there; I am still more conscious of it from all that I hear. It makes me sad at heart."(9)

Cornelius was a better prophet than he knew.

4

After Carolyne's departure Liszt became the old Liszt once more, trying to find an anodyne for his melancholy, a support in his hours of bitter self-criticism, in wine, in company, in feminine flattery and affection. It is to this epoch that the episode belongs of one of his "pupils"—ostensibly a "young Englishman"—who pursued him in boy's clothing to the country house of his friend Prince Hohenzollern in Löwenberg in the autumn of 1861, and later forced herself on him in Rome. (The male costume had to be adopted to escape the observation of a jealous husband). In Paris, in June, 1861, he annoyed Wagner by neglecting him for his aristocratic acquaintances, though he was friendly and kind enough when they happened to meet. Liszt was not in Paris during the famous production of *Tannhäuser* at the Opéra (in March, 1861), though there was nothing to prevent his being there to give his old friend his support at that critical time had he wished to do so. He seems to have deliberately delayed his trip to Paris until he thought he could count on Wagner having left. A reference to this matter in Wagner's letter of 3rd May, 1861, to Bülow is significant as showing the general opinion of the time as to the strain of snobbishness in Liszt's nature that made him so untiring a tuft-hunter. "I wish," says Wagner, "I could know how to be something to Liszt! But he has other and deeper-lying norms for his ways and doings than a poor plebeian like myself can fathom."(10)

---

(9) CAB, I, 474, 478, 522, 601, 602, 604, 605.

(10) WBB, p. 159. Liszt was being fêted, as usual, in Paris society, and though he pretended that he did not like being asked to play the piano

As it happened, Wagner had to return to Paris in May. Liszt, he found, had reverted to type; he was too busy visiting his titled friends to have much time to spare for Wagner. "Liszt," he says, "had already fallen back into his old way of life"—the expression is significant—"and even his daughter Blandine could manage to get a word with him only in his carriage as he drove from one visit to another," though, as Wagner sarcastically admits, "he *did* manage to find time to invite himself to my house for a beefsteak."(11) Liszt, who by this time had not seen Carolyne for more than a year, had, in fact, become completely the man of the world again, whose sole delight was in being fêted in the salons of aristocrats and notabilities. It would not have required much knowledge of human nature on anyone's part to see that it would be a miracle if ever the broken link between him and the Princess were to be forged anew. A sense of duty might conceivably still draw him back to her; but at heart he had become once more the rudderless Liszt of the eighteen-forties. In fact, if not in name, there was an end to Carolyne's long ascendancy over him.

Cornelius at last yielded to pressure and visited the Altenburg again. He left there in August, 1861, Liszt's parting words to him being, "Now I go to Rome for my marriage!" Cornelius was convinced that Liszt was never wholly sincere in that matter; and when even the death of Prince Wittgenstein in 1864 failed to bring about the marriage, he had no doubt that his suspicions had been correct. "Recollections of painful scenes, dissatisfaction with Liszt, and sympathy with the Princess," says his son, "all awoke in him once more, and wrung from him the bitter reproach that at bottom Liszt had been playing false with her, and had treated cruelly the woman to whom he owed

---

in aristocratic salons, he was obviously too flattered to be willing to refuse. He was also very busy calling on and dining with everybody who, he thought, could be useful to him in a project he had at heart at that time—though he pretended, as usual, to have no appetite for "honours"—his election to the Institute. He knew, as he told the Princess, that Wagner was angry at not being able to get a sight of him. (See his letter to her of 5th June, 1861, in LZB, V, 179).

(11) WML, II, 880.

everything." Cornelius was not alone in this opinion: another acute observer—Tausig—who was sometimes given to a brutal frankness of speech, merely shrugged his shoulders when he heard of the final abandonment of the plan for marriage, and wrote to Cornelius, "Liszt's whole journey to Rome was simply a *blague*."(12)

Carl Maria Cornelius sums the matter up thus:

"Liszt's nature was the last in the world to be suitable for marriage; and to tie himself now to an ageing woman was more than could be expected of him. The Princess, in days gone by, had followed him from Russia and had thrown herself at his head. He had been chivalrous enough to comply with her humour; and to his own astonishment the adventure developed into a passionate love, which, however, cooled down in the course of years. Liszt still wanted to be chivalrous, or at any rate to appear to be so, and outwardly to make it look as if he were willing to fall in with her plan for marriage. But in Rome he was so undisguisedly cold towards her that the woman in her compelled her to renounce this plan. It assuredly was not external events [the opposition of the Wittgenstein family and the machinations of the ecclesiastics] that drove her to abandon the plan that had been so close to her heart, but 'profounder feelings, more urgent causes.' "(13)

Adelheid von Schorn, who was Carolyne's regular confidante during these years, bears similar testimony.

"I feel it my duty to repeat," she writes, "what the Princess assured me and others in tones of the utmost sincerity and the deepest sorrow, that during the·period when they were separated from each other Liszt had become indifferent; the thought of a legal union with her no longer appealed to him as a necessity. She was conscious of this change in him when he arrived in Rome on 21st October [1861]; and he himself supplied the confirmation of it, for he never asked her again whether the marriage was possible or not. He was, of course, ready at any time to stand before the altar with her; but her womanly fine feeling sensed that if he did so it would be merely to fulfil a duty. And so she never spoke of it to him again."(14)

(12) CMC, II, 77, 78.
(13) Ibid. 78.
(14) SZM, p. 107.

PRINCESS CAROLYNE SAYN-WITTGENSTEIN, IN LATER LIFE

LISZT IN 1885

From " Franz Liszt," Dr. Julius Kapp, Hesse-Verlag, Berlin

He was manifestly undergoing a racking crisis, physical, mental, and moral, in the first Roman years. Ferdinand Gregorovius records in his diary on 13th April, 1862, his first meeting with Liszt—"a striking, demoniac figure, tall, lean, with long grey hair. Frau von S. maintains that he is burnt out, that there is nothing left of him but the walls, that are licked by spectral flames."(15)

Human thoughts and actions are too subtle in their roots and ramifications to be glibly set forth in terms of this simple formula or that; and no one with the least understanding of human nature can persuade himself that to the leading actors in this Liszt-Wittgenstein drama either the first two acts or the tragic third were as psychologically simple as they now appear to the biographers. We can be tolerably certain that the particular neat simplification of it that now constitutes the Liszt legend is in large part false. The tendency of the idealising biographer is always to dramatise his subject, to shape him into the desired heroic figure by cutting away from him all the facts that do not square with the preconceived opinion of him. Contemporaries usually have a better sense of the man as he really is, in all his complexity, all his self-contradictions. It suits the biographer's book to present Liszt from first to last as a model of unselfishness, rectitude and chivalry, and to paint a pathetic portrait of him as the victim of the malignity of the Fates in this matter of the Wittgenstein marriage—a victim frustrated in the deepest wish of his heart, and driven, by this frustration, into a twenty-five-years' loneliness in which there was nothing left to him but religious resignation. But that romantic picture can hardly hold its ground against the plain facts as Liszt's contemporaries saw them. Their view of him was precisely the one that has slowly emerged in the foregoing pages as a result of the study of him in first-hand documents the authenticity of which cannot be challenged—no simple saint, but an exceedingly complex human being who was torn in twain, his whole life through, between his religious instincts and the imperious demands of the flesh, a man with undoubtedly

---

(15) GRT, p. 201.

P

a strong strain of chivalry in him, but also a man to whom play-acting was second nature, who dramatised himself more thoroughly than any of his biographers have done for him, and who, both in his public life and in his letters, consciously worked at the establishment of his own noble legend.

As the years went on, all his old friends became more and more convinced that at bottom he was an actor; their love for him, their admiration for what was great in him, their gratitude for all he had done for them and for music, remained unchanged; but they could no longer be under any delusion as to the shoddier elements in his composite being. The demoniac quality in the Zigeuner half of him, that was answerable for the incomparable quality of his piano-playing and for a good deal of what is best in his original music, had its false and common side; and it was this other side of him that ultimately alienated almost everyone who at some time or other had come under his magic spell. His long public career as an admired virtuoso and his training in the ways and manners of high cosmopolitan society had combined to give him a touch of brilliant insincerity even in some of his best moments. There was an element in him that rubbed the more solid Germans the wrong way. There emanated from him, both in his conduct and in his music, a subtle something that they felt to be non-German; Schumann, indeed, called him on one occasion "a French man of the world." It was this something, no doubt, that made Schumann, as early as 1840, feel that his own purely German nature was fundamentally irreconcilable with that of Liszt.

> "How extraordinarily he plays!" he wrote to Clara after one of Liszt's recitals—"boldly and wildly, and then again tenderly and ethereally! I have heard all this. But, Clärchen, this world—his world I mean—is no longer mine. Art, as you prac-tise it, and as I do when I compose at the piano, this tender intimacy I would not give for all his splendour—and indeed there is too much tinsel about it."(16)

It was this tinsel element in Liszt, again, that estranged Brahms and Joachim and many others, in spite of their willing admiration for many of his qualities; they were conscious of a

---

(16) LCS, I, 285.

touch of the charlatan in him. He created this impression not only by the character of his piano-playing when he happened to be in one of his more extravagant Zigeuner moods and by the quality of a good deal of his own rather too effusive music, but by his conduct in social intercourse. The Princess, with her too comprehensive idolatry of him, did much to strengthen his tendency to dramatise himself in the Weimar days. We have only to look at the absurdly theatrical pose he adopted in some of his portraits of this period, especially the one for which he sat to Kaulbach, to realise that there was a good deal of the posturing mountebank in him; no other composer, before or since, has attitudinised so grossly as this. It was all very much to his own rather flamboyant taste and that of the Princess, no doubt, but it occasionally set other and more sensitive people's teeth on edge. Cornelius noticed that with one or two intimates he was always simple and natural, but that in a larger company he was inclined to become an actor. When the pair met again at a festival in Meiningen in 1867, after an interval of six years, Cornelius succumbed at once to the old spell so long as he was with Liszt alone, but again observed that in public the Master could not refrain from striking the accustomed attitudes. Cornelius did not like the *pontifex maximus* airs he adopted with other musicians.

"Liszt," he wrote to Bertha Jung, "was very nice; but it is a curious thing, Wagner, for all his caprices and his tempestuousness, is dearer to me. With Liszt one is always uneasily conscious of the mask he puts on for the world. Yet he wants *himself*, *himself*, and again *himself;* no doubt about that. Is it so with Wagner, with Berlioz? God preserve us from having genius!"(17)

Fanny Ewald, who adored Liszt, and whose reminiscences were based on a thirty years' friendship with him, also gives us a hint of the difference between his private and his public manner.

"I had heard," she writes, *à propos* of her first meeting with him in Weimar in 1848, "a good deal of talk about the swagger with which he used to make his entry into a salon or a concert room, of the affected way in which he proudly threw back his mighty head, of his carefully calculated trick, when he seated himself at the piano at a concert, of letting his gloves slip from his hands on to the floor, to be snatched up by his enthusiastic female listeners and preserved as priceless mementoes. He was described as a man who was bent on making a sensation by means of empty externalities."

Fanny Ewald obviously feels that she cannot deny all this: the most she can do is to urge in his defence that "it is natural that a man who, from earliest childhood, has known that the eyes of others were turned inquisitively and admiringly on him, should gradually come to adopt a certain attitude in front of people," and to say that she always found Liszt "natural enough in intimate intercourse"—the obvious inference being that, as Cornelius also hints, he was inclined to pose on other occasions.(18)

6

In view of the genuine love and devotion of Cornelius, Bülow and a score of others for Liszt, it seems curious, at first sight, that Raabe should say that it was one of the great misfortunes of his life that he never had a male friend. Yet in the strict sense of the term this is true. It was always to women—Marie, the Princess, Agnes Street, Adelheid von Schorn—that Liszt fled when he wished to indulge himself in the whimpering self-pity to which he was periodically prone. There are no pitiful revelations of this kind in his correspondence with men, and very few instances are recorded of it in his personal intercourse with them. It may have been precisely because with men he always tried to conceal the softness of his real features behind the stiffness of his buckram mask that they became

---

(18) See LZBL, pp. 335, 336. Carl Maria Cornelius (CMC, I, 160) says that at Weimar Liszt "exaggerated to the point of the theatrical the French salon tone he had acquired, when there were guests present on whom he wanted to make an impression." Elsewhere Carl Maria Cornelius speaks of his father having been grieved by Liszt's "fatal habit of posing and pontifying, which he had picked up in Paris." It was generally only when numbers were present that Liszt became an actor (see CMC, I, 167).

suspicious that there *was* a mask, and, behind it, something that he would rather not reveal. It is surely significant that in the end they were inwardly all more or less alienated from him, feeling no enmity or dislike, indeed, but resigning themselves sadly to the conviction that the division of soul within him, and particularly the irrepressible actor within him, had flawed his life and his work from the beginning, and that now he was past curing. In the latter years even the disciples who had done most to propagate the gospel of his works denied their former faith. Even during the Weimar days, when the personal spell he exercised upon these young people was at its maximum, they were rather more critical of his music than is generally supposed. They did not, like Brahms, Joachim and others, give public expression to their doubts—they loved him too much for that; nor, indeed, could they criticise him publicly without damaging the progressive cause whose standard-bearer he was. But almost from the beginning there was much in his music that they did not like. As early as 1866 Bülow confessed to Alexander Ritter that his first enthusiasm for Liszt's music had lessened; if he still made propaganda for him, it was only out of piety and gratitude.(19) Five years before that, he had told Louis Köhler that while he subscribed to every note of the *Faust Symphony* he could not bring himself, without a certain amount of sophistry, to do that where the symphonic poems were concerned.(20) In his final years his reaction against Liszt's music was complete. He thought that the symphonic poems compared badly, in their own genre, with the *Hebrides* and other overtures of Mendelssohn.(21) And to Hans von Bronsart he admitted in 1888—two years after Liszt's death—that "the works and even the name of the 'great master' whom I worshipped idolatrously for several decades are to me now the object of an abhorrence

---

(19) BB, IV, 131.

(20) Ibid., III, 411, 412.

(21) See his letter of 5th July, 1884, to Emil Breslauer, in BBL, p. 418. He energetically rebuts the charge that he is a Liszt "renegade." He is still conscious, he says, of all he owes to his old master, but he can no longer feel the former enthusiasm for his music.

that is almost as unlimited as it is unconquerable: in this respect
I am completely of Joachim's way of thinking."(22)

Bülow, it is well known, became a little "queer" in his last
years—the result in part of sheer satiation with the exciting
music of Wagner, in part of degenerative changes in his
physical system, due to a lifetime of the grossest overwork.
But his final revolt against Liszt cannot be wholly explained in
these terms, for we find him expressing the same sentiments
in the eighteen-seventies. His widow tells us that during that
decade his old admiration for Liszt's music had changed to
positive aversion: the *Faust Symphony*, in particular, now seemed
to him "unmusic, quack music, antimusic."(23) In 1875 Liszt
offered him the post of piano professor at the National Conservatoire in Pesth. Bülow set forth his reasons for declining it in a
letter to Cosima of 3rd July:

> "The true, the essential, the principal motive for my refusal
> is that I find it morally and intellectually impossible to justify
> the valued confidence of Monsieur l'Abbé Liszt. Perhaps my
> beliefs of former days have been somewhat modified by time,
> by life, and by habit. For a long while this has been a real and
> lively grief to me. But if I can conceal from other eyes the
> metamorphosis to which, in some degree, I have been subject,
> if I can conceal it in practice by affirming to the full extent
> of my powers all that my musical conscience permits me to
> affirm, or to help others to affirm, I am frankly incapable of
> undertaking the task of an apostolate—forgive the presumptuous-
> ness of the expression!—for which the necessary faith and
> enthusiasm (necessarily exclusivist) have long forsaken me.
> I have become too much of a reactionary in the matter of
> instrumental music, which is now my province, for me to be
> the humble sacristan which your respected father has the right
> to expect. . . . I am no longer qualified for the post your father
> has had the kindness to offer me. The gratitude I shall eternally
> feel towards him will make me keenly watchful for any occasion,
> upon which I shall joyfully fasten, to testify my devotion to
> him. But these opportunities to serve him I am more likely to

---

(22) BB, VII, 203.

(23) BLW, p. 169.

find elsewhere than in the very dubious temple of a people that is half-barbarian, half-Israelitish or Israelised."(24)

7

Liszt, in fact, became intellectually a more and more lonely man in the last twenty years of his life. A number of young people, especially his later piano pupils, who came directly under the influence of his personal charm and profited by his sometimes excessive kindness, did indeed continue to fight for him; but virtually without exception the great figures of an earlier day who had once stood by his side—Bülow, Cornelius, Wagner, Berlioz and others—now drew away from him. Joachim, we are told, was to the end of his days convinced that a man of Wagner's penetration must really have held the same opinion about Liszt's music as he and Brahms and others did. Hermann Levi, in 1876, wrote to Clara Schumann thus: "The people who call themselves Wagnerians and lift on their shields, side by side with Wagner, a talented humbug like Liszt, are as nauseous to me as those who oppose Wagner on principle are incomprehensible."(25)

Liszt's services to Wagner during his Weimar days are undeniable, even though there is reason for holding that they have been exaggerated by the biographers: but there can be no question that, in general, the linking of their two names in a common cause was often a disadvantage to Wagner; he had to share in the dislike and distrust that Liszt's music and Liszt's character aroused in many quarters.

All this later criticism of Liszt by his old friends was not, as is commonly alleged, a matter of "ingratitude"; it was purely and simply that there was something both in Liszt's music and in his personality to which many of them could no longer reconcile themselves.(26) We have a valuable light on this matter in a

---

(24) BNB, p. 507.

(25) LCS (German edition), III, 341.

(26) Much has been made by the biographers of the "ingratitude" of Berlioz, for whom Liszt had done so much. Berlioz's estrangement from Liszt in the later years was certainly due, in part, to jealousy over the latter's unshakable admiration for Wagner. But in part also it came

letter of Cornelius in which (about 1868) he declined the
suggestion of a German publisher that he should write a biography of Liszt. The inflexibly honest Cornelius felt, as his son
says, that he "could not fulfil the duty of a biographer to be a
panegyrist." "The biographer who wishes to give pleasure,"
Cornelius wrote to the publishers, "must have in him something
of the evangelist: he must be able to speak with the utmost
conviction of the divinity of his hero. . . ." He has the fullest
appreciation of Liszt's aims, he says, but "my own artistic
development has brought me to a point at which I can no longer
take the tone of a panegyrist with regard to the majority of his
works." Cornelius's likes and dislikes in this connection make
very interesting reading today: he accepts wholeheartedly the
Gran Mass, the piano sonata, *Ce qu'on entend sur la montagne*,
St. Elizabeth, *Prometheus*, *Hungaria*, the *Totentanz*, and other
works. He regards Liszt as "the classical piano composer of our
epoch," making a third with Bach and Beethoven. He is "convinced that his Hungarian Rhapsodies, his two concertos, the
Totentanz, the *Wandererphantasie* and his *Rhapsody with
Orchestra* will still be played and admired centuries hence."
But he now has his doubts about *Orpheus*, *Hamlet*, *Hunnenschlacht*, *Mazeppa*, the *Ideale*, the majority of his songs, and
even the *Faust* and the *Dante*.

So much, he says, for Liszt the artist. As regards the man
also he finds himself in a difficulty. He pays a warm tribute to
Liszt's generosity and magnanimity; but, he says, there is a
second point to be considered by a Liszt biographer—

---

from an honest inability to like some of Liszt's later music. Liszt could
hardly complain of this, since he himself, as he told Göllerich, turned
against Berlioz's music to some extent in his later years, especially the
Symphonie fantastique, the third movement of which he now preferred
to the other four, and the *Damnation de Faust*, which, he said, "contained some fine things," though as a whole he "did not like it" (see
GFL, p. 43). "Ingratitude" has nothing whatever to do with matters
of this kind: they represent simply an honest revision of opinion. Artists
who have worked together enthusiastically in their youth, feeling themselves to be brothers in the fight for progress, often become more
conscious of their dissimilarities than of their common qualities as their
personalities develop with the years.

"the moral centre of his life, the ethical conflict, with regard
to which I ask myself, without being able to supply an answer
to the question, whether Liszt has succeeded in emerging from
it as a victor. My lack of clear vision in this respect, in conjunction with his later entering upon a spiritual career [Liszt
had taken minor orders in the Catholic Church in 1865] constitutes a hindrance to me as a biographer, brings an element of
doubt into my mood."

Then he gives his opinion upon Liszt's action in throwing up
his work in Weimar after the episode of *The Barber of Bagdad*—
an opinion to which insufficient attention has been given by the
biographers. He holds that there was no real necessity for
Liszt to have taken this drastic step, and that he had been
morally wrong in doing so; he puts it down to pique "at not
being accepted by the Germans during his lifetime as a demi-
god after he had boldly and adroitly soared to distinction on
Wagner's shoulders"; and he claims that in suddenly turning
his back on the movement of progress Liszt had "thrown away
the baby with the bath." The charge will give offence to the
uncritical believers in the Liszt legend, but it cannot be dismissed with a shrug of the shoulders. Cornelius knew Liszt
inside out; he had observed him critically at close quarters for
some two years in Weimar, and he was there when Liszt, in his
rage at the opposition to *The Barber of Bagdad*, resolved to
sever his connection with the town. He was therefore in a better
position than any modern writer to see the situation as it was
and to know the real workings of Liszt's mind; and if he decided
that there were other reasons than the ostensible one for Liszt's
sudden abandonment of his ideal, he must be listened to
attentively.

"Without censuring this behaviour of the energetic artist,"
he continues, "[I hold that] the Liszt I have in mind, and whose
praises I would sing in the loudest tones, ought to have remained
at his post in spite of every misunderstanding: self-renunciation
in this sense was the touchstone by which the gold of his labours
proved itself, to the outer world, not to have been free from
alloy. Kammerherr(27) and Abbé are snakeskins of vanity; the

(27) The Grand Duke of Weimar had given him the rank of Chamberlain
as a solatium for his disappointments.

God-sent musician Franz Liszt is the only person with whom
I am concerned. How then could I, during his lifetime, peel the
bark off the tree, without running the serious risk of doing
justice in no quarter and to no one?"

And he recommends to the publishers as biographer, in place
of himself, Heinrich Porges, "who unites a congenial point of
view with an unqualified enthusiasm for Liszt."(28)

It is impossible to resist the cumulative weight of all this
evidence; it is clear that, for all the consummate quality of
Liszt's acting, the sharper-eyed among his contemporaries, at
any rate, were not duped by it. They were acutely aware, being
at close quarters with him, of currents and motives in him that
we today can only reconstruct laboriously from the relevant
documents; they felt there was something fundamentally insincere in him. The insincerity may have been largely unconscious on his part, so persistently had he dramatised himself
to himself and to the world; but about its existence there can be
no doubt.

8

One point in connection with this gradual setting of the
current against Liszt even within his own circle deserves a little
attention. It is a curious fact that all these people, when trying
to make up the debit and credit sides of their account with
Liszt's music, ignored completely the piano works of his first
period. Their talk is mainly about his orchestral works: Cornelius is almost the only one who specifically mentions the
piano sonata, and that also is a work of the Weimar years. The
earliest Liszt seems to have been forgotten by everybody.
Cornelius, when he called Liszt "the classical piano composer
of our epoch," plainly had in mind the sonata and the two piano
concertos, for in the first place the piano works of Liszt's first
period would be regarded not as classical but as romantic in
the second half of the nineteenth century, and in the second
place Cornelius's coupling of Liszt's name with that of Beethoven is clearly due to the recognition of Liszt's original achievements in the way of large-scale construction in solo piano music
and in works for piano and orchestra.

_____

(28) CMC, II, 132, 133.

But in the eighteen-thirties and early 'forties there had been quite another Liszt, whose piano works are in their smaller way as significant as those of his middle period. The man who had conceived these early works was fully justified in believing that, given a mode of life in which he would have leisure for concentration and self-cleansing, he had it in him to produce something epoch-making in a larger genre. Liszt's works of his first period fall into three main classes—the fantasias, arrangements, and studies, in which the incomparable virtuoso surrenders himself to the delight of exploiting all the known and a multitude of the yet unrealised possibilities of the piano; the original works, such as the *Mazeppa* Study (which in its first form dates from about 1838), in which the thinking itself is to some extent conditioned by technical problems of "l'exécution transcendante;" and the quieter, more thoughtful works, that present hardly any technical difficulties, but in which Liszt poured out the ecstasy or the trouble of his youthful soul. The division here made is a rough-and-ready one, but it will serve our present purpose.

The technical brilliance and audacities of the virtuoso works no doubt distracted the general attention of his contemporaries from the more solid qualities of them, and blinded them to the evidence they afforded not merely of the youthful Liszt's present powers as a pianist but of his latent possibilities as a composer. As Saint-Saëns has pointed out, some of Liszt's fantasias upon and transcriptions of other men's works indicate more talent for composition than many an "original" work by this composer or that; Liszt's musical imagination often played upon his material in a fashion of its own that may almost be called creative.

"If we take the trouble to study Liszt's fantasias," says Saint-Saëns, "we discover how very different they are from the ordinary pot-pourri, in which themes have been taken from an opera only to serve as a pretext for arabesques, festoons, and astragals. We see how Liszt can take any bone and extract the marrow out of it, how his penetrating mind has cut through trivialities and platitudes and got to the hidden artistic germ, which he proceeds to fertilise; how, if he is dealing with a work

of a high order, such as *Don Giovanni*, he not only illuminates
the beauties of it but adds a commentary of his own that gives
us a new insight into them and helps us to appreciate more fully
their supreme perfection and their immortal modernity."(29)

   In the wholly original works of this first period Liszt already
reveals himself as potentially the subtlest harmonist of that
epoch. More than that: he creates a new type of piano thinking,
the direct recording of intimate personal moods, of *choses vues*
and *choses veçues*, in a language and a form that are the native,
the organic counterpart of them. One is sometimes tempted to
censure the star concert pianists for hardly ever playing these
works. But on further reflection one is glad, on the whole, that
they do not: these pieces belong to that genre of music that is
best savoured in the quietness of one's study, where a composer
seems to be talking confidentially to us alone of the things that
have most concerned his soul. Now the curious thing is that
practically all this music, which is so significant to us today, and
so calculated, by its expressiveness and its sincerity, to commend Liszt to us, appears to have fallen out of the reckoning of
musicians in the second half of the nineteenth century. A few
people may still have played these works in private, but there
was no public discussion of them. The reason is that, not long
after the turn of the mid-century, Germany became sharply
conscious that it was standing on the threshold of a new era in
music, mainly as the result of the controversy that Wagner's
revolutionary theory and practice had called forth. By 1860
the difference between the partisans of "the music of the future"
and those of "the classical spirit" had become so acute that
Brahms and Joachim were moved to issue their famous public
protest against the ideals and tendencies of the "New German
School." For that generation, for his friends as for his foes, the
only Liszt that mattered was the Liszt who was engaged in the
composition of large-scale works embodying a new ideal of
aesthetic—the "fertilisation of music by poetry"—and a new
principle of symphonic design: the great piano sonata had been
published in 1854, while the first six of the symphonic poems

---

(29) SSPS, p. 20.

(*Tasso*, *Les Préludes*, *Orpheus*, *Prometheus*, *Mazeppa* and *Fest-klänge*) had been floated in one breath, as it were, in 1856, to be followed in 1857 by *Ce qu'on entend sur la montagne*, in 1858 by *Die Ideale*, in 1859 by the *Dante Symphony*, and in 1861 by *Hamlet*, *Hunnenschlacht* and the *Faust Symphony*. (The *Faust* and the *Dante* had both been performed, before publication, in 1857).

9

It was over these works that the journalistic war raged, and in the din of it the earlier Liszt was either forgotten or regarded as of minor significance. Now the Liszt of the Weimar orchestral works was in some respects a different Liszt, spiritually, from the Liszt of the years in which he had written the earlier pieces of the *Années de Pélerinage* and the *Harmonies poétiques et réligieuses*. It was inevitable that the discussion should mostly take, in the press, the form of arguments for and against the mere externalities of the new works; critics and professors always prefer to talk about this aspect of music because it seems to offer them concrete material for judgment in terms of objective "values." But, as is always the case in matters of this kind, most of the arguments for and against the "form" of Liszt's music were only attempts to find a justification in theory for an attraction or repulsion that was in essence temperamental and instinctive. It is himself that a man expresses in his music, if he has a self to express at all: and we are either drawn to it and to him by a similarity of constitution and of spiritual experience on our part, or alienated from it and from him by a vague sense that the inner world of this music is not, and never will be, ours. There was a good deal in these Weimar works that grated on the sensibilities of certain temperaments: for all their fine qualities, it cannot be denied that occasionally there is something theatrical in their pose, something rank in their sentiment, something too rhetorical in their gestures. Every composer's mind has a certain odour, so to speak, that either strikes pleasantly on our nostrils or does not: it is the somewhat corrupt odour of Meyerbeer's mind, for instance, that makes us turn away from him today. In the Weimar days Liszt's mind had taken on a peculiar odour, largely as the result of his daily association with the mind of the Princess. In basic essentials, it is true, this odour is the same as that of his first period; but it has now become more pungent, with an occasional drift into downright rankness. It was this, not the mere "form" of Liszt's music, that really alienated so many of his contemporaries.

We may be tolerably sure that many of his partisans too were conscious of it and did not take kindly to it. But they would be unwilling to dwell upon it in public: their business just then was not to see Liszt steadily and see him whole but to take their stand by his side in the battle for freedom that he and Wagner were waging. While a war is on, the allies sink their individual differences for the sake of the common cause; it is only when the victory has been won that they become acutely conscious of each other's failings. However subconsciously aware Liszt's Weimar friends and colleagues may have been from the first that there were elements in his music of which they did not approve, it was impossible for them to give expression to these views in public; to have done that would have been to furnish arms to the enemy. But there is a fair amount of internal evidence that there was something in this music to which they could never quite reconcile themselves: and when the victory had at last been won for the new aesthetic, not so much by Liszt as by Wagner, even Liszt's old friends began to feel themselves at liberty to say more or less openly what they had previously dared to say only to themselves. Hence the apparent "desertion" of him in the later years by many of those who had constituted his bodyguard in the days when the battle was still raging between the "old" art and the "new."

Once more we must bear in mind that those in close contact with Liszt were conscious of correspondences between the man and his music that have become obscured for the rest of us during the passage of the years. They saw clearly how his mind had been coloured, not always to its advantage, by the Princess; and they were less tolerant than we, with our historical sense, can now be of certain elements that had spread from her to his music. They saw him as a man divided against himself, too weak to withstand an influence that was in many ways bad for him as an artist. The Princess's perfumed religiosity, her passion for crude effect, her mountebankery of thought and tumidity of expression, all left their mark upon him, and led to the exaggeration of certain elements in him of which, under a different influence, he might perhaps have purged himself. And it was these elements that in time made it impossible for his old friends to admire his music unreservedly. All talk of "ingratitude" in this connection is beside the mark. Wagner, for instance, was anything but ungrateful to Liszt: it angered him, indeed, to see Liszt's great services to the musical life of his generation meeting with such inadequate recognition in the later years. In Cosima's diary we see Wagner protesting against this public forgetfulness; "without Liszt," she reports him as saying, with a pardonable touch of exaggeration, in 1878, "I cannot imagine how things would have turned out." He went on to speak of her father's "experiences at the hands of Joachim, Raff, and so on;" "he has been able to do far more for others," said Wagner, "than I have."(30)

10

Wagner and Cosima often discussed Liszt's works together. In 1869, at a time when he was alienated from them over the Bülow affair, Wagner often talked about him purely as an artist. He paid tribute to his original achievements in the matter of form, but, he said, he was distressed at the turn Liszt's mind had gradually taken. "He had a strong liking," says Cosima, "for the *Faust Symphony*, and for the *Mazeppa* because of the big impulse that ran through it; but he deplored Liszt's fatal apotheosis-mania, the triangle, tamtam and chain-clanking effects in the *Tasso*, and so on. His church music, he said, was a childish play with intervals"—a judgment that was probably provoked by one of the weaker specimens of this music, and must not be taken as applying to the religious works as a whole. "He regretted all the more that he had never lived in real union with Liszt, and he deplored the influence of the Princess

---

(30) DMCW, p. 822.

Wittgenstein, who, like a savage, was susceptible only to the crudest effects in music."(31)

In the final days of Wagner's life Cosima exhorted him more than once to express his opinion frankly to Liszt about the latter's new works, but he could not bring himself to do so; it was too devastating for that. Cosima herself felt that something had crept into her father's music that indicated degeneration from what he once had been. When *Die Glocken von Strassburg* arrived she noted in her diary, "A strange work: very effectively put together, but so alien to us." Some time before that, after going through the score of the *Christus* with Wagner, she had written in her diary.

> "What I know of this work so far does not make a very beautiful impression on me. For a man to renounce the achievements of great art in order to imitate the gabble of priests argues poverty of intellect. We are sad over this development of my father, the main responsibility for which certainly rests with the Princess Wittgenstein."(32)

Liszt's life seemed to both of them the saddest of tragedies, owing to the unhealable dissensions within his own soul.

And when Berlioz, after hearing the Gran Mass in Paris in 1861, turned over to d'Ortigue the distasteful task of writing a notice of the work in the *Débats*, and, a few days later, left the Erard concert hall while one of the symphonic poems was being played, it was not because he had become unmindful of all that Liszt had done for him in days gone by, but because there was something in the odour of this music that nauseated him. For us of today all this revolt against Liszt's music on the part of his friends does not influence our own judgment of the personal and historical merits or demerits of that music. Our present concern is simply with the evidence the revolt affords as to the existence of something, partly in the music, partly in the man, that gradually alienated practically all those who, from long experience of them both, were best able to correlate the two in their intertwined development during the years since Liszt

(31) DMCW, pp. 458, 459.

(32) Ibid., pp. 989, 720, 612.

had given his artistic soul into the keeping of the Princess. Most of all, perhaps, they objected to the odour of patchouli that clung to so much of Liszt's religious and ethical music: it was this element in it that made the friendly-disposed Ambros say of some of these works that they reminded him of "those cakes that are set out in the cloisters during church festivals: they are good, dainty cakes, adorned not with the ordinary tragacanth cupids or opera figurines but with apostles, evangelists, and saints."(33) The tone of the criticism is courteous; but under it we detect the note of ironical amusement that runs through so many discussions of Liszt and his music in that epoch.

---

(33) ABB, p. 65.

Q

CHAPTER VIII

PULL FRANCISCAN, PULL ZIGEUNER

I

Raabe holds that Liszt's love for Carolyne made him her "slave." "She made it her life's task," he says, " to save Liszt by prayer and work. Wholly obsessed by this task, she did everything, according to her knowledge and her power, that would, in her belief, help him to develop in the direction she desired for him. Whether she succeeded as regards prayer we do not know; but unhappily there is no doubt that she mostly chose the wrong means to further his work."(1) This may or may not be true. She was undoubtedly answerable for certain dubious elements in both his music and his literary work; but the question arises whether Liszt would really have allowed himself to be drawn, even by Carolyne, in a direction which in his heart of hearts he did not want to take. If he did, he was an even weaker character than we have supposed: we cannot imagine Wagner working according to the prescriptions of Minna, or Berlioz according to those of Marie Recio, or Beethoven according to those even of the Immortal Beloved. It may be, again, that in taking minor orders in the Church of Rome in 1865 he allowed himself to be influenced in some degree by the Princess, whose ambition for him now was the dual one that he should endow the world with a new type of religious music and that he should become the official head of church music in Rome. But here again, considering Liszt's strong natural bias towards religion and the passionate interest he took in his own religious works, which he regarded as so many chapters in spiritual autobiography, it seems superfluous to assume that the Princess did more than, with her usual energy, cross his own t's and dot his own i's. All this, however, is no

---

(1) RLL, pp. 146, 147.

more than a side issue: what more immediately concerns our present enquiry is the inveterate tendency of Liszt to let the attractions of the worldly life stand in the way of the consistent development of the best that was in him as a composer. And as to that the evidence is conclusive. He had often bewailed his indolence and impotence in the d'Agoult days; and the rift between himself and Marie, as we have seen, was largely due to the fact that she was angered by the vulgarian element in him that made him prefer the flashy life of the virtuoso and the man of the salons to the solitude, whether physical or simply spiritual, in which alone great works can be conceived and carried out. In the Weimar days he worked so well because the Princess's hand, at once loving and compelling, was always on his shoulder. In the Rome-Pesth-Weimar days of the final twenty years of so of his life he was visibly a ship without a rudder because that hand was withdrawn.

At first, in Rome, he had tried to persuade himself that now he would give himself up heart and soul to his true vocation of solitary and saint. He settled down in a cloister that had been placed at his disposal in the church of Santa Maria del Rosario, on the Monte Mario. There was no one in the vast place but Liszt, a Dominican priest, and a servant. The priest read mass every morning; Liszt was always present, sitting in a stall a few yards from his cell. In the latter he had a long work-table, a small library, about a dozen pictures of saints, a marble cast of Chopin's hand, and a small piano of advanced age, badly out of tune, and with a D in the bass missing. But, as usual, he was making the best of both worlds. His tribute having been paid to the spirit in the morning, in the evening he let the flesh have its fling in the kind of company it loved. Shrewd observers were conscious of something suspiciously like a pose in his way of living: Schlözer, for example, who saw a good deal of him at this time, opined that it was "only one of his bizar-reries for the benefit of the world—to make people talk about him," and foresaw the probability of his one day doing some-thing that would surprise the world.(2) There were already

(2) SRB, pp. 71, 72. Schlözer's letters are especially valuable for this period in Liszt's life.

rumours, Schlözer notes in March, 1864, that Liszt was about ·
to enter the church; but he can see no foreshadowing of that
step in Liszt's gay behaviour at the dinner table or in the drawing
room. He is the most charming company when he is in a good
humour, and "as pleased as any beginner when he sees that one
of his own works is appreciated." When he plays the piano he
still indulges in the old showman trick of his virtuoso days
—commented on by more than one observer—of suddenly
turning round to his audience and fixing them with a carefully
calculated demoniac look that bores into them like a gimlet.
But when he is in a bad humour, especially when he is asked
to play and does not want to, he can be very unpleasant indeed.

The real reason for his taking minor orders in 1865 will
never be known. Perhaps there was no one reason, but several
reasons, so interwoven that Liszt himself would have been
unable to disentangle them. As most of the people with whom
he came into contact were conscious of the strange mixture of
sincerity and play-acting in him, it is not surprising that the
oddest rumours circulated in Rome. Due credit was given in
some quarters to the Princess's desire that he should now devote
his art to religion. But even *her* motives were the subject of
speculation: Schlözer, who knew everyone in Rome in the
Liszt-Wittgenstein circle, opined at first that Carolyne was
anxious to plant Liszt in the church because she was afraid he
was going to marry some young girl or other; to frustrate this
plan she induced the Roman ecclesiastics to work upon his
religious feelings. She and they, it was said, were aided and
abetted by the Wittgenstein family, which, scenting a misalliance on the composer's part, got Cardinal Hohenlohe (the
brother of the Prince Hohenlohe who had married Carolyne's

Another friend of his Roman days, Frau Nadine Helbig, writing her
reminiscences of him some forty years later, still remembered that
while his breakfast was of a "Spartan or Franciscan" frugality, at a
lavish dinner in some rich house or other he was once more the gay
man of the world (see HLR, p. 74). No doubt many a guest cocked an
amused eye at the easy way in which Liszt could abandon his Franciscan
pose when the food and wine were good and the conversation merry.
Frau Helbig, by the way, had still, in her old age, a lively recollection of
his "horribly strong Tuscan cigars."

daughter) to use his influence with Liszt.(3) Marriage was in all probability no part of Liszt's plans, either then or at any other period: but he may quite possibly have been showing signs of his perennial infatuation with some young petticoat or other about this time. That these rumours were in circulation in Rome is proved by the fact that Carolyne took the trouble to assure Schlözer that there was no truth in them—that Liszt had not taken orders either to escape marriage with her or any-one else, or to achieve some day the ambition of a Cardinal's hat; his motives, she said, were partly religious, partly artistic.

We may be permitted to conjecture that there was another motive also—the desire to attain inward peace. This, the close student of him finally concludes, was the central desire of his whole life, a desire never gratified, because he had not the strength of mind to will firmly enough the many renunciations that alone would have brought him to inner harmony with himself. As on a hundred previous occasions, he may have deluded himself in 1865 that the way to inward peace was by way of an outer demonstration, to himself and to others; by visibly marking himself off from the world by means of the cassock and the tonsure he may have thought he could assist his weak will to renounce the world. This, in substance, was Fanny Ewald's reading of his problem in 1865. He was fifty-five, she says. "The *allegro con brio* of his life lay behind him. His plans for Weimar had come to nothing. He had been unable to bring his association with the Princess to a tranquil-lising end by means of a marriage. He must have felt that it was time to impose a barrier between his past and his future; and he assured Stahr later . . . that he had gone to Rome to achieve a decision." In taking minor orders, Fanny Ewald thought, Liszt was obeying an instinct "to bring beauty and dignity into his life, to shape it to a living work of art."(4)

---

(3) SRB, pp. 210-211. Schlözer's letter is dated 25th April, 1865. It was in Monseigneur Hohenlohe's private chapel in the Vatican that Liszt received the tonsure.

(4) SZBL, p. 378. As usual with her where Liszt was concerned, Fanny Ewald takes the purely idealistic line.

It was a revival of the old hope for spiritual equilibration; but the hope was as far from fulfilment as in the d'Agoult days. The soft and rotten matter in his soul could not be cut away from the outside, but only from within; and he lacked the strength of will and the steadiness of hand to be his own surgeon.

2

The old vanity, the old love of titles and orders, was still strong within him. Schlözer tells us how one evening, after a gala dinner, he went with him to a concert and ball of the German Künstlerverein in Rome. Liszt had been wearing some twenty crosses, and round his neck "not his four or six Commander crosses, for which he had a weakness, but simply the Prussian Order of Merit." As they entered the hall he put all these away, but said to Schlözer "When we go in, please, my dear fellow, address me as Herr von Liszt, or Kammerherr von Liszt: I possess both the 'von' and the 'Kammerherr'. In France they quite rightly call me Monsieur Liszt; but for the Germans I must hang out the Kammerherr."(5) Schrader thinks that this was just a piece of irony on Liszt's part, which Schlözer took too seriously; it is inconsistent, Schrader thinks, with all we know of Liszt as he really was.(6) On the contrary, it is perfectly consistent with all we know of him; it is inconsistent only with the popular Liszt legend. His passion for the display of his decorations was notorious: he himself tells the Princess, in his letter of 17th October, 1877, that in an article in *L'Univers* he has been gently castigated for wearing his "numerous decorations" on the occasion of the fête-day of the Emperor Francis.(7) His amused contemporaries found it a little difficult to reconcile this naïve delight in worldly honours with the renunciation of the shows and shams of the world that was implied in the cassock of the Abbé.

We are told that it was a great satisfaction to his admirers, especially the feminine portion of them, to discover that after

---

(5) SRB, p. 181.
(6) SFL, p. 28.
(7) LZB, VII, 203.

the drastic step of taking minor orders the unbecoming tonsure was "hardly noticeable" in that mass of "world-historic hair." Nor was a malign influence of the tonsure particularly noticeable in any other quarter: Liszt dined out assiduously with the same old carnal gusto, his newly-donned and quite impressive Abbé's robe never preventing him, for example, from doing full justice to the excellent Amontillado of the Prussian Ambassador, Arnim. He had no intention, he told Schlözer, of giving up music: "I will show them," he said, "what music in a cassock can be like."(8)

But at heart he was not happy. He could be alternately charming, rough and sarcastic, but Schlözer noted that at bottom he seemed to be possessed by a profound melancholy. As usual, he both longed to retire from the world and to live in it and enjoy it; and the contrary pull of the Franciscan and the Zigeuner in him gave him the old sad feeling of futility and waste. In the salon he enjoyed being fêted; on his return to his cell he loathed it, and loathed himself for having enjoyed it. "Believe me," he said to Schlözer on one occasion, "celebrity is the punishment of talent and the chastisement of merit."(9) After a charity concert that Liszt had arranged, and at which the usual flattering homage had been paid to him, Schlözer remarked how wonderful it must be to be able to kindle the world to such enthusiasm. The tears came into Liszt's eyes: "Believe me, my friend," he said, "I would gladly give up all this applause, all this enthusiasm, if I could only produce one really creative work."(10) That, in fact, was the secret sorrow of his being. Without the Princess to lead him to their common *prie-dieu* he now too often lacked the strength to believe in himself sufficiently to bend all his energies to the task of composition. Gregorovius notes in his diary on 30th April, 1865, that immediately after his taking orders Liszt "looks well and is contented. This is the end of the great virtuoso, who was a truly sovereign personality." But on 26th November of the

---

(8) SRB, pp. 210-217.

(9) The aphorism is by Chamfort. Liszt was fond of quoting it.

(10) SRB, p. 187.

same year he records, "I met Liszt—now an Abbé—at Fräulein von Stein's. They say he already regrets his metamorphosis."(11) He could be everything by turns, but nothing long. At this time he was manifestly wilting under the strain of the incessant pull between the two sides of his nature: Gregorovius observed in February, 1866, that he was looking very old and shrunken, though his manner was still lively.(12)

3

It was the constant complaint of the Princess, all through these years, that he was surrendering himself to his natural indolence. At first his reception into the church appeared to have worked beneficially on him. Adelheid von Schorn, who saw him again in Weimar in 1866, thought he seemed "tranquillised."

"He had come from Rome purified and calm. He was delighted to be musically active again [he had come back to Germany to take the rehearsals for the approaching festival at Meiningen and at the Wartburg, where his *St. Elizabeth* was to be performed]; he was brisk and eager both in body and mind. The conflicts of the earlier Weimar days lay far behind him; with the donning of the Abbé's robe he had translated himself to another sphere. Although he had received only minor orders, was not a priest and could not read the mass, yet as a secular ecclesiastic he had entered upon a path along which his life could have moved tranquilly to the end, had he himself not brought instability and unrest into it again later."(13)

By 1869, when Adelheid saw him once more in Weimar, he had aged greatly, though he was still only fifty-eight; and while he was as charming and as courteous as ever, he seemed changed in many ways. His wandering life, his inner discontent with himself, were telling on him. He had to bear as best he could the Princess's constant reproaches that he was wasting himself on society and not working hard enough. Not that he did not put in a considerable number of hours at his desk. He was not idle

---

(11) GRT, pp. 298-299, 313.

(12) Ibid., p. 320.

(13) SZM, p. 118.

in the literal sense of the term; but his arrangements, transcriptions, fantasias and so on were not what Carolyne wanted from him. In May, 1865, he informs her that his day has been spent in reading some fifty pages of the *Catechism of Perseverance* and in making an arrangement from *L'Africaine*. Presumably she found fault with him for this, for in his next letter he writes, "Do not scold me for prolonging my musical indolence(14) for another week. It would be difficult for me to work here, but I promise to make up for lost time."(15) This was a *leit-motiv* of which both Carolyne and Marie knew all the permutations and combinations!

Another *leit-motiv*, the first statement of which we have in his letters of thirty-five years earlier to Marie, also drags its slow length through the pages of his correspondence of this later time. His hunger for the good things of the world drives him into the world; but he has no sooner tasted what it has to offer him than he longs, or imagines he longs, for solitude. "My true nature," he writes to Carolyne from Munich in 1867, "is for martyrdom. You alone have understood this. If it has sometimes happened that I have blessed existence, it is only because of you." A year later he tells her that his thoughts and his desires are "of an infantine simplicity." If at one time he had had dreams of glory, these have now completley disappeared: "neither success, nor distractions, nor honours of any kind now have the smallest attraction for me." To achieve the little he can do in music, he continues, he is convinced that it is better for him to live apart from the world. "If I had my choice, I would live in some country place far from a railway—live in my own fashion, without troubling anyone. Were it not for a certain inclination towards personal independence which I do not think I ought to combat, I would willingly turn Franciscan."(16) He returns to this theme more than once; he is always sure he will manage to find "some corner or other of the earth

---

(14) He often calls or signs himself "Fainéant" ("sluggard") in his letters to her. It was a name she had given him in the Weimar days.

(15) LZB, VI, 79, 80.

(16) Ibid., 175.

where I can write my music, and read my breviary as I understand it."(17) In 1880 he tells the Princess that his celebrity
weighs heavily on him, "but it is a tyrannical *impasse!* I could
wish henceforth simply to work and pray in my corner; but that
corner, alas, I cannot find!"(18) He could have found it had he
desired it ardently enough. More than forty years before this
he had bewailed to the Abbé Lamennais the waste of his life in
fashionable society: "Will my life," he cried, "always be soiled
with the idle uselessness that frets me? Will the hour of devotion and of *virile action* never come? Am I condemned for
ever to this trade of a buffoon whose business it is to entertain a
salon?"(19) But to the end of his days the "buffoon" in him
could not resist the temptation to take the easy salon line
towards popularity and applause.

4

He was sincere enough when he told Carolyne that he meant
to "leave the world and live in the country, in order to read,
educate myself, and work without intermission and without
repose to my dying day;" but, as usual, he was deluding himself.
There was nothing whatever to hinder him from living the life
of a Franciscan in fact, if not in name, had he really desired to
do so. But he loved the world too much to give it up: the
potential martyr was willing enough to get an ecstatic shudder
from the contemplation of his cross, but to have been stretched
upon it would have been too uncomfortable. It is understandable that he should travel about a good deal to hear performances of his works or take part in them; like every other artist,
he felt fortified by any sign of public appreciation, however
much he might affect to despise the judgment of the public.
But apart from that there was the element in him that made
dining out, and gay conversation, and adulation, and, above all,
the company of adoring women, a sheer necessity to him.
Carolyne knew him too well, as Marie had formerly done, to

(17) LZB, VI, 180.

(18) Ibid., VII, 275.

(19) Ibid., I, 17.

believe in the ultimate validity of his desire for solitude. In 1872 she writes to thank Adelheid for taking care of him once more in Weimar. "Continue to take this place in my name, so that others may not take it. Liszt cannot endure solitude. It is true that a *single* companion has never sufficed him; but when he has good company at home he wastes himself less on useless or superfluous things." That is true, Adelheid comments: "Liszt could not bear to be alone, except when he was occupied with some work that absorbed him wholly. This, however, was not the case in Weimar [in the eighteen-seventies]. Here he lived in the world, among his pupils and in society."(20) "The Princess," she writes later, "suffered at seeing Liszt fritter away his time instead of working." The biographers make it a grievance against Carolyne that she wished him to devote himself entirely now to writing music for the glory of the church; but it is evident that the *fons et origo* of her complaints was not so much that he was not working at religious composition as that he was often hardly working at all, preferring to squander himself on anyone or anything that would save him from realising the Franciscan solitude that he both so desired and so dreaded.

"Liszt," says Adelheid, "knew best what he was doing when he remained a man of the world even after becoming an Abbé—a point that distressed the Princess, who would have preferred him to live in Rome and Tivoli and work for the glory of God. Liszt *could not* be always composing, however; he needed outer stimulants, he needed the world. When he was in the mood to write serious things he was happy to be doing so; but the mood was not always there. Every true artist knows that it must be so. When he merely wanted to *work*, he made transcriptions, arrangements, etc. He had done so much original work at Weimar because Carolyne's influence could there be exerted upon him daily. In Rome he escaped from this influence, and, to her great grief, went his own way."(21)

The complaints against the Princess would be better justified had Liszt used his independence during the last twenty-five

---

(20) SZM, pp. 221, 222.

(21) Ibid., pp. 260, 261.

years of his life to produce a notable quantity of first-rate work, in whatever genre he might have chosen. But apart from some of his sacred works he wrote, in all this time, comparatively little that is of the first importance, while the list of his transcriptions of other men's work is enormous. The conclusion is irresistible that without the daily moral support of the Princess he no longer believed in himself as he had done in Weimar; and his self-doubt, as Schlözer saw, was one of the causes of his secret unhappiness. Not only the Princess but Liszt's friends must have been grieved to see the man who had produced the piano sonata, the *Faust Symphony*, and other works of the same calibre now complacently turning out arrangements of the Waltz from Gounod's *Faust*, of pieces from *Rienzi*, the *Flying Dutchman*, *Tannhäuser*, *L'Africaine*, the *Ruins of Athens*, *Norma*, *La Sonnambula*, *Aida*, of the songs of Schubert, Schumann, and even Clara, the *Danse Macabre* of Saint-Saëns, and so on. The energy put into work of this kind would have been much better employed in original creation. It may be pleaded, in extenuation, that these transcriptions were undertaken in order to make money. The answer to that would seem to be that a genuine Franciscan would not have needed much money.(22) Liszt, however, had all the desire but none of the will to be a genuine Franciscan. Nor, one suspects, was the creative impulse strong enough in him to produce much great work during all these later years. He *had* to be always filling up music paper, as more than one passage in his letters proves; for only at his desk could he forget his troubles and to some degree or other

---

(22) While complaining of his "poverty," and pleading that he had to turn out a lot of musical rubbish in order to get a little money, he was as lavish as in his young days in showy expenditure on others. In Rubinstein's honour, for instance, he gave a dinner to which forty guests were invited. His "poverty" during this period of his life has been exaggerated by his sentimental biographers. If he travelled cheaply—sometimes meanly—that was, in part, only one of his Franciscan poses. There was really no necessity for him to do so, and his friends often remonstrated with him about it; but the gratification of the pose outweighed, for him, the physical discomfort. He left, at his death, about 82,000 kronen, apart from the settlement on his daughter Cosima. (See KBG, p. 258).

believe in himself. But much of his musical work was merely in the nature of a narcotic for the conscience; and for that purpose a transcription from *Norma* or *Faust* seems often to have been good enough. With his pen in his hand, even for a paltry task of this kind, he could still somehow or other persuade himself that he was not "Fainéant."(23)

One suspects that the wandering life he led during his last period—from Rome to Weimar, from Weimar to Pesth, from Pesth back to Rome, with many an excursion to other French, German and Belgian towns and to the country houses of his friends—a life that everyone who loved him saw to be physically and spiritually bad for him, and that filled them with an intense pity for the homeless and secretly unhappy old man, was motived in part by a desire to escape from the control of the Princess. His respect for her, his gratitude to her, were theoretically as great as ever; but having tasted his youthful freedom once more he had no desire ever to resume his chains. Life with Carolyne, he knew, meant daily exhortations to give up the social world and devote himself entirely to original composition; but on the one hand he loved the world too much to give it up, and on the other hand he lacked the confidence in himself that would have made tolerable to him a life wholly devoted to work. It was much easier for him to keep at a safe distance from Carolyne and fend off her anxious enquiries with repentant excuses and promises to reform. It is impossible, he keeps assuring her, to settle down to serious work where he is now, but it will be different next week or next month. In June, 1873, after telling her how his time has been taken up lately, he continues, "You will say that I would have been better engaged working at my *St. Stanislas*.(24) I am quite of your opinion; but I can't get the time to write with anything like

---

(23) His total output was enormous. He wrote very fluently—at hotels, between visits, in the intervals of conversation, anywhere and at any time—when the mood was on him; and of course with his consummate knowledge of the piano and his insight into the music of other men the majority of his transcriptions would cost him no more effort than an ordinary article costs a practised journalist.

(24) An oratorio which he never finished.

continuity. My involuntary *Fainéantise*, I assure you, is often a heavy burden for me to bear; pray to God that He may deliver me from it. Although I have no illusions as to my talent, I suffer greatly at seeing it dwindle away in the multitude of obligations that have me in their net."(25)

In October, 1869, Cardinal Hohenlohe placed at his disposal agreeable quarters in the Villa d'Este, in Tivoli, where he was near enough to Rome not to lose touch wholly with society, yet sufficiently removed from Rome to have the feeling of solitude. He entered into possession of his rooms filled with the usual passion for retirement and work. "Liszt came yesterday," Gregorovius writes in his diary on 24th October, 1869, "and told me that he was retiring to the solitude of the Villa d'Este, where he would remain for some months in order to escape from the crowd. . . . He seems to feel a profound necessity for work."(26) It was about this time that, when conducting Adelheid von Schorn over Rome, he looked enviously at a monk with whom he talked in one of the churches. Once more he spoke of his youthful longing for the cloister; but, he told Adelheid, the solitary life would not have suited him for long. "These contradictions in his nature were always revealing themselves, and made a deep impression on me," she adds.(27) He stayed in Tivoli at various times during the next few years, but never for very long; always the Wandervogel in his blood drove him to the towns, where he could temper solitude with company. And even in the Villa d'Este his solitude was not much more than, at its best, an aspiration, and, at its worst, a pose.

"Madame Minghetti," he writes from there to the Princess on 1st January, 1876, "is a thousand times right when she says that I am wasting my time in salons. I will give up this unfortunate habit. I hope that your symbolical watch [a present from Carolyne] will help me to make my definite retreat from the factitious world—a retreat to which I have aspired for the last twelve years."(28)

---

(25) LZB, VII, 23, 24.

(26) GRT, p. 442.

(27) SZM, p. 310.

(28) LZB, VII, 123.

He was full, indeed, of virtuous resolutions. He had no intention, he told Franz Servais, of ever quitting his retreat, except to spend a day or two occasionally in Rome. He was refusing several invitations to Paris.

"Henceforth my object will be not to exhibit myself but simply to get on with my composing in full tranquillity and freedom of soul. For this purpose I will have to sequestrate myself; I must keep away from the salons, the open pianos, and the thousand tasks imposed by the large towns, in which I soon find myself out of place."(29)

So it goes on for ever, each year a further milestone along the road to spiritual bankruptcy. And unfortunately a new element of discord had arisen in his relations with the Princess. She had become more and more jealous of the enormous success of Wagner, more and more anxious to alienate Liszt from the man whom she now regarded as merely his triumphant rival. He, for his part, gave his artistic soul into the keeping of this great musician and dramatist whose work he felt to be the most vital factor in the German culture of the epoch; and all the nobility in him, all the magnificent disinterestedness where other men's fine work was concerned, made it impossible for him to swerve an inch from his loyalty to Wagner, especially now that the latter needed all the help he could get in the terrific task of founding Bayreuth. So, as he says, there were now "three black points" in his life upon which he and Carolyne could not hope to agree—Rome, Weimar, Bayreuth; Rome, which he cordially disliked, but to which he felt committed in part for her sake; provincial Weimar, in which she regretfully saw him wasting himself on the Grand Duke and on a crowd of pupils, many of whom imposed upon him shamefully; and Bayreuth, the growing fame of which was a constant thorn in her flesh. And always there was the Zigeuner restlessness in him, the inability to retire into himself and to concentrate, which, she saw, was slowly wrecking him both as man and as composer. It was in vain that he kept assuring her that "the seductions of the world have very little attraction for me, and

---

(29) Letter of 20th December, 1869, in LZB, II, 153.

my small successes have rather plunged me deeper into the
solitude that is the right thing for my soul than turned me away
from it." She knew him better than to be able to believe that all
this was anything more than words.

5

Most great men owe their salvation to the fact that their
strength exists in a watertight compartment to which their
weaknesses have no access. Liszt's misfortune was that every
element of strength in him was also, to some extent, a weakness.
His generosity with his money and with his time, for instance,
was boundless; but apparently he had not the strength of
character to fix a limit to the demands that could be legitimately
made on him in these respects. He would certainly have come
under the censure of Goethe, who said once, "I have no patience
with people who cannot control their benevolent impulses.
They are like people who cannot contain their urine." Now and
then indeed, we find Liszt protesting against the unconscionable
demands made by all the world upon his purse and his time;
but the protests were half-hearted, and they rarely translated
themselves into action. To be bled of money as he was all his
life by all sorts of unworthy people was perhaps not so serious
as his constant sacrifice of his time to them. All the world sent
him scores to read; all the world wrote to him about its own
affairs and expected a reply. He weakly complied with all the
demands made upon him, partly out of sheer goodness of heart,
but partly also, one suspects, because on the one hand he had
not the force of character to tell people bluntly to attend to
their own business and let him get on with his, while on the
other hand it is just possible that in this matter, as in others, he
was given to dramatising himself. He had a *rôle* to play—that
of the most generous, disinterested musician who had ever
lived; and rather than not speak the noble lines in his part he
would submit to any imposition. Where his own music was
concerned he could be fairly indifferent, at any rate in outward
appearance, to other people's dislike, preferring this to any
tampering with his artistic conscience. But the unwillingness to
do anything that might damage his own Franciscan legend

made him deplorably weak where suppliants were concerned. He could refuse no demand, however unreasonable, made on his time and his money. He tells the Princess in 1875 that after a concert given in Pesth to raise funds for Bayreuth, Wagner declined to attend a banquet in his honour, and the suggested celebration had accordingly to be abandoned. "Wagner has also refused a banquet in Vienna; he absolutely will not have anything more to do with mere social *convenances*. He visits no one, except in a case of ultra-necessity; and even then he often backs out." Wagner's object in life just then was not to be flattered and fawned upon either in public or in private, but to carry through his vast plans before the strain it all meant on him should ruin his failing health beyond repair. He had not the least objection to hurting susceptibilities by secluding himself from his flatterers: his view was that any admirer whose susceptibilities could be hurt by so rational an attitude on his part was an admirer with whom he could perfectly well dispense; true admiration and understanding would have shown itself, in his opinion, not in an anxiety to brush shoulders with him but to make it easier for him to economise his strength for his work.

Liszt was incapable of standing out in this sturdy way against the unreasonable demands of his admirers. For one thing, he loved to be fêted; for another, he weakly shrank from giving offence. He must have been well aware that an artist or writer who is very much in the public eye can get through his work only if he turns a callously deaf ear to the hundreds of thoughtless egoists who write to him in the course of the year, assuming that because he is a public character he is also a public institution, existing to attend to everybody's business but his own.(30) To ignore four-fifths of the quite unnecessary letters

---

(30) Liszt was perpetually lamenting the amount of time he spent in answering letters, at the rate of about 2,000 a year; but it was only in his last years, when he had become physically incapable, as he said, of giving up ten hours a day for weeks at a time to this kind of thing, that he rebelled against the monstrous imposition: sheer weakness of body at last did for him what his mind and his will had never had the strength to do. Sometimes, in these final years, he would lose his temper and throw

that reach him will mean, no doubt, making a number of enemies; but if he is a sensible man he will decide that it is better to have enemies and maligners and to get on with his work than to earn the goodwill of all these pestering flies at the expense of it. Liszt, however, could never brace himself to front the hard realities of a situation of this kind; and so he wasted an enormous amount of his time every year in letter-writing. He grumbled about it; but he lacked the strength of will to put a summary end to it. When Huckleberry Finn was told that altruism meant living for others, his dry comment was that that was very fine—for the others. Liszt's altruism was very much to the liking of the others.

So it was with his charities. His vast generosity is as much a psychological mystery as everything else connected with him: how much of it was due to real goodness of heart, how much to sheer inability to listen to the voice of common sense, how much to the love of display, how much to the conviction that at all costs he must live up to the legend he had created with regard to himself, it is impossible to say. Many of his benefactions, public and private, in the years when he was making money easily, were due to the noblest of impulses; but, as we have seen, a great deal of his expenditure during that period was of a senseless and sometimes rather vulgar kind. In his later years he was bitterly conscious that he had been foolishly extravagant in his youth. In 1851 we find him rebelling against his mother's attempt to force her family on him: he knows, he says, that if he is too polite to them all he will soon have his thirty or forty uncles, aunts, nephews and nieces all borrowing from him. He could exhort his mother earnestly not to be cajoled into lending money, that would never be repaid, to all sorts of unworthy people; but in this matter he was never able to live up to his own precepts.(31)

---

piles of letters in the waste paper basket, furious, as Adelheid von Schorn tells us, at the writers' shameless attempts to exploit him. Sometimes Adelheid would reply for him, imitating his signature. He struck her as being pitifully weak in these matters (see SZM, pp. 222, 223).

(31) Yet even here we meet with another of the many contradictions or

He knew perfectly well that he was frequently imposed upon. He took as his motto *caritas;* but he more than once assured the Princess bitterly that he "had no illusions about charity." If it ever occurred to him, as it may sometimes have done, that he was merely making life easier for all kinds of plausible knaves, and therefore behaving anti-socially in order to enjoy the sweet luxury of his own private glow of benevolence, he never acted upon this knowledge. We are face to face with one more of the complexities of a character in which every virtue has its countervailing vice; and it is difficult to resist the conclusion that his "Christian charity" finally became, in part, just another of his poses. A story is told of his frequently missing money from his desk at one time in his latest years. His servant, who did not share his accommodating views on these matters, made up his mind to catch the thief. Entering the room one day he found one of Liszt's oldest friends opening the bureau with his master's keys. A struggle ensued, the noise of which brought Liszt down to them. He took the situation in at a glance; but he merely told his servant to release the man, to whom, he said, he had given his keys to get something for him. He took no further action, and even maintained outwardly his customary relations with the man in society. It seemingly did not occur to him that what he was doing was to let loose a dangerous knave upon the community in order to gratify his own passion for posing as the embodiment of Christian charity.

6

With all our admiration for his virtues—and they were many and great—it is impossible not to decide that he sometimes loved to act the man of super-virtue. We cannot read the letters in which he gave his opinion upon some of the manuscript scores that had been sent to him without feeling that often he

---

paradoxes of his being. Carolyne's daughter, Princess Marie von Hohenlohe, told Ludwig Karpath that "for all his geniality and his really boundless liberality, Liszt was no waster: he knew to a *heller* [farthing] exactly where his gifts had gone, and for what purpose. It was easy to see that he was the son of an official" (KBG, pp. 263-264).

carried benevolence to the point of sheer insincerity. It was one of his most insistent delusions that he was a man of inflexible truth and frankness: we often find him assuring the Princess of this. His letters are evidence to the contrary—not, of course, that he ever stooped to actual mendacity, but that, for one reason or another, from politeness, or the unwillingness to hurt, or the desire to earn the good opinion of his correspondent, he frequently praised a man or a work beyond his or its merits, and knew perfectly well that he was doing so. He was incapable, where palpable mediocrity was concerned, of the tonic frankness of Bülow, who, in a matter so serious as art, believed in calling a fool a fool.(32)

Liszt's classical achievement in this respect, perhaps, is his letter of 28th June, 1866, to Rossini, who, breaking the silence that had lasted from the appearance, in 1841, of his *Stabat Mater* (most of which had been written in 1832), now sent Liszt the score of his *Messe solennelle*, which he had played to him a little while before in Paris. Liszt, in his reply, becomes positively fulsome:

"The Swan of Pesaro [Rossini] remains quite as classic as, and much more popular than, the Swan of Mantua [Vergil]; even the birds vie with each other in celebrating him. Without troubling myself about their warbling, permit me, dear master, to tell you again of the profound impression your Mass has made on me. When I was reading the manuscript with you I said to you, 'We are in St. Peter's!' and when I lately went into that basilica again I imagined I was listening to the swelling waves of your music in all its magnificence. No other temple, in my opinion, has such affinities with the splendour, the sumptuousness, the vast dimensions and the majestic harmony of your inspirations."(33)

The fact was that Rossini, almost alone among Liszt's former

---

(32) Bülow's withering letter to Nietzsche, who, fancying himself as a musician, had been indiscreet enough to send him one of his wretched scores with a request for an opinion upon it, is a model of the kind of plain-spoken reply that every man with an artistic conscience ought to make in a case of this kind.

(33) LZB, VIII, 180.

colleagues in Paris, still maintained at this time the old friendly and admiring attitude towards him, and Liszt was duly grateful for his approbation. When telling the Princess of the meeting in Paris, he had merely remarked that Rossini had shown him the Mass, which he found "beautiful—superior to the *Stabat*, but in the same style."

In a letter of 23rd June, Rossini adroitly reminds Liszt of the love and admiration he had felt for him since 1822, assures him that, unlike certain other people, he fully approves of his taking minor orders, praises his "celestial harmonies," and then gets down to the real business of his letter. He is anxious to have the Mass performed in Rome, but unfortunately the Roman Church forbids the participation of women's voices in the service, and Rossini cannot resign himself to having his work "misrepresented by the untuneful voices of boys." Does Liszt think he can influence the Holy Father to issue a new bull, authorising a performance of the Mass with women singers? Liszt had no liking for such a commission, which he knew in advance to be futile; and his reply to Rossini must have cost him a great deal of trouble. "I have elaborated my answer to Rossini," he writes to the Princess from Rome in June; "I should like to know that it has your approval." The answer, running to three pages of print, is typical of Liszt's procedure in cases of this kind. He could have said politely and soothingly, in fifty words, all that was necessary to be said—that while he personally liked the Mass, there was not the least hope of the Pope raising the ban on women's voices in a Roman church.

But Liszt could never content himself with anything so simple and direct as this where an opening for diplomatic verbiage presented itself; and the present opportunity was too good to be lost. So he speaks of the "beautiful, equitable, noble cause" that Rossini is "pleading," "a cause, moreover, which the authority of your great name makes as persuasive as possible," while all the time he knew perfectly well that the grand old joker who had created the best of Figaros was not in the least concerned with a reform theoretically desirable in the interests of piety, but simply and solely with floating his Mass in Rome under the best technical conditions possible. But Liszt cannot turn down so fine a chance to become flowery.

"Looking at the matter in another way," he writes to Rossini, "and considering the question solely from the point of view of religious sentiment, would it not seem that women, who are more assiduous than men in taking part in the services of the church, who participate more frequently in the grace of the sacraments, who make collections inside the churches and at the doors, who watch and pray at the bedside of the sick, who tend them in the hospitals and on the battlefields, who devote themselves with such abundant ardour to so many works of charity and edification—would it not seem, I say, that women are called even more than men are to the celestial expansions of their souls, to *chanted prayer*, and that to deprive the music of the church of its most touching accent, its accent of purest piety, by excluding them from that music, would be rigorous in the extreme?" As for his own suggested intervention at the Vatican, "although there is no question of faith involved in all this, but simply one of discipline, you will understand, very dear master, that a particular reserve is imposed on me. Attached as I am by heart and conviction to the Catholic Church, it is my duty to conform absolutely, in all humility and submission, to the decision of the authority to which our Lord Jesus Christ has given the power to teach the nations."

And to soften still further the blow of his implied refusal to approach the Pope on the matter he indulges in the fulsome adulation of the *Messe solennelle* that has been quoted above. He must have known perfectly well that he was being fulsome; but he had his *rôle* to act—the *rôle* of generous admirer of other men's work in general and the work of his correspondent of the moment in particular. In face of a letter of this kind, we understand better how he could bring himself to overpraise, as he did, so many scores that were sent to him, especially if they were the work of anyone of title or position. The only way in which, in many instances, we can salvage his reputation as a judge of music is to believe that in his desire to be polite and benevolent he was not always strictly sincere.(34)

---

(34) We have a typical example of his weakness in this respect in his letter of 10th May, 1874, to the Princess Julie Waldburg, whose amateurishness

By conduct of this sort he generally achieved his object, the double one of ingratiating himself with his correspondent and of having his praises for generosity and sympathy sung far and wide. But some of his contemporaries, not being the dupe of the later Liszt legend, must often have curled a contemptuous lip in secret over these matters. Tchaikovsky was one of the few who spoke their minds frankly on the subject. "Last year," he wrote to Frau von Meck on 27th November, 1877, "I met Liszt. He was sickeningly polite."(35) On 18th November, 1879, he tells her that

"Liszt, the old Jesuit, speaks in terms of exaggerated praise of every work which is submitted to his inspection. He is at heart a good man, one of the very few great artists who have never known envy, . . . but he is too much of a Jesuit to be frank and sincere." On 1st July, 1892, six years after Liszt's death, he writes to Jurgenson that "Liszt was a good fellow, and ready to respond to everyone who paid court to him. But as I never toadied to him or any other celebrity, we never got into correspondence."(36)

In the German edition of Modeste Tchaikovsky's book there

---

as a composer, no doubt, counted less with him than her title. She had sent him some songs of her own composition. "I feel my conduct to be inexcusable," he writes to her. "You are kind enough to send me some charming Lieder and to accompany them with the most gracious letter in the world. Why did I not thank you for them immediately? What rudeness! Deign to forget it, Princess, and permit me, not to 'criticise' your Lieder—for I am totally lacking in magistral competence—but to tell you that I have read them with pleasure. The one that pleases me most, by reason of its passionate tone, is . . ." and so on at some length (LZB, II, p. 201). He wasted an incredible amount of his time over futilities of this kind.

(35) Liszt was once asked what he would have been had he not become a musician. "The first diplomat in Europe," was his complacent answer. The actor in him made him cultivate diplomacy and Jesuitry in his manner to an extent that often made people smile. Nadine Helbig (HLR, p. 71) tells us how, when playing four-hands arrangements with a bad pianist, he would condescend to address her as "chère collègue." By charming flatteries of this kind he made himself very popular in society; but he could be impolite enough when his vanity was hurt.

(36) TPT, pp. 241, 356, 685.

is a further reference to Liszt that has been omitted from the
English edition: writing to Jurgenson on 10th December, 1881,
Tchaikovsky says,

> "I have just been to a quartet matinée where I heard a new
> quartet by Sgambati. The Jesuit Liszt sat in the middle of a
> bevy of ladies (mostly old), and pretended to be delighted with
> his pupil's work, than which I have never heard anything so
> destitute of talent."

All this agrees with the opinion which, it will be remembered,
Bernhardi had formed of Liszt some thirty years earlier.

7

We have the suspicion that in his dealings with his pupils
also there was, in addition to the sincere desire to "serve," as
Kundry would have put it, a trace of the actor unwilling to do
anything contrary to the noble *rôle* for which he had cast himself. As usual, he was the soul of generosity with his pupils: he
not only took no money from them but in many cases gave them
money. But his generosity itself was seen, by impartial observers, to have in it an element of toadying weakness. He was
disgracefully imposed upon; yet, although he would occasionally, in a moment of irritation, tell a particularly incompetent
young woman that her line in life was matrimony rather than
music, he never had the moral courage to assert himself against
these pupil-parasites as a whole. He shut his eyes to the fact
that the manners and the conduct of many of them made them
cordially detested in Weimar. Through sheer reluctance to do
anything that would be likely to get himself disliked, he allowed
his house (37) to be turned topsy-turvy by the rabble of so-
called pupils who quartered themselves on him. The soberer
and worthier among them and among his disciples generally
lamented his weakness, but could do nothing against his
determination to preserve the pose of the steadfast well-doer and
the patient sufferer of evil. One day, in July, 1880, taking advantage of the fact that Liszt was confined to his room with a

---

(37) In the later years Liszt occupied the Hofgärtnerei when staying in
Weimar.

sprained foot, Bülow descended upon the place and, as he put it, cleaned out the Augean stable. Having made some of the pupils play to him, he ordered the worst of them to leave; "You have no right," he told them, "to pester the master any more." Calling them together, Bülow addressed them thus: "Ladies and gentlemen, do not forget that the Master was born as long ago as 1811, or that he is the essence of goodness and gentleness; and do not misuse him in this revolting way. You ladies in particular; most of you, I assure you, are destined for the myrtle rather than the laurel." "All trembled," we are told; the majority of them disappeared. A certain Fräulein P. played the *Mazeppa* Study in frightful style. Bülow, to the delight of the others, told her that she had only one qualification for performing this piece—she had the soul of a horse.(38) But the next day the stable was as full of the filth as ever. Having learned from Kellermann what had happened, Liszt said, "Yes, as a matter of fact Bülow was quite right. But he was too hard. I suppose you will see all these people tonight in the Sächsischer Hof? Just tell them to wait until Bülow has left, and then to come back here." Liszt refers to the incident in his letter of 3rd July, 1880, to the Princess(39), in which he censures Bülow for being too thoroughgoing in his methods and too uncompromising in his speech. Bülow's opinion of the affair, as expressed to Adelheid von Schorn, was that he had done Liszt the same service as he did to his own dog in ridding him of his fleas.

Matters were no better two years later.

"*À propos de vermine*," Bülow writes to his daughter Daniela on 1st July, 1882, "let us not rejoice too much on your grandfather's account over the little revolution at the Hofgärtnerei. I believe that in matters of insecticide things are destroyed only to be replaced. You may take it for granted that Mlle. D. P. will have been expelled indirectly by some Co-Guenon or other such as Mlle. Schmalhausen, for example . . . and

---

(38) KE, pp. 25, 26; BLW, p. 273. Many of these people were, of course, merely using Liszt for their own commercial purposes, taking advantage of his weakness in order to be able to go back to their home towns and advertise themselves as "pupils of Liszt."

(39) LZB, VII, 292.

that the Abbé's studio will remain the stable it has always been."(40)

It is perhaps not very difficult to win for yourself a reputation for infinite goodness and generosity if you will only allow yourself to be imposed upon as monstrously as Liszt was. It would have been better for his work had he possessed a little more of Bülow's directness. Bülow had a short way with fools and nuisances: at one time, being pestered by unwanted callers, he affixed a printed notice to his front door—"Not at home in the mornings. Out in the afternoons"; while he used to pass on superfluous letters straight to what he called "the silent secretary"—the waste paper basket. "I wish," said Liszt to the Princess with a sigh, "I could run my life like this!" He could easily have done so had he really wanted to: it merely meant adding a few more enemies to the number that every public man must count on having. But Liszt had to live up, at any cost, to the part he had cast himself for—the universal helper and provider. It is surely evident, also, that no man could indulge as Liszt had done in tobacco and coffee and spirits for nearly half a century without his mental as well as his physical tissues becoming softened. A good deal of Liszt's resigned benevolence can be explained quite simply as the inability of his soddened nerves to brace themselves to face an unpleasant situation. He knew his own weakness, and there is something more than humour—there is a sad truth—in his comparison of himself and the more resolute Princess to the little dog and the lion he had seen occupying the same cage in the Paris Jardin des Plantes.(41)

Bülow was not the only one who turned with a mixture of pity and disgust from the paltry music-making that went on at the Hofgärtnerei. In 1884 Joachim and his son spent an evening there with a numerous company that included the Grand Duke and members of the Court. Music being called for, a pupil of Liszt's played a poor piece of his own; a tenor sang the serenade from *Don Giovanni*, the mandoline accompaniment to which

(40) BNB, p. 594.
(41) LZB, VII, 54.

Joachim had to supply with pizzicati on his violin (he was not asked to play anything else); Liszt and one of the Court ladies played the Flea-Waltz as a duet, Liszt taking the bass. As they left the house, Joachim said sadly to his son, "Once more a horrible music-making! It has always been the same here!"(42)

8

The record of the last ten or twelve years of Liszt's life is a melancholy one. The Princess grieved without ceasing over his waste of himself. One of the most unfortunate elements in his being was his lack of any real feeling for nature. He had, it is true, especially in his earlier period, occasionally felt himself moved to composition by some exquisite scene or other, but this was part of the standard romantic apparatus of the artist in those days. Nature, in and by itself, he could not endure; and his distaste for it grew with the advancing years. He consequently lacked the ultimate resource of troubled souls that periodically resort to solitude in order to steady their lives and concentrate on their work. The country boring him as it did, he could escape from himself, by paradox, only in a crowd: the more dissatisfied he felt with himself and with the world, the more he was driven into society. During one of his periodical efforts to seclude himself at the Villa d'Este (in 1874), the Princess rejoices, in a letter to Adelheid, at what he has been able to do in spite of all his distractions, and looks forward to his settling down at last to the writing of his greatest works, especially the *St. Stanislas*. But a few weeks later the old lamentations over his *fainéantise* break out again. "Liszt has left Tivoli," she writes to Adelheid on 12th October, "and so he has ceased to work on his oratorio. The irony of Fate! I stayed in Rome this summer in order that he might remain in Tivoli and get on with his oratorio—and it was I who was the cause of his leaving Tivoli for Rome(43), where, of course, he did not write a note of the oratorio, but occupied himself with a mass of transcriptions,

---

(42) MJJ, II, 54.
(43) The Princess had been ill for some weeks.

which I regard as puerilities."(44) He had no doubt been glad
of the excuse afforded him to leave his irksome retreat. In
December of the following year the Princess is once more
lamenting that "Liszt dines and sups in town very often—too
often—never goes near Tivoli, acts *l'homme charmant*, and so
squanders his time. He has not lost his creative power; but he
has lost his pleasure in work, and that is the saddest result of
these last sad five years."(45)

Two years later:

"Liszt stayed here for a fortnight after 4th November, and
then went to Pesth. His health is a great anxiety to me. The
climate there is too cold for him. His Zigeuner life is not suitable
for a man of his age; he is wearing himself out; his digestive
system is in a bad way; his régime is fatal; every night he has a
fever. . . . His constitution is strong, but he is nearing his
seventieth year."(46)

It rejoices her, however, that once more he has found his
inspiration flowing. But it is not long before the laments begin
again. In 1880, though Liszt is composing once more, it appears
that he finds work difficult. It is not because of his age, she
says:

"Humboldt, Thiers, and many others worked until they were
nearly ninety, with the old freshness, and with an ease born of
vast experience. These men, however, always kept on working,
while Liszt, since he began to run about, has completely lost the
faculty of concentration. But I will not indulge for ever in these
vain laments. If God will help him to finish the work he now has
in hand, I will ask for nothing more: should he produce, in
addition, a trifle or two, this will be a gift from God."(47)

From 1880 he declined steadily until the end, six years later.
His unwise way of living had brought on dropsy: his body
swelled, the once shapely hands lost their beauty, the tired eyes
looked out dully upon the world; reading became difficult for
him. But the Princess never quite lost faith in his powers of
recuperation if only he could be persuaded to alter his régime.

---

(44) SZM, p. 248.
(45) Ibid., p. 315.
(46) Ibid., p. 339.
(47) Ibid., p. 379.

In June, 1882, she could still write to the faithful Adelheid, to whom had fallen the lot of Liszt's guardian angel in Weimar, "I hope that this year the vicious circle will be broken, at any cost to me—anything will be better than this perpetual Zigeuner life from Rome to Pesth, from Pesth to Weimar, from Weimar to Bayreuth, and again *da capo*."(48) As early as 1883—three years before the actual end came—she could no longer disguise from herself the fact that his spiritual light had gone out. In April of that year she was still hoping that he would complete *St. Stanislas*. "It is natural that the progress with it should be slow. Thank God that he has given up the cognac! His new works are full of life: there are no signs of old age in them." But less than a month later she welcomes the news that a certain X. . . . has joined the Weimar circle, whose company, she hopes, will be better for Liszt than that of his ordinary hangers-on—people "whose emptiness of soul, affording him only a futile and puerile nourishment, have brought about the gradual apathy of this mind that was once so luminous and so happily strong. You can imagine how my heart is torn—I who knew him in all his strength and ardour!"(49) And so it went on until that day when, on a train journey from Weimar to Bayreuth in July, 1886, he caught the cold that brought him to his death ten days later. The episode, in its commonplace way, was symbolic: Liszt, true to his ideal of resignation and renunciation, or perhaps merely lacking the courage to assert himself, sat during the night in a cold draught rather than suggest to the other occupants of the carriage that the window might be closed.

---

(48) SZM, p. 419.

(49) Ibid., p. 442.

CHAPTER IX

THE QUESTIONABLE EVIDENTIAL VALUE OF LISZT'S LETTERS: THE OLGA JANINA EPISODE

I

As the intelligent reader has no doubt surmised by this time, one of the purposes of the present volume is to show the general untrustworthiness of the type of musical biography cultivated in the nineteenth century and the early twentieth. In Liszt's case the wells of truth were poisoned at the outset by the Princess Wittgenstein and by Liszt himself, operating through their hireling Lina Ramann. The Ramann record of Liszt's life and presentation of his character must have caused, at the time, an incredulous raising of many an eyebrow. Survivors from that epoch who knew Liszt are now comparatively rare; but we are fortunate enough to have one still among us in the person of Cosima Wagner's biographer, Richard Graf Du Moulin Eckart, whose father was a friend both of Wagner and of Liszt; of the latter the young Du Moulin saw a good deal as a boy. Young as he was, he seems to have sensed, at any rate in part, the mournful mystery of Liszt's complex being. "Since then," he says (*i.e.* since the publication of the Ramann Life), "no biography of Liszt has ever roused in me any feeling but one of illimitable vexation—often, I must confess, downright anger. When I read, soon after its appearance, the first volume of the Ramann biography, I said, 'But this is quite another man than the one I knew'; whereupon my father said with a smile, 'You prescient angel!'(1) He said nothing more; but I felt that there was

---

(1) "Du ahnungsvoller Engel, du!"—the words Goethe puts into Faust's mouth when Gretchen voices her mistrust of Mephistopheles.

something wrong, and my opinion is unchanged today, now that I know how this so-called biography came into being."(2)

On a later page Du Moulin tells us of the unpleasant impression Lina Ramann's first volume made on Wagner and Cosima. "The worthy old Ramann," he says, "reminds me of a captive metal-worker who is compelled to coin false money in his cell. The captor was the Princess Wittgenstein; the metal she supplied was genuine, but the die with which it was stamped was false. It is easy to imagine, then, the impression this book produced in Wahnfried."(3)

Cosima's concern was mainly over the Princess's portrait of her mother, for she knew both women well. The reader of the present volume, however, will have gathered by now that not only are the current Liszt biographies untrustworthy with regard to this subject—where they have blindly followed Lina Ramann—but that they are equally untrustworthy in their general reading of Liszt's character and psychology. But while it is true that the writers cannot be blamed for not having known a number of documents that appeared after their books were written, it is equally true that they have failed to deal critically with such documents as were available, and especially Liszt's correspondence. They have not perceived that, he being the actor he was, his letters are not always to be taken at their face value. The early correspondence with Marie d'Agoult is unconstrained: at that time Liszt had not yet realised the possibility of his letters being some day laid open to the world's inspection. In later life, when he had begun to dramatise himself and to labour at the creation of his own legend, he probably wrote many of his letters with a diplomatist's eye to the future, asking himself how they would look in the eyes of posterity. It is the business of the modern biographer to try to get behind the mask he persistently wore in his middle and last periods—to discover to what extent his letters correspond to the realities of this situation or that, and to his contemporary reaction to them.

---

(2) DMCW, p. 3.

(3) Ibid., p. 925.

2

We can test the degree of conformity between a fact as it was and the same fact as dealt with by Liszt in a letter, by the episode of the Countess Janina. Her revelations have either been loftily ignored by the biographers—by Raabe, for instance—or have been passed off with an indulgent smile as merely one more amusing illustration of the length to which an angry woman can go in the way of defamation. As a matter of fact, her book is one of the most valuable documents we possess for the reconstruction of the real Liszt. We are accordingly justified in devoting to it, on psychological grounds, more space than the story told in it would otherwise deserve.

Briefly the external facts are as follows. Olga Janina was a Cossack girl of aristocratic birth who became Liszt's pupil in Rome in 1869. By her own showing she was a wild creature of the steppes with a passion for dangerous adventure and an imperious will. In one respect she resembled the Countess d'Agoult—in spite of her birth and her wealth she had considerable contempt for her own class, resenting its pride of position and its social injustice. "Strange words were heard on my lips," she records of herself as a child—"kindness, fraternity, social life, liberty. I looked around me: I saw miserable peasants, my vassals, putrefying in the mud, ignorant even of the names of their fathers, treated like beasts of burden, idiots, brutes." The trait is important in view of her later disgust with Liszt for his toadyism to wealth and titles. Olga's democratic sympathies brought her, as those of Marie d'Agoult had done, into conflict with her family and her friends; and we gather, in general, that her temperament, exasperated by what she calls "the irritating electricity of the steppes," made her a difficult proposition to handle. She would have met with Nietzsche's full approval as one of those who have the courage to live dangerously: a mad rider, killing horses under her, she developed a spirit of domination that in later years was to make Liszt a helpless victim of her will. She married at the age of fifteen. The wedding night was sufficient to fill her with something of Turandot's hatred of men, and the change of her husband's manner from that of a sleek courtier before marriage to that of a cynical tyrant after it completed her disgust. The pair separated in a few weeks' time, the husband renouncing his rights in consideration of the addition of a large sum to his wife's dowry. At sixteen Olga was a mother.

She found consolation mainly in her piano, at which she worked hard for three years. Chance brought some music of Liszt to her notice: she at once succumbed to the charm of this new idiom, at once so strange and so insinuating; and as her conservative teacher declared the music to be antipathetic to him she resolved to take lessons from Liszt himself, of whom, as yet, she knew nothing except that after a career of unexampled triumph as a virtuoso he had retired from the world to devote himself to composition. She wrote to him at Rome, begging him to take her as a pupil. Liszt's reply was that he would do so "if your talent seems to me to be one that is worth encouraging." The envelope, however, was addressed to "Monsieur ——, at ——, in the Ukraine": Liszt had assumed that his correspondent was a young man. A fortnight later Olga was in Rome.

The question now arises of the trustworthiness of her account of Liszt and of her relations with him. After their parting she published her story (in 1874), under the title of *Souvenirs d'une Cosaque*, by "Robert Franz";(4) the work caused a great sensation—for of course the whole musical world recognised Liszt as the X*** of the story—and it quickly ran through several editions; there were at least eight of these in the year of publication. After a careful study of the book in the light of all we know about Liszt, we are bound to accept it as a perfectly truthful record. On every point with regard to which we can now check her statements she is accurate; while her reading of Liszt—which alone concerns us here—tallies with all we have independently discovered about him. Olga Janina did not set out to counter the Liszt legend. Of that, indeed, she knew nothing, for it had not yet been invented by the biographers. Yet everything she says about him flies in the face of that legend. She was writing not about a distant historical character but

(4) She followed this volume up with another—*Mémoires d'un pianiste*—that purported to be a reply on Liszt's part. I have not been able to obtain a copy of this.

S

about a living man whom she and many of her readers knew; and the portrait she paints of this man agrees in the most unexpected ways with the one I have tried, in the present volume, to reconstruct from the evidence of his life, his letters, and the testimony of his friends and acquaintances.

3

Liszt was agreeably surprised to find that his correspondent from the Ukraine was not a young man, but an attractive girl. Olga's impression of him at their first meeting was of "a man of high stature, distinguished carriage, and grand manner; ugly, with an abundance of beautiful hair, now almost white, which he wore long and thrown back from the forehead; profound, thoughtful eyes, that could be hard upon occasion; and a smile that was like a shaft of sunlight." He seems to have set out at once upon the conquest of her; seating himself at the piano after a few words with her, he launched into a performance of Chopin's C sharp minor Polonaise that shook her impressionable young soul to its foundations. He knew well the effect his incomparable playing would have on her; it was the practised old amorist's usual opening gambit in the game of love. He could never resist, where rich and aristocratic women were concerned, the temptation to play with fire, if it were only to warm his hands; he was soon to discover that in this case he had plunged his hands into a furnace. That his immediate interest in Olga was personal rather than artistic is shown by the fact that he at once accepted her as a pupil, although ostensibly he did not "take pupils," and though he informed her frankly, after she had played to him, that she "knew nothing." She was to come to him on Fridays, the day on which he received his other "pupils."

On the first Friday she found herself in a crowd of young men and women, their fathers, their mothers, their cousins and their aunts, awaiting the arrival of the Master. When Liszt entered, they all flung themselves upon him and covered his hands with "long and unctuous kisses"—behaviour that obviously gratified him. He greeted Olga, however, to her astonishment, coldly and drily; he was annoyed at her for being the only one who had *not* kissed his hand. "Quel drôle de grand homme!" she thought to herself. She noticed that in the course of his instruction he could not bear the smallest contradiction or even question; towards the end of the lesson he became "almost coarse." She was a little alienated by his "airs de hauteur," already a trifle disillusioned about him; but she resolved to conquer his interest and good opinion by hard work.

That same evening, to her astonishment, he called on her in her apartment. "He was no longer the same man. He took my head between his hands and kissed it." He apologised for his rudeness in the afternoon, and told her that in future he would take her alone on Tuesdays, either in his rooms or in hers. He was already feeling the agreeable warmth of the new fire. He questioned her about herself and her family; and at once she became conscious of the toady in him. "When I told him of my birth and my fortune he swelled, as it were, with pride and satisfaction in a way that struck me, though I could not fathom it then. It was only much later that I understood." No more on this occasion than on any other could Liszt resist an aristocrat, especially when the aristocrat happened to be of the female sex, young, pretty and rich. By this one quick stroke of observation Janina at once unconsciously reveals herself as an accurate reader of the man.

She soon fell a victim to his extraordinary fascination, and one day she confessed that she loved him. For a moment she feared that he would put on his severe manner and "condemn me to exile." He folded her in his arms and held her for a long time against his breast; but he seems to have had an intuition of the danger that lay ahead, for he said to her in a low voice, "Never speak to me of love: I must not love." She fled from him in some confusion. Alone, she ran over in her mind the stories she had heard of his countless amorous caprices, his facile conquests, his complacent acceptance of the most banal feminine passions; and her Cossack blood, afire with all the romanticism of her years, boiled over at the thought that he could in this case refuse a love that was "as superb as the magnificent, fabulous Brazilian plant that flowers once only in a hundred years." "He shall be mine, or I will kill him!" she resolved.

She was annoyed to find, in conversations with other pupils, that the Abbé Liszt was everywhere regarded as a joke by reason of his notorious exploits in the field of love. "I was scandalised," she says, "by the irreverence and frivolity with which people spoke about him; I was particularly struck by the small importance they attached to his having taken orders." He had gone for a while to Munich, which, her friends told her, was "the rendezvous of his friends and his numerous female admirers whenever he went there. He was fêted, petted; crowds attended his *petits levées;* Madame **** used to hand him his shirt." Olga began to reflect about him. "Until now, X*** had been, for me, a man great in virtue of his genius, great by the austerities of his life, austerities I had believed to be sincere; even his religion, which he had carried to the extent of donning the ecclesiastical robe, did not offend me. I now began to take stock of this weak and ailing soul, this spirit excited by the exaggerations of an artificial way of living, this imagination exasperated by unappeased desires." She understood the attraction exercised on him by Catholicism, "with its theory of the divine will and grace, its submission of the heart and the mind," this religion "according to which personal enquiry and judgment and initiative are sins, and mystical sensualities a glory." The longer the talk among the pupils went on, the more Olga learned as to the cynical estimate of Liszt in the circles that knew him best. "Detail about X*** was added to detail— stories of his amours with plain or ancient women whose titles, or position, or the luxury of their establishments, flattered his amour-propre; of his colossal vanity; of his boundless ambition to be talked about at any cost; of his passion for approbation, for flatteries of the cheapest kind, for the commonest sort of adoration." This was the general estimate of him, indeed, in his own circle before the biographers, headed by Lina Ramann and the Princess Wittgenstein, had begun to labour at the creation of the saintly legend. "I was stupefied, "continues Olga; "I fought against the impression that was being made on me. 'I will believe only what I see,' I said to myself. I promised myself that I would observe him closely—and I bravely closed my eyes!"

On Liszt's return to Rome she visited him in his retreat: he folded her in his arms and laid her head on his shoulder. Then comes one of those touches in the narrative that convinces us today of the essential truth of it. Olga's reading of Liszt, let us remember, was based on none of the documents now open to us. She knew very little more of him than what she saw of him at their meetings. If, then, she gives us an analysis of the shoddier side of his nature that agrees down to the minutest detail with all that we of a later age have been able to discover with regard to that side of him from a multitude of letters and reminiscences unknown to her, the only conclusion we can come to is that her story is at no point fiction, but sober truth. The words she puts into Liszt's mouth from time to time are precisely those the reader of the present volume would by now expect. The sensualist in him could not resist the appetising amorous bait: his vanity would not allow him to renounce so flattering a conquest—a young girl, apparently good-looking, decidedly attractive, and, above all, rich and an aristocrat. He said to her, " 'My answer to your letter is my return. I could not write. I ought not to love; but I do love and cannot conceal it. I beg you'—and here his voice became so caressing that I trembled from head to foot—'to have pity on me now that you have torn this confession from me. Let your love be sweet to me; do not let it make me perjure myself'." She replied, "in a choked voice," " 'Your wish shall be sacred to me.' " " 'Call me Ferencz,' he said; 'tutoie me'; and he covered me with passionate kisses."

The next day, having had time to reflect on the dangers of the abyss that was opening beneath his feet, he wrote to her exhorting her to love him, indeed, but not to do anything that might lead to his forgetting his duty and give him reason for shame and regret. She saw at once what had happened: the religious element in him had for the moment overridden the sensual. Her resolution was taken: "I will fight the Church for him." And she already read him so accurately that in a flash she saw the right line of strategy to take. "His mind delighted in the follies of Catholicism: a combat would only strengthen his objections and the feeling of what he called his duty. There came back to my memory our conversation of the evening before.

Yes, that was it; the one thing necessary was to flatter all the paltry vanities of this immense amour-propre."

She took a handsome apartment close by his, and furnished it with a luxury which she knew would captivate this luxury-loving Franciscan. He visited her frequently, even taking his friends there. Her love for him, a savage love that was ready to give everything but demanded everything in return, developed to the point almost of madness. Her jealousy was aroused by certain evidences that other women were making an impression on Liszt's susceptible heart by the luxury of their toilettes.(5) She flew off to Paris, returning with the most dazzling creations of Worth, in one of which she attended a reception of Liszt's at Santa Francesca Romana. And now comes another touch the psychological penetration of which is on a par with her whole reading of his character. Her costume made a great impression on the company. "X*** also came towards me. When I saw how enchanted, almost tender, he was, putting his arm round my waist before them all, by way of establishing his intimacy with the rich Countess who had come to Rome from the depth of the Ukraine in order to find him—he who, had I arrived in my Cossack clothes, would barely have noticed me—I could not repress a feeling of rage." She had seen through him on this occasion as she was destined to do on so many others. In her fury she smashed her ivory fan and threw the pieces out of the window. "When I left, I said to myself that all was finished, that with my own hands I had dug the grave in which my dignity lay buried, and that henceforth nothing could hold me back on the fatal incline that led to every concession, every baseness."

Talk of love between them ceased, but she still saw him frequently. He complained of the inefficiency of his copyists: she volunteered to undertake this tedious work for him, and spent her nights making copies that won his amazed approval.(6) So it went

---

(5) He once confessed that "women could not wear enough lace, furs, jewellery, and so on" to please him.

(6) This is one of the many points of fact in her story that are confirmed by his contemporary letters.

on till the winter. She was maddened by the complacency with which the would-be Franciscan accepted the most inane of worldly attentions so long as it flattered his vanity. Adoring women pressed round him at the piano, and, with little tweezers, drew from his hair, as he played, a silver hair or two, which they religiously folded in a piece of paper. "It was not only of his hair but of his time that people robbed him," says Olga: "he spent his whole time in distributing photographs of himself and playing the *Invitation to the Waltz* or the *Erl-King*." At last he fled to Cardinal Hohenlohe's Villa d'Este, in Tivoli: the sixteen Italian miles from Rome to Tivoli, involving in those days a journey of three hours and a half by coach, dismayed all but the most persistent of his pursuers. For three months Liszt enjoyed the solitude for which he was always crying out. Olga's narrative thus once more tallies point by point with all we know of these matters from other sources.

"The first time I went to see him at Tivoli," she continues, "he showed such joy that I could see how terribly solitude weighed on this soul that was so passionately in love with the world and its homage." The pseudo-Franciscan's retreat became more and more an abode of love as the weeks went on, until at last the inevitable happened: one day Liszt turned the key of his room, took her in his arms, and said, "I can no longer deny myself you." He slept exhausted after the possession of her; in the morning, as she looked at him, she was struck by the "dolorous sadness" of his face even in his sleep. At once the thought occurred to her that she would lose him. "He was mine; but when he waked he would perhaps recoil from me, and, weeping, take refuge at the feet of a crucifix. . . . Yes, I must lose him: on awakening he would seek out some priest or other, and, his face in the dust, he would implore God's pardon for the crime of love, which, at the tribunal of penitence, he would sully with names of the most hateful kind." The wild Cossack determined to kill him before this could happen. She reached for the poisoned dagger she was used to carrying with her. "One tiny puncture, and he was mine to all eternity, for we would lie under the same winding-sheet in the same tomb. I held the dagger in the hollow of my hand and waited for his

first word. It was one of love. He was saved." He saw the
blade and understood her intention. "You would have killed
me, child!" he said. He took her in his arms, covered her with
kisses, and swore that he would fight no more against his love
for her. It all sounds very romantic now; but there is not the
slightest reason to doubt a single word of the story.

4

Towards the end of February he returned to Rome and
resumed the salon life that was so dear to him, visiting Olga
every day. At "the beginning of April"(7) he went to Weimar;
she accompanied him there. She gives an entertaining if slightly
malicious account of the comic provinciality of the little town,
and of Liszt's life among his many *maîtresses en retraite*. There
was Madame **** (an easily recognisable former member of
the Weimar opera company), the story of whose liaison with
him in days gone by Liszt himself related, with cynical frankness,
to Olga. A Mlle. **** is evidently Adelheid von Schorn, the
"Providence" of Liszt in the absence of Carolyne: Olga is
cruelly candid about her pathetic old-maidishness. And there
were others. Olga gives us an acidly humorous picture of the
daily scenes of feminine adoration wherever and whenever Liszt
appeared, and of his grotesque satisfaction with them. He
appears to have reached the topmost heights of fatuity when he
said to Olga one day, "These women are good. There is a
striking thing about them which you do not appear to have
noticed. All who know me are brought into sympathy with
each other. *They love each other in me.*" "Ah, Lord Jesus
Christ!" was Olga's cynical comment to herself; "Lord Jesus
Christ, at one time the focal point of divine love, You have been
supplanted!"

Before a week was out Olga had made herself cordially
detested in Weimar. She could not conceal her critical opinion
of the women to whom Liszt introduced her, and she was
angered at the way he allowed them to waste his time, unable
as he was to deny himself the luxury of their attentions and

---

(7) Actually it was the end of March.

flatteries. One elderly lady was a particular trial to her. "She did not take snuff, she did not smoke, she changed her linen regularly; and yet, for a quarter of a century, she had exhaled a horrible odour," without anyone being able to say why. Olga somehow or other won her confidence, and one day the secret of the odour was revealed: the lady drew from her corsage the remains of a cigar-stump that had once rested between the sacred lips of Liszt! She had purloined it after a dinner given in his honour by the Jena Philharmonic Society as long ago as 1843. "She replaced the odorous relic in her bosom, buttoned her cape again, and resumed her weeping."(8) The story would be incredible in the case of any other man, but not in that of Liszt. There is abundant testimony to the follies that women used to indulge in where he was concerned, especially in the days when his piano-playing was drawing the eroticism out of the sex as a poultice draws out inflammation. They would invade his hotel bedroom in his absence and carry off in bottles the used water from his wash-bowl. They would fight each other for the privilege of drinking what was left in his teacup. In the Roman days we read of a lady—we learn with surprise that she was an American—who cut out, *faute de mieux*, the cover of a chair cushion on which the least dignified portion of his anatomy had rested, had it framed, and hung it up in her boudoir.(9) There was no limit to the lunacy of these sex-crazy females—or to Liszt's vain satisfaction with their lunacy.

In the week before Easter he startled Olga by having one of his religious fits. He suddenly became cold and sombre towards her, and tried to avoid being alone with her. He told

---

(8) Perhaps this was the lady of whom Lehmann speaks as having appropriated a half-smoked cigar of Liszt's (see LAR).

(9) The story is told by Gregorovius, whose informant was Countess Tolstoi. "She told Liszt," says Gregorovius, "who was at first annoyed, and then asked if it was true. If a man like this does not despise humanity, one must count it a virtue in him" (GRT, p. 320). There is abundant reason to suspect, however, that Liszt derived great pleasure from the inanities of his female admirers, though perhaps the comic grossness of this particular one was too much even for *his* palate and for his very limited sense of humour.

her that "the Church had commanded him to repent." When
she reminded him of his promise on the morning she had
thought of slaying him, "his eyes became veiled, he turned a
timid glance towards heaven. He spent the whole of the
afternoons of Good Friday and the following day in church:
on his knees before the image of Christ he poured forth tears
in abundance and smote his breast. All Weimar wept with
edification." Then comes another touch in the narrative that
Olga could not have invented, for she had no biographical
documents upon which to base such an invention: she merely
sets down her own experience. She was sitting alone in her
room, cursing the church bells that were the symbols of the
religious ecstasies that had stolen Liszt from her, when he
suddenly entered. All trace of the contrition appropriate to
the season had disappeared. "He was radiant. He carried his
head proudly. His eyes were ardent, passionate. He embraced
me: never did Christian celebrate better the resurrection of his
Saviour. 'You see, my dear,' he said, 'there's nothing like putting
your conscience in order.' I understood then that he was accustomed to these periodical repentances." "Every six months, in
fact," she continues, "he consecrated a week to the salvation
of his soul. . . . This lowered him in my eyes, but I loved him
so much that my scorn, my hatred, the impulses of revolt that
formerly made my heart swell as if it would burst at the spectacle of hypocrisies on this scale, now melted into bitter sadness.
This man no doubt believed in the efficacy, in the sight of
heaven, of his pitiable trickeries."

As I have said, Olga's narrative proves correct in every
detail that we can check from other records. She tells us that
Weimar soon became "odious" to her, because of the rapturous
crowd of women who surrounded Liszt during "the festival in
celebration of the anniversary of the birth of Beethoven." This,
of course, gives us the date of 1870. Lest any reader should
point out that Beethoven was born on 26th March and that
Olga's story has by now taken her beyond Easter, it may be as
well to say that the Beethoven celebrations in Weimar took
place at the end of May, at a festival of the Allgemeine Deutsche
Musikverein. Liszt conducted, among other things, the Ninth

Symphony. Quite unaware, as of course she is throughout, that half a century or so later it would be possible to check one after another of her statements of fact by contemporary documents, Olga tells us that the centre of the crowds of adorers from other towns that descended upon Weimar for the festival was another of Liszt's "former friends and joyous *compères*," a certain Mme. M***, "the belle of the Berlin balconies." Of this Mme. M*** she paints one of her most pitiless portraits.

"What false graces, what false ideas, what false sentiments, what false hair, what false posterior! There was nothing genuine about her but an issue in her leg, and her breath. This invalid of sentiment always walked with a crutch; but in Weimar X***, the most obliging of men, offered to do duty for this. Leaning on his arm, wearing a white wrap lined with pink, this ruin wandered along the shady paths in the park, cooing her whole repertory of recitatives, nocturnes, and cantilenas. She evidently desired to serve up to him a *macédoine* of his cosmopolitan amours."

Mme. M*** is clearly the once beautiful Marie von Kalergis, now, by her second marriage, Countess von Mouchanoff; she had been a pupil of Chopin, and a close friend of Liszt in the days of her beauty and splendour. In her later years she was a cripple. That she was in Weimar for the festival is proved by her letter of 2nd June, 1870, to her daughter.(10)

Olga, of course, was consumed with jealousy of all these women.

"As for X***, he was radiant. All these women, fluttering round him like butterflies and caressing his divinity, made him quiver with vanity and joy. His weaknesses betrayed themselves in a thousand little ways that were like so many pebbles thrown at the windows of the magic palace of love in which I was dreaming. But soon the pebbles became large stones. X*** shamelessly indulged in infidelities towards me. I recognised that he loved women, and that he must have a profound faith in the immensity of the divine mercy!"

Yet though she saw him thus clearly for what he was, in all his weaknesses, vanities and hypocrisies, he had only to give

---

(10) See LMMM, p. 235.

her one glance or lay his hand on hers to enmesh her in the web of the old illusion.

5

Finally, however, the nerves of the excitable Cossack gave way; for a while she resorted to opium. Liszt began to look bored: "he reproached me with being jealous of the esteem, the friendliness that surrounded him." He complained of her desire to play the "despot" with him; and when she pointed out that she had not complained, his reply was that her silence itself was a complaint. The old situation with Madame d'Agoult, in fact, was beginning to repeat itself, down even to the very words. Unable to endure any more, Olga, whose system by this time was probably deranged by drugs, fled to Heligoland; but a letter from Liszt was enough to reconcile her to him again. What did all these other women matter? "What was there in common between the sentiments of that crowd and mine? He was prodigal, he lied, he betrayed me. I loved this man who was frivolous, a liar, and unfaithful." She went to Vienna, where she learned that Liszt was now in Hungary. She telegraphed to him that she was coming, and the next day was in Pesth. As usual, she does not give the exact date, but Liszt's letters show that at the end of July or beginning of August he was staying at Sexard [Szegard], the country house of his Hungarian friend Baron Augusz. (Olga, who never gives us actual names, refers to the place as Sz., and to Augusz as Baron von O. Once more we find that she is not indulging in fiction but conforming to the facts as we now know them). Liszt met her at Gemencz and took her to Sexard, where he lodged her in the miserable local hotel, "a hovel with filthy floors and white-washed walls. . . . But what did it matter? I was near *him*." He introduced her at the château, his vanity no doubt finding its usual satisfaction in the exhibition of this appetising young mistress. He was fêted by the company like a king; and Olga once more observed his passion for exercising his despotism upon people who adored him.

She describes his daily round—out of bed at six in the morning, a mass in the local church, some hours of work after breakfast and again after lunch, and the normal social life of a

country house, interspersed with readings with Olga and long
walks with her in the fields.(11) She was in the seventh heaven
of happiness; at last he was hers alone, and, in the absence of
other feminine attractions, expending all his famous art of
fascination on her. "There were certain intonations in his
voice," she says, "that would have persuaded me to commit any
crime." She is disturbed, however, by the arrival of Mgr. H***
(Cardinal Hohenlohe), who has come to try to fix Liszt permanently in Hungary as the official head of Hungarian music,
sacred and secular.(12) She fears the worst: "My old fear for
X's vanity where an offer of honours and titles was concerned
had never left me. I determined to show frank hostility to the
scheme." She describes an amusing talk between herself and
the Cardinal on the subject of *The Song of Songs, which is
Solomon's.* Olga, who seems to have been a free-thinker, had
been enlarging on the physical nature of the passion in that
curious piece of ancient sacred literature, and the Cardinal, as in
duty bound, had tried to persuade her that the real object of the
love whose praises it sings was "the Church." The irreverent
Olga cited, among other passages, the one about the "ivory
belly" of the beloved. "These images, Countess," said Hohenlohe gravely, "are lofty ones in the true Biblical vein, and are
the invention of the Holy Ghost. You must not laugh at them."
Unable to escape from her irony or to answer it, he turned to
Liszt, who had just arrived on the scene. "My dear Abbé," he
said, "has the Countess ever paraphrased the *Song of Songs* for
you? Ask her to do so." "Monseigneur," was Olga's bright
reply, based on a profound knowledge of her tonsured lover,
"the Abbé prefers the real thing."

---

(11) The truth of her account of these days is confirmed by Liszt's letter
of 11th August to the Princess: "The Augusz live a very retired life,
and I spend three-fourths of my time in the way I like—alone in my
room. In the evening I make a little four-hands music with the two
daughters, Anna and Helène, with no audience but papa and mama, or
occasionally Franz Servais" (LZB, VI, 258, 265, 268). Needless to say,
there is no mention of Olga in his contemporary letters to the Princess,
at any rate in the published version of them.

(12) All this is confirmed by Liszt's letter of 20th October to the Princess
(LZB, VI, 270).

As she had foreseen, Liszt was unable to resist the new appeal made by Hohenlohe to his vanity and love of domination. His letters to the Princess during this period show him, as usual, vainly trying to accommodate his desire for solitude and work with his passion for what Carolyne described as "the world, success, external effect." Olga was a witness of the latest stage of this inner conflict between the two halves of his being. We, who know him by now, can see fairly well what was happening. He had had a long spell of self-indulgence, and the usual virtuous reaction was due, a reaction that gathered strength from the appeal to his vanity involved in the offer of honours and titles in Hungary. One day in November—his contemporary letters prove Olga's date to be correct—he told her that he had resolved to accept the invitation; he was tired, he said, of his nomad life, Rome was "anti-musical," and he would now devote himself to the musical life of his native land. "Later," she says,

> "the Austrian Court offered him a title and granted him a pension. It meant servile dependence; he submitted to it. His conduct neither astonished nor grieved me: I had gradually become accustomed to seeing him descend from the pedestal on which my admiration had placed him. I dreaded these changes only as one always dreads the unknown, and to the extent that they might threaten danger to my love. I was reassured, however, by the tenderness he continued to show towards me: this tenderness soothed the vague fears that pursued me everywhere. He loved me: my passion had been contagious. Even in society he could not exist without me: I had to accompany him everywhere, be always at his side. A year of sunshine passed thus."

Towards the end of this year (1870), however, she received word from her banker that she was ruined; and at once she thought apprehensively of Liszt. She knew him by this time.

> "He loved luxury; like the artist he was, he could conceive of love only as surrounded by every refinement, every delicacy. He could expand only in rooms lit by alabaster lamps that exhaled perfumes: under his feet he needed soft white carpets: his eyes demanded the satisfaction of rare fantastic shrubs:

love, for him, was inseparable from silks and the finest tissues of all kinds."

She remembered that one day she had said to him, "What would happen to me if I were ruined?" His dry reply had been, "You would go and take an airing in your own country." As a last desperate resort she alienated the fortune she had settled on her child. Six months later this too had been dissipated.

6

At the beginning of April, 1871, Liszt went to Vienna, while Olga, after accompanying him there, went to Rome to try to find some way out of her difficulties. A friend in whom she confided assured her that if Liszt really loved her the loss of her fortune would make no difference to him. "You do not know the man," was Olga's reply. "He is rotten with vanity. He loved me only because I was rich. I knew it: I was one of the rays of his pride. My poverty would humiliate him before his public; he would place a distance between it and him, without shame, with the utmost tranquillity of soul." She wrote to him, telling him what had happened. "His reply appalled Myriam [her friend]. It was nothing but vague phrases, larded with old German proverbs and pious hopes for my future." She made a desperate attempt to retrieve her fortunes at the gaming tables at Baden, but lost her last franc. There was nothing for it now but to try to make money as a pianist in America.

But in America she found, of course, that there was nothing to be done in the way of music in July, while the music publisher S*** [Schuberth], to whom she had a letter of introduction, benevolently pointed out to her the many difficulties she would have to face unless she had plenty of money to spend on agents, advertising, bouquets and so on. He passed her on to the leading impresario, the great Barnum, who made two characteristic and eminently practical propositions—that he should bill her as a daughter of Liszt, and that she should sleep with him. As she would not consent to either, his interest in her was soon at an end. She wrote to Liszt. His reply was pitiless, "a masterpiece of coldness and calculated cruelty." A further letter of hers, humble in tone, remained without an answer, although, as she says, he could find time to write to everyone, including his servants. A third letter brought a reply which she quotes in her book: it is so consistent with all we know of Liszt that we can hardly doubt the authenticity of it. "The violence of your sentiments troubles the peace that is one of the conditions of my existence. Permit me therefore to abstain from receiving your strange lucubrations until the time comes when you realise that happiness is possibly only when one obeys the divine laws. You must reconcile yourself to your fate, which, indeed, is the result of your many imprudences."

This, of course, was the end. She found, she says, that a boat was leaving for Europe on 15th November. She booked her passage, wrote two lines to Liszt—"Monsieur, I am returning to Europe—to kill you"—and went to a medical friend from whom she obtained some wourali—a poison which, he assured her, would bring on death after six hours of torpor—and an antidote. (It is hardly credible that he actually gave her the poison; but he no doubt pacified the half-crazed creature by giving her something resembling it in its effects. She seems always to have been able to obtain drugs and poisons in Europe).

"Three weeks later" she burst unannounced into Liszt's room at Pesth.(13) To do him justice, the old actor played his part well. He made to take her in his arms: she laughed and called him a coward. With one of his finest theatrical gestures he pointed out that he had received her threatening letter, and yet he was there! She promptly deflated that balloon by telling him that wherever he had gone she would have found him, and that he knew it. She assured him once more that she intended to kill him, but not till the evening: she would have a last few hours with him. He rang for his servant and gave orders that no one was to be admitted. The servant handed him a letter; having read it, Liszt turned to Olga and said it was imperative that he should go out. He gave her the letter to read.

"It was a Princess who was sending for him; she was to make her début that evening in the theatre, and, she said, she needed

---

(13) Actually she was there on the 26th.

his encouragement. A Princess! Could he fail to respond to the appeal of a Princess? Even at the point of death his vanity would fain drink in the homage of this last incense! It is true that he counted on *not* dying. I took pity on this monstrous weakness, and, without imagining that it might be his intention to escape me, I said, 'Go! I will wait for you.' "

On his return they had dinner together: she noticed that he would not taste his wine till she had drunk hers. After dinner a number of people came in, for the news of Olga's being in Pesth had spread. "I discovered later that he had shown his friends the letter in which I announced my arrival. Hence his courage! I recognised that he counted on them." When all the visitors had left he dismissed his servant for the rest of the evening. They were alone. She produced a little box containing two pilules. Telling him that she had intended one of them for him, she swallowed both of them herself. Liszt gave a cry, fell on his knees, and broke into prayer. She laughed at him. The distracted man broke out into sobs and protestations of love. But his presence of mind had not quite deserted him: he was still sufficiently master of himself to suggest that she should go to her hotel to die, as *he* would be accused of a crime if she died in his room. She offered to write out a confession of suicide, but this did not satisfy him: enquiries would be made, he said, a report drawn up: "and my priest's robe!" She laughed again: "my pity and scorn for all this feebleness restored my strength." They went to the hotel, where a doctor was called. She told him she had taken wourali. He exhorted her to take the antidote, but she refused, and insisted on Liszt's dismissing him. Liszt now begged her to take the antidote, swearing eternal love if she would; having no great faith in his mere word, she made him take an oath on the medallion of St. Francis that he habitually wore next his skin. She showed him where the antidote was concealed, and fainted. When she awoke, at dawn the next day, she was in his arms; her first thought was that he loved her still. He soon disillusioned her: looking at her coldly he said—and once more the words are so characteristic of Liszt that there is no reason to doubt her story—"My sentiments are still the same. We must separate. If I lied to you last night, it

T

was because anything is justifiable to save a fellow-being from suicide." Being, no doubt, in something like her right mind by now, as a result of the reaction after the experiences she had gone through, she decided that her love for him was dead. She left Pesth the same evening.

In spite of the febrile strain in which she writes throughout, for she was clearly a very unbalanced creature, it has to be reiterated that there is not the slightest reason to question the essential truth of her story from start to finish. It will be observed that this was the second occasion in Liszt's life on which a woman, maddened by what she took to be his hypocrisy and heartlessness, had resorted to literature by way of public revenge. And, as was the case with Madame d'Agoult, Olga had no need to invent: she had only to set forth the facts as they were to demonstrate, as she thought, the reality of her grievance and the accuracy of her diagnosis of the character of the man.

7

If now we turn to the references to her in Liszt's correspondence we get a perfect illustration of the unreliability of this as a complete record of facts and motives, for Liszt, as I have said, wrote many of his letters with a view to the maintenance of his legend. Had we only his letters to go upon in this matter, he would appear, as usual, to be the composed, patient, saintly figure the biographers have loved to make of him.

"You know," he writes to the Princess from Weimar on 10th May, 1871, "that Madame Janina has been in Rome for the last fortnight, staying with her friend Mme. Szemere. [Apparently this is the "Myriam" of Olga's story]. Your views concerning her are very just; and it grieves me to see a woman gifted with such intelligence, so much talent, and a thousand-devils sort of feeling for art, persist in a kind of fury in her way of living, that is conducting her to ruin, material and moral. Unhappily Gregorovius's sad opinion of her seems to me to err on the side of moderation. For some years she has nourished her mind exclusively on the most perverse theories and sophisms. [He knew that there was no better way of prejudicing the Princess against her than by painting her as a free-thinker!] The blasphemies, imprecations and extravagances of Proudhon and the new atheistic, agamist and anarchist school are her familiar litanies. She thinks Madame Sand timid and insipid. As for poetry, she is crazy about Baudelaire's *Fleurs du mal*. Last year I hoped that her assiduous musical studies and her exceptional artistic talent, which is not devoid of imagination and charm, would bring her back, if not to the true path, at any rate to a more rational one. This was an illusion on my part; you are not deceiving yourself when you say that 'she has formed herself greatly to her own disadvantage.' What will become of her? The loss of her fortune and several attempts at suicide do not augur well for her future. I beg you, out of Christian charity, to keep all that I just told you to yourself."(14)

Had the *Souvenirs d'une Cosaque* never been published, who would have guessed from this pious epistle that the subject of it was a young girl of twenty-two or so who, for the last couple of years, had accompanied him almost everywhere as his mistress, and that the breach between them had only come when the loss of her fortune had made her less desirable in his eyes? It is one of the many illustrations we have of a fact that becomes clearer and clearer to us as our study of Liszt becomes more intensive—that it is unwise to take any one of his later letters at its face value. The letter we are now considering dates from about the time when Olga was telling Madame Szemere, in reply to the latter's attempts at consolation, "You do not know the man. He is rotten with vanity. He loved me only because I was rich."

The next reference to her in Liszt's letters is in that of 29th November, 1871, from Pesth, to the Princess.

"My letter of today is a little late. You know I do not care for mixing tonalities! Last Saturday a terrible dissonance befell me; I was unable to resolve it until the evening of the day before yesterday. Mme. the Countess Janina—this is now the title on her Austrian passport—has spent three days here. Spare me the story of her violence and furies, and do me the favour not to talk about her to anyone. My good angel preserved me from danger. After another attempt to poison herself in my room, Madame

---

(14) LZB, VI, 299.

Janina left for Paris, where she will probably settle. But once more I suggest your not mentioning her, even to me, for I want to forget, as well as I can, this crisis, which, thanks to my good angel, has ended in neither a catastrophe nor a public scandal. My friends Augusz and Mihalovich, knowing in advance my resolution, of which I had told them by letter last year, not to allow Mme. Janina to stay long in Pesth, behaved with the most perfect devotion. Your beautiful views on the development of music and the pre-eminence of religious music have interested my greatly. I labour in the field you mention, and I share your convictions—except as to my personal value, which, without false modesty, I find extremely modest. May the good angels of God be with you!"(15)

The Princess having evidently pressed him for further information about Olga, in his letter of 3rd February, 1872, he narrates what he calls "the horrible incident" in more detail: .

"She telegraphed me from New York to Rome in October—'I am sailing this week to pay you back for your letter.' This letter of mine was couched in the mildest terms, implying that after our quite frequent meetings I could hardly avoid expressing myself with a certain degree of veracity. I understood at once what she meant by paying me back; in mid-November two letters from Schuberth, in New York, and from Hébert, in Paris, had warned me to be on my guard against the frenzy of an exasperated woman bent on revenge. It appears that Mme. Janina had openly announced to her friends and acquaintances her resolve to come to Pesth, to kill me and herself. As a matter of fact she came into my room, armed with a revolver and several bottles of poison—ornaments which she had already exhibited to me twice in the preceding winter. I said to her tranquilly, 'What you are contemplating doing is wicked, Madame; I advise you to change your mind, but I will not prevent you.' Two hours later Augusz and Mihalovich found her still in my room: Mme. Augusz came in later. She repeated to them categorically that nothing remained for her to do in this world but to assassinate me and then commit suicide. I protested point-blank against the intervention of the police, which in any case would have been useless, for Mme. Janina is perfectly capable of employing her revolver before anyone could seize her.

---

(15) LZB, VI, 316.

Enough and too much of this subject! The next day but one she went to Paris. Seven weeks ago I arranged with Mihalovich, who has often met her at Weimar, Sexard and Pesth, to send back to her, sealed, any letters she might write to me; and Mihalovich informed her of this intention on my part. I beg you again not to talk about Mme. Janina with anyone whatsoever. Do not even write to Augusz: I shall be honoured by your silence!"(16)

It will be noticed that this letter agrees generally with Olga's account of the scene; the only difference between the two is that Olga describes Liszt as she saw him and read him, while he, naturally enough, is at pains to exhibit himself as the perfectly good man dealing with a difficult situation with the detachment that comes from the possession of a clear conscience. Few students of Liszt will doubt that Olga's story is the truer to the facts of the moment.

8

As I have already remarked, the Janina affair would not have been worth the space here devoted to it had it been merely the record of just another erotic episode in a life that was agreeably rich in such episodes from its fifteenth year to its seventy-fifth. The value of the *Souvenirs d'une Cosaque* resides in the parallelism it shows between the case of Olga Janina and that of the Countess d'Agoult. Each of these women noted in Liszt the perpetual conflict between what Marie had called "pride and concupiscence" on the one hand and his religious aspirations on the other; the ease with which he could be led astray from his artistic ideals by the attractions of the world; his vulgar infatuation with titles and honours; the sheer inability of this "Don Juan parvenu" to resist the flattery of an amour offered him by an aristocrat; his vanity, his love of adulation, his exasperating way of purging his conscience periodically by a resort to penitence and confession before reverting to type; his command of fluent pious verbiage when the time came to defend himself against criticism—a verbiage that has imposed on the readers of his letters, but that only maddened the immediate victims of his Tartuffism, who saw clean through him. It is

(16) LZB, VI, 330.

surely not without a certain significance that each of these women should have felt herself driven to tell the world what she knew of him and thought of him in a book of pitiless analysis; the extent of their seeming malice is the measure of their detestation of his shifts and evasions and hypocrisies and love of unctuous acting. They felt impelled to give the world what they felt to be the real portrait of him precisely because their gorge rose at the spectacle of the success with which this consummate comedian, by one device after another, was imposing an idealised portrait of himself on the world.

They did not, of course, do him full justice; an angry woman, smarting under her wrongs, is rarely capable of an achievement of that kind. They could not take the objective psychological view of him that is made possible to us today by the copious documentation we possess regarding his life. They could not see his vacillation between aspiration and performance for the tremendous inner tragedy that it was; they were simply exasperated beyond endurance by his conduct as it affected them daily. During those months at Sexard in 1870 Liszt was once more fighting out within himself the eternal battle between his desire for solitude and his desire for the world, between the saint in him and the *arriviste* in him. His contemporary letters to the Princess show clearly the division in his soul at the time when he was debating within himself whether to accept or refuse Hohenlohe's invitation to become the official head of music in Hungary. He knew well that acceptance would mean not only still less time and energy for his creative work but an explicit recantation of his earlier ideals—for of what avail would it have been that he had renounced the career of a virtuoso in the eighteen-forties in order to realise himself as an original artist, if now he was to sell himself into public slavery once more?

"In Rome," he writes to the Princess on 20th October, "I confessed to you my main desire—to make a good end. Pray to God that in pity He may grant me His grace, that He may fix my soul and my feet in the straight path for the rest of my life! I have never foreseen, still less desired, any external position whatever for my old age. If it were a question only of myself,

I would cut myself off entirely from the exigencies of society, which have already robbed me of too much of my time. To please others while becoming discontented with oneself is not a good rule of conduct! . . . Nevertheless it seems that I ought not to succeed in what I have most desired—to live in and for myself; I ought to submit, in the hope of doing a little good in the other way. Without enlarging further on the subject, I have decided to accept the reversion of a very honourable position which the country and government will offer me shortly—a kind of general direction of the whole of Hungarian music, sacred and secular."(17)

A week later he is vacillating once more. On the occasion of his birthday (the 22nd), kind and flattering things have been said about him in the Pesth papers; they were no doubt inspired from high quarters for the special purpose the ecclesiastical authorities had in view.

"I am sincerely grateful for all this; but still I cannot, as yet, quite reconcile myself to the idea of being tied to the new post, for this would subject me to dependencies and constant derangements that are very contrary to my taste. For years I have aspired only to escape from the world, to spend my time in working a little and occasionally a little idle dreaming. And now they are launching me into full external activity again; my friends want to load me with the heavy task of working for the prosperity and the glory of music in Hungary! What ought I to do? Apollo himself would be embarrassed to advise me!"(18)

As usual, he professes that the title and the honour do not attract him, and, as usual, we are bound to believe that there was in him a sincere desire to be of service to others. But at the same time we are bound to give due weight to the analysis of Olga, who was with him in Sexard at this very time, and who saw, in his acceptance of the post, simply another manifestation of the vanity and the love of orders she had already noted in him, and upon which so many of his contemporaries have commented. Once more it must be said that his public actions, and the idealistic colouring he manages to give them in his

(17) LZB, VI, 269.
(18) Ibid., 271.

correspondence, are not always to be taken at their mere face value. A certain altruism there undoubtedly was in many of these actions; but it is impossible to resist the conclusion that vanity and the desire to weave a legend of altruism around himself also played their part in some of his decisions. Our judgment of his complex psychology must be based on the whole of the evidence, not on fragments of it carefully selected to support the legend.

He had acted, in part, on a generous impulse when he offered, in 1839, to supply the funds for the completion of the Beethoven memorial. But that there were other motives at work, including that of self-advertisement, is shown by the fact that before the letter containing his offer had reached the Committee he himself had already made haste to announce his benefaction in the Paris press.(19) It is only the innocence of the modern musical biographers—the most credulous, the least scientific body of men to be met with anywhere outside the medieval literature of hagiology—that has enabled them to imagine they were giving us the whole Liszt by selecting just the facts that suited their idealistic book and ignoring all the rest. Liszt may seem a smaller man after we have taken all the facts into consideration, but psychologically he is certainly a far more interesting man. And the last fatuity of biography or of analysis is blandly to ignore the testimony of people who knew him as well as Olga and Marie did, merely because this testimony is irreconcilable with the accepted hagiography. Olga Janina, like Madame d'Agoult, has been superciliously elbowed aside by the biographers for no other reason than that she told the truth, and the truth happened to be unpalatable. We have seen a generally shrewd writer like Julius Kapp dispose of Madame d'Agoult with the remark that a man of Liszt's generosity and chivalry would not have shown such implacable hatred towards her in later life unless she had deserved it; apparently it never occurred to Kapp that the falsehood may not have been in the lady but in the Liszt legend. *Nélida* is now, in the light of all the contemporary evidence we have concerning Liszt, and in particular

---

(19) For further details see *infra*, p. 228 ff.

that of his own letters, established as a perfectly veracious portrait of him in all his complex weakness. The *Souvenirs d'une Cosaque* have been regarded as the mere hysterical outpourings of an unbalanced woman whose love had been scorned.(20) As a matter of fact they are a penetrating study of Liszt as he really was.

The Janina affair prompts another reflection. From Liszt's unctuous letters to the Princess no one today would be able even to guess at the realities of the long affair; and, in particular, no one who knows Liszt's gift for plausibly colouring facts according to his fancy will believe that the final interview between himself and Olga ran precisely on the lines of his letter of 3rd February, 1872, to Carolyne. We are surely entitled, then, to ask whether the now famous accounts he gives the Princess of his last meetings and conversations with the Countess d'Agoult are essentially any more trustworthy. One does not suggest that they are actually false, any more than the story of his last evening with Olga Janina is false: one merely permits oneself to doubt whether they are complete, and whether they are such a record of what really happened and was really said as the other party to the matter would accept. Olga would certainly not have accepted the record in her case. Would Marie have accepted it in hers? Is it not at least probable that the consummate actor has appropriated to himself the best lines in the big final scenes in the d'Agoult drama, as we have seen him doing in the big scene of the drama in which Olga was the leading lady?

To the end of his days Liszt exercised a curious fascination over women. Shortly before his death, when he was seventy-five

---

(20) James Huneker, for example (HFL, p. 41), dashes off a confident remark about the "falsity of the picture" of Liszt in Olga's book. In what respect the picture is "false," and how he knew it to be "false," he does not tell us. Manifestly he assumed it to be false merely because it clashes with the generally accepted view of Liszt: but that it was this view that was "false" does not seem to have occurred to Huneker. Olga Janina's book was published almost on the heels of the events she describes, at a time when almost every statement in it could be checked by the many persons who figure in the story. Is it likely that she would indulge in outrageous fiction?

and mentally and physically not far from a complete wreck, he received a letter from a former pupil of his who signed herself "Ossiana," begging to be allowed to leave husband and child and accompany him, in any capacity, to London.(21) In his last years Liszt fell under the spell of another young woman, Lina Schmalhausen, who seems to have looked after the desolate old man in a way that, in part at least, was filial. Cosima had to deal firmly with her in Bayreuth in the last few days of Liszt's life. "Lina Schmalhausen"—Bülow writes to Karl Klindworth in June, 1885—"how diverting! Arthur Friedheim, whom I met at the station, told me the whole scandal. How sad it is for our Master's dignity!"(22)

The Princess told Adelheid von Schorn that "Liszt's soul is too tender, too artistic, too impressionable, for him to live without the company of women. He must have a number of them round him, just as in his orchestra he needs many instruments, with various rich timbres."(23) Adelheid tells us that he plumed himself on his respect for chastity: "I have never seduced a maiden," he assured her. The Princess also pleaded for him: if his triumphs, she said, would look, to posterity, like a bacchanal procession, it was never he who called the bacchantes to him, but they who flung themselves at his head. Adelheid says that even in his old age "many women regarded him as a desirable prey."

9

It is a mistake to suppose that Liszt, as a composer, was the victim of a universal neglect or contumely that saddened his life. On the contrary, a good part of his time during his last

---

(21) The curious in these matters will find her letters in KFL, pp. 535-537. Kapp does not tell us how these letters were obtained, but presumably he had satisfied himself as to the authenticity of them. (It is said that Liszt's last servant, Mischka, abstracted a number of letters from a portfolio and sold them after his master's death).

(22) BNB, p. 122. Another woman who exercised an extraordinary influence over Liszt in his last years was the Baroness von Meyendorff; 380 of his letters to her (all but two are as yet unpublished) were put up for sale at Sotheby's in April of the present year.

(23) SZM, p. 236.

fifteen years was spent in travelling from one town to another to be present at performances of his works, or in replying to letters telling him of their success in this place or that. The biographers have gone astray, as in the parallel case of Wagner, by paying too much attention to the attacks of the critics on him; in spite of these, his music had a not inconsiderable popular vogue. What weighed most heavily upon his heart was the consciousness that many of his oldest friends and acquaintances had become alienated from him and his music: and the question arises, what did he really feel towards them in this connection? We may reasonably doubt whether his correspondence, in this as in so many other matters, is a true mirror either of events or of his thoughts regarding them. Adelheid von Schorn tells us, as I have said, that in his later period he was studiously careful in the composition of his letters—for many of which he made elaborate drafts—because he knew that they would come under other eyes than those of the actual addressees. We may hazard a guess at another reason for this care—the knowledge that some day his correspondence would be published: a man who dramatised himself as Liszt did would certainly look further ahead in his letters than the immediate moment, would ask himself how the written word would look in the eyes of posterity.

We have seen Bernhardi noting that Liszt "is not a man of great intelligence, but he has a certain worldly wisdom, and he possesses in a high degree the tact that goes along with this. It is a settled system with him never to express an opinion upon anything, however unimportant it may be, so as not to compromise himself or offend anyone." We may reasonably ask ourselves whether Liszt did not carry out these principles of "tact" and "worldly wisdom" in his correspondence also—whether his scrupulous abstention from dispraise of his contemporaries is always a trustworthy guide to his real opinion of them, or just another facet of the art with which he laboured at the creation of the legend of himself as a man above all considerations of ill-will. We shall probably never know how much healthy, commendable resentment he hid from the outer world under the saintly mask he had trained himself to wear. He wins admiring credit for his noble attitude towards Joachim and

Brahms, for instance, who had given him some cause for offence; and certainly in no part of his conduct that had a public side to it, or in his correspondence, does he show anything but the utmost magnanimity towards the pair. But one would like to know what this man of an easily wounded amour-propre and an often uncontrollable temper said about them, and about several others, in private. A few of his sayings have been recorded that suggest a pungency of criticism that never appears in his letters: Cosima tells us, for example, that his true opinion of Brahms was that "this is music for people who, for preference, would rather not have music at all."(24)

There is a curious passage in the Ramann biography that seems to have escaped general notice; Ramann's informant, of course, was the Princess. We are told that after that evening at Schumann's house in Dresden in 1848, at which Schumann and Liszt had a violent quarrel over Meyerbeer,(25) Wagner was for some time suspicious of, and inimical to, Liszt, whom, of course, he knew only slightly at that time. (The Princess, by the way, seems to have been somewhat confused in her facts and dates. That is quite understandable after the lapse of more than thirty years. This confusion, however, does not invalidate her general testimony as to the psychological essentials of the matter). Her story was that for some time before the meeting of the pair in Weimar during Wagner's flight from Dresden in May, 1849, Wagner had cherished an ill-feeling against Liszt "to which he gave free and angry expression to others." Liszt heard of it,

---

(24) WFL, p. 117. His capacity for saying the diplomatic thing without committing himself in any way descended, in an even greater degree, to his daughter Cosima. When Brahms died, in 1897, the Committee of the Vienna Gesellschaft der Musikfreunde, of which Brahms was an honorary member, sent an official notice of the event to Cosima Wagner. The situation was a difficult one, for the name of Brahms was not one upon which Wahnfried could dwell with affection. Cosima got out of the difficulty by means of a letter to Hans Richter that is a masterpiece of diplomatic phrasing; she conveys the full sense of her and Wagner's inner alienation from Brahms, without a single reflection upon him, or the smallest lapse from dignity on her own part.

(25) Wagner's account of the evening will be found in WML, I, 463.

and "it estranged him, though it did not affect his willingness to help Wagner."(26)

There is no reason whatever to doubt the accuracy of the Princess's story; and there could be no greater proof of Liszt's essential generosity of soul than his assistance of Wagner in the dark days that followed May, 1849, in spite of the fact that as yet there had developed no warmth of personal feeling between the pair. Knowing Liszt as we do, his pride, his vanity, his resentment when these were hurt, we can all the more appreciate the real bigness of soul in him that made it impossible for him to act upon this resentment when it was a matter of helping a fellow-artist in his dire distress. The point to be stressed here is that nowhere in the whole of Liszt's correspondence is there the smallest hint of this secret temporary resentment, of the very existence of which we should have remained in perpetual ignorance but for this chance remark of the Princess to Lina Ramann. It is yet another proof that Liszt's voluminous correspondence is anything but a complete revelation of his real thoughts and feelings: from the first Weimar days to the end of his life, he turned, in his letters, his mask to the world.(27)

---

(26) RFL, III, 52-54.

(27) There is a marked difference in tone and in style between his early and his later letters, the dividing line being about 1848. Previous to that year he writes unconstrainedly, and, as regards style, carelessly, like a man of the world, with no thought beyond his correspondent and the matter of the moment. His letters to Prince Felix Lichnowsky (BAYB, 1907) are the last in which this non-dress air is maintained. After 1848 the Princess manifestly began her work of shaping him into the grandiose world-figure she had planned him to be; and his correspondence after that date takes on a new tone, acquires a new and sometimes factitious polish, and, in general, conveys the impression of a certain prudent calculation, a certain hiding of the real play of his features behind a mask.

CHAPTER X

THE ACTOR

I

Occasionally, as in the Wagner instance just cited, the motive and the consequences were of the noblest kind. But there is abundant reason to believe that in many other instances the motives were less noble—that Liszt, in his letters, did not permit himself the frankness in which he indulged in conversation, only because he was determined not to furnish the addressees of his letters, other readers of them, or posterity, with the slightest evidence that would tell against the legend he had built up around himself of the man of perfect, all-embracing Christian charity. His perception of new values in music was remarkable:(1) it is impossible to over-estimate the service he did to music by his encouragement of composers, such as the "nationalistic" Russians, who were bringing into the art a new spirit that was as yet not wholly appreciated. But it is equally impossible to deny that in many instances he over-praised mediocre composers to their faces, from an unwillingness to deny himself the pleasure of earning their good opinion and having his praises sung far and wide. Seroff was one of the few second-rate composers to whom he seems, for some reason or other—perhaps because he was nettled at Seroff regarding

---

(1) Perhaps, however, not so surprising as it is generally supposed to have been. It must not be forgotten that Liszt was the one musician in Europe to whom every budding composer sent or brought his scores. He therefore had opportunities, denied to other men, of being in at the birth, so to speak, of many a new work or new movement. One can hardly blame other musicians of the epoch for not similarly recognising the value of new music that never came their way. Still, it is beyond dispute that Liszt rarely made a mistake with regard to a significant work, even if he frequently overpraised works that were insignificant.

himself as "the Russian Wagner"—to have been frankly dis-
respectful. In general it was not without reason that he prided
himself on being "the first diplomat in Europe." He made
himself popular by his ingratiating flatteries not only in private
life but in public—at banquets or meetings, for example, at
which he would roll over his tongue some sonorous platitude
or other that was thoroughly insincere, but that happened to be
very much to the taste of his audience of the moment. There
was an occasion of this kind at a dinner given him in Pesth in
1865 after a festival at which his *St. Elizabeth, Dante Symphony*
and *Rakoczky March* had been performed. Speaking, no doubt,
when the wine had done its generous work within him, he
assured the other diners that "You are all of you greater artists
than I am, gentlemen!" Even Bülow, who was present at the
banquet, and who was at that time in the full flush of his
personal admiration of Liszt, had to admit, in his report of the
proceedings in the *Ungarische Nachrichten*, that this was a trifle
"exuberant."(2) Less partial critics turned with a feeling of
nausea from characteristic Lisztian poses and insincerities of
this kind. The fact was that Liszt, who in general had no great
opinion of the musical intelligence of the public, was in this case
gratified by the enthusiasm showered on him in his native land.
Like all composers, he was inclined to measure the musical and
the moral value of the public by the extent of its appreciation
of himself.

"I could not reasonably have expected," he wrote to the
Princess on 30th August,(3) "so complete, so extraordinary a
success! If the two concerts at Rome were successes, the four
at Pesth during the last fortnight went far beyond that. . . . *St.
Elizabeth* given twice, the *Dante* applauded and re-demanded,
my name and my character fixed in the enthusiastic respect of

---

(2) "The Master . . . spoke with such enthusiasm of the action and
reaction between the artist and the public, of the necessity and fruitful-
ness of this mutual action for both parties and for the development of
public musical life, that the exuberance [gush] of his conclusion—'You
are all of you greater artists than I am, gentlemen!'—could pass as an
oratorical licence, in spite of its monstrosity" (BAS, II, 90).

(3) LZB, VI, 88.

the whole population, such are the sheaves of the harvest I now offer you. . . ."

2

Flattery, indeed, as everyone observed, was the very breath of his nostrils. It was largely for this reason, no doubt, that he wasted so much of his time in his later years in salons and among budding pianists. He could not always command the regard of other musicians or of the public: but in private circles he could at the same time enjoy the exercise upon his admirers of the extraordinary fascination he knew himself to possess, gratify his generous desire to help others, and sun himself in the admiration showered upon his good deeds and in the love evoked by his personality among those who had benefited by his kindness. He would have been either less or more than human had it been otherwise; and only biographers ignorant of the merest simplicities of human nature could have failed to recognise how closely bound up his weaknesses were with his strength. "L'intérêt," says La Rochefoucauld, "parle toutes sortes de langues, et joue toutes sortes de personnages, même celui de désintéressé." The remark is cynical, it will be said; but it is none the less true for that: the cynical French makers of aphorisms may not tell us the whole truth about human nature, but they at least remind us of many a truth which, in our sentimental romantic moments, we are apt to forget. A man one of the central forces of whose being, as in the case of Liszt, is vanity is hardly likely to deny himself the luxury of the contemplation of his own good deeds, or the glow of satisfaction that comes from knowing that he has given the world reason to speak well of him. "Il semble," says the shrewd Frenchman in another aphorism, "que l'amour-propre soit la dupe de la bonté, et qu'il s'oublie lui-même lorsque nous travaillons pour l'avantage des autres. Cependant c'est prendre le chemin le plus assuré pour arriver à ses fins; c'est prêter à usure, sous prétexte de donner: c'est enfin s'acquérir tout le monde par un moyen subtil et délicat." Liszt in his old age needed something to sustain him against the depression he must often have felt when he contrasted his present comparative failure with the brilliant promise of his early and middle years; and he found the needed support in the adulation of his friends and his pupils. He could no longer persuade himself that he was shaping the destinies of musical Europe as he had done, to some extent, in his Weimar days. He could not delude himself either that the world in general was recognising what he took to be his real value as a composer, or that he was now conducting his life in such a way as to make it yield consistently the best that was still in him as a creative artist. But there were things he could still do to gratify his insatiable appetite for applause. He could exercise upon the young people who came to him the personal fascination he knew himself to possess, and every trick of which, from the ingratiating smile to the condescending attention, from the rather over-mannered courtesy to the spell of his playing, he had at his easy command. And while playing the part of the Great Renouncer, the Great Resigned, the humble servant of his God, he could at the same time nourish his colossal pride on the sweets of humility; for, to quote La Rochefoucauld a third time, "L'humilité n'est souvent qu'une feinte soumission dont on se sert pour soumettre les autres. C'est un artifice de l'orgueil qui s'abaisse pour s'élever; et bien qu'il se transforme en mille manières, il n'est jamais mieux déguisé et plus capable de tromper que lorsqu'il se cache sous la figure de l'humilité." There were no limits to Liszt's humility, so long as nothing was done to offend his equally illimitable pride.

We have some amusing sidelights on the old actor in the eighteen-seventies in the letters of Amy Fay, an American pupil of his at Weimar, who, vastly as she admired him as a pianist, and greatly as she loved him as a man, still could not help being conscious of the little weaknesses and absurdities of his nature. At their first meeting she noted, anything but unkindly, his "most crafty and Mephistophelean expression when he smiles," and the "sort of Jesuitical elegance and ease" of his manner. He went about in Weimar, she says, "bowing to everybody just like a king," for "all Weimar adores him, and people say that women go perfectly crazy over him." Fascination had become so much second nature with him that he could not

U

refrain from exercising it when there was nothing in particular
to be gained by it, just as a great fiddler will dazzle us with his
virtuosity for pure virtuosity's sake and for the sake of the pure
love of dazzling. "I can't give you any idea of his *persuasiveness*
when he chooses," Miss Fay writes to her friends in America.
"It is enough to decoy you into anything." "His personal
magnetism is immense"—and he knew it: if he could not
instantly conquer his interlocutors by his feline grace of manner,
he had only to sit down at the piano and play them something
as only he could play it, at the same time toying with his victim
with equal delight on his part—the delight of the virtuoso in his
technique of seduction—and on theirs. He never, to the end of
his days, gave up his old trick of holding his audience with his
mesmeric eye while he was playing:

> "Liszt knows well," says the enraptured Amy, "the influence
> he has on people, for he always fixes his eyes on some one of us
> when he plays, and I believe he tries to wring our hearts. . . .
> But I doubt if he feels any particular emotion himself when
> he is piercing you through with his rendering. He is simply
> hearing every tone, knowing exactly what effect he wishes to
> produce and how to do it."

(We are reminded of Balzac's description of the singing of
Conti).

> "Liszt is a complete actor," Miss Fay writes later, "who
> intends to carry away the public, who never forgets that he is
> before it, and who behaves accordingly. Joachim is totally
> oblivious of it. Liszt subdues the people to him by the very way
> he walks on the stage. He gives his proud head a toss, throws
> an electric look out of his eagle eye, and seats himself with an
> air as much as to say, 'Now I am going to do what I please with
> you, and you are nothing but puppets subject to my will.' . . .
> Joachim, on the contrary, is the quiet gentleman-artist. He
> advances in the most unpretentious way, but as he adjusts his
> violin he looks his audience over with the calm air of a musical
> monarch, as much as to say, 'I repose wholly on my art, and I've
> no need of any ways or manners.' In reality I admire Joachim's
> principle the most, but there is something indescribably fas-
> cinating and subduing about Liszt's wilfulness."

3

She observed, as Bernhardi had done twenty years before, that "he never gives a direct answer to a direct question:" to have done that would have been to surrender one of the most potent weapons in his armoury, to have dissipated something of the mystery with which he loved to surround himself. She saw that he could be cruel at times. "With this Machiavellian bent," she says, "it is not surprising that he sometimes indulges himself in playing off the conceited or the obtuse for the benefit of the bystanders. But the real *basis* of his nature is compassion. *The bruised reed he does not break, nor the humble and docile heart despise.*" For all this "compassion," however, he could be "bitter, sarcastic;" "I've seen him snub and entirely neglect young artists of the most remarkable talent and virtuosity, merely because they did not please him personally"—presumably because they did not fawn on him in the way he loved. For this incarnation of Franciscan humility had in him the pride of Lucifer, and woe to anyone who offended it. "Liszt is just like a monarch," says Miss Fay, "and no one dares to speak to him until he addresses one first, which I think no fun." She noticed, as so many other people did, that in the company of aristocrats he was not himself: he put on a special manner for their benefit. The impression one gets from these as from other reminiscences of Liszt in his later Weimar days is that many loved him, few could resist the demoniac fascination that was half natural to him, half carefully cultivated technique, and all more or less saw through him and laughed at him. The artist Rudolf Lehmann, who saw a good deal of him in Rome and elsewhere, tells us that the triumphs of Liszt's career as a virtuoso, followed by "the incense burnt from morning till night by the Princess and her charming daughter on their idol's altar," had left their indelible mark upon him: he was addicted to "a certain self-consciousness and love of posing." Lehmann noted in 1861, as many others did before and after that date, that Liszt could be "most natural and attractive in his behaviour" when he was alone with a friend or two; "but if there was anything in the shape of an audience he would become self-conscious and a poseur, and would sometimes make himself

insupportable." The Lehmann's Italian servant used to announce him, when he called on them, as "*l'inamidato*" ("the
starched gentleman"), "from the solemn stiffness of his gait
when he knew himself to be observed."(4) He even carried into
questions of art the pomposity that he called chivalry where
women were concerned, for his sense of humour was rudimentary. He amused Wagner, when the latter read the text of the
Valkyrie to him and the Princess, by objecting to the rating that
Wotan gives Brynhilde for disobeying him: that was not a nice
way, he thought, for any man to speak to a woman!

In his last years the vanity that had been in him from the
first had become perhaps the strongest element in his nature.
He could easily be manoeuvred into seating himself at the
piano; hostesses and guests soon realised that *not* to ask him to
play to them was the surest way to get him there, for the king,
of course, while anxious to dispense his royal largesse, had to do
so at his own time and of his own free will. To *ask* him to
play, however, was *lèse-majesté*, to be punished with all-highest
severity. He probably did not know that he was merely acting
once more the eternal farce of the executive artist whose head
has been turned, and his sense of comic values destroyed, by
excess of flattery. Ancient Rome knew the type: he appears at
the commencement of the third Satire of Horace:

> "Omnibus hoc vitium est cantoribus, inter amicos
>   Ut nunquam inducant animum cantare rogati,
>   Injussi nunquam desistant."(5)

---

(4) LAR, pp. 260, 268.

(5) In Theodore Martin's translation:
> "All singers have their failing: asked to sing,
> Their minds to do so they can never bring;
> But leave them to themselves, and all night long
> They'll go on boring you to death with song."

The Tigellius of Horace seems, indeed, to have resembled Liszt in
other respects than this, and especially in his passion for titles and his
vacillation between a life of luxury and one of asceticism:
> "Nil aequale homini fuit illi: saepe velut qui
> Currebat fugiens hostem, persaepe velut qui
> Junonis sacra ferret; habebat saepe ducentos,

He would graciously condescend to play four-hands arrangements of the most trivial music with aristocratic amateurs—at his own winning invitation, of course; but at the smallest request that *he* should play, his vanity was up in arms, and for a moment all the temper upon which, as a rule, he managed to keep so tight a hand would overflow. Alexander Wolkoff-Mouromtzoff has described for us an incident of this kind which he witnessed at a party at Princess Metternich's in Venice in the eighteen-eighties.

"While she and I were looking at and criticising a family portrait, painted by Kirchmayr, in the next room, a young lady, well known in Venetian society, came into the room, and going straight up to Liszt, said to him, 'Sir, they have asked me to sing something. Will you accompany me?' The cheek with which she asked this favour gave the measure of her ignorance as to the

---

Saepe decem servos; modo reges atque tetrarchas,
Omnia magna, loquens, modo: 'Sit mihi mensa tripes et
Concha salis puri et toga quae defendere frigus
Quamvis crassa queat.' Decies centena dedisses
Huic parco, paucis contento, quinque diebus
Nil erat in loculis; noctes vigilabat ad ipsum
Mane, diem totum stertebat; nil fuit unquam
Sic impar sibi."

"That man was made of inconsistencies:
Oft would he scour along, like one that flies
A foe; as often with majestic stalk,
As though he carried Juno's symbols, walk;
One day he'd have two hundred serving men,
The very next as probably have ten;
Of kings and tetrarchs now his talk would be,
And all things splendid, like some great grandee;
Anon he'd say, 'Give me an oaken chair,
A three-legged table, and the humblest fare,
A coat, however coarse, so 'twill prevent
The cold from pinching me, and I'm content.'
Give him ten thousand pounds, this frugal soul,
And in a week he would have spent the whole.
He waked the livelong night, and snored all day;
Such contrasts never did one man display."

(Martin's version.)

exceptional position which Liszt occupied in the world, and the . impossibility of suggesting such a thing to him. Princess Metternich and I could only smile, but Liszt without even turning to the lady in question, said drily, 'No, madam.' After two or three minutes Liszt went back to the drawing-room, which was full of people, and said rather loudly, 'Hohenlohe, come and sing *The Two Grenadiers* of Schumann. I will accompany you.' "(6)

Such was the courtesy, the Christian charity and humility, of the Franciscan Liszt when his vanity was hurt. He could forgive and shield a thief; because this gave him an opportunity both to indulge his passion for *caritas* and to strike one of his favourite attitudes—for it was he himself, apparently, who told the story to Lina Schmalhausen; but he could rudely snub a lady who had been guilty of the enormity of asking him to accompany her, and he could shake the life out of a young man who had not been listening respectfully enough to his piano-playing! Of contradictions like these is our absurd human nature made up.

4

We are brought back again and again to the same problem— a problem that is perhaps finally insoluble. How much of the generosity for which Liszt was admired was genuine saintliness, how much due to the satisfaction he found in playing the part of the supremely benevolent man? "You are too much preoccupied with being grand," Marie had warned him in 1840, when he was passing like a flaming meteor through Europe. Many of the people who came into contact with him in his earlier and middle years were astounded at his vanity, his love of adulation; and we may reasonably ask ourselves whether a man of this cast did not occasionally perform his public good deeds with at least one eye to public applause. More than once we find him feeding the Paris press with his own hand with accounts of his triumphs abroad. There were few nobler acts in his life than his offer to the Committee for the Beethoven monument in Bonn to bear part of the expense of the monument himself. But have we

(6) WMM, p. 208.

perhaps been led to exaggerate the extent of his contribution?(7)
As the accepted story runs, he was revolted at the slowness of
the progress of the fund, a concert in Paris, for instance, having
yielded only 425 francs; and the impression has been given that
Liszt saved the scheme from collapse by contributing the greater
part of the funds. This was apparently not so: in a letter of 17th
December, 1839, to Marie he says that the Committee has
40,000 francs in hand, and only another 20,000 are needed,
"which," he says, "will easily be raised." As always happens on
these occasions, the moment a big private donation was announced the grateful public felt itself relieved from the necessity
of subscribing: as the Committee said in their letter to Liszt,
the 40,000 francs in hand "would doubtless have been aug-
mented had your generous proposal not become so soon and so
generally known." Is there, perhaps, a touch of quiet irony
in this last sentence? That the proposal became "so soon and so
generally known" was due entirely to Liszt himself. His letter
to the Committee is dated 3rd October, 1839. On the 2nd he
had already sent to the Paris *Gazette Musicale*, for publication,
an open letter (addressed to Berlioz), dealing with art and music
in Italy. Towards the end of the letter he introduces, with
calculated casualness, the names of Mozart, Beethoven and
Weber: this gives him the desired cue for his public announce-
ment that he has written to the Bonn Committee asking them
to close the lists, as he will subscribe the remainder of the sum
required himself. This article was published in the *Gazette
Musicale* of 24th October.(8)   It is difficult to resist the

---

(7) Göllerich, for instance, tells us that "Liszt gave more towards the
Beethoven monument than forty million Germans had subscribed
between them"! (GFL, p. 200).

(8) LZPR, pp. 257-267. Even this, however, is not the whole story.
Though his letter to the Committee is dated 3rd October, he did not
send it to them until about 10th December, as is evident from their
letter of acknowledgment, in which they speak of it having reached
them on the 12th of that month. Meanwhile, for some six weeks, he had
had the benefit of the *réclame* of his *Gazette musicale* article of 24th
October, the passage in it relating to his offer having been reproduced
in the German press.

suspicion that Liszt was well acquainted with the uses of advertisement. It was just at this time that he was angling for a title
of nobility in Hungary; and we are probably not doing him any
great injustice if we surmise that he may have reflected that his
prospects of receiving the honour would not be damaged by
a magnificent public flourish of this kind. Certain it is that we
find him sending Marie the letter of the Committee thanking
him for his offer: this he asks her to have inserted in the Paris
papers, where it will make, he says, "a good effect."(9) How
many other generous acts in his life, one wonders, were performed not merely out of sheer goodness of heart but also with
the knowledge that they would "make a good effect"? He could
never stir out of his retreat in Tivoli without being surrounded
by a swarm of waiting beggars to whom he distributed largesse.

---

(9) LZAC, I, 336. The further history of this affair is anything but clear.
Liszt's offer to the Committee was made in October, 1839, and the
impression we have been given is that Liszt now paid the remainder of
what was required out of his own purse. But, as we have seen, he earned
so little money in 1840 and 1841, and part of 1842, that he was sometimes
financially embarrassed. In January, 1841, he was anxious to establish
himself once more in Paris. He evidently thought the best way to
ingratiate himself with the Parisian public, which at that time was not
particularly well-disposed towards him, was to "take one day a week
(a Thursday or a Friday) at Erard's, and commence with the Beethoven
monument. In this way I could form a coterie and definitely take the
position I want" (see his letter to Marie, in LZAC, II, 106). On 20th
April he accordingly gave a concert of his own in Paris, and on 25th
he played at another concert—for the monument—given by the Conservatoire Orchestra (conducted by Berlioz), at which Geoffroy, of the
Théâtre-Français, recited a poem by Antony Deschamps. Manifestly,
then, Liszt's offer to the Bonn Committee was still unfulfilled eighteen
months after it had been made. Further, in November, 1841, we find
him contributing his transcription of the Funeral March from the *Eroica*
to an Album to be issued by the Vienna publisher Mechetti, of which,
he hopes, 500 copies will be sold for the benefit of the monument
(LZAC, II, 178). Apparently, then, other people were still raising funds
for the cause, although Liszt, in his letter of 3rd October, 1839, to the
Committee, had undertaken to provide *out of his own pocket* all that was
still needed at that date. There is plainly some little mystery about the
matter, and it would be interesting if some one with access to the official
documents could clear it up.

Can we be sure that he was quite unconscious of the extent to which all this would contribute to his legend?

Janka Wohl tells us admiringly of an incident she witnessed in Pesth in 1867, when some music of Liszt's was to be performed at the ceremony of the coronation of the Emperor of Austria as King of Hungary. All Pesth was in the streets to see the King "go and take the traditional oath on a hillock formed of a heap of earth collected from all the different states of Hungary, which had been built up opposite the bridge on the left bank of the river."

> "When the feverish suspense grew intense, the tall figure of a priest, in a long black cassock studded with decorations, was seen to descend the broad white road leading to the Danube, which had been kept clear for the royal procession. As he walked bare-headed, his snow-white hair floated on the breeze, and his features seemed cast in brass. At his appearance a murmur arose, which swelled and deepened as he advanced and was recognised by the people. The name of Liszt flew down the serried ranks from mouth to mouth, swift as a flash of lightning. Soon a hundred thousand men and women were frantically applauding him, wild with the excitement of this whirlwind of voices. The crowd on the other side of the river naturally thought it must be the King, who was being hailed with the spontaneous acclamations of a reconciled people. It was not *the* King, but it was *a* king, to whom were addressed the sympathies of a grateful nation proud of the possession of such a son. . . ."(10)

Was the "effect" quite unpremeditated on Liszt's part?

The legend he has succeeded in creating about himself paints him as a man to whom honours and the adulation of the world meant nothing. But that was not how the contemporaries who studied him most closely regarded him: to them he was a man who could not exist without the approbation of others, especially aristocrats and women. Hence his surrounding himself, his whole life through, with Puzzis, as Marie had said; hence his constitutional inability to break loose from the crowd of "pupils" of whose general worthlessness he must have been

---

(10) WFLR, pp. 20, 21.

inwardly conscious, but whose flattering attentions he could not do without. In 1869 Bülow complains to Wagner that his projected meeting with Liszt will not take place, because Liszt is staying in Pesth "to be fêted." "I have perceived clearly once more," he says, "that if Liszt's life is to be prolonged he needs resounding compensations for the immeasurable injustices he has suffered."(11) A quarter of a century before then, Georg Herwegh had summed him up thus in a letter to Madame d'Agoult:

"Liszt remains entirely true to his nature. Just as it is impossible for him to shake himself free of the present and of the thousand good-for-nothings who fasten themselves on him at every step, so he will never free himself of his past. . . . Liszt is an abyss that will never give back what it has once possessed. . . . He will never have the courage to take the resolution to break with anything. In order to assimilate everything, including the most disparate things, a man must be a *character*. Liszt will never be that as long as he persists in his virtuosism: this virtuosism has infected his whole conception of things: it has made him a veritable 'man-eater' who will never find enough people to devour.(12) His unparalleled success, which has been won less by his genius, his soul, than by his mechanism, has led him astray to the point that he in turn judges men only by their mechanism, their virtuosity, without considering their moral basis: this success has brought him into contact with all those beggars whose influence on him is so malign, and who will perhaps in the end ruin him. But I admire in Liszt the splendid force that unhappily projects itself too much to the outside and splits him up into a thousand rays. . . . If it were possible to steady him by a violent shock of some sort, that would impel him to penetrate more deeply into the depths of things instead of spreading himself over the surface of them, we might save him."(13)

The portrait is not by any means wholly true of the later Liszt, who, under the domestic influence of the Princess and the

(11) BNB, p. 465.

(12) Compare Bernhardi's diagnosis of him, *supra*, p. 181.

(13) HPD, pp. 71, 72.

artistic stimulus of Wagner, did indeed succeed in steadying himself to some extent and giving direction to his life for a few years: but there are several traits in the sketch that remain true of him to the end of his days.

5

We have seen him, in his first period, bewailing to Marie his inability to bring the various parts of his nature into anything like harmony, to shape his life, by an effort of the will, to what he would have liked it to be. Every thoughtful observer who studied him then and at a slightly later period was struck by the war of impulses and of passions that went on within him. Through all his outer triumphs, during the years when, as a pianist, he was dragging all Europe behind his chariot, there ran a current of secret dissatisfaction with himself: it was probably this spiritual tension within him that, even more than his dazzling technique, made his performances something the like of which had never been known before. In the Weimar archives there exist the still unpublished diaries of Ludwig Preller, to which Peter Raabe has had access. Preller, in his earlier years, was Professor of Philology at the University of Dorpat; he later became, curiously enough, head librarian at Weimar during Liszt's residence in that town. Preller heard Liszt at Dorpat in 1842, and, with almost uncanny instinct, deduced from his playing the spiritual dis-harmony of the man, and forecast the regimen of isolation and self-concentration that alone could save him.

"If this man," he wrote in his diary, "could withdraw for a time from the wild, restless whirl of activity that even to himself seems something uncanny, could he implant peace and tranquillity in his soul, he would probably write some very fine things, whereas at present he is only a musician of the type that Plato and Aristotle would have driven out of the state. . . . From what his biographers tell of him, it would seem that the man in him oscillates widely between the two poles of extremest passion; apparently he has not yet found that centre of gravity for his innermost being that is so difficult for the greatest man to find, but from which, when it is found, calm and clarity are diffused over all they do and feel—that stability of character which, just as it alone makes a man a real man, alone makes the artist a real artist. That his soul is struggling to achieve this is revealed by his whole playing, his whole being."(14)

In his middle period those who loved him most truly and most anxiously were conscious of the split that ran right through his complex nature. In 1859, when the death of Daniel, coming at a time when his domestic and other troubles in Weimar had already brought Liszt near the cracking point, seemed likely to break him utterly, Wagner wrote thus to Bülow:

"I hope to hear from you soon that Liszt has not suffered too greatly in his sorrow. I fear terribly for him, for it was clear from his last passionate disturbance that now, more than ever, he is in need of the peace that unfortunately has always been so harshly denied him. I fear that he is irresponsibly allowing his life to be interfered with: he will lose in the end the strength to withstand the *unavoidable* encroachments upon his nature. I am very concerned about him."(15)

Liszt never solved the problem of his dual nature; the seeming peace of his last years was due not to a solution of it but to a flight from it, a flight that was the tacit recognition that with a will so weak as his the problem was fundamentally insoluble. "I love peace so much," he said once, "that I would do base things to achieve it, did I not know that the basenesses would only compromise it still more." Basenesses he could not commit so far as the outer world was concerned; but within his own soul he resigned himself to every kind of spiritual baseness, seeking refuge from his intellectual discontent, his mournful self-criticism, in tobacco and cognac, in company that flattered him, in the exploitation of the rapidly growing legend of his saintliness, of his Franciscan renunciation of all that other men strive for in the world. The mask models itself more and more closely to the face, till in the end the natural lineaments and the play of their expression become almost completely hidden. The letters of his last years are virtually no guide

---

(14) RLL, pp. 91, 92.

(15) WBB, p. 141.

whatever to his mind as it really was in the depths of it, so completely had he schooled himself to silence about his profounder feelings. Nor do the reminiscences of his pupils help us much towards the understanding of him. He was happy, or relatively happy, in their company, basking in the love they showed to the pathetic ruin he was now rapidly becoming: they, for their part, were mostly too full of the sense of the honour his friendship would do them in the eyes of posterity to be at all critical of him, or to leave on record anything that did not tend to confirm the legend of his infinite goodness. Besides, they were all young people who knew nothing at first hand of his past life and his inward struggles, and were incapable of sensing the profound mystery of his psychology. And so they have painted for us a portrait of Liszt that has influenced all the biographies of him, but which, as we now see, has only the most superficial resemblance to the man as he was.

It is a curious paradox that in the early days, when there was still strength enough in him to rebel against his weaknesses, he could confess them to others, while in the latest years, when he could no longer conceal from himself the fact that the battle was irrevocably lost, he draws between himself and his friends a veil that almost completely hides his innermost life from them and from us. In 1851 he could write thus to the Princess:

"However crushed I may feel, as a rule, by the thought of my insufficiency, my sterility, my irresolution, my sad memories of the past, by the lack of conformity—nay, the shocking disparity—between what I must appear to others to be and what at times I feel myself to be, but which it will never be given to me to reveal either by actions or by works worthy of you, my gentle guardian angel—yes, crushed as I generally feel by the *me* that others have made of me, I never cease to hope in you and through you. May the Lord bless this hope!"(16)

And again, a few days later,

"There is an unhappy contradiction between my tastes, my needs, my natural vocation, and the obligations of my outer career. . . . This contradiction sometimes afflicts me painfully; sometimes it reduces me to a state of fatigue, of

(16) LZB, IV, 43.

inexpressibly painful languor, traces of which are visible in this last Vienna portrait. That is why I like it better than any of the others except the bust by Bartolini."(17)

So it goes on to the end. Yearning for solitude, he wastes himself on the world: longing to be an original creative artist, he wastes himself on transcriptions of other and often inferior composers' works; relinquishing much of his ambition, he gives himself up to the relatively sorry task of producing pianists: the soul of him aspiring to heaven, the body squanders itself on women: professing to despise the poor prizes of the world, he clasps feverishly to his breast the paltriest prizes of all—titles, honours, adulation. He ends as he began, with a thrill of delight at the thought that royalties and aristocrats approve of him. Three months before his death he was in London for the performance of his *St. Elizabeth:* the Duchess of Cambridge, the old man proudly tells Carolyne, has sent for him; he has dined with the Prince of Wales at Marlborough House; the Prince has come into the artist's room at St. James's Hall to congratulate him on his work, and has presented him to the Princess and the Duchess of Edinburgh; the Queen has commanded him to Windsor. It is flattering condescensions of this kind that bring the real balm to the soul of one in whom the artist and the genuine nobleman were from first to last at war with the vulgarian.

---

(17) LZB, IV, p. 49.

POSTLUDE

LISZT'S PERSONALITY
AND HIS ART

I

Although this book is concerned with Liszt the man, not with Liszt the musician, a final word on the connection between the two may not be out of place.

Mr. Calvocoressi, in his thoughtful book on *Musical Criticism*, has thought it advisable to warn the budding critic against the use of what he calls "indirect data" when appraising a composer's work. "Indirect data," he says, "are of two kinds: they may occur in the author's [composer's] biography and letters, and refer to his disposition, his ideals, the events of his life, and so on; or they may consist of his statement of what his intentions were in composing a work, or whence he derived the impulse that led him to compose it—*i.e.* constitute a positive clue to the work's trend, meaning, or *raison d'être*." A large number of these "indirect data" may indeed be dismissed as fundamentally irrelevant to the work. It may please the lover of romance, for instance, to associate *Tristan* with Frau Wesendonk; but the sober truth is that not a semi-quaver in *Tristan* would have been different from what it is now had Frau Wesendonk's parents never been blessed with a daughter named Mathilde. One of the sections of Elgar's "Enigma" Variations would be neither better nor worse, as music, if instead of its being the portrait of his friend Miss N., it should turn out to be that of Miss X. Our aesthetic estimate of the *Symphonie pathétique* would be no different had Tchaikovsky lived happily for another twenty years after writing it, instead of dying miserably by his own hand some three months later.

But another class of "indirect data" to which Mr. Calvo-coressi refers, the data implicit in Sainte-Beuve's avowal—which Mr. Calvocoressi quotes disapprovingly—that he found it impossible to judge a work without knowing all about the man who wrote it, is another matter altogether. Mr. Calvocoressi's prejudice against this order of data comes from his being pre-occupied with the problem of "criticism" as an affair of "judg-ing," of giving the composer so many bad marks or good marks according to what the critic imagines to be the merits of his performance. Manifestly "indirect data" may be of little or no importance from that point of view: our judgment of the aesthetic value of an oratorio should be the same whether the work was written by Dr. Watts or by Dr. Crippen; the final musical value of a song is not in the least impaired by the fact that it was "inspired" by the composer's neighbour's wife instead of by his own. But there is another and deeper sense in which "the author's biography and letters, his disposition, his ideals, the events of his life, and so on" are not merely interest-ing in themselves but valuable to us in our study of his work. I say "study" because the process I have in mind has nothing whatever to do with the lower activity that is at present called "criticism."

There are some composers whose lives, so far as we can see, have had practically no bearing on their work. Even if we knew, for instance, that the Aria of the D major Suite had been written by Bach immediately after the death of a favourite child, it would be fatuous to suppose that that event had any-thing whatever to do with either the genesis of the work or the nature of the music; Bach's impulses to compose came out of a general fund of musical feeling that was independent of external incitations of the moment. In other composers some emotional shock or upheaval, the chance impact of some blinding exper-ience or other, of some book or scene or work of art or other, may have been the primal germ from which the impulse to create the work arose; but between the germ and the full-grown organism there has intervened a psychological something that makes the provenance of the germ of virtually no account at the finish. Wagner explained this process very lucidly.

The composer, he said in effect, must not sit down immediately after the moving experience and straightway project a tonal equivalent of it; he must leave it to germinate for some time within him according to its own unconscious inner law and according to the peculiar nature of music; in this way a particular mood is in time generated that constitutes the composer's starting-point; but from this point he will proceed purely and simply as a *composer*, without reference to the external event that had moved him in the first place—he will allow his ideas to evolve purely and simply in terms of *music*. In its way, the statement is just a variant of Wordsworth's well-known dictum as to poetry being emotion remembered in tranquillity.

2

Another type of composer does not wait for this remembering in tranquillity, for the slow metamorphosis of the first outer stimulus into an inner spiritual substance out of which the work of art will grow organically according to its own laws and those of the special artistic medium, but hastens to record the stimulus while it is still diffusing its first heat within him. To this type Liszt may be said to have belonged; many a work of his was not merely embarked upon but finished while he was still under the shock of the experience. There are composers, in fact, whose life is mirrored in their art, and their art elucidated by their life; and Liszt was one of them. Our perception of this fact, however, has nothing to do with "criticism"; we are content, for the time being, to put on one side the question of whether the resultant work is "good" or "bad": we simply note the mirroring, the parallelism, as an interesting phenomenon.

In Liszt's case the parallelism between his life, his character and his work is often obvious; few composers have painted themselves so accurately in their music. Peter Raabe is not being in the least fanciful when he points out that "Liszt's whole nature" is reproduced in the great piano sonata—

> "all that was given to him in the world, all that he had to win by bitter conflict, and that, for all the splendour of his life, barred him perpetually from happiness. Hardly anywhere else in the whole of his works has he so uncompromisingly laid bare

the sorrow of struggle as in this psalm that cries out towards enlightenment and salvation, in this poem that speaks with the same intimacy of jubilation and lament, of defiance and humility." "The hesitating, mysterious opening is a revelation of the Liszt who stood in an attitude of expectancy towards everything that was great, not groping timidly, but with the calm that is needed to recognise how we should bear ourselves towards what is great. This greatness is here *Combat*. How his will asserts itself in the first allegro energico! It is as if he had caught sight of the enemy. Then"—here Raabe quotes the main theme—"the malediction of the restlessness that burdened his life. He pauses, horrified. The theme returns, more clearly defined, more threateningly. Now he no longer recoils. The storm breaks; and now comes a struggle between resolution and doubt, a struggle that becomes ever more passionate, more embittered, till the tense gathering up of the foaming masses in the unison culminates in a hymn—'God alone it is who decides in such a fight.' Faith brings peace. . . . There is no parallel in other music to the way in which Liszt carries out the re-mainder of the sonata—the course of the combat—always evolving something new by means of the repetition of the assaults and the repulsion of these, exactly in the same way as in the course of his own life. . . . The fight is renewed, but it is never the same; the flight to God recurs, but never in the same form; sternness is succeeded by mildness, but always in a different form. Finally his confidence in God becomes a roar of jubilation; sinking back upon the earth he reaches the simple but moving conclusion—humble resignation, in the distance the call to combat, a deep sigh, a reminiscence of the commence-ment of all this torment and pain, a last tired look towards heaven."(1)

Of the *Faust Symphony* Raabe writes thus:

"The first movement is a self-confession the analogue of which is to be found only in the B minor sonata. The brooding protagonist whom he has drawn with such uncanny certainty in this first movement, the ardent lover, the aspirant towards the ideal, who again and again sinks back into darkness when victory seems at hand, is Liszt himself. If anyone wishes to know Liszt's inmost thoughts about the soul of woman he needs to read no

---

(1)   RLS, pp. 60-62.

books about his relations with women; he has only to listen to the Gretchen movement.(2) . . . And who has ever known better than Liszt that there is a power that falsifies and disintegrates everything that is great and noble? So he shows us, in the Mephistopheles finale, the themes of the Faust movement in a horrible distortion. Not only the first but the second and third movements are thus pictures of the Faust that was in the soul of Liszt."(3)

This correlation of the moods, the sequences of moods, and the outcome of the conflict of them in a given piece of music with what we know of the nature and the life of its composer would in most cases be illegitimate. But in the case of Liszt it is not only legitimate but actually forced upon us by the most obvious features of the man's life and those of his music. The two are here interrelated in a way that is without parallel anywhere else in musical history. Perception of this fact has within recent years set a few musicologists at work at the task, not of "criticising" Liszt, but of trying to understand him. "Criticism" of him, in the ordinary sense of that word, will never take us much further with regard to Liszt than we are at present. His music will always appeal strongly to some temperaments and as strongly repel others, and the opposing camps may be left to fight out their tiresome quarrel in their own way; neither will ever convince the other, or make the least impression on spectators who are not of their particular way of thinking. Apart from the futility of this wrangling about what is at bottom merely a temperamental difference between the disputants, there is the curious fact to be faced that, as Raabe points out, Liszt and rational criticism have come together rather too late. In his own lifetime, for one reason and another, intelligent discussion of him, intelligent appraisement of what

---

(2) This, of course, is an exaggeration. The Gretchen movement may tell us Liszt's inmost thoughts about the soul of a virgin, but it tells us nothing of his inmost thoughts, which must have been no less interesting, about that of a Lola Montez; and it was of the Montez type, not the Gretchen type, that Liszt had by far the more experience. He may have "respected chastity," as he told Adelheid von Schorn; but in the matter of female companionship he generally preferred the other thing.

(3) RLS, p. 83.

was really significant in his music in spite of its many faults, was
relatively scarce;(4) while the present generation, that is willing
to do justice to him, has lost the key to many chambers of his
soul.

We can no longer respond as the generation of 1830 did to
all the ardours, ethical no less than emotional, of the French
romantic movement; and it was as one of the spirits that were
the very incarnation of that movement that Liszt began. As
regards his second period, the literary and pictorial and didactic
impulses that played so large a part in the music of the "New
German School" have lost some of their force for us of today,
through pure satiation. We are critical of Liszt's halting construction in his symphonic poems because, in the eighty years or
so that have passed since they were conceived, composers in
general have learned a new logic of building; a minor orchestral
composer of the present day, with only half Liszt's originality
of conception, can give his work the appearance of hanging
together twice as well as some of that of Liszt does. In an epoch
when consummate virtuosi of the piano or the violin are ten a
penny we have completely lost the sense of what so dazzling a
virtuoso as Liszt must have meant to a more naïve generation,
that on the one hand saw something miraculous in men like
Liszt and Paganini, and on the other hand, lacking the vast
music-cultural background that we possess today, could not
separate the performer from the works he performed. Many of
Liszt's hearers in the epoch 1830-40 listened to some of the
great music of its own and a previous generation for the first
time at his recitals; the result was that his own playing was
credited with some of the potency that rightly belonged to the
music, while he himself added to the music something of his
own volcanic creative personality. The distinction between a
great work and the performer of it, that is always present in
the minds of even ordinarily instructed listeners today, hardly
existed for the average concert-goer of the days of Lisztomania.

---

(4) A certain amount of intelligent discussion of him there assuredly was,
even in his own epoch. See, for example, the defence of his music in
LCD, pp. 329-337. I do not know when this essay originally appeared,
but it was reprinted in book form in 1869.

At that time the public performer was still something of the improvisator, even in music not his own. Still more was he the improvisator in music wholly his own; and so we of today have lost many a clue to the real nature and the real contemporary force of many a Liszt work as he himself played it. He unconsciously carried over into his first orchestral compositions many of the ideals and the methods of musical expression that had become second nature to him through his association with the piano and through the early influences on him of the great violinists and singers of his time; with the result that we listen now to more than one passage in Liszt's symphonic poems with ears incapable of tuning-in with the local and temporal conditions out of which this music evolved. The upshot of it all is, as I have said, that now, when students of the music of the nineteenth century are turning with renewed eagerness to the examination of Liszt, they do so lacking the qualities of ear and of mind and the historical perspective that could alone enable them to see the significance of much of Liszt's work as an intelligent contemporary of his might have seen it.

3

Recognising, then, that in Liszt's case our ordinary "critical" apparatus is slightly flawed at the base, thoughtful students of him are tending more and more to leave questions of "values" in his work to be settled by individual tastes, and to concentrate on the effort simply to understand the man's mind. And once we begin to do that, we realise how closely the man is paralleled in his music. An admirable commencement in this understanding of him was made by Arnold Schering a few years ago in an article in the *Jahrbuch der Musikbibliothek Peters* on *Liszt's Personality and His Art;* and Peter Raabe, in his second volume, has carried the investigation a few points further. Liszt's music invariably reflects his nature and his life. He had no real nationality, a fact that has undoubtedly stood in the way of his full appreciation by any country. Though there was something of the Zigeuner in him, his music is not specifically Hungarian. His early romanticism was of the French, not the German, variety, a fact that made him seem an alien to the ordinary

German mind of the mid-nineteenth century. In his middle period he took up certain lines of musical development that were specifically German; but he never projected himself with complete success into the purely German mentality of which these lines of development had been, and still were, the natural, inevitable expression. He had as little a fixed spiritual home, his long life through, as he had a fixed physical home. It was probably this feeling that Liszt was fundamentally non-German that accounted for much of the German opposition to him in his own day: Germans sensitive to their own poetry must have turned with a wry face from some of his mishandlings of German verse-rhythm and accentuation in his songs—the opening line of *Kennst du das Land*, for instance—and from his tendency, as shown, for example, in his setting of Goethe's *Ueber allen Gipfeln ist Ruh*, to load the pithiest of poems with repetitions that destroy the very breath of their being. The psychical essence of a work like the *Faust Symphony* was too French for the nineteenth-century Germans and too German for the French. No approach to an understanding and an appreciation of Liszt can be made until we have learned to avoid trying to categorise him under any of the usual national heads, and to see him just as he was.

4

Raabe calls this non-national quality of Liszt by the name of universalism. It was universal, however, only in the negative sense that it was not local. It can hardly be called universal in the sense that it corresponds to a basic something in his music in which humanity in general, regardless of its geographical and cultural divisions, can find itself with full conviction, as it can, for instance, in the music of Bach, Mozart, Beethoven, Schubert or Wagner. It seems truer to say that Liszt was not universal, but simply himself—a personality of a peculiarly self-centred kind, which, while it reaches out now to the French, now to the Italian, now to the German, now to the Hungarian spirit, is not sufficiently French, Italian, German or Hungarian to allow either of those nations to claim him positively and wholly for its own, or to find its own historic culture faithfully mirrored in him. Schering, for example, has pointed out that while the ethical element in Liszt's nature attracted him to German ethical subjects, his treatment of them was not German enough for the Germans.

"Liszt certainly aimed at the highest idealism," he says, "and ardently strove to convert the ethical problems of his matter into the general-human; but in few instances, apart from the two symphonies, did he succeed in this. While in his idealism he was as German as any of the Weimar great ones [Goethe and Schiller], in his emotions he was never able, even in the years of his maturity, to shake himself quite free from French romanticism. In the excessively raised spiritual temperature of these works, in their sentimental exuberance, their frequent hypertrophy of moods that in themselves are quite simple, in their appeal to pathos and their attempt to make everything clear in the medium of tone, in a word, in the very essence of their spiritual mentality there are traces of that artistic attitude towards life which Liszt, with a touch of exaggeration, described as the 'romantic fever' of the eighteen-thirties. This is the reason why, of all these ethically so high-toned works, so few evoked a general response. The antipathy of the Brahms-Joachim group certainly did not spring from a lack of perception of the artistic quality of Liszt's compositions, but came from the impossibility of understanding his 'exalted' nature from the standpoint of the Germanic soul. The opposition between him and them was a matter of a difference between their respective ways of looking at the world."(5)

Schering speaks of "the religious," "the idyllic," "the heroic," and "the erotic" as the "four powers of Liszt's soul." His music is, indeed, as his life was, a perpetual oscillation between these; frequently within the same short work we pass from the idyllic or religious aspiration to a stormy outburst that reminds us of those episodes in Liszt's life in which the suppressed fury of his being had to clear the air for itself with a Donner-stroke at the black clouds around and within him. His mournful sense of his general inability to master himself and shape his life as he would have wished to shape it is curiously reflected in his choice of certain poems for his songs and as epigraphs to his piano works—

(5) SLPK, p. 37.

306 THE MAN LISZT

a feature of his work that cannot be dwelt upon in detail here, but that will well repay the student's investigation. In work after work, and in the different sections of each long work, we come upon the musical equivalent of the traits that can be seen to make up the zigzag pattern of his life—religious aspiration, perfumed eroticism, the heroic gesture, the theatrical attitude, the over-elaboration of manner, the studied effect, the alternation of the noble and the flashy, the prayer, the male-diction, peace succeeded by tempest and tempest by peace, the eternal combat between a higher and a lower element, and so on. There is no musician whose music so closely resembles his life, and whose life is so manifestly his music made flesh, as Liszt. The more clearly, then, we see the man as he really was, the more thoroughly we may hope to understand the many contradictions of which he was constituted, and so with all the more interest shall we renew our study of his music. Hence the necessity for the re-writing of his biography in the light of all the information about him with which modern research can supply us: if we are to follow up the clues we already possess as to the parallelism between his art and himself, the more we know about that self the better. That fact, it is hoped, will constitute the justification of the intention, if not the achievement, of the present volume.

INDEX

Ad nos, 11, 12 *n.*

Adelaïde, Liszt's additions to, 9 *n.*

Agoult, Count Charles d', 24

Agoult, Countess Marie d', Corder on, 4; Lina Ramann describes, 4 *n.*; *Mémoires* of, 4, 7-8, 20, 27 *n.*, 29, 40; falsehoods concerning, 5 *n.*, 6, 16-19, 21-3; *Esquisses Morales* of, 6; literary ability of, 6, 125; Liszt's vindictiveness towards, 6-7, 15, 84, 124, 145-7; "unveracity" of, 7; her knowledge of Liszt, 15, 20, 145-6; as "Muse" of Liszt, 17, 29, 76; story of extravagance of, 17, 19; reproves Liszt, 19 *n.*, 87-8, 91; *Souvenirs* of, 20 *n.*, 25; journal of, 20, 74, 76; *Nélida* of, 20, 23 *n.*, 112, 124 *et seq.*, 274-5; Princess on, 21-2; religion of, 22; Hillebrand on, 22 *n.*; Bäumer on, 22 *n.*; Liszt's letters to, 23, 29, 36-9, 41-50, 53, 58-61, 78-81, 92-4, 104, 138, 152-5; early life of, 24; marriage of, 24; victim of *mal du siècle*, 24; early meetings with Liszt, 24, 27-9; invites Liszt to visit her, 27-8, 34; her letters to Liszt, 27 *n.*, 39-40, 42, 102; on the young Liszt, 32-5; has thoughts of suicide, 39, 47; expresses her love for Liszt, 40, 42; and amours of Liszt, 43, 78, 91-2, 96, 100-2; death of daughter of, 47-8; elopes with Liszt, 49-53, 55 *n.*; birth of Blandine, 50, 53 *n.*; in Switzerland, 54-9; suffers odium of misalliance, 56, 97; and George Sand, 66, 114, 116 *n.*; writes Liszt's articles, 67 *n.*; on virtuoso in Liszt, 74, 84 *n.*, 221; praises Liszt, 74; in Italy, 76-7, 85; on Liszt's departure for Vienna, 77; strained relations with Liszt, 83, 94-7, 137 *n.*; returns to Paris, 85-6; in England, 85, 96-7; salon of, 86, 99-100; and Lytton, 86; Liszt reads journal of, 94, 136; separated from children, 95, 147-50; Liszt's love for, 98; final breach with Liszt, 100, 102, 139; sees worst side of Liszt, 110-11; portrayed in *Béatrix*, 112-13, 121; portrayed in *Horace*, 114; portrays Liszt, 124 *et seq.*, 271-2; idealises herself, 125, 154; against social injustice, 127; life in Weimar impossible for, 141-2; sacrifices of, 141; death of children of, 146; death of, 146; reissues *Nélida*, 147, 155; on Liszt's mother, 148 *n.*; change in style of Liszt's letters to, 154-5; later meetings with Liszt, 155-6, 275

Allgemeine Deutsche Musikverein, Der, 260

Altenburg, 164; oratory in, 166; Cornelius on, 174; Bernhardi in, 178-9; after departure of Princess, 198-9

Ambros, on Liszt's church music, 219

Années de Pélérinage, 48 *n.*, 215

Apponyi, Count, 89

Augusz, Baron, 262, 263 *n.*, 270

Austria, Empress of, 78 *n.*

Austria, Liszt in, 77-8, 80, 85

B minor piano sonata, 12, 299-300

Bach, J. S., 298

Bacheracht, Therese von, 183

Balzac, Honoré de, *Béatrix* of, 112-13, 115-23; and George Sand, 116 *n.*; Faguet on, 121; Sainte-Beuve on, 123 *n.*

Barber of Bagdad, 165, 173, 175, 211

Barnum, P. T., 265

Basel, 51-2

Batta, 67 *n.*

Bäumer, Gertrud, on Countess d'Agoult, 22 *n.*

Bayreuth, 233; Liszt's death in, 247, 276

Béatrix, 112-13, 115-123

Beethoven, Ludwig van, legend of, 1; raising of funds for monument to, 9 *n.*, 288-90; unveiling of monument to, 100 *n.*; celebration of anniversary of birth of, 260

Beker, 107

Belgiojoso, Princess, 100

Bellagio, Liszt in, 76

Belloni, on extravagance of Countess, 17-18, 19 *n.*; "swindles" Liszt, 19 *n.*; and Liszt's biography, 108; Liszt gives snuff-box to, 110

Bériot, 26, 67 *n.*; Liszt's duet with, 88

Berlin, Liszt conducts in, 140 *n.*; Liszt's children sent to, 170

Berlioz, Hector, 140; and Liszt's sabre, 91; orchestration of, 168 *n.*; "ingratitude" of, 209 *n.*, 218; Liszt on music of, 210 *n.*

Bernhardi, Theodor von, memoirs of, 177; on Liszt and Princess, 178-81, 183-5, 187-9, 277

Bethmann, Johann Philipp, 24

Bethmann, Marie Elisabeth, *see* Flavigny, Vicomtesse de

Bex, Liszt in, 55

Boissier, Madame, on Liszt, 56-7

Bologna, Liszt in, 88

Bonn, 9 *n.*, 100 *n.*

Bory, Robert, inaccuracies of, 56

Bourges, Liszt in, 75

Brahms, Johannes, 204; protests against New German School, 214; Liszt's attitude towards, 278; Cosima on death of, 278 *n.*

Brandt, Marianne, 146 *n.*

Brendel, Liszt's letter to, 8 n.

Breslau, Liszt conducts in, 140 n.

Briefe an eine Freundin, 171 n.

Brussels, Liszt's children in, 182 n.

Budapest, Franz Liszt Musical Academy in, 91 n.

Bülow, Hans, on Bülowmarsch, 14; on Romance oubliée, 14; daughter of, 84 n.; his love for Liszt, 150; on Countess, 150-1; on Princess, 151; letters of, 151; and Princess, 161; on Servais's likeness to Liszt, 182 n.; on Liszt's music, 207-8; last years of, 208; directness of, 238, 244; and Liszt's pupils, 243-4; on Liszt's "exuberance," 281; on Liszt, 292

Bülowmarsch, 14

CALVOCORESSI, M. D., Musical Criticism of, 297-8

Carl Alexander, Grand-Duke, and Liszt, 105, 143, 185, 187; marriage of, 162

Carl Friederich, Grand Duke of Sachsen-Weimar, 162

Ce qu'on entend sur la montagne, 158, 210, 215; second version, 11

Cessiat, Countess Valentine, 157

Christus, 218; Ramann's brochure on, 23 n.

Cohn, Hermann, 53, 57 n.; in Geneva, 57-8

Como, Liszt in, 79

Conradi, 140 n.

Corder, Frederick, on Countess d'Agoult, 3

Cornelius, Carl Maria, on people of Weimar, 174, 176; on children of Princess and Liszt, 182 n.; on projected marriage, 198, 201-2; on Liszt's theatricality, 206 n.

Cornelius, Peter, on Liszt's "mask," 61 n., 205; Barber of Bagdad of, 165; on Princess, 168 n., 181, 199-200; on people of Weimar, 174; on separation of Liszt and Princess, 197-201; declines to write biography, 210-12; on Liszt's music, 210

Correspondance de Liszt et de la Comtesse d'Agoult, 5, 8, 58; second volume of, 97; gaps in, 97-8

Croissy, Countess at, 27 n., 34, 40, 42, 47-8; Liszt at, 34-6, 45

Dante and Goethe, 84 n.

Dante Symphony, 83 n., 158, 160, 168, 210, 215, 281; ending of, 169; Princess's foreword to, 169

Danube floods, 77-8, 80

David, Ferdinand, 10, 10 n.

Die Glocken von Strassburg, 218

Die Ideale, 210, 215

Die Kinder der Haide, 169

Dietrichstein, Prince Moritz, 90 n.

Dingelstedt, and Barber of Bagdad, 165, 175

Donizetti, 106 n.

Dorpat, Liszt in, 293

Dubois, on Belloni, 19 n.

Duplessis, Marie, 101

ECKART, R. Du Moulin, on Ramann biography, 5 n., 248-9

Elizabethgrad, Liszt in, 158

England, failure of Liszt's tour in, 18; Liszt and Countess in, 96-7; Liszt in, 296

Erard, lends Liszt apartment, 36; salons of, 67 n., 290 n.

Esquisses Morales, 6, 146

Essai sur la Liberté, 109

Esterhazy, Count Casimir, 88

Esterhazy, Count Paul, 89

Ewald, Fanny, on Liszt, 176, 183, 195 n., 205-6, 223

FAGUET, Emile, on Balzac, 121

Fantasia quasi Sonata, après une lecture du Dante, 83 n.

Fantaisie symphonique, 48

Faust Symphony, 12, 83 n., 140 n., 168, 210, 215, 217; Bülow on, 207-8; Raabe on, 300-1; Liszt's self portrayed in, 304

Fay, Amy, 283-5

Festklänge, 215

Fétis, Open Letter to Liszt, 66

Flavigny, Marie Catherine Sophie de, see Agoult, Countess d'

Flavigny, Maurice de, 65

Flavigny, Vicomte de, 24, 27

Flavigny, Vicomtesse de, 24; marriage of, 27; in Basel, 51

Florence, 85, 101, 137 n.

Flying Dutchman, Liszt's essay on, 167

France, mal du siècle in, 24-5; arrangement of concerts in, 26; romantic movement in, 302

Frankfort-on-the-Main, 24

Franz Liszt, by Lina Ramann, 5; Princess's hand in, 5 n., 16; unveracity of, 16-19, 21-3, 28, 40, 51, 58, 104, 246; early publication of, 21; prejudices world against Countess, 21-2; English edition of, 51; Du Moulin Eckart on, 248-9

Fritsch, Countess, 189

Gaudeamus igitur, 12

Geneva, Liszt and Countess in, 53 n., 66, 73

Genoa, Liszt in, 78-9

Germany, New School of music in, 11, 143-4, 165, 214, 302; division between social classes in, 25 n.; Liszt's tours in, 79, 85, 108; Liszt alien to mind of, 303-5

Girardin, Emile, 99

Göllerich, August, 90 n., 141 n., 148 n., 210 n., 289 n.

Gran Mass, 210, 218

Grande-Chartreuse, Liszt at the, 67 n.

Gregorovius, Ferdinand, on Liszt, 203, 225-6, 259 n.

HAGN, Charlotte, 100

Hague, The, Liszt-Rubini concert at, 110

Haineville, Madame d', 43

Halle, Liszt in, 109
Hamlet, 210, 215
Hanska, Countess, 63 *n*.; Balzac's letter to, 116 *n*.
Harmonies poétiques, 48, 215
Hartig, Count, 89
Heine, Heinrich, 91
Helbig, Nadine, 222 *n*., 241 *n*.
Heligoland, Liszt in, 195, 262
Heroïde funèbre, 11
Herwegh, Emma, 102 *n*.; Countess's letter to, 147-8
Herwegh, Georg, Countess's letter to, 102 *n*.; 126 *n*.; *Wo solch ein Feuer*, of, 109 *n*.; on Liszt, 292
Herz, 26
Hevesy, André de, 98
Hillebrand, Karl, on Countess d'Agoult, 22 *n*.
Hohenlohe, Cardinal, 222, 232; and Olga Janina, 263
Hohenlohe-Schillingsfürst, Prince Konstantin zu, 159
Hohenlohe-Schillingsfürst, Princess Marie zu, 158-9, 161 *n*., 189; on Liszt and his money, 237 *n*.
Hohenzollern, Prince, 200
Horace, Countess portrayed in, 114
Hugo, Victor, 44, 99
Huneker, James, 275 *n*.
Hungaria, 210
Hungarian Rhapsodies, 210; preface to, 154
Hungary, Magnates of, and Liszt, 30; Liszt in, 78, 85; Liszt's successes in, 89, 90-1; and "ennoblement" f Liszt, 90-1, 264; Liszt offered post in, 263-4
Hunnenschlacht, 210, 215

Il Pensieroso, 83 *n*.
Italy, Liszt and Countess in, 76-7

JANINA, Olga, 250; *Souvenirs d'une Cosaque* of, 250-1, 268, 271, 275; becomes Liszt's pupil, 251-3; her love for Liszt, 253, 256-8, 262; sees through Liszt, 256, 261-2, 265; in Weimar, 258-61; takes to opium, 262; at Sexard, 262-4; loses her money, 264-5; Liszt's cruelty to, 265-6; in America, 265-6; determines to kill Liszt, 266-7; takes poison, 277; Liszt on, 268-71
Jena, culture in, 186
Joachim, Joseph, on Liszt as composer, 2, 209; on Liszt's pranks with music, 12; and Liszt, 204, 277-8, 305; protests against New German School, 214; on music-making of Liszt's pupils, 244-5; oblivious of his public, 284
Jurgenson, 241-2

KALERGIS, Marie von, 261
Kapp, Julius, on Liszt, 6, 274
Karpath, Ludwig, 161 *n*., 237 *n*.
Karr, Alphonse, 91

Kaulbach, portrait of Liszt, 205
Kellermann, B., 243
Kennst du das Land, 304
Kiev, Liszt in, 158-9
Knopp, Herr, 52
Koettlitz, 107
Krusenstern, Charlotte von, 178

LA Chênaie, Liszt at, 31, 41, 46-7
La Mara, 193
Lafenestre, George, 98
Lafont, 26, 67 *n*.
Lagarde, Count August de, 24
Lamartine, niece of, 157
Lamennais, Abbé, 31, 41, 46-7, 228
Laprunarède, Countess Adèle de, 43
Lausanne, Liszt in, 74
Le Prophète, 11
Le vieux vagabond, 83 *n*.
Lehmann, Rudolf, 285
Leipzig, Liszt in, 108
Les Adieux, 14
Les Préludes, 215
Lettres d'un Bachelier ès Musique, 67-72
Lettres Republicaines, 154
Levi, Hermann, on Liszt and Wagner, 209
Lichnowsky, Prince Felix, Liszt's letters to, 152-3, 279 *n*.
Lichtenstein, Prince, 90
Liszt, Daniel, death of, 146, 294; Liszt's letters to, 170
Liszt, Franz, legend of, 2, 8, 181-2, 203-4, 280, 291; unreliable biographies of, 3 *et seq*., 249; as composer, 2, 11, 187, 207-10, 212-19, 299 *et seq*.; of Weimar years, 3, 11, 40, 164 *et seq*.; publication of letters of, 5, 23; supplies material for Ramann *Life*, 5 *n*., 16, 24 *n*., 53; "goodness" of, 6, 171, 288; his vindictiveness towards Countess, 7, 15, 124, 145-7; on *Mémoires*, 7, 84, 145; dual nature of, 8-9, 14-15, 40, 73, 84, 93, 203-4, 225-6, 264, 271-2, 293-6, 306; on self-correction, 8 *n*.; fantasias of, 9, 213; delights in applause and flattery, 9, 13, 56, 87-9, 98, 139, 225, 252-4, 282-3, 288; plays pranks with music, 10, 12, 69; as pianist, 10, 74, 107-8, 204, 222; virtuoso in, 11, 13, 74, 139, 204-6, 213, 284, 292, 302; his lack of discrimination, 12-14; idealism. of, 13, 185, 305; influence of Princess on, 15, 40, 149, 152, 155, 165-70, 184, 279 *n*.; poverty of, 18-19, 230 *n*.; extravagance of, 19 *n*., 65, 230 *n*., 236; his first meetings with Countess, 25, 27-9; as infant prodigy, 25, 30, 68; defective education of, 25, 32, 165-6; social inferiority of, 25, 28, 88, 91 *n*., 126; at aristocratic concerts, 26, 129; grand manner of, 26, 65, 187, 205, 253; articles written by, 27 *n*., 167, 170; Countess's letters to, 27 *n*., 39-40, 42, 102; religious aspirations of, 29-30, 68, 220; early life of, 30; and Caroline de St. Cricq, 30; at La Chênaie, 31, 41, 46-7; and George Sand, 31, 48, 116 *n*.; his fascination for

Liszt (continued)

women, 31, 78, 89, 258-9, 257-6; conversation of, 32, 57; rationalist tendency of, 34 n., 57; Sainte-Beuve on, 34 n.; insincerity of, 35 n., 145, 187, 204, 212, 238-42, 281; his letters to Countess, 36-9, 41-50, 53, 58-61, 79-81, 92-4, 104, 138, 152-5, 249; expresses his love for Countess, 35-9, 41, 44-7, 58, 99; goes into "retreat," 36-7, 221, 332-3, 257; his letters to Princess, 37 n., 61, 145, 160, 162, 171-2, 196, 227-8, 231-3, 268-73, 295; periods of gloom, 38, 41-2, 169, 171-2; his dependence on women, 40, 157, 160, 206, 276; amours of, 43, 78, 91-2, 96, 98-103, 172, 186, 253-4, 261, 276; self-doubts of, 44, 81-2, 144, 167, 169, 230; elopes with Countess, 49-53, 55 n.; children of, 50, 159 n., 182 n.; in Switzerland, 54-9; religious music of, 54, 217, 219-20, 229-30; Mme. Boissier on, 56-7; "mask" of, 61-4, 171, 205-7, 249, 277, 294; uncontrollable temper of, 62-3, 107, 278; in Tivoli, 63, 232, 257, 290; his carefulness in letters, 63 n., 64, 153, 182, 249, 269-71, 277, 279; dealings with Thalberg, 64-6, 70-2, 80; dramatises himself, 65 n., 204-5, 212, 234, 249; Lettres d'un Bachelier ès Musique of, 67-72; actor in, 68-9, 145, 204-7, 242, 275, 283-4; and life of solitude, 69, 92, 155, 227-8, 232-3, 245, 257, 272-3; transcriptions of, 73, 215, 230-1, 245; in Italy, 76-7, 85; his passion for society, 77, 167; goes to Vienna, 77, 80, 85; on his successes, 77, 80, 88-90, 108, 296; armorial bearings of, 78, 90; tours of, 79-80, 85, 88-94, 108; journal of, 81-3; rift between Countess and, 83, 94-7, 137 n.; in London, 85, 94, 96-7, 296; tires of chains, 85, 191-2, 197, 231; hectic life of, 86-90, 93, 99, 197, 200; vanity of, 87-8, 90-1, 180-1, 186, 224, 254, 257, 265, 273-4, 282, 285-8; arrogance of, 87, 108, 175; his love for aristocracy, 88-91, 107, 157, 253, 296; "ennoblement" of, 90-1, 290; and Thalberg's parentage, 90 n.; presented with sabre, 91; indulges in stimulants, 92, 99, 141, 169, 193-5, 196 n., 244; cigars of, 92, 195, 196 n., 222 n.; his love for Countess, 98; his love for Princess, 98, 160, 202; jealousy of, 100; final breach with Countess, 100, 102, 139; hostility to, at Bonn, 100 n.; self-justification of, 101, 103; worldly aims of, 105; operatic ambitions of, 105, 167; his position at Weimar, 105-6, 143; produces Wagner's operas, 106, 164, 185; seeks post in Vienna, 106; income of, 106, 157; hardening of character of, 107; asks Countess to write biography, 108; benefactions of, 108-9, 236, 288-90; and advantages of publicity, 109, 274, 290; episode of snuff box, 110; large scale compositions of, 110, 141; portrayed in Béatrix, 112, 115-19; portrayed in Nélida, 112, 124 et seq.; on Béatrix, 112-13, 119; disparages Countess, 113, 115, 145; and George Sand's attack on Countess, 114; on living people portrayed in novels, 119 n.; on Nélida, 119 n., 125, 152-3; repartees of, 135 n.; Weimar's attractions for, 139-41, 144; turns to orchestral work, 140 n., 142, 168, 212; as conductor, 140 n.; and Raff, 140 n., 187; and death of Countess, 146; separates Countess from

Liszt (continued)

her children, 147-50, 170; growing animosity of, to Countess, 152, 154-5; later meetings with Countess, 155-6, 275; meets Princess, 158-9, 180; Princess's letters to, 160-1, 192-3; decorations of, 162, 224; appointed Kapellmeister at Weimar, 162; at Altenburg, 164, 166, 198-9; Weimar works of, 164, 168, 214-16; resigns post, 165, 211; has difficulty in expressing himself, 166 n.; and Princess's sacrifices, 166-7, 169; indolence of, 167, 221, 226-7, 229, 245-6; ambition of, 167, 181, 183; and Wagner, 168, 185, 200-1, 209, 233, 278-9; his lack of application, 169; influence of Princess on work of, 169-70, 216-18; 220; his letters to his son, 170; sufferings of, 171-2, 225, 230; deterioration after separation from Princess, 173, 194, 197-200; and people of Weimar, 173-7, 186, 260-1, 283; appearance of, 176, 178 n., 203, 252; pupils of, 177, 191, 200, 209, 242-5, 252, 291, 295; Bernhardi on, 178-81, 183-5, 187-9, 277; and Catholicism, 179, 254-5; start of liaison with Princess, 180-3, 202; and Servais, 182 n.; on marriage, 183; suggests founding a journal, 183-4; never expresses opinion, 184-5, 277, 285; and marriage with Princess, 190-1, 198-9, 201-2; in Rome, 190-1, 195, 202-3, 221; Rome-Pesth-Weimar days of, 191, 221, 231, 247; religious moods of, 194, 199, 259-60; as seen by contemporaries, 203-6, 241, 254, 291-9; poses of, 204-5, 285; portraits of, 205, 296; has no male friends, 206, 209; contemporaries on music of, 207-8, 302 n.; symphonic poems of, 207, 214-15, 218, 302-3; "desertion" of, 209, 216, 218, 277; Cornelius on, 210-12; takes minor orders, 211, 220-3, 226; appointed Kammerherr, 211 n., 224; early works of 212-14; subtle harmonies of, 214; Wagner on works of, 217-18; allows himself to be imposed upon, 234-5, 242-4; wastes time in answering letters, 235 n.; generosity of, 236-7, 242, 274, 279, 288; overpraises mediocrity, 237-8, 240, 280; and Rossini, 238-40; diplomacy of, 241 n., 281; last years of, 245-7; death of, 247; and Olga Janina, 250 et seq.; the collecting of relics of, 257, 259; offered post in Hungary, 263-4, 272-3; cruelty of, 265-6, 285; on Olga Janina, 268-71; contemporary popularity of music of, 276-7; his perception of new values in music, 280; fascination of, 283-4; and Beethoven monument, 288-90; and royal ceremony in Pesth, 291; interrelation of life and music of, 299 et seq.; B minor sonata of, 299-300; French romanticism of, 302; has no real nationality, 303-5; "four powers" of his soul, 305

Liszt, Madame, Liszt's letter to, 52; and Koettlitz, 107; and Liszt's and Countess's children, 148 n., 149-50; Liszt and family of, 236

Lohengrin, Liszt's production of, 106, 164, 185; Liszt's essay on, 167

London, Liszt in, 85, 94, 96-7, 296

Lucca, Liszt in, 85

Ludwig, Grand Duke, 78 n.

Lugano, Liszt in, 85

Lyde, Mlle., 18

Lyon, 48
Lyons, Liszt in, 64
Lytton, Henry Bulwer, 86

MALTITZ, M., and Princess's divorce, 187-8
Mantius, 100
Maria Pavlovna, Grand Duchess of Sachsen-Weimar, 162-3
Mazeppa, 210, 213, 215, 217
Meck, Frau von, 241
Mémoires d'un pianiste, 251 *n.*
Mendelssohn, on Liszt's playing, 10; on Liszt, 11; social footing of, 90 *n.*
Messe solennelle, Rossini's, 238
Metternich, Princess, 135 *n.*, 287-8
Meyendorff, Baroness von, 276 *n.*
Meyerbeer, Jakob, 215, 278; *Les Huguenots* of, 31 *n.*
Meysenbug, Malwida von, on Princess, 159
Miethe-O'Connell, Mme., 102 *n.*
Milan, Liszt in, 76, 79, 82, 85, 87, 92
Minghetti, Madame, 232
Mischka, 276 *n.*
Molènes, Gâchons de, 154
Montez, Lola, 100
Moscheles, Ignaz, 26
Moser, on Liszt's playing, 10, 12
Mouchanoff, Countess von, 261
Munich, Liszt in, 254
Musset, Alfred de, 31

NADERMANN, 26
Nélida, 23 *n.*, 112, 124 *et seq.*; Liszt's portrait in, 20, 124 *et seq.*; "Zepponi" incident, 94 *n.*, 134-7; a genuinely historical document, 125, 274-5; passages from, 127-30, 133, 135-8; final stages of, 142-5; reissue of, 147, 155
Niemizov, Liszt in, 193
Nietzsche, Bülow's letter to, 238 *n.*
Nohant, Countess and Liszt at, 66, 69 *n.*, 74-5; Balzac at, 116 *n.*

ODESSA, Liszt in, 158
Ollivier, Blandine, 201; birth of, 50, 53 *n.*; death of, 146
Ollivier, Daniel, and Liszt-d'Agoult papers, 98, 146
Ollivier, Emile, 146
Orpheus, 210, 215
Ortigue, Joseph d', 34 *n.*, 49

PADUA, Liszt in, 93
Paris, Liszt in "retreat" in, 36-7; flight from, 51-3; Liszt's successes in, 64, 66, 192, 200 *n.*; Liszt on, 67-8; Liszt and Countess return to, 85; Liszt's concerts in, 108, 290 *n.*; Liszt not liked in, 140; *Tannhäuser* performed in, 175, 200
Pater Noster, 11
Patersi, Madame, 150, 170

Pensees des Morts, 48
Pesth, Liszt's successes in, 65 *n.*, 80, 89, 281; Liszt conducts in, 140 *n.*; Liszt's post in, 191; Bülow offered post in, 208; Wagner refuses banquet in, 235; Liszt and Olga Janina in, 266-70; Liszt and royal ceremony in, 291
Pixis, 87
Planché, Gustave, 116 *n.*
Pleyel, Camille, 100
Plötz, Frau von, on Liszt and Princess, 180-85
Pohl, Richard, 150
Porges, Heinrich, 212
Potocki, angered by Liszt, 87; and Balzac, 116 *n.*
Prague, Liszt in, 89
Preller, Ludwig, 293
Pressburg, Liszt's success in, 80, 88
Prometheus, 11, 210, 215
Pückler, Prince, 89
Puzzi, *see* Cohn, Hermann

RAABE, Peter, 196 *n.*; on revision of Liszt's inferior works, 12; on Liszt's liking for the showy, 14; inaccuracies in biography of, 41; on Liszt's family, 91 *n.*; on *Nélida*, 124, 128-9, 138; on Countess, 141; on Princess, 160; on Liszt's deterioration, 173; on Princess's letters, 192-3, 196; on Liszt as seen in his music, 299-301, 303
Raff, Joachim, on *Ad nos*, 11; collaboration with Liszt, 140 *n.*, 187
Raiding, 29
Rakoczky March, 281
Ramann, Lina, 23 *n.*; describes Countess d'Agoult, 4 *n*; *Life of Liszt* by, 5, 21, 248; Princess and, 5 *n.*, 23 *n.*; on Liszt-d'Agoult affair, 16, 48; on the flight from Paris, 51
Reischach, Baron, 89
Rhapsody with Orchestra, 210
Rheinweinlied, 109
Richmond, Liszt in, 96-7
Richter, Hans, 278 *n.*
Ritter, Alexander, 207
Robert the Devil, Liszt's Fantasia on, 9
Rohan, Prince de, 90
Romance oubliée, 14
Rome, Liszt and Countess in, 76; Princess Wittgenstein in, 159, 190, 192 *n.*, 197; Liszt's life in, 221, 224, 245-6, 258; Olga Janina in, 251, 265
Ronchaud, Louis de, on Countess, 6; on Liszt, 87; and Countess's correspondence, 97-8; and *Horace*, 114; lines on death of Countess, 146
Rossini, at aristocratic concerts, 26; *Messe solennelle* of, 238-40
Rubini, 110
Russia, Liszt in, 158; Princess banished from, 163-4

SACHSEN-Coburg-Gotha, Grand Duke of, 141 *n.*

St. Cricq, Caroline de, 4, 30

St. Cricq, Comte de, 30

St. Elizabeth, 168, 210, 226, 281, 296

St. Stanislas, 231, 245, 247

Sainte-Beuve, C. A., on young Liszt, 34 *n.*; Liszt's letter to, 49; attracted by Countess, 99; on Balzac, 123 *n.*; on criticism, 298

Saint-Saëns, C. C., on Liszt's behaviour to audiences, 108; on Liszt's fantasias, 213

Samoyloff, Madame, 100

San Rossore, 85

Sand, George, on Countess d'Agoult, 4 *n.*; and Liszt, 31, 48, 116 *n.*; *Lettres d'un voyageur* of, 45; Countess stays with, 66, 74; *Horace* of, 114; attacks Countess, 114; portrayed in *Béatrix*, 115 *n.*; supplies data for *Béatrix*, 116 *n.*, 121

Sayn-Wittgenstein, Prince von, *see* Wittgenstein, Prince Nicholas von

Sayn-Wittgenstein, Princess von, *see* Wittgenstein, Princess von

Schering, Arnold, 303, 305

Schlick, Count, 90

Schlözer, Kurd von, 177; on Liszt's manner in playing, 13; on Liszt's taking orders, 221-3; on Liszt's love of titles, 224

Schmalhausen, Lina, 276, 288

Schorn, Adelheid von, 23 *n.*; marriage of parents of, 25 *n.*; on Liszt's temper, 62-3; on Princess, 159; cares for Liszt, 168, 197, 229; on Liszt's intemperance, 194-5; on Liszt's indifference to Princess, 202; on Liszt's taking orders, 226, 229; on Liszt's dislike of solitude, 229; and Liszt's letters, 236 *n.*; Princess's letters to, 245-7; Olga Janina on, 258

Schorn, Ludwig, 25 *n.*; in Bonn, 101 *n.*

Schrader, Bruno, on Liszt's flight from Paris, 52 *n.*; inaccuracies of, 82

Schuberth, 265, 270

Schumann, Clara, ingratitude of, 3, 171

Schumann, Eugenie, 161 *n.*

Schumann, Robert, on Liszt as composer, 2; on Liszt in Leipzig, 108; on Liszt as pianist, 204; Liszt's quarrel with, 278

Schwarzenberg, Prince Fritz, 89

Sedlnitzky, Count, on Liszt, 78 *n.*

Seroff, 280-1

Servais, Adrien François, 182 *n.*

Servais, Franz, 232, 263; parentage of, 182 *n.*

Sexard, Liszt and Olga Janina at, 262-4; 272

Sgambati, G., 242

Sontag, Henriette, 26

Souvenirs d'une Cosaque, 250-1, 271, 275; Huneker on, 275 *n.*

Stahr, Adolf, 184

Stern, Daniel, *see* Agoult, Countess d'

Street, Agnes, 171 *n.*

Switzerland, Liszt and Countess in, 54-9, 66

Symphonic poems, 207, 214-15, 218, 302-3

Szécheni, Count, 89

Szemere, Myriam, 265, 268-9

Tannhäuser, Liszt's production of, 106; Liszt's essay on, 167; produced in Paris, 175, 200

Tasso, 215, 217

Tausig, 202

Tchaikovsky, on Liszt, 241-2

Thalberg, Sigismond, Liszt's rivalry with, 64-6; Liszt on compositions of, 70-2; parentage of, 90 *n.*

Thode, Daniela, 84 *n.*

Thode, Henry, on Liszt, 8

Thun, Count, 90

Tivoli, Liszt in, 63, 232, 245, 257, 290

Tolstoi, Countess, 259 *n.*

Totentanz, 210

Tulou, 26

UNGER, Caroline, 100

Urhan, Christian, 31, 67 *n.*

VENCKHEIM, Baron, 88

Venice, Liszt and Countess in, 76-7, 85

Vial, Madame, 39

Victoria, Queen, 296

Vienna, Liszt studies in, 30; Liszt visits, 77, 80, 85, 198; his successes in, 77-8, 80, 88; aristocratic supper in, 89; Donizetti's post in, 106

WAGNER, Cosima, 27, 152; on *Life of Liszt*, 5 *n.*, 16, 249; daughter of, 84 *n.*; on her mother, 149-50; marries Bülow, 150; on Princess's influence on Liszt, 170, 218; Bülow's letter to, 208; diary of, 217-18; on Liszt's work, 218; diplomacy of, 278 *n.*

Wagner, Richard, legend of, 1; befriended by Liszt, 3, 164, 185, 209, 279; on Liszt's outburst of rage, 62; Liszt produces operas of, 106, 164; revolution effected by, 143-4; estranged from Liszt, 168; and *Dante Symphony*, 169; and Liszt, 200-1, 233, 278-9, 286; Cornelius on, 205; on Liszt, 217-18; 294; refuses banquet in Pesth, 235; and the Ramann biography, 249; on musical composition, 298-9

Waldburg, Princess Julie, 240 *n.*

Waldstein, Count, 89

Wales, Prince of, 296

Wandererphantasie, 210

Wetzlar, Baroness von, 90 *n.*

Weimar, segregation of social classes in, 25 *n.*; Liszt and Wagner at, 62; Liszt's position at, 105-6, 179; as centre of German culture, 105-6; as musical centre, 106, 165, 185; Liszt and post at, 106, 139-41, 162; Wagner and, 143; culture in, 163, 174, 186; Princess in, 164, 176-7; opposition to Liszt in, 165, 173-7, 186-7; Bernhardi in, 177-85, 187-9; Wagner's cause in, 186; Prince Wittgenstein in, 187-8; Liszt's pupils in, 191, 242-5; Liszt Museum in, 193, 196; Olga Janina in, 258-61; Liszt's popularity in, 260-1, 283

Wittgenstein, Prince Nikolaus von, 158 at; Weimar, 187-9; death of, 190, 201

Wittgenstein, Princess Carolyne, and *Life of Liszt*, 5-6, 16, 21; her influence on Liszt, 11, 15, 40, 110, 149, 152, 155, 165-70, 184, 279 *n*.; prejudices of, 16, 22 *n*.; on Countess d'Agoult, 21-2, 40; literary work of, 21, 190; Liszt's letters to, 37 *n*., 61, 145, 160, 162, 171-2, 227-8, 231-3, 295; writes Liszt's articles, 67 *n*.; Liszt's separation from, 85, 173, 191-2, 197-200; Liszt's love for, 98, 160, 202; and Countess's children, 147, 149-50, 170; eccentricities of, 151, 159 *n*., 176, 190; meets Liszt, 158, 180; marriage of, 158-9; daughter of, 158, 189; appearance of, 159, 164, 178; cigars of, 159, 164, 176, 190; wealth of, 160, 163, 178; culture of, 160, 165-6; her love for Liszt, 160; religiosity of, 160, 166, 190; her letters to Liszt, 160-1, 192-3; seeks divorce, 163, 166, 186-8, 190; sequestrated estates of, 163, 166; in Weimar, 164, 176, 180, 195;

Wittgenstein (*continued*)
    banished from Russia, 164; sacrifices of, 166-7, 181; her ambitions for Liszt, 167-8, 184; and Wagner, 168, 273; on Liszt's lack of application, 169, 245-6; her influence on Liszt's work, 169, 216-18, 220; disliked in Weimar, 176-7, 186; Bernhardi on, 178-81, 183-5, 187-9; children of, 182 *n*.; visit from husband of, 187-9; and marriage with Liszt, 190-1, 202; in Rome, 190, 197, 199; reproaches Liszt, 193, 196-7, 226; and Liszt's taking of orders, 220, 222-3; points of disagreement with Liszt, 233

Wohl, Janka, on Countess's anger at *Béatrix*, 112-13; on Liszt in Pesth, 291

Wolkoff-Mouromtzoff, Alexander, 287

Woronince, 158; Princess's chapel at, 166

ZIMMERMANN, 72 *n*.

Zychyi, Count, 88